GRE® Prep
by Mag✓✓sh

D0690768

RTC Team	Publisher **Corey Michael Blake**
	President **Kristin Westberg**
	Editor **Amanda Ronan**
	Content Coordinator **Christian Panneck**
	Designers **Sunny DiMartino, Christy Bui**
	Coloring Page Illustrator **Nathan Lueth**
	Proofreaders **Adam Lawrence, Carly Cohen**
	Project Manager **Leeann Sanders**
	Facts Keeper **Mike Winicour**

Magoosh Team	Project Leads **Jessica Wan, Maizie Simpson**
	Content Specialists **Chris Lele, Mike McGarry**
	Copy Editors **Lucas Fink, Adam Lozier**
	Student Editing Coordinator **Anne Bercilla**
	Proofreaders **Peter Poer, Kristin Fracchia, Travis Coleman**
	Cover Designer **Mark Thomas**

Copyright © 2017 Magoosh

All rights reserved. Except as permitted under the US Copyright Act of 1976, no part of this publication may be reproduced, distributed, or transmitted in any form or by any means, or stored in a database or retrieval system, without the prior written permission of the publisher.

Writers of the Round Table Press
PO Box 511, Highland Park, IL 60035
www.roundtablecompanies.com

Printed in the United States of America

First Edition: January 2017
10 9 8 7 6 5 4 3 2 1

Library of Congress Cataloging-in-Publication Data
Magoosh.
GRE prep by magoosh / Magoosh.—1st ed. p. cm.
ISBN Paperback: 978-1-939418-91-3
Library of Congress Control Number: 2016961821

RTC Publishing is an imprint of Writers of the Round Table, Inc. Writers of the Round Table Press and the RTC Publishing logo are trademarks of Writers of the Round Table, Inc.

GRE®, TOEFL®, and Praxis® are registered trademarks of Educational Testing Service (ETS). This workbook is not endorsed or approved by ETS nor any of the following trademark holders:
ACT® is a registered trademark of ACT, Inc.
GMAT® is a registered trademark of the Graduate Management Admission Council (GMAC).
LSAT® is a registered trademark of the Law School Admission Council, Inc.
MCAT® is a registered trademark of the Association of American Medical Colleges.
SAT® is a registered trademark of the College Board.

GRE® Prep
by Mag✓✓sh

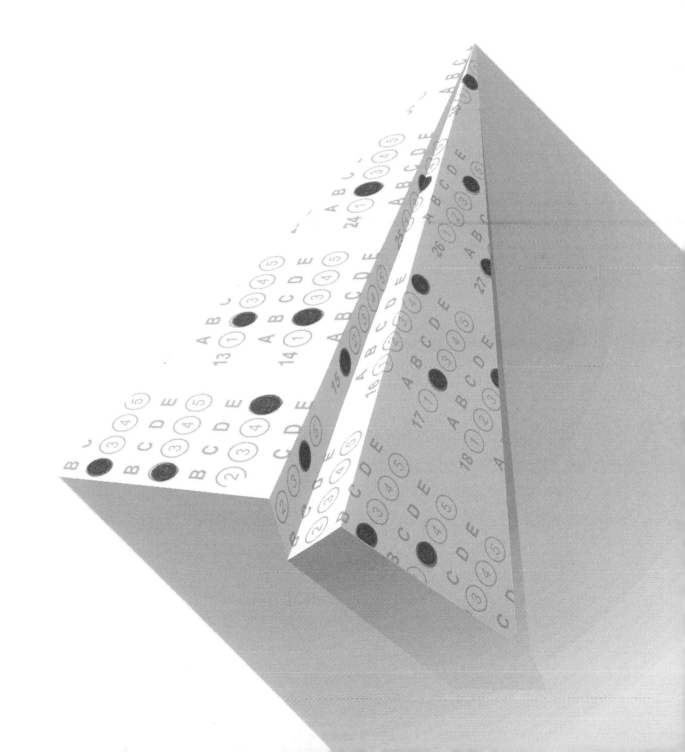

Contents

Chapter 4

211 GRE Verbal Reasoning

Chapter 5

309 GRE Analytical Writing Assessment

Chapter 6

333 GRE Practice Test

423 Off to the Test!

Appendix

Magoosh Vocabulary Word Lists 427

Hi there!

First, we want to take this opportunity to thank you for checking out this book by Magoosh. You'll soon discover that the content of these pages, combined with our online product, packs a gigantic GRE-prep wallop.

You see, what you're holding in your hands is a companion guide for the Magoosh GRE-prep program offered online at magoosh.com. You're not going to find thousands of practice questions in these pages. Instead, you're going to find two hundred of the highest-quality, best-explained, and most robust questions that have helped thousands of students succeed on the actual GRE. On top of the thorough explanations and step-by-step directions, we rank the difficulty level of each question and tell you what percentage of our online students answered the question (or one like it) correctly. These stats are there to help you size up each question before you dive in. You can use them to figure out what actually makes a question *easy*, *medium*, or *hard*. Getting a feel for the difficulty level of the questions on the GRE will help you approach the test with more confidence. "Look at that," you'll say to yourself. "I just sailed through a hard question like it was no big deal!"

With the help of this book and all the useful features in Magoosh online, you'll rock the GRE.

That's because the preparation you do with Magoosh online mimics the real experience of a computer-based test like the GRE. You'll have all the tools you need and know what to expect when you sit down to take the real test. In addition to the thousand-plus practice questions online, we also provide a text explanation and a video explanation for every question. Yes, every single one. And we don't just offer practice questions. To help you cover the basics, we also provide more than two hundred video lessons that cover every topic on the test.

We hope you're getting the sense that we really care about your success, because we do. That's where this book comes in. We started wondering how we could help you study even more efficiently for the GRE and figured that an actual book might come in handy. Sometimes books can go places laptops can't. You can toss this book in your bag and study whenever you find yourself lacking an Internet connection, wanting to review handwritten notes, or feeling like you might learn something better from a physical book. This book extends the Magoosh content to help keep you studying whenever and wherever it's convenient.

Magoosh isn't just about practice questions and tests, though. We also have a free blog (magoosh.com/gre) full of great study tips and other info. In fact, we've used some of our most popular posts to help write this book. In addition, you'll find free math and vocabulary flashcards in the iOS and Google Play app stores. You can flip through these online resources whenever you have a few free minutes.

We hope you find this book useful, and we would love to hear your feedback. If you have any questions, comments, or want to send a virtual high five, get in touch with us at book@magoosh.com. Happy studying!

All the best,
The Magoosh Team

Meet Magoosh

The Team

We at Magoosh are a bunch of education nerds who get super stoked about helping students achieve their academic dreams.

This is Bhavin Parikh, our CEO and founder. He has a BS/BA in economics and computer science from Duke University and an MBA from the Haas School of Business at University of California, Berkeley. Now, he's on a mission to change the way people learn and how they think about learning, which is why he started Magoosh in 2009. Fun fact: when he's not hard at work with our team, you'll usually find Bhavin playing ultimate Frisbee or Smash Bros.

And here's the rest of the fantastic Magoosh team!

The Magoosh Experts

Learn more about the Magoosh test-prep experts who helped write this book! All the tips, tricks, and lessons you're about to read came from the minds of these two instructors. If you have any questions for them, send an email to book@magoosh.com. We're always happy to speak with students!

Chris Lele

GRE and SAT Curriculum Manager at Magoosh

Chris is the GRE and SAT curriculum manager (and vocabulary wizard) at Magoosh Online Test Prep. In his time at Magoosh, he has inspired countless students across the globe, turning what is otherwise a daunting experience into an opportunity for learning, growth, and fun. Some of his students have even gone on to get near perfect scores. Chris is also very popular on the internet. His GRE channel on YouTube has over eight million views.

Mike McGarry

GMAT Curriculum Manager at Magoosh

Mike wrote the GRE Quantitative chapter of this book. At Magoosh, he creates expert lessons and practice questions to guide GRE and GMAT students to success. He has a BS in physics and an MA in religion, both from Harvard, and over twenty years of teaching experience, specializing in math, science, and standardized exams. Mike likes smashing foosballs into orbit, and despite having no obvious cranial deficiency, he insists on rooting for the NY Mets.

Our Mission

We create products that give students *everywhere* access to enjoyable, affordable, and effective test prep.

Our Core Values

We want to share these with you so you know what we're all about.

Accessible > Exclusive	⇨	We're open to ideas from everyone, inside and outside of Magoosh.
Challenge > Comfort	⇨	We challenge ourselves to learn new skills by tackling tasks we've never done before.
Friendly > Formal	⇨	We always show respect and kindness to our teammates, customers, and partners, whether online or offline.
Wow > Profit	⇨	We go above and beyond in our work and never say, "It's not my job."
Done > Perfect	⇨	We have a bias toward action and won't delay for perfection tomorrow what can be done today.
Data > Intuition	⇨	We run experiments to test ideas and gather data.
Passion > [Something]	⇨	We love what we do! Helping students is too much fun to be considered work.
Communication > Efficiency	⇨	We set clear expectations, communicate when we've completed a task, and follow up when necessary.
Change > Status Quo	⇨	We adapt to difficult situations and reevaluate our priorities, so we'll always be a work in progress.

Our Products

Magoosh offers test prep for the GRE, GMAT, LSAT, SAT, ACT, TOEFL, IELTS, MCAT, and Praxis. And we're expanding to new tests soon!

Magoosh GRE Online

Our premium online product offers:

- More than two hundred lesson videos on the GRE Quantitative Reasoning, GRE Verbal Reasoning, and GRE Analytical Writing Assessment (AWA) categories— that's about twenty hours of video!
- More than one thousand GRE Quantitative and GRE Verbal practice questions, with video explanations after every question
- Material created by expert tutors who have in-depth knowledge of the GRE
- Email support from our expert tutors
- Customizable practice sessions and mock tests
- Personalized statistics based on performance
- Access anytime, anywhere from an Internet-connected device

When you sign up for the premium product, you can access all your stats at any time. This is what the Magoosh dashboard looks like:

| Mag♥♥sh | Admin Dashboard Lessons Practice · Review Resources · Students · | Help Account · |

Dashboard

Suggested Lessons	See all lessons
Intro	
General Introduction	
What's on the GRE?	
Math	
Intro to Data Interpretation	
QC Questions & Inequalities	
Intro to GRE Math	
Data Interpretation Strategy	
QC Strategies - Picking Numbers	
Verbal	
Intro to Text Completion	
Elements of the Argument	
Intro to Vocabulary	
Intro to Reading Comprehension	
Elimination Method	
Writing	
Intro to AWA	
Essay Organization	

Suggestions are based on your lesson progress

Quick Practice Take or review practice tests | Customize your practice

Practice Math — 573 questions left

Practice Verbal — 503 questions left

Results Summary See detailed results | Reset stats

Math	Verbal
Estimated Score: 142 - 147	Estimated Score: 141 - 146

Math pie: Correct 21% / Incorrect 79%
Verbal pie: Correct 35% / Incorrect 65%

	Math		Verbal
Questions Answered:	67	Questions Answered:	51
Your Average Pace:	0m 34s	Your Average Pace:	0m 45s
Others' Average Pace:	1m 20s	Others' Average Pace:	1m 6s

Your Notes View all notes

You have taken 1 note on Math   You have taken 1 note on Verbal

What Students Say about Magoosh

We're your biggest fans when it comes to your GRE studies. And our support doesn't go unnoticed. Check out what some of our current and former students have said about us below and on magoosh.com/stories and gre.magoosh.com/testimonials.

Stephenie L.

"Finding Magoosh was like stumbling upon a pot of gold."

Liliane S.

"Thank you so much for the help, Magoosh team."

Giancarlo S.

"There is great customer care behind Magoosh."

Sanchari G.

"These features are unique and a refreshing change from the commonplace prep tools."

Additional Resources from Magoosh

In addition to this book and our full online GRE prep, we offer many other resources (yes, even more!) to help you get the most out of your GRE prep journey.

- **Magoosh GRE study plans:** Whether you have one, three, or six months to study, we've created these daily and weekly guides to tell you exactly what and when you should study so that you'll be fully prepared for test day. Find all of the guides by visiting this page online: magoosh.com/gre/gre-study-plans-and-guides.

- **Magoosh GRE apps for iOS and Android:**
    - **Magoosh Prep:** Practice GRE Quantitative, GRE Verbal, and GRE AWA on the go.
    - **GRE Vocabulary Flashcards from Magoosh:** Quiz yourself every day with these flashcards to learn the 1200+ most important words on the GRE. You'll master different tiers of vocab difficulty and unlock new levels along the way. Play an opponent for an extra challenge!

- **Magoosh GRE Blog:** Visit magoosh.com/gre for tips and advice from our test-prep experts on how to prepare for test day and dominate the exam.

- **Magoosh GRE eBooks:**
    - The Ultimate GRE Guide (magoosh.com/gre/ultimate-gre-guide)
    - GRE Vocabulary eBook (magoosh.com/gre/2012/gre-vocabulary-ebook)
    - GRE Vocabulary Flashcards (magoosh.com/gre/2013/gre-vocabulary-flashcards)
    - GRE Math Formula eBook (magoosh.com/gre/2012/gre-math-formula-ebook)

- **Magoosh GRE YouTube channel:** Learn from our expert tutor Chris Lele, whose "Vocab Wednesday" videos walk you through some of the trickiest vocabulary you'll see on the GRE.

- **Magoosh GRE forum (official questions and explanations):** On this page, you'll find links to all of Magoosh's video explanations for official GRE material. You can leave responses to questions or upvote answers that you find particularly helpful. (gre.magoosh.com/forum)

Chapter 1

Meet the GRE

The Test Breakdown

The sections

The GRE consists of two Quantitative Reasoning sections, two Verbal Reasoning sections, and one experimental section, which can be either Verbal or Quantitative. In addition, there are two timed essay-writing assignments in the Analytical Writing Assessment (AWA) section of the GRE. The experimental section won't count toward your score, but you won't know which section is the experimental one. You should treat all sections like they're the real deal. Both the overall GRE Verbal and GRE Quantitative scores can range from 130 to 170. The essays are scored from 0 to 6 in half-point increments.

Number of questions and time limit

The GRE Quantitative sections contain twenty questions each. You'll be given thirty-five minutes to complete each section. The Verbal sections also consist of twenty questions each, but you'll have just thirty minutes to complete those sections.

GRE Quantitative overview

The two sections in this category are made up of approximately seven quantitative comparison questions and thirteen non–quantitative comparison questions (don't worry, we'll explain comparison and non-comparison questions soon). Possible question types include the following (these four example practice questions will be explained starting on page 35; no need to worry about solving them now!):

Multiple choice: a standard question type in which you just have to identify the **one** correct answer.

Which of the following equations is true for all positive values of x and y?

- (A) $\sqrt{x} + \sqrt{y} = \sqrt{x + y}$
- (B) $\sqrt{x^4 y^{16}} = x^2 y^4$
- (C) $(x\sqrt{y})(y\sqrt{x}) = x^2 y^2$
- (D) $y\sqrt{x} + y\sqrt{x} = \sqrt{4xy^2}$
- (E) $(x^y)(y^y) = (xy)^{2y}$

Multiple answer: a question type that can have up to ten answer choices; you'll have to "select all that apply," which means that the number of correct answers isn't provided.

$2x^2 + 6 > 40$

Which values of x satisfy the inequality above?

Indicate <u>all</u> such values.

- A   −8
- B   −6
- C   −4
- D   −2
- E   2
- F   4
- G   6
- H   8

Numeric entry: an open-ended question type in which you'll have to type in the correct value.

Two trains starting from cities 300 miles apart head in opposite directions at rates of 70 mph and 50 mph, respectively. How long does it take the trains to cross paths?

Quantitative comparison: a question type that lists two quantities and asks you to compare them and select one of the following: A is equal to B, A is greater than B, A is less than B, or the relationship between the two quantities cannot be determined from the information given.

Column A	Column B
The number of positive multiples of 49 less than 2000	The number of positive multiples of 50 less than or equal to 2000

(A) The quantity in Column A is greater

(B) The quantity in Column B is greater

(C) The two quantities are equal

(D) The relationship cannot be determined from the information given

For more information on question types, see the information in chapter 3.

Also, don't forget that there's a basic on-screen calculator that you'll have access to while completing the GRE Quantitative sections! See page 33.

GRE Verbal overview

The two sections in this category are each made up of about six text completion questions, four sentence equivalence questions, and ten reading comprehension questions.

Text completion: questions that can have one to three blanks and range from short sentences to four-sentence paragraphs. For double- and triple-blank text completion questions, you must answer each blank correctly to receive full points—there's no partial credit!

Sentence equivalence: questions that have six possible answer choices. For every sentence equivalence question, there will be two correct answers. To receive any credit, you must choose both correct answers.

Reading comprehension: passages that range from twelve to sixty lines. Topic matter is usually academic in nature and covers areas such as science, literature, and the social sciences. Question types include standard multiple-choice questions, highlight-the-passage questions, and multiple-answer questions, which require you to choose any number of three possible answer choices.

GRE AWA overview

At the beginning of your GRE, you'll have to write two essays: the Issue task and the Argument task. The essays are timed at thirty minutes each. Neither is part of your 130–170 score. Each essay receives a score ranging from 0 to 6. Your final essay score is the average of both essay scores.

How Is the GRE Scored?

The GRE scale may seem pretty arbitrary. After all, who has ever seen a test graded on a 130–170 scale? A range of 0–100, yes, but 130–170? Weird! Well, according to ETS, when they revised the GRE scoring back in 2011, they wanted to stick to three digits so that schools wouldn't have to overhaul all the textbox entries that call for that specific number of digits. Fair enough. Also, to avoid confusion, ETS made sure the current scoring system didn't overlap numbers with the old GRE scoring system.

The GRE scoring system makes up for the limited range (just 40 points!) by giving more significance to the extreme ends of the scale. For example, on the GRE, the difference between a score of 165 and a score of 170 will be the difference between being in the 96th percentile and being in the 99th percentile.

At the end of the day, you're not going to be tested on these statistical nuances. The important thing to remember is that many admissions offices base their evaluations on a percentile score, which you'll also receive as part of your score report.

Questions are static, but the GRE is adaptive

The GRE is adaptive, but not in the way some other tests are. Many tests (such as the GMAT, for instance) will adapt to your proficiency level. The more questions you get right, the harder they'll get; if you get more questions wrong, they'll get easier and easier. The GRE isn't adaptive in this way. Question difficulty within a section doesn't change depending on whether you answer questions correctly. However, your performance on the first GRE Verbal and Quantitative sections will determine whether the next sections of the same type are easier or more difficult than the first.

Questions have random levels of difficulty

Questions might be static, but that doesn't mean a section can't become progressively harder or easier, theoretically. There is no order of difficulty on the GRE. The first question can be the hardest and the last question the easiest.

Each question is weighted the same

Each question is basically weighted the same. So the question that seems like it will take fifteen minutes to answer is worth the same as the question you can answer in fifteen seconds.

How Difficult Is the GRE?

Simply put, the GRE can be a very difficult test, especially if you've been out of school for a while. Typically, this tends to hold truer for the GRE Quantitative than for the GRE Verbal or AWA. So let's break it down by category.

How hard is GRE Quantitative?

The truth is, as soon as you leave college, the likelihood of using math diminishes drastically. Compounding the "rusty math-brain syndrome" is the fact that GRE math is different from the math you probably did in college; it's much closer to the math you did in your junior year of high school. That's not to say it's easy. It's generally much trickier than anything you ever saw in your algebra class. Throw in the high-pressure testing environment, and it's understandable why the mere mention of GRE prep can fill a student with utter dread.

How hard is GRE Verbal?

Believe it or not, as you read more and are exposed to different kinds of text, the parts of your brain that are wired for reading and language skills will continue to expand. Of course, knowing your brain is getting better probably doesn't help you *feel* better about facing a four-hundred-word passage on user-experience design theories or a text completion task that asks you to distinguish between *extenuating* and *corroborating*. The simple fact is that the GRE Verbal is very hard, even for PhD candidates. The writing is dense and stylistic; the vocabulary is esoteric and daunting.

How hard is GRE AWA?

The real difficulty of the GRE writing section stems from rusty writing skills. For many students, it has been years—or even decades—since they last wrote a five-paragraph essay. Whether you fall into that group or not, trying to score a "6" is hard, even for confident writers.

Don't worry!

With lots of study, you can still do very well on the GRE! Remember, it's a test that puts you in competition with others. You don't have to answer every question correctly to score well. Another way of looking at it is this: just as you struggle on a very difficult three-blank text completion or a probability question involving the combinations formula, so do 99 percent of the other students taking the test.

Don't forget to do the following:

- Give yourself plenty of time to prep.
- Learn how to take the GRE (you're already doing that by reading this book and using Magoosh online!).
- Believe that improvement will come gradually. At times you may plateau. So be patient.

Performance Statistics on the GRE revised General Test

	Verbal Reasoning	Quantitative Reasoning	Analytical Writing	
Number of Test Takers	1,585,305	1,587,610	1,579,373	51% female, 43% male (6% did not provide their gender)
Mean	150	152	3.6	
Standard Deviation	8	9	0.9	

Data source: ETS.org

Is the GRE Important?

This is a very interesting question, and one that even we at Magoosh debate internally. Some people think it's not important at all and that it's just an arbitrary test that attempts to measure IQ. On the other hand, some people think the GRE is a valid measure of the intellectual skills required for success in grad school.

Ultimately, since much of the reading in the test itself is lifted from academic journals, being able to understand such writing *will* make a difference in grad school. The math sections may not be as defensible, especially for someone looking to write his or her dissertation on motifs of fifteenth-century frescoes. At the same time, though, the math found on the test isn't that "mathy"—it's more a test of your logical reasoning with numbers, which, especially for the majority of you who will have to dabble in the statistics side of things, is somewhat relevant. Then there's the GRE AWA, which tests your ability to write competently about complex issues—maybe not so useful to engineers, but not totally irrelevant to students who hope to have their work published in academic journals.

For now, the GRE is important in that it's a piece of an application—though only a relatively small one—that gives grad school admissions officers a somewhat accurate sense of an applicant's intellectual ability in a highly artificial—and stressful— environment. That said, relevant work experience, excellent letters of recommendation, and a strong undergraduate GPA can strengthen a weak score, just as a lack of any related experience or a terrible undergraduate GPA can neutralize a perfect score.

Chapter 2

How to Study

Whether you're taking the GRE for the first or the fifteenth time, you'll need to come up with a plan of action when it comes to studying. You know your schedule, attention span, strengths, weaknesses, and study habits better than anyone else. To complement, in this chapter, we offer all kinds of study-related tips, tricks, and thoughts, from a sample study schedule to time-saving tips to morale-boosting reminders. We want you to know that you're not going this alone. We at Magoosh will have your back the whole way.

Find the Time to Study

Possibly the most challenging aspect of preparing for the GRE is exercising the self-discipline to study for it in the first place. Many people convince themselves that it will be impossible to carve out any time to study while working a full-time job and maintaining some type of work-life balance, so they don't even try. But, as it turns out, they're wrong about there being so little time. According to a study by the Bureau of Labor Statistics, working adults in the US have on average approximately four and a half hours of leisure time each day. The trick to excelling on the GRE is to leverage the free time you do have and use time-management techniques that work for you. Here are some ideas on how to do just that:

1. **Take public transportation.** If you have the option to use public transportation to commute to and from work, take it. Yes, it may make your commute longer and it may be a little inconvenient. However, it will provide you with a routine study time where there are few distractions. When you're sitting on the metro, subway, or bus, there's nothing better to do than study, so take advantage of this alone time. An added bonus? By taking public transportation, you avoid the frustration of driving in traffic, save gas, and avoid wear and tear on your car.

2. **Study on the go—always.** Download our flashcard apps or keep a set of flashcards in your purse or backpack so you can study whenever you happen to have a spare minute. If you're an auditory learner, you can listen to recordings of vocabulary words. Another option is to use a study app on your smartphone. For example, the Magoosh GRE app provides convenient access to video lessons that can help you prepare. Whether you prefer to use an app, flashcards, or audio recordings, the key is to take advantage of any opportunity to incorporate more studying into your day.

3. **Spend an extra hour at work.** Consider arriving at work an hour earlier or staying there an hour later so you can study for the GRE. Why should you do it at work? Some people are too distracted at home, and if that's you, it may be better to either study at your desk or in a conference room—especially if the building is nice and quiet before and after business hours.

4. **Study at your peak focusing hours.** Some people study better in the morning, while others are able to focus better in the evening or at night. You know yourself and your strengths and weaknesses better than anyone else.

5. **Schedule the exam.** Once you've decided to take the GRE, take a practice test to gauge how much you need to increase your score. Then, schedule the exam and give yourself approximately twelve weeks or so to prepare. If you need to increase your score dramatically, you may want to allow even more time than that—twenty weeks out might be a better target date. It may seem premature to schedule the exam before you've even started studying for it, but this is actually a great motivator. Once you've registered and paid for the exam, you're more likely to take it seriously. By registering, you've moved your "one day" or "someday" to a definitive date.

Preparing for the GRE is a time-consuming task. However, it's also one of the best ways to prepare for graduate school and kick-start your study habits. Whether you're considering a full-time, part-time, or online master's program, carving out a set study time for the GRE will also help you develop a study regimen that will benefit you in graduate school.

Good, You Got It Wrong

For some students, getting answers wrong can be interpreted too easily as some kind of negative personal message (e.g., "I'm dumb," "There's something wrong with me," etc.), and it becomes a negative and frustrating experience.

But here's a different perspective about mistakes. Every mistake, every wrong answer, is an *opportunity for growth and self-improvement*. The truly excellent student lives by this very high standard: absolutely never make the same mistake twice. That requires incredible perseverance, but even falling short of that, each wrong answer is a chance to improve and clarify some necessary concept about which you previously were unclear or confused.

Think of how grateful you would be if, before some important event, you happened to walk by a mirror and notice you had something smudged across your face. Now you can wipe that smudge off and improve your appearance before the important event. Metaphorically, every question you get wrong is such a mirror—a chance to look at yourself, remove the smudge, and improve your understanding.

Our study plans are designed with this in mind. We have you jump into mixed content questions right away, well before you have a chance to complete all the Magoosh video lessons. One reason is, of course, that the GRE itself will throw nothing but mixed content at you, and we want you to get comfortable with this "gear-switching" as early in your study process as possible. That being said, we know this means you'll probably get many questions wrong at the beginning, and we believe this is a good thing. Obviously, we aren't trying to punish you or make you feel bad about yourself. Rather, we know that making mistakes and consciously reflecting on these mistakes is exactly what will prime your mind for the content of the video lessons.

It takes a good deal of confidence and emotional security to adopt this attitude—to look beyond the frustration of getting questions wrong, and to embrace, with courage and optimism, the opportunity for self-improvement in each mistake. In the face of an apparent lack of success, it's very hard to maintain any sort of courageous optimism. It takes a very strong and secure individual who can say, "I've gotten two hundred GRE questions wrong so far, and that's great, because from those mistakes I have learned two hundred new concepts that I can use!" But remember, if you want to stand out, you must *be* a standout. If you want extraordinary results, you need an extraordinary perspective. Wherever you are in your GRE preparation, that's exactly the kind of success we wish for you.

Beating Exam Stress

If you're already overwhelmed with anxiety about the test, in addition to studying, you should focus on managing that stress. To combat this problem, you may want to try to make future mock tests as stressful as possible. For instance, when you're giving yourself a practice test, don't stand up except at the appointed breaks of the exam. Maybe even turn on the television in the background just so you can learn to cope with distractions.

Another important way of coping with stress is to notice your breathing. When we become stressed, our breath becomes shallower and our bodies tense up. You can ease stress by taking longer, deeper breaths. Just a few deep breaths should calm your nerves and help restore your breathing and, most importantly, your focus.

Tips to Study More Effectively

When you're trying to focus on studying, and especially when you're following a pretty intense study plan, it can feel like the whole world is trying to distract you. Between texts from friends, social media messages from family, and adorable pictures of kittens, it can be hard to stay true to the study schedule.

But there are tried-and-true ways to cut through the distractions and focus on the job at hand—studying for the GRE. Here are a few tricks:

1. **Change the way you think about studying.** Research shows that how you feel about a task is just as important as how you do it. If you can flip that switch in your brain that takes you from thinking, "Ugh, studying!" to thinking, "Woohoo! Look at all this cool stuff I get to learn!" you'll set yourself up for success.

2. **Look for good study vibes.** Where you study is important. Try a quiet room in your house or a study carrel at the local library. Try studying in a few different spots until something feels right. Then come back to that place often.

3. **Stick to a schedule that works.** Be deliberate and work significant chunks of study time into your daily routine. Every time you repeat your routine, it'll get easier, until it feels totally natural.

4. **Turn off your phone.** Don't put it on vibrate or airplane mode. Turn it off. You're not available to others during study time.

5. **Close the tabs on your browsers.** Yes, even email. Yes, even social media. Yes, even fantasy football. Resist the urge to surf by closing all tabs at the start of your study session.

6. **Add some variety to your study routine.** Try something new if you keep seeing spots while reading the book. Make flashcards. Watch a lesson.

7. **Take breaks and reward yourself.** Every hour or so, make sure you get up and give your mind and body a break. Take a walk. Eat something delicious. Play with a puppy. Breaks help your mind process all that stuff you've been learning. You deserve breaks!

Arm yourself with strategies to avoid distraction, and nothing can stop your GRE study sessions—except you, of course, when you take a break. Which we absolutely recommend!

How to Register and Other Commonly Asked Questions

As we've mentioned before, getting your test date and location all set is a great way to begin your GRE study cycle. Here are some frequently asked logistical questions about the test. Knowing the answer to these ahead of time can put your mind at ease and let you focus on the important stuff—like, you know, studying.

How do I register for the GRE?

You can register for the GRE by visiting ets.org/gre and creating a GRE account with ETS. The test is computer-delivered year-round, with the option of taking it up to three times a year.

What do I have to bring?

The most important thing you need to bring to the testing site is a valid photo ID that includes your name, photo, and signature. If you're testing outside of the United States, we recommend bringing your passport. If you arrive without any form of identification, the testing center will turn you away.

The next most important thing you need is something nutritious to eat. The GRE is a long test, and you'll need some brain fuel to help you avoid crashing during the sixty-five-line passage on the use of isotope dating in glaciers. We recommend bananas, dates, nuts, and other natural foods with a high caloric density. However, you know yourself best. If you got through college by keeping yourself awake on Snickers bars, then that's what your body is used to. If this is the case, chomping on pistachios for the first time in your life, right before the test begins, may not be the best idea.

Do I need to know which schools I want to send my scores to that day? How many schools can I pick?

The GRE has a feature called Score Select, which allows you to send your scores to up to four schools for free. You'll get this option at the end of the test.

If you want to send your scores to more than four schools, you'll have to pay twenty-five dollars per additional school. You don't have to select any schools when asked. However, the downside to not selecting schools is that sending the score reports in the future won't be free.

Do I need to know the codes of the schools I'm applying to, or will that information be provided?

The test will provide you with the relevant codes for each school. So don't worry, you won't have to burden your brain with even more information.

When will I receive my scores?

If you take the computer-based test, you'll be able to see your unofficial GRE Verbal and Quantitative scores at the test center the day of the test. Your official scores will be available in your ETS account online about ten to fifteen days after your test date, at which time your scores will also be sent to the schools you chose on test day. Scores of paper-based tests are available approximately six weeks after your test date.

What's the testing center like?

Usually the labs are drab and sterile. Essentially, you'll be asked to empty your pockets and leave everything behind in the registration area. Luckily, there will be a trusty locker in which you can put your stuff. You get to keep the key when you go into the testing room. You're allowed to run to the locker during breaks in testing for an emergency snack.

The important thing is to mentally prepare for the testing center experience. You don't want any surprises: bad traffic, poorly marked buildings, or a testing center staff that moves at the pace of glaciers. Some GRE test takers even visit the testing center a day before to trace their exact steps.

How long is the test?

The test will take you close to four hours. This includes checking into the testing center, answering a few background questions, and then diving into two thirty-minute essays and five GRE Quantitative/Verbal sections (including that one experimental section).

The good news is that you'll get one scheduled ten-minute break after the third section and one-minute breaks between all the other sections. While you're free to take a break at any other time, the clock will keep on running if you choose to do so. In other words, unless you're about to pass out, don't get out of your seat, except during a scheduled break.

Study Schedule

At Magoosh, we know everyone has different needs for studying. Some people like to do a little each day over a long period of time, while others prefer to cram in a lot of studying over a short period. We offer suggested study schedules for all different types of learners. From our one-week study schedule to our six-month schedule, we've got all of you covered.

As it turns out, our one-month schedule is the most popular plan we offer. For those who are focused and ambitious, this four-week study guide plan is great, as long as you have the time to put in. If you feel like you might not be 100 percent committed to an intense study schedule, or if you need to improve your score drastically, then this study plan for the GRE may not be for you. If this is the case, check out our two- to three-month study schedules on magoosh.com/gre.

1-Month GRE Study Schedule

What You'll Need

- ○ This book
- ○ An online Magoosh GRE account (see the last page in the book for your 20% off coupon)
- ○ Magoosh GRE Math Flashcards (available at gre.magoosh.com/flashcards/math)
- ○ *The Official Guide to the GRE revised General Test* (Second Edition), from ETS
- ○ About three hours to study each day (it sounds like a lot, but you got this!)
- ○ Optional: the Magoosh GRE Vocabulary Flashcards app, or the Magoosh GRE Vocabulary Builder app

Note: For those of you with more than a month to study, this one-month study schedule can be stretched out over two months. Magoosh also offers a variety of more specialized versions, including daily schedules, two- to three-month schedules, and six-month schedules.

Week One

Primary Goals

- ◯ Brush up on math fundamentals.
- ◯ Learn basics for approaching GRE Verbal questions.
- ◯ Read two articles from recommended resources.
- ◯ Learn one hundred and fifty new words (either with your magoosh.com account or the Magoosh vocabulary apps). Remember the importance of context.
- ◯ Begin watching Magoosh lesson videos (especially the "Intro to the GRE" module) and reading through this book.

Secondary Goals

GRE Quantitative

- ◯ Read chapters 1 and 2. Also read the beginning of chapter 3, up to the "Quantitative Concept #1" section.
- ◯ Log in to your account at gre.magoosh.com and watch all of the general math strategies lessons, the arithmetic and fraction lessons, the percents and ratio lessons, and the integer properties lessons. *Note:* It will be more helpful to stop and work on practice problems as you go. Pause and try some problems after every three or four videos that you watch. You'll want to make sure you apply the techniques you learned about. Watching too many videos in a row can result in false confidence.
- ◯ Practice concepts seen in lesson videos by using the magoosh.com "quiz" feature.
- ◯ Go through every easy and medium question relating to arithmetic, percents, ratios, and powers and roots using your online Magoosh account. Watch videos whenever necessary. Return to all questions you initially miss and be able to answer them accurately.

GRE Verbal

- ◯ Read chapter 4 up to the "Verbal Question Types: Text Completion" section.
- ◯ Go to magoosh.com to watch overview lessons on text completions all the way up to "Text Completion Sentence Shifts." Practice with easy questions in the online product.
- ◯ Practice thirty online text completion questions at easy to medium difficulty
- ◯ Watch about half of the Magoosh reading comprehension lesson videos online.
- ◯ Practice approximately thirty reading comprehension practice questions online, watching videos when necessary.
- ◯ Make flashcards of words you don't know and use references such as vocabulary.com to help.

Supplemental/Optional

- ◯ Read two articles, four to fifteen pages each, from the *New Yorker/Atlantic Monthly/Economist*. Reading articles that are similar in style to what is found on the GRE Verbal will help with your reading comprehension. These magazines have many such articles, especially in the arts and culture or science and technology sections.
- ◯ Find fifty words you don't know in the articles. Reference those words using vocabulary.com and make flashcards on quizlet.com.
- ◯ Write a quick summary/review of one of the two articles you read. Include GRE words you studied this week.
- ◯ Practice the first four decks in Magoosh's GRE Math Flashcards (available online and on mobile).

Week Two

Primary Goals

- ( ) Learn one hundred and fifty new vocabulary words and review words from last week.

- ( ) Make sure you're caught up on your assigned reading in this book (chapters 1, 2, and parts of chapters 3 and 4).

- ( ) Make sure you're confident with the material covered in last week's lessons. Revisit whatever topics you feel need review. Many concepts we'll introduce this week will build off of last week's topics.

- ( ) Work your way through the magoosh.com lesson videos, making sure you do the follow-up quizzes after each lesson group. Remember: practice, practice, practice! Don't become a video-watching zombie. Keep your mind active by pausing lesson videos and trying actual practice problems!

- ( ) Learn the concepts covered in this book.

Secondary Goals

- ( ) Finish reading through chapters 3 and 4 in this book. Work through the GRE Quantitative and GRE Verbal practice questions and check your answers. It's okay if you're not getting the *hard* and *very hard* questions correct yet. Those will seem easier with practice.

- ( ) On magoosh.com, work through the algebra, equations, and inequalities lessons, the word problem lessons, and the powers and roots lessons.

- ( ) Also online, complete at least seventy-five practice GRE Quantitative questions dealing with the above concepts.

- ( ) Finish watching all GRE Verbal lessons on magoosh.com.

- ( ) Complete at least seventy-five questions on magoosh.com covering text completions, sentence equivalence, and reading comprehension.

- ( ) Take and grade a practice test from either the back of *The Official Guide* or its CD supplement.

- ( ) Watch the video explanations for the questions you missed or that you were not 100 percent confident on. Before you watch each video, though, try to figure out for yourself where you made a mistake.

Supplemental/Optional

- ( ) Read two articles. Make sure the content is different from the articles you read last week. If you read something scientific last week, focus on business topics, history, or social commentary this week. Write two summaries or reviews. Remember to include GRE vocabulary words you have studied so far.

- ( ) Take the full-length practice test at the end of this book. Check your answers and review your mistakes with the answer key section. You can also review your mistakes by watching lesson videos on magoosh.com.

- ( ) Practice the next four decks in our GRE Math Flashcards.

Week Three

Primary Goals

- ○ Complete all math modules except probability.*
- ○ Customize sessions to focus on areas where you need the most work.
- ○ Learn two hundred new vocabulary words.
- ○ Revisit lessons that cover topics where you need more review.
- ○ Learn about the Analytical Writing Assessment (AWA) portion of the GRE.

Why skip probability? The test will have only one or two probability questions. Because probability questions are so rare on the GRE, it's better to focus on other "low-hanging fruit." If you feel strong at other areas in math, a basic overview of probability couldn't hurt. Otherwise, you might want to skip studying it.

Secondary Goals

- ○ Read chapter 5 of this book and work through both the practice "Analyze an Issue" and "Analyze an Argument" writing tasks.
- ○ Quiz yourself on vocabulary from the first two weeks. Total: three hundred words. Try fifty words at random. A passing rate is 80%.
- ○ Complete one hundred and fifty GRE Quantitative problems on magoosh.com based on those areas in which you need the most practice.
- ○ Complete another seventy-five-plus GRE Verbal questions on magoosh.com.

Supplemental/Optional

- ○ Read three articles—the more challenging, the better. Make sure you're getting your vocabulary from these articles, as well as from practice questions. Attempt to use twenty-five GRE vocabulary words in a three-page review and summary of all three articles.
- ○ Take a practice test from *The Official Guide*. Review your mistakes by watching Magoosh videos online. For the bold, take a second practice test this week.
- ○ Finish going through the decks in the GRE Math Flashcards.

Week Four

You're in the home stretch and have done a good job getting this far, but now you need to really push full steam ahead.

Primary Goals

- ◯ Feel confident in your approach to the different types of questions.

- ◯ Prepare yourself, as much as possible, for the high-pressure environment of the actual test.

- ◯ On magoosh.com, start doing the hard questions (and very hard, if you've answered more than 70 percent of magoosh.com questions correctly).

- ◯ If you weren't able to complete the "hard" and "very hard" questions in the book before, try them again now and review your answers.

Secondary Goals

- ◯ Take a full-length practice test on magoosh.com.

- ◯ Even if you've seen the questions in your mock test before, it doesn't matter. Do them again.

- ◯ Learn one hundred and fifty new words. Also make sure you review every vocabulary word listed in the appendix at the back of this book.

- ◯ Take a final vocabulary quiz, testing yourself on at least six hundred words you've studied.

- ◯ Keep reviewing several Magoosh GRE Math Flashcards each day.

- ◯ Take another practice test in *The Official Guide.*

Supplemental/Optional

- ◯ Take yet another test from *The Official Guide.*

What to Do If You Fall Off the Study Wagon

Even the best-laid plans are imperfect. Studying for the GRE is a demanding process that takes time, and even after all the planning, sometimes you're going to find yourself veering off track. But you don't have to give up completely just because you didn't meet some of your goals. Instead, consider it a good place to start over.

You already have a plan that you know *didn't* work, so you'll be able to craft a better plan this time around.

Let's examine what might have thrown you off course, how to correct the issue, and how to make plans to begin again.

1. **Be specific.** Part of the problem might have been the goals that you set for yourself. Goals that are too vague or too broad lend themselves to failure. When your goals aren't specific, you won't know what to do next or when you've achieved them.

2. **Be realistic.** Try setting smaller, more attainable goals. This practice allows you to achieve goals with greater ease. For example, here's a hard-to-reach goal: "I am going to get a perfect score on the GRE Quantitative." In contrast, here's a much more tangible, reasonable goal: "I am going to memorize all the prime numbers from 0 to 100 and the conversions of common fractions to decimals."

3. **Be flexible.** Sometimes life happens and you have to abandon your studies for personal issues, family emergencies, or professional deadlines. There are unexpected events that are impossible to plan for and can throw your schedule completely out of whack. There's very little that you can do to avoid these hiccups. One way to make them less of an issue is to build a plan that has some wiggle room in it. Plan to miss days in your study schedule by scattering free days throughout. These days can be used to adjust your schedule when the unexpected happens.

4. **Be forward-thinking.** Whatever path you have chosen, anticipate times when you might fall off the wagon. Did you just plan a trip? Are you going to a wedding or surprising your mom for her birthday? These need to be accounted for in advance. If you know something is coming, make changes—don't just trot along with the same plan. By foreseeing bumps in the road, you can account for them and adjust now.

Don't beat yourself up over a small derailment in plans. Go on, dust off those GRE-prep materials, and get back to it. You have a test to dominate!

What to Do If You Hit a Study Plateau

If you've been studying for the GRE for a good amount a time, it's likely you'll start to feel frustrated and unmotivated. No matter the skill you're trying to sharpen, there will come a moment when you feel you've hit a plateau. By no means should you give up. Your brain could very well be telling you that you need to take a break or that you at least have to mix it up a little.

The GRE is no different. Your practice test scores, even after you've studied diligently for weeks, may not be going up. It's easy to come to the conclusion that all your work means nothing. But don't despair: we've put together some important pointers to review when you feel you've hit the proverbial wall.

1. **Go somewhere new.** It's possible that GRE prep has become too regimented for you. Structure and discipline are critical to success, up to a point, but after a while, you may start to lose interest because of the repetition. One great way to break the monotony is to study in a different place than usual.

2. **Change your study routine.** You might start each study session by doing a few GRE Verbal exercises. You review your mistakes and then move on to a set of math problems. After following this pattern for a month, your brain starts to become bored. Surprise it! Any of the following should do the trick:

   ○ Do a mini-test in which you immediately follow up five math problems with a long reading passage.
   ○ Try out the Magoosh GRE Prep app.
   ○ Spend a half hour testing yourself with Magoosh's Vocabulary Builder app or GRE Flashcards.
   ○ Review material from a day or two ago. Do you remember what you learned that day? Revisit questions you missed.

3. **Take a break.** Our brains, like our muscles, need rest. By taking a break from something you're learning, you'll have time to process all that information. Understandably, you don't want to take too much time off. But even a three- to four-day break from studying vocabulary won't cause you to forget all you've learned. Coming back after a few days' rest, on the other hand, will give you a renewed perspective. Suddenly, the word *polemical*, which you were having so much difficulty learning because you couldn't get the image of a pole out of your head, conjures up new—and more applicable—images.

4. **Focus on different parts of the test.** Many students become too fixated on doing just one question type or just one section on the test. Breaks from studying the test as a whole aren't the only way to process better: taking a break from a specific section can also help cement what you've learned.

The Week Before the Test

You've probably heard this a hundred times before: Always get a good night's sleep the day before something important. Prepping for the GRE is no different. The GRE is a long, taxing experience. And you don't want to find yourself nodding off at any point during the four-plus hours that you'll be sitting in the testing center. So a good night's rest is crucial to your performance.

Also, don't do anything that isn't usually part of your routine. For instance, if a friend asks you out for dinner, reschedule. We're not telling you to be antisocial, but people tend to stay up later when engaged in social activities. Conversely, don't turn off your phone and hide under the covers, hoping for a twelve-hour sleep session. Just try to keep to your weekday routines as much as possible.

And if you're not an early riser but were forced to make an eight a.m. testing appointment, be sure to start waking up a little bit earlier each day during the week before the test. That way, you'll get used to wrestling yourself out of bed at six in the morning before test day.

Finally, don't feel obligated to cram, and definitely don't stay up late cramming. The GRE tests knowledge built up over a lifetime—or at least a few months of intensive prepping. Cramming the night before won't lead to a higher score, and because it will most likely fray your already frazzled nerves, cramming may actually hurt your score. That doesn't mean you shouldn't do a few practice questions the day before the test. But otherwise, try to relax, as much as it's possible to do so.

How to Study for a GRE Retake

If this section applies to you, then it's very important to ask yourself what you can do differently in preparing for the GRE this time around. If you find yourself retaking the test, then most likely some part of your study process the first time around was not optimal. Of course, "something" is a terribly vague word. So we'll try to help you figure out what might have happened.

Maybe you didn't take enough practice tests. Nothing prepares you for test day better than a mock exam. And not just any mock exam, mind you. Magoosh tends to be as difficult as, if not more difficult than, the actual GRE. Of course, nothing beats taking an official test. There are two ETS mock tests at the end of the *The Official Guide to the GRE* book and and two tests on the Powerprep II CD that comes with the book.

This time around, try spacing out practice tests every five days. The assumption is that you have already prepped sufficiently and therefore don't need to learn all the fundamentals over again. Much of your time in between tests should be focused on dissecting your performance. What did you do wrong? What could you have done better? Any insights gleaned should be used in the following test; i.e., you're anticipating making similar mistakes and will thus be on guard.

It's possible you used mediocre prep resources. Not all prep materials are equal. If you felt the GRE was very different in the types of question asked in your practice material, then you should consider using new materials. To solve this problem, you should do some research and use the material that will best help your score. And, if possible, don't just settle on one resource.

It can be hard to identify your weaknesses. And if you can't identify them, then it's possible you didn't focus on those areas while studying.

Keeping an error log can help tremendously. This log can be highly systematized or it can be very basic. For instance, you can simply file a difficult question in your mental Rolodex. Try to remember how the question tricked you and what you should do the next time you come across something like it in order to avoid the same mistake. Of course, remembering things isn't always the best way to improve. In fact, we recommend that you first jot down the question number and source of the question in a notebook. Then answer the following questions:

1. Why did you miss the question?
2. Why was your answer wrong?
3. Why is the correct answer correct?
4. What will you avoid doing the next time around?

Come back to this log often, especially before you take a practice test. Review your errors, so that on the practice test you'll be careful not to make a similar mistake. By the time your test rolls around, you'll be on guard against any careless errors, and hopefully you'll never again have to ask yourself how to study for retaking the GRE!

In Sum

We've provided a whole bunch of tips and tricks for studying for the GRE. Now it's time to get to it. The rest of this book is dedicated to helping you understand GRE question types and practice the thought processes and procedures necessary to answer them. Remember to come back to this section whenever you need a boost of confidence or a pat on the back. We know the life of a person studying for the GRE is busy and complicated, but we also know that you can totally do this!

MANTRA

Each mistake is an opportunity to learn. During your worst moments, while prepping for any test, and especially the GRE, you'll feel inclined to hurl the book or laptop against the wall. Remember that even if you miss a really easy question, doing so is an opportunity to learn. That is, you can try to better understand what led you to miss an easy—or even difficult—problem, so that you can avoid the same mistake in the future.

Chapter 3

GRE Quantitative Reasoning

Brought to you by Mike from Magoosh

Meet the GRE Quantitative Section

What do integral calculus, trigonometry, and geometry proofs all have in common? Well, besides being three things you probably don't enjoy doing for fun, they also don't show up on the GRE. That's right: no higher-level math will show up on the test. We know. *Phew*, right? It's okay to take a minute to sigh with relief and jump for joy right now.

The type of math that *does* show up on the GRE is the stuff you most likely learned from middle school to junior year of high school. To give you a little refresher, in case you've forgotten some of this stuff, the common topics include the following: basic properties of shapes (circles, quadrilaterals, etc.), integer properties, exponents, and word problems (including rate questions and probability). And really, there's not much beyond that.

What makes the GRE so tricky is the complexity and density of many of the questions. Once you figure out what the question is *actually* asking, though, the math involved isn't nearly as long-winded as what you probably did in high school. You know, those homework questions that your teacher exactingly checked to make sure that you followed each of the thirteen steps to arrive at the solution. In fact, with the GRE, you don't even have to show your work. You just have to pick the right answer.

Keep reading to find out how to prepare for GRE quantitative problems. We've included tips on topics such as how to pace yourself during the test and what to do when facing what seems like a really tough question.

Commonly Tested GRE Math Concepts

Based on the practice tests in the second edition of *The Official Guide to the GRE revised General Test*, word problems will be plentiful. There are also a fair number of algebra-related questions. And even a few combinatorics problems rear their fearsome heads. If you're wondering how many questions on the GRE will deal with

> Did you know?
> The ancient Greeks were the first to do true mathematics.

statistics—a topic often given scant attention in many prep books—it can pop up in spades. Most interestingly, coordinate geometry only shows up once, and there isn't a single rate problem.

The breakdown of concepts based on the fifty quantitative questions in Practice Test #2 of *The Official Guide* detailed below will likely be similar to what you see on test day. That said, you'll probably see more than one coordinate geometry question and may also see a rate question. Remember, just because a concept didn't show up on the published practice test doesn't mean you won't see that concept on test day. Interest problems, both simple and compound, will probably show up, too.

What is the takeaway from all this? If you're weak in a certain area—say, word problems that deal exclusively with adding a series of numbers—don't sweat it. You may only see one problem dealing with that concept. On the other hand, if you're only somewhat comfortable with statistics, it's a good idea to strengthen your skills in that area, as you're likely to see several questions on such a broad topic on test day.

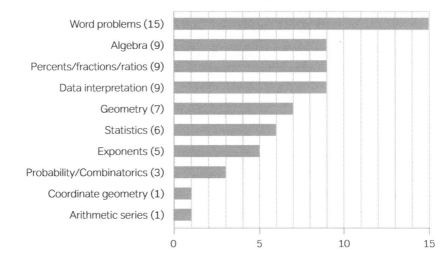

GRE Quantitative Concept Frequency

How to Study GRE Math

So you've bought a few of the major test prep books, including the one you're holding in your hands right now, and you're ready to rip into the GRE Quantitative. You'll read through each book, page by page, and by the end, GRE math mastery will be yours. If only!

Studying for the GRE Quantitative is much more complicated than just reading a book. You could easily get through hundreds of pages of text and feel like you've learned very little. The GRE Quantitative takes knowledge and practical application.

Keep in mind the following important points on how (and how not!) to study for the GRE Quantitative.

1. **Watch for the GRE math formula trap.** You may ask, *"How can formulas be bad? Aren't they the lifeblood of GRE math?"* Actually, formulas aren't all that helpful. And they definitely aren't the crux of the GRE Quantitative. The real key to being successful on the GRE is to have sharp problem-solving skills.

The reality is you must first decipher what the question is asking. All too often, students let the formulas do the thinking. That is, they see a word problem—say, a distance/rate question—and instead of deconstructing the problem, they instantly come up with a formula and start plugging in numbers from the question. In other words, they expect the question to fall neatly into the formula.

To illustrate, take a look at the following question:

Two cyclists, Mike and Deborah, begin riding at 11 a.m. Mike rides at a constant rate of 40 kilometers per hour (kmh), and Deborah rides at a constant rate of 30 kmh. At noon Mike stops for lunch. At what time will Deborah pass Mike, given that she continues at a constant rate?

Students are tempted to immediately rely on the $d = rt$ formula. They think, *Do I use the formula once for Mike and once for Deborah? Or for only one person? But which person do I use it for?*

This is an unfortunate quandary; the solution to the question actually relies on figuring out how many kilometers Mike has gone in one hour and how many kilometers behind him Deborah is. There's no formula for this conceptual step. It's only once the conceptual step has been completed that we can use the $d = rt$ formula. The answer, by the way, is 12:20 p.m.

Remember that the essence of problem-solving is just that: solving the problem logically, so you can use the formula when appropriate.

2. **Use training wheels to start, then get out of your comfort zone!** Many students learn some basic concepts, memorize a formula or two, and feel that they have the hang of the GRE quantitative content. But, as soon as they actually sit down to solve a few problems, they feel confused and uncertain of exactly what problem type they're dealing with.

Starting with basic problems is an excellent study strategy early on. You can build off the basic concepts in a chapter and solve problems of easy to medium difficulty. This phase, however, represents the "training wheels."

Actually riding a bike, much like successfully answering an assortment of questions, requires you to get out of your comfort zone. In other words, you should try a few questions chosen at random. Opening up *The Official Guide* and doing the first math questions you see is a good start. Even if you haven't seen the concept, just go for it. You'll get a feel for working through questions with limited information.

Sometimes students don't love this advice. It makes them uncomfortable to tackle problems they haven't studied for yet. But the reality is that you can actually solve many problems based on what you already know, especially when you take your time and consider the question carefully.

3. **Avoid tunnel vision.** Some students become obsessed with a certain question type, at the expense of ignoring equally important concepts. For instance, some begin to focus only on algebra, forgetting geometry, rates, counting, and many of the other important concepts.

   This "tunnel vision" is dangerous; much as the "training wheels" phase lulls you into a false sense of security, only doing a certain problem type makes it harder for your brain to get into the groove with other mathematical topics.

4. **Don't focus too much on the really high-hanging fruit.** Try not to spend a lot of time studying topics that may not even show up on the test. This is a subset of "tunnel vision." For example, some students get totally wrapped up in learning permutations and combinations concepts. Instead, they could be using that time to study a more important area, such as number properties and geometry, which show up much more frequently on the test.

   Would you climb to the very top of the tree to grab the meager combinations/permutations fruit, when right within your grasp are the luscious number properties fruit?

5. **Be wary of test-prep material.** Many of the sources out there don't offer practice content that's as difficult as what you'll see on the test. Some offer too few sets with a mixture of question types. Basically, they never take you out of the "training wheels" phase.

   Other content has questions in which you can easily apply a formula without first having to "crack" the problem. Such material will leave you feeling pretty unprepared for the actual GRE.

Understand Where You Can Go Wrong

GRE math can be tricky, but the test still rewards fundamentals. If you have a solid grounding in all of the fundamentals, you have a strong chance of scoring above 160. Speed and concentration will play a large factor in your score, so remember to watch out for those careless errors!

The wrong answers—as well as lucky guesses—can fall into several categories listed below:

1. **Conceptual errors.** Getting confused by a conceptual question should be no reason to give up, throw your arms in the air, and scream. Rather, you should have the exact opposite attitude. *Wow, I just found something that I need to work on in order to better understand the concepts. Doing so will help me prepare for test day.* So go back to your resources, read up more on whatever that concept may be, and find practice problems to help you conquer that concept.

2. **Falling for the trap.** The GRE is a tricky test. ETS has decades of experience writing questions meant to trip up test takers. Did you forget to consider that the value of x could be a fraction between 0 and 1? Maybe you missed the word

isosceles, or maybe you only considered rectangles and not irregular quadrilaterals.

Whatever the case may be, identify why you fell for the trap and the assumptions you made that led you to the wrong answer. Here's a hint: if a question seems a little too easy, that may be a sign that the test is trying to trick you.

3. **Careless mistakes.** Careless errors range from selecting the wrong letter to making a small computational error. Identifying the type of careless errors you make can help you avoid repeating those specific mistakes when you're answering questions.

4. **Misinterpretation**. Sometimes you misread the problem and end up solving a different problem. ETS can actually predict ways that test takers might misinterpret a problem, so they provide a wrong answer choice that matches these common misunderstandings. To fight back, be sure to read word problems carefully, and pay attention to small but important words such as *positive*, *integer*, and *not*.

How to Approach Complicated Math Problems

Every GRE test is going to have a few math questions that are very difficult. Try not to get flustered. You'll be able to figure them out with practice.

Below are three important points to keep in mind when you're dealing with a difficult GRE math problem.

1. **Don't get rattled.** It's very easy to become anxious when you come across difficult math problems, especially word problems. One reason is that we start reading and rereading the same question, hoping that by the fourth read we'll finally get it. At this point, rereading is clearly an example of diminishing—and frustrating—returns. What to do?

2. **Read the question carefully.** Sometimes a problem seems much more complicated than it actually is. The reason is that we're misreading a word or inserting our own word into the question. We spend several minutes trying out difficult equations only to realize that none of the answer choices matches up with our answer. To avoid this, make sure you don't rush through the question. Instead, read carefully and know what the question is asking before attempting to answer it.

3. **Let your brain decipher the question.** It can take about thirty seconds—and a careful, calm rereading—to understand what the question is asking. Then you'll need to find the solution path. To do so, think—or even write down—the necessary steps to get to the solution step by step.

One piece of good news: you can take longer on complicated questions. After all, there aren't too many of them. Just make sure to solve the easy and medium questions first. Remember, you can always come back to a question. Sometimes it's easier to decode the second time around.

Tips for Quickly Solving GRE Math Problems

Students who are reasonably comfortable with math itself often complain, "I *could* solve most GRE quantitative problems if I had enough time, but I always seem to run out of time," or "I just wish I could do GRE math faster." Does this sound like something you've said? Then this section is for you.

Solve this question. Allot yourself a strict one-and-a-half-minute time limit.

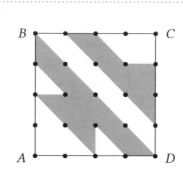

In the figure, *ABCD* is a square, and all the dots are evenly spaced. Each vertical or horizontal distance between two adjacent dots is 3 units. Find the area of the shaded region.

Ⓐ 60

Ⓑ 72

Ⓒ 81

Ⓓ 96

Ⓔ 120

(Answer and explanation below.)

The brain

First, let's quickly review a few things about the brain. Before we do, though, please know that we're not neurologists. Instead, our goal here is to introduce you to another way of thinking about the problem above. So below is just a little background to set the scene. The brain, of course, is much more complex than the amount of space we have in this book!

The cerebrum, the "intelligence" part of our brain, is divided into two halves—the left and right hemispheres. Each half controls all the sensation and muscular movements on the opposite side of the body. So when you move your left leg, it's the right half of your brain that controls it. The two hemispheres also process information very differently.

The left hemisphere is all about logic, organization, precision, and detail management. It specializes in *differentiation*, that is, telling the exact difference between closely related things. It's very good at following clear rules, recipes, formulas, and procedures in a step-by-step, logical way. The left brain controls the grammar and syntax of language. If someone said, "I are happy," it would be your left brain that recognized that as incorrect.

The right hemisphere controls intuition and pattern-matching. It specializes in *integration*, that is, seeing the underlying similarity or unity behind things that seem pretty different. It's often called the "artistic" side of the brain, and it's good at interpreting information presented as symbols or images. It's also good at facial recognition and voice recognition.

Math and the brain

Okay. So which hemisphere is better for math? Well, the detail-management, organization, and precision of the left brain are a huge help in arithmetic and algebra. Meanwhile, the right brain's pattern-matching skills can play a role in some branches of math, such as geometry. Now, we're going to make an oversimplification in order to illustrate two ways of approaching GRE math. Imagine that we're all split up into "left-brain people" and "right-brain people," each with a "dominant" hemisphere that has a larger influence over the way we think. In general, left-brain people usually feel reasonably comfortable with math and can certainly follow the methodical procedures with ease. Typically, right-brain people tend to have a more difficult time keeping all the details straight, although many times they tune into the "big picture" ideas faster.

The magic of right-brain thinking

Left-brain people usually know the rules reasonably well. They're often the "good-at-math" kind of students. Faced with most GRE quantitative questions, they could figure out the right answer, given enough time. The catch, of course, is that they don't have unlimited time on the GRE—just thirty-five minutes for twenty questions, or 1:45 per question.

An overwhelming number of GRE math questions are designed specifically to punish someone who is overly left-brained. In other words, the questions are written to be looked at in different ways. Yes, the methodical, step-by-step, plodding approaches can work, but they take too much time. The best test takers can reframe a question or see it in a different way—one that can be answered more quickly.

Example: the practice problem

Let's take a look back at the practice problem. Yes, you could figure out separately the area of each triangle, each square, each trapezoid, and then add all of those shapes together. That would take some time. So let's look at it a different way.

Here's a right-brain solution to this question: rearrange the pieces!

First, slide the little triangle up into the corner.

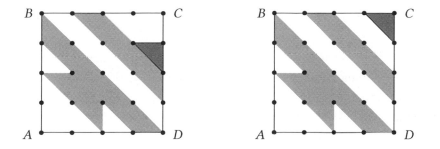

Now, notice that the left-most trapezoid would fit nicely into that blank space on the upper right.

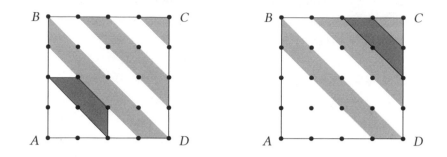

Now, flip that remaining long trapezoid over the diagonal *BD*:

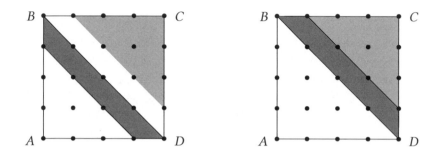

Would you look at that! The shaded region accounts for exactly half the area of the big square. The big square is 12 × 12 = 144, so the shaded region is 144 ÷ 2 = 72. Answer = **(B)**. Once you see the trick, the pattern, there's only the most minimal of calculations needed.

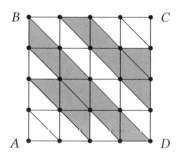

Another reasonably quick right-brain approach would be to simply count all of the little triangles.

The original shaded figure can be broken into 16 equal triangles. The full square is 16 little squares or 32 triangles. Therefore, the area of the shaded figure is exactly half the area of the square.

Learning to see

Some right-brain readers might celebrate such a process, while some left-brain people might be frustrated or annoyed at this point. They may be thinking, *Great! Now that it's pointed out, yes, that's an efficient way to solve, but how am I supposed to see that on my own?*

Mastering the strengths and skills of your non-dominant hemisphere is never an easy task, but it can be done.

There are a wild variety of things you can do to enhance right-brain function. Read poetry. Look at art. Make art. Read about patterns in comparative mythology. Free-associate. Imagine. Follow chains of word associations. Slow down and really look at things.

Specific Tips for Doing GRE Math Faster

1. If the problem asks for the value of an expression involving variables, chances are good there will be some way to solve for the value of the expression directly, without solving for the individual variables.
2. For a "find the area of the shaded region" question in which the region is particularly complicated (as in the practice question), look for a way to rearrange and simplify.
3. If the problem is a geometry one stated in words, always sketch a rough diagram, unless you can visualize the diagram easily.
4. If the problem is purely numerical or algebraic, consider whether there would be a way to visualize the problem (number line, xy-plane, etc.)

From this point forward, whenever you practice GRE quantitative questions, first of all, always practice against a strict time limit. Second, the criterion is no longer whether you got the answer right or not. Even if you got the correct answer, compare your solution to the official solution. If your solution was a slow methodical approach and the official solution shows a shortcut, then for your purposes, **consider this a question you got wrong**. For every such question, force yourself to write down the shortcut and consider what you could have done to "see" that shortcut. Force yourself to put it into words and explain it—a practice that will strengthen your interhemispheric connections. As you collect more and more write-ups, go back to reread the collection. Keep doing this consistently. Learn from your mistakes, and before you know it, you'll start "seeing" solutions to GRE quantitative problems!

Pacing Strategies

Each GRE Quantitative section contains twenty questions. You're given thirty-five minutes for each section, which works out to 1:45 per question. Below are some helpful tips to help you use these thirty-five minutes wisely.

1. **Go for the low-hanging fruit.** Each question within a given GRE Quantitative section is worth the same number of points. That's an extremely important point to remember.

   That's right, friends. Let's say ETS devised a question such as the following:

   $$\frac{[(100! - 99!)^{100}] - [(99! - 98!)^{100}]}{(98! - 97!)^{100}}$$

Even someone really good at math might take five minutes to solve this question—if they can solve it all. Yet, the correct answer would yield the exact same number of points as this question:

If $2^x = 4^2$, what is the value of x?

So what's the takeaway from this—other than "Factorials scare me!"?

Well, why waste time on a very difficult question when you can simply skip to an easier question? Think of it this way: in thirty-five minutes you want to score as many points as you can, and each question is worth the same.

If you were paid one thousand dollars for every apple you picked from a tree in thirty-five minutes, what would you do? You would go for the low-hanging fruit. You wouldn't waste your time climbing to the very top of the tree to pluck an apple that's worth the same amount of money as an apple that you can simply reach out and grab with both your feet planted on the ground.

Of course, after a certain point—once all those easy questions are complete—you must grab the fruit up high and go for the difficult questions. But make sure you've answered the easy ones first.

2. **Budget your time wisely.** There are easy questions, medium questions, and difficult questions. Easy questions should take between forty-five seconds and one minute. Medium questions should take between one and two minutes. And difficult questions should take no longer than three minutes. The ratio of easy, medium, and difficult questions varies per section, but in general you can expect to see a smattering of each. Within an easy section, the ratio will skew toward easy; in a difficult section that ratio will skew toward difficult.

3. **Learn to let go of a question.** If you're staring at a question and have been unable to come up with a solution after a minute, you should seriously consider moving on to the next question. Again, keep the low-hanging fruit metaphor in mind.

   If, however, you're dealing with a difficult math question (and it's clear that it's difficult and that you're not just missing something obvious), then take a couple of minutes, as some questions will clearly take that much time. Don't freak out over a question that's clearly tortuous just because you've taken two minutes. As long as you're headed toward the solution, persevere.

4. **Don't be sloppy, but don't obsess over easy questions.** Using the time breakdown above, we can see that easy questions should take less than a minute. It's important to answer these questions confidently and move on. If you dither, you're wasting time that could be spent on a more difficult question. That's not to say you should race through an easy question, because that defeats the whole low-hanging fruit lesson. Missing a question that you could easily have answered correctly had you spent that extra second doesn't make sense, especially if you're racing toward difficult questions that you may not even answer correctly in the first place.

5. **Make sure you guess.** As we've established, it's okay to skip some questions. But make sure, at the very end, that you guess on any questions remaining, because there's no penalty for guessing. So if you skipped a lot of questions, give yourself enough time at the end to select an answer for the questions you left blank. A little bit of luck can go a long way!

Calculator Strategies

Can I use a calculator on the GRE?

This is a very popular question, and the answer often elicits an audible sigh of relief. So, yes, you can use a calculator.

But don't celebrate just yet.

First off, many problems don't require a calculator. In fact, using a calculator may very well slow you down because you can either do the arithmetic faster in your head or on a piece of paper. Then, there's always the case of what to calculate. While a calculator won't make a careless error, neither will it tell you how to answer a question. Basically, the GRE math is still testing your ability to logically deconstruct a problem. In many cases, the challenge isn't the math but the approach to a problem.

When is it advantageous to use a calculator?

There are times when the calculation is simply too difficult to multiply on paper and the question isn't asking you to estimate. Problems such as compound interest fit this description. Maybe you have to find the hypotenuse of a right triangle with sides of 51 and 31. Figuring out the square root of a large number could be very difficult without a calculator.

Of course, if the problem asks, *What is the unit's digit of* 3^{1000}*?* then you then have to come up with a clever way to approach the problem; a calculator doesn't hold that many digits.

Getting a feel for the calculator

The best way to determine whether you'll benefit from a calculator is to take a practice test using Magoosh's online GRE prep. By doing so, you should get a feel for the number and types of questions in which the calculator will help you save time and those in which using it will only eat up time.

To the right is what the online calculator looks like.

You've probably used a calculator before, so the digits, decimal point, four operations (+, −, ×, ÷), and parentheses buttons are all probably quite intuitive. The ± changes the sign of the entry currently on the display. The √ button takes the square root of the entry currently on the display.

Many students are confused about CE vs. C buttons. The CE button is "clear entry" and C is "clear all." What's the difference? Suppose for some reason, you have to compute 23 × 41 × 72—that would be an unlikely thing to calculate on the GRE, but pretend you had to calculate that product. Let's say you type 23 × 41 ×—but then, by accident, type 27 instead of 72. If you hit CE, the screen goes to 0, but the calculator remembers your previous steps. After CE, you just type 72 and = and voila! The correct

One person who definitely didn't need a calculator was Srinivasa Ramanujan (1887–1920), the Indian supergenius who made mind-boggling contributions to many different branches of mathematics.

answer of 67,896 appears. Using the CE button is the way to tell the calculator to remember the previous steps of a calculation. By contrast, if you hit C, the calculator forgets everything and you're starting over fresh with a brand new calculation. Use C often, whenever you want to start something new, and use CE sparingly, only when you need to change the most recent input in a long calculation.

The three M buttons are also confusing and underused. These memory buttons allow you to store one number in memory and save it while you're performing a difference calculation. The M+ adds whatever is on the display to the memory. The default in memory is 0. When you use M+ to put some non-0 value into memory, an M will appear on the screen, to let you know that something is in memory. If you press M+ again when another number is on the display, this action adds the number currently on the display to the number in memory. MR is the memory recall button, which calls the number from memory back to the screen. MC is the memory clear: this resets the value in memory to 0 and it makes the M on the screen go away because there's no longer anything stored in the memory. These buttons can be very useful if you have to do a multi-step calculation.

For example, suppose you had the extremely unlikely task of computing the value of the following:

$$N = \sqrt{51^2 + 68^2 + 204^2}$$

You can compute this on the calculator as follows:

1. Make sure memory is empty (i.e., no M on the screen)
2. 51 × 51 =, then M+. At this point, M will appear on the screen. Then C.
3. 68 × 68 =, then M+, then C.
4. 204 × 204 =, then M+, then C. At this point, the sum under the radial will be in the memory.
5. MR and $\sqrt{}$

At this point, if you like, you can hit MC to clear the memory again. The advantage of the memory buttons is to break a long calculation into bite-sized pieces so you can focus on the pieces one at a time. The disadvantage is that you can only use the M+ function when you're doing addition.

Finally, let's discuss the "Transfer Display" button. On ordinary multiple-choice questions and multiple-answer questions, this has no function, but on a numeric entry question, this button will transfer the number on the calculator's display to the answer box in the question. This prevents you from making any awkward copying mistakes.

Quantitative Question Types

Let's take a look at some of the types of questions you'll see in the GRE Quantitative. Knowing beforehand how questions are formatted and what kind of answers you'll have to provide can ease some stress and make you feel better prepared.

Multiple Choice

You've definitely seen this type of question before. It's a typical five-choice multiple-choice question with only one right answer.

Here's an example—try it out for yourself before checking the explanation below.

Which of the following equations is true for all positive values of x and y?

- (A) $\sqrt{x} + \sqrt{y} = \sqrt{x + y}$
- (B) $\sqrt{x^4 y^{16}} = x^2 y^4$
- (C) $(x\sqrt{y})(y\sqrt{x}) = x^2 y^2$
- (D) $y\sqrt{x} + y\sqrt{x} = \sqrt{4xy^2}$
- (E) $(x^y)(y^y) = (xy)^{2y}$

This question is really testing your knowledge of roots and exponents. If anything doesn't make sense here, you can brush up on all the roots and exponents rules in the "Quantitative Concept #4: Exponents and Roots" section later in this chapter.

$\cancel{(A)}$ $\sqrt{x} + \sqrt{y} = \sqrt{x + y}$ $\quad\Rightarrow\quad$ $\sqrt{4} + \sqrt{9} \neq \sqrt{4 + 9}$

$\cancel{(B)}$ $\sqrt{x^4 y^{16}} = x^2 y^4$ $\quad\Rightarrow\quad$ $\sqrt{x^4 y^{16}} = x^2 y^8$

Proof: $(x^2 y^8)(x^2 y^8) = x^{2+2} \times y^{8+8} = x^4 y^{16}$

$\cancel{(C)}$ $(x\sqrt{y})(y\sqrt{x}) = x^2 y^2$ $\quad\Rightarrow\quad$ $xy\sqrt{xy} \neq x^2 y^2$

(D) $y\sqrt{x} + y\sqrt{x} = \sqrt{4xy^2}$ $\quad\Rightarrow\quad$ $y\sqrt{x} + y\sqrt{x} = \sqrt{4xy^2}$

$2y\sqrt{x} = \sqrt{4y^2}\sqrt{x}$

$= \sqrt{4xy^2}$

$\cancel{(E)}$ $(x^y)(y^y) = (xy)^{2y}$ $\quad\Rightarrow\quad$ $(x^y)(y^y) = (xy)^y$

Multiple Answer

The GRE calls these "multiple-choice questions—select one or more answers." For brevity—and clarity—at Magoosh, we call them "multiple-answer questions." We do include "multiple-choice questions," but we identify those type of questions that ask for more than one answer as "multiple-**answer** questions."

Imagine a question that has ten possible answer choices, any number of which could be correct—that's a multiple-answer question. So, unsurprisingly, they can be a little more difficult than a typical multiple-choice question.

Those well-versed in combinations and permutations know the chance of guessing correctly on this question is 1 in 1,023, odds so slim the question might as well have been a big empty fill-in-the-blank. But that's okay because you won't be guessing—you'll know the material, so you'll feel confident and prepared to tackle multiple-answer questions.

Luckily, most multiple-answer questions will have only five or six possible answer choices, not ten. The bottom line is that if you know the concept being tested and are careful and methodical, then you should be able to get this cumbersome question type correct.

Here is an example of a multiple-answer question:

$2x^2 + 6 > 40$

Which values of x satisfy the inequality above?

Indicate <u>all</u> such values.

A −8
B −6
C −4
D −2
E 2
F 4
G 6
H 8

Note that on the actual GRE, each answer choice will have a square around it. If there's a circle around the answer choice, then it's multiple choice, business as usual—one answer only. But when you see the square, you know you're dealing with multiple-answer questions. Another telltale sign of these questions is giveaway text such as "indicate <u>all</u> such values," with the word *all* underlined.

As for this particular multiple-answer question, the first trick is to notice that the inequality isn't stated in its simplest form. To simplify, divide all terms by 2, then subtract 3 from both sides. This leads to a much more straightforward inequality: $x^2 > 17$. Of course, [G] and [H] satisfy this, while [E] and [F] do not. Remember that when you square a negative, you get a positive—for example, $(-6)^2 = +36$. Thus, [A] and [B] also work. The complete correct answer set for this multiple-answer question is {A, B, G, H}.

Make sure you write something down when tackling multiple-answer questions. Trying to juggle all the information in your head will surely get you in trouble on more challenging questions!

Numeric Entry

Two trains starting from cities 300 miles apart head toward each other at rates of 70 mph and 50 mph, respectively. How long does it take the trains to cross paths?

$$\boxed{}$$

This is a classic problem that sends chills up students' spines. And now we're going to add another bone-rattling element: the empty box.

That's right—the GRE will have fill-in-the-blank/empty-box math problems, called "numeric entry." There won't be too many, judging from official ETS materials, but even facing a few questions like this is enough to unsettle most students.

Let's go back and attack the above problem. When you have any two things (trains, bicyclists, cars, etc.) headed toward each other, you must add their rates to find the combined rate. The logic behind the combined rate is that the two trains (as is the case here) are coming from opposite directions, straight into each other.

This yields 120 mph, a very fast rate. (Incidentally, that's what accounts for the severity of head-on collisions. Don't worry; the trains in the problem won't collide!)

To find the final answer, we want to employ our nifty old formula $d = rt$, where d stands for distance, r stands for rate, and t stands for time.

We've already found r, which is their combined rate of 120 mph. They're 300 miles apart, so that's d. Plugging those values in, we get $300 = 120t$. Dividing both sides by 120, we get $t = 2.5$ hrs.

Now we can confidently fill that box in and let the trains continue on their respective ways.

Quantitative Comparison

Quantitative comparison is a huge part of the GRE, making up roughly one-third of the questions in the GRE Quantitative. Often, when prepping, students forget this fact and spend much more time on problem-solving. Quantitative comparison is a unique beast; while the math concepts are the exact same as those covered in problem-solving, quantitative comparison questions can be very tricky. In fact, the GRE test writers work very hard to make these questions seem simple and straightforward. In reality, there's usually a trap or twist waiting to catch the unsuspecting test taker.

The format of quantitative comparison questions will always be the same: comparing two quantities (column A vs. column B), with the same four answer choices that evaluate the relationship between the two quantities. However, the quantities for column A and B can be anything from expressions with variables to references to a quantity in a geometric shape.

Take a look at this example on the following page:

Column A	Column B
The number of positive multiples of 49 less than 2000	The number of positive multiples of 50 less than or equal to 2000

(A) The quantity in Column A is greater

(B) The quantity in Column B is greater

(C) The two quantities are equal

(D) The relationship cannot be determined from the information given

To start, you've got to know that a multiple is any number that results when multiplying an integer, x, by 1, 2, 3, 4 ... .

If x is equal to 5, then the multiples of 5 would be:

$5 \times 1 = 5$

$5 \times 2 = 10$

$5 \times 3 = 15$

$5 \times 4 = 20$

$5 \times 5 = 25$

$5 \times 6 = 30$

...

In the table above, you can see that any multiple of 5 is divisible by 5. For instance, $\frac{1,000}{5} = 200$. Therefore, 1,000 is a multiple of 5.

The question above asks you how many multiples of 49 are less than 2,000. You can divide 2,000 by 49 to see how many multiples of 49 are less than 2,000. Doing so may take a while. A faster way is to see that 49 is very close to 50. Quick math allows you to determine that 50 × 40 is 2,000. Therefore, 49 × 40 equals 40 less than 2,000, or 1,960. If you were to multiply 49 × 41, you would be adding 1,960 + 49, which equals 2,009. This number is greater than 2,000. Therefore, you know that there are only 40 multiples of 49 less than 2,000.

What about column B? Well, you've already figured out that 40 × 50 equals 2,000. But here is the tricky part. Whereas column A specifies that the number has to be less than 2,000, column B says the number has to be less than OR equal to 2,000. Therefore, there are 40 multiples of 50 that are less than or equal to 2,000, etc.

The answer is **(C)**.

There's a good chance that your first instinct was (A). Clearly, 49 is lower than 50, so it has to have more multiples. Usually, when the answer to a quantitative comparison question appears obvious at first glance, there's some twist to the problem. In this case, the twist was the wording in column B: "less than or equal to 2000." So be wary of any quantitative comparison questions that seem too easy.

Quantitative Concept #1: Fractions/Ratios/Percents

We're putting the three concepts of fractions, ratios, and percents together because they're intricately linked. After we break these topics down for you, it'll be time to practice!

Fractions

Of all the math topics that raise dread, fear, anxiety, and confusion, few do so as consistently as fractions. Why is that anyway? Well, at Magoosh, we have this theory. Think back to when you learned fractions—maybe the third, fourth, or fifth grade. That's when fractions are usually taught, but there are two problems with that. First of all, that's before the tsunami of puberty hit and virtually obliterated all previously held logical connections in your head. More importantly, fractions, like many other topics in math, involve sophisticated patterns, but in the fourth grade, the brain isn't capable of abstraction, so instead you had to rely on reproducing patterns mechanically. And when those patterns don't fit a particular question, you basically don't know what to do.

The solution to getting over fractionitis is to approach those mechanical procedures with the understanding that comes from having an adult brain capable of seeing abstract patterns. When you understand why you do each thing, then (a) you can remember it much better and (b) you can figure out what to do in a moment of confusion.

So are you ready to rekindle your relationship with fractions? Let's start with the basics.

What is a fraction?

A fraction is a way of showing division. The fraction $\frac{2}{7}$ means the number you get when you divide 2 by 7. The number at the top of a fraction is called the *numerator*, and the number on the bottom of a fraction is called the *denominator*.

The fraction $\frac{2}{7}$ also means two parts of something broken into seven equal parts. Imagine dividing something whole into seven equal parts—one of those parts is $\frac{1}{7}$ of the whole, so $\frac{2}{7}$ is two of those parts, or $2 \times \frac{1}{7}$. This diagram representing $\frac{2}{7}$ will probably call up dim memories from your prepubescent mathematical experiences.

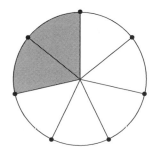

The first quasi-fractions were used by the ancient Egyptians about 4000 years ago. It was the brilliant twelfth-century Moroccan mathematician Abu Bakr al-Hassar who initiated the use of the horizontal bar to separate a numerator and a denominator.

Notice that if you have the fractions $\frac{4}{14}$ or $\frac{10}{35}$, they both cancel down to $\frac{2}{7}$. **Canceling is division.** Thus, when you have $\frac{4}{20}$, and you cancel (i.e., divide) the 4s in the numerator and the denominator, they don't simply "go away," but rather what's left in the numerator is $4 \div 4 = 1$, and what's left in the denominator is $20 \div 4 = 5$, so we get $\frac{4}{20} = \frac{1}{5}$.

Adding and subtracting fractions

When you add fractions, you can't simply add across the numerator and denominator.

$$\frac{a}{b} + \frac{c}{d} \neq \frac{a+c}{b+d}$$

You may dimly remember that you can add and subtract fractions only when you have a common denominator. That's true, but why? Believe it or not, the basis of this fact is what's called the Distributive Law, $a(b + c) = ab + ac$. For example, if you add $3x$ and $5x$, you get $3x + 5x = 8x$. According to the Distributive Law, you can add two terms of the same thing, but if you want to add $3x + 5y$, you can't simplify that any further and must keep it as $3x + 5y$. Basically, you can't add apples and oranges.

When the denominators aren't the same, as in the example $\frac{3}{8} + \frac{1}{6}$, then you can't add them as is, but you can take advantage of a sleek mathematical trick. You know that any number over itself, say $\frac{3}{3}$, equals 1, and you can always multiply by 1 and not change the value of something. Therefore, you could multiply $\frac{3}{8}$ by some fraction $\frac{a}{a}$, and then multiply $\frac{1}{6}$ by some other fraction $\frac{b}{b}$, and both would retain the same value. You'll want to multiply each to find the least common denominator (LCD), which here is 24. Thus,

$$\left(\frac{3}{8}\right) + \left(\frac{1}{6}\right) = \left(\frac{3}{8}\right) \times \left(\frac{3}{3}\right) + \left(\frac{1}{6}\right) \times \left(\frac{4}{4}\right) = \left(\frac{9}{24}\right) + \left(\frac{4}{24}\right) = \left(\frac{13}{24}\right)$$

The same thing works for subtraction:

$$\left(\frac{3}{8}\right) - \left(\frac{1}{6}\right) = \left(\frac{3}{8}\right) \times \left(\frac{3}{3}\right) - \left(\frac{1}{6}\right) \times \left(\frac{4}{4}\right) = \left(\frac{9}{24}\right) - \left(\frac{4}{24}\right) = \left(\frac{5}{24}\right)$$

Multiplying fractions

This is the easiest of all fraction rules. To multiply fractions, multiply across the numerators and denominators.

$$\frac{5}{7} \times \frac{2}{3} = \frac{10}{21}$$

What's a little tricky about multiplying fractions is knowing what you can cancel. If you multiply two fractions, of course you can cancel any numerator with its own denominator, but you can also cancel any numerator with *any* denominator. Here's a horrendous multiplication problem that simplifies elegantly with the liberal use of canceling.

$$\frac{26}{48} \times \frac{18}{56} \times \frac{64}{39} = \frac{26}{48} \times \frac{18}{7} \times \frac{8}{39} = \frac{2}{48} \times \frac{18}{7} \times \frac{8}{3} = \frac{2}{6} \times \frac{18}{7} \times \frac{1}{3} = \frac{2}{1} \times \frac{1}{7} \times \frac{1}{1} = \frac{2}{7}$$

Dividing fractions

To get started with division, it's important to remember that multiplying by $\frac{1}{3}$ is the same as dividing by 3. That's just the fundamental definition of fractions as division. This also means that dividing by $\frac{1}{3}$ is the same as multiplying by 3. This pattern suggests, correctly, that dividing by a fraction simply means multiplying by its reciprocal:

$$\boxed{\frac{5}{12} \div \frac{3}{8}} = \boxed{\frac{5}{\cancel{12}} \times \frac{\cancel{8}}{3}} = \boxed{\frac{5}{3} \times \frac{2}{3}} = \frac{10}{9}$$

Notice, as always, that you cancel *before* you multiply. Dividing a fraction by a number follows the same pattern:

$$\boxed{\frac{\frac{6}{13}}{3}} = \boxed{\frac{6}{13} \div \frac{3}{1}} = \boxed{\frac{6}{13} \times \frac{1}{3}} = \frac{2}{13}$$

Notice the similarity with the previous rule: dividing by 3 means the same thing as multiplying by $\frac{1}{3}$. Also, again, notice that you cancel before you multiply.

Ratios

Suppose a big group has two kinds of members. Let's say that all the baseball players in a certain high school student body are divided into varsity and junior varsity players, two mutually exclusive groups. Suppose we're told that the ratio of junior varsity to varsity players is 3:5. What does this mean? It would be wrong to assume that there are only 3 junior varsity players and 5 varsity players—it's hard to play baseball with so few players! Instead, the ratio tells us about overall makeup of a larger group.

A ratio of 3:5 could mean that the numbers of junior varsity and varsity players are 6 and 9, or 15 and 25, or 30 and 50, or 60 and 100. In other words, it *could* mean any multiples of 3 and 5. What it *does* mean, though, is that if we made a fraction with the number of junior varsity players in the numerator and the number of varsity players in the denominator, that fraction would simplify to $\frac{3}{5}$.

It's also possible to have more than two groups related in a ratio. Let's say that we can group all the employees in a company by how they travel to work. Group D are the employees that drive, group P are the ones who take public transportation, and group W are the ones who walk. Let's say that, at Company KX, the ratio of D to P to W is 2:5:1. Once again, this doesn't necessarily mean that there are only $2 + 5 + 1 = 8$ employees at Company KX. Instead, we could have any multiple of those:

- 8 drivers, 20 on public transit, and 4 walkers
- 14 drivers, 35 on public transit, and 7 walkers
- 26 drivers, 65 on public transit, and 13 walkers

Also, this triple ratio doesn't give us just one fraction but several: $\frac{D}{P} = \frac{2}{5}$, $\frac{W}{P} = \frac{1}{5}$, and $\frac{W}{D} = \frac{1}{2}$, for example. There's a lot of information in that ratio!

Mathematically, a ratio between two quantities is simply a fraction: whether we write 3:5 or $\frac{3}{5}$, we're conveying the same basic mathematical information. The good news is that if you learn all the rules for fractions, then you know all the mathematical rules for ratios also. We'll talk a little more about the mathematics of ratios.

Ratios and proportions

Mathematically, ratios and fractions are exactly the same thing. A proportion is an equation in which one fraction equals another; in other words, it's an equation in which we show two ratios as equal. For example:

$$\frac{x}{12} = \frac{33}{28}$$

One legitimate move is to *cross-multiply*, although doing so here would violate the ultra-strategic dictum: cancel *before* you multiply. And it's precisely this issue—what you can and can't cancel in a proportion—that causes endless confusion.

Let's look at the general proportion $\frac{a}{b} = \frac{c}{d}$.

First of all, as always, you can cancel any numerator with its own denominator—you can cancel common factors in a and b, or in c and d. What's more, a proportion, by its very nature, is an equation, and you can always multiply or divide both sides of an equation by the same thing. This means you can cancel common factors in both numerators (a and c) or in both denominators (b and d). The following diagrams summarize all the legitimate directions of cancellation in a proportion.

$$\boxed{\frac{a}{b} = \frac{c}{d}} \quad \boxed{\frac{a}{b} = \frac{c}{d}}$$

The following are highly tempting but completely illegal ways to cancel in proportions:

$$\frac{a}{b} = \frac{c}{d} \quad \frac{a}{b} = \frac{c}{d}$$

Let's solve the proportion above with proper canceling:

$$\frac{x}{12} = \frac{33}{28} \quad \Rightarrow \quad \frac{x}{3} = \frac{33}{7} \quad \Rightarrow \quad x = \frac{99}{7}$$

Notice in that last step that to isolate x, all you had to do was multiply both sides by 3. Cross-multiplying, while always legal in a proportion, is often a waste of time that simply adds extra steps.

Ratios and portioning

Okay. We have discussed some of the mathematical moves we can do with ratios and proportions, but there are many other ways of thinking about ratios. Let's say, that in a particular town, there are just two kinds of residences: rented and owned.

A few sections ago, we discussed how a given ratio might mean that the actual numbers are any multiple of those in the ratio. For example, if the ratio of the number of rented residences to the number of owned residences is 7:4, then the numbers are some integer multiple of 7 and 4; for example, 70 rented and 40 owned, or 700 rented and 400 owned, or 1400 rented and 800 owned, etc.

One way to say this is that there's some unknown integer N, the factor that multiplies the numbers in the ratio. This generalizes the idea that we can multiply a ratio by any positive integer: rather than pick a specific integer, we'll use a variable that can represent an integer. In other words, for this unknown value of N, the number of rented residences is $7N$ and the number of owned residences is $4N$. One bonus fact we learn from thinking this way is that the total number of residences is $4N + 7N = 11N$. Using this factor N allows us to set up all kinds of equations from a ratio. Here's a practice problem:

In a certain town, the ratio of the number of rented residences to the number of owned residences is 7:4. Those are the only two kinds of residences in this town. If there are 150 more rented than owned residences in this town, what is the total number of residences in the town?

Ⓐ 200

Ⓑ 350

Ⓒ 550

Ⓓ 700

Ⓔ 1100

Let's say that, for some value of N, the number of rented residences is $7N$ and that the number of owned residences is $4N$. Then the difference is 150.

$$7N - 4N = 150$$
$$3N = 150$$
$$N = 50$$

Now that we have the value of N, we know that there are $7 \times 50 = 350$ rented residences, and $4 \times 50 = 200$ owned residences. The total would be $350 + 200 = 550$. That's answer choice **(C)**.

Let's consider another example. Let's say that in a certain stable, all the horses are classified as either stallions (males) or mares (females). Let's say that we're given that the ratio of stallions to mares is 7:3. One way to look at this is that, for some unknown N, the number of stallions is $7N$ and the number of mares is $3N$. Then it's clear that the total number of horses is $7N + 3N = 10N$. Thus, we could figure out fractions or percentages for each group. The stallions are $\frac{7}{10}$ or 70% of all the horses, and the mares are $\frac{3}{10}$ or 30% of all the horses. We can always make these fractions of the whole from a ratio: this is called portioning. Here, since the whole was 10 "parts," we also could easily express the numbers as percents as well; of course, if the denominator of a fraction is, say, 17 or 23, then it would be more difficult to express the fraction as a percent.

We can also use portioning if there are more than two groups. Let's say that all the cars in a city can be classified as compact (C), family-sized (F), luxury (L), or trucks (T). Suppose we're given that the ratio of C to F to L to T is 12:7:1:5. We know that $12 + 7 + 1 + 5 = 25$ would represent the whole, so $\frac{12}{25}$ of the cars are compact, $\frac{7}{25}$ of the cars are family-sized, etc. We can also create all the fractions relating individual groups ($\frac{L}{F} = \frac{1}{7}$, $\frac{T}{C} = \frac{5}{12}$, etc.). This single ratio is absolutely packed with mathematical information.

We can also go backwards from portion information to the individual ratios. Suppose, in a certain class, there are boys and girls, and suppose girls are $\frac{8}{13}$ of the class. If girls are $8N$ and the whole class is $13N$, then boys must be $5N$. The portion of boys is $\frac{5}{13}$, and ratio of boys to girls must be $\frac{5}{8}$. Given the ratio information, we can get the portions, and given the portions, we can get the individual ratios.

Here's another practice question, a quantitative comparison, using this example:

In a certain class, every student is either a boy or a girl. The boys constitute $\frac{5}{13}$ of the students in the class.

Column A	Column B
The ratio of boys to girls in the class	The fraction of the class that are girls

---

As we saw in the paragraph immediately above the problem, the ratio in column A equals $\frac{5}{8}$, and the ratio in column B equals $\frac{8}{13}$. We have to compare the size of these two fractions. As we'll learn in the chapter on quantitative comparison strategies (page 190), we're always allowed to multiply both columns by any positive number. Thus, we're allowed to cross-multiply in quantitative comparisons: cross-multiplication doesn't change the underlying relationship between the two columns.

Column A	Column B
$\frac{5}{8}$ ⇨ 5×13 ⇨ **65**	$\frac{8}{13}$ ⇨ 8×8 ⇨ **64**

Column A is bigger, so the answer is **(A)**.

Percents

Fundamentally, a percent is a fraction out of 100. The word comes from the Latin *per centum*, meaning "per one hundred." It's easy to change a percent to a fraction or a decimal. For example, 37% means 37 parts out of one hundred or $\frac{37}{100}$. As a decimal, that's just 0.37. Changing a percent to a decimal simply involves sliding the decimal two places to the left.

Percent changes as multipliers

This is one of the **big** math ideas in the GRE. A *multiplier* is a factor by which you multiply a number to get a desired result. There are three percent-related multipliers you will need to understand:

- **X% of a number.** Suppose you have $400 in an account and need to know what 30% of this account is. The multiplier = the percent as a decimal, so 30% as a decimal is 0.30, and $400(0.30) = $120; therefore $120 is 30% of $400.

- **An X% increase.** Suppose you have $400 in an account, and over a period of time you're going to get an additional 5% of interest; in other words, your account is going to increase by 5%. Here, the multiplier = 1 + (the percent as a decimal). Thus, $400(1.05) = $420, so that's the amount you would have after a 5% increase.

- **An X% decrease.** Suppose you have $400 in an account, and because of some kind of penalty, you're going to be nailed with a 15% deduction; in other words, your account will decrease by 15%. Here, the multiplier = 1 − (the percent as a decimal). In this case, the multiplier = 1 − 0.15 = 0.85, and the result after the deduction is ($400)(0.85) = $340.

Calculating a percent change

Basically, a percent is a simple $\frac{part}{whole}$ ratio times 100. The GRE will ask you to calculate percent changes, and here you have to be very careful with order; that is, you need to know the starting number and the ending number. It's important to note that in a percent change problem, the starting number is always 100%. So …

$$percent\ change = \frac{amount\ of\ change}{starting\ amount} \times 100$$

Here are a couple of examples:

- **Price increases from $400 to $500; find the percentage increase.** Of course, that's a change of $100, so $\frac{\$100}{starting\ value\ of\ \$400} = 0.25 \times 100 = 25\%$. A move from $400 to $500 is a 25% increase.

- **Price decreases from $500 to $400; find the percentage decrease.** Change is still $100, but now the starting value is $500, and $\frac{\$100}{\$500} = 0.20 \times 100 = 20\%$. A move from $500 to $400 is a 20% decrease.

You can see in these examples that order matters. When you change from one value to another and want the percentage change, it matters which value was the starting value.

A series of percentage changes

On the GRE, you may be asked a question that involves a series of percentage changes, some increases and some decreases. These may seem like a nightmare. But using multipliers will surely simplify your approach. Let's take a look at an example.

The ancient Romans didn't have the idea of decimals, so they expressed the parts of something as a multiple of 1/100 of that thing. For example, the first Emperor, Caesar Augustus, levied a 1/100 tax on any goods sold at an auction. This fraction, "per 100" (or "per centum" in Latin) evolved into our idea of a percent.

> Profits increased by 40% in January, then decreased by 30% in February, then increased by 20% in March. Express the change over the entire first quarter as a single percentage.

Don't get tripped up by adding a series of changes. That's what many people will do, and on multiple choice, it's always an answer choice. Here, that would be 40 − 30 + 20 = 30. That's not the way to go about answering the question.

The way to attack this question is with a series of multipliers:

In January, a 40% increase makes the multiplier = 1.40
In February, a 30% decrease makes the multiplier = 0.70
In March, a 20% increase makes the multiplier = 1.20

For a series of percentage changes, simply multiply the respective multipliers. Aggregate change = (1.40)(0.70)(1.20) = 1.176. That's a 17.6% increase for the quarter.

The increase-decrease trap

This is a predictable GRE trap: the result of a percentage increase, followed by a percentage decrease of the same numerical value. For example, look at this problem:

> The price of the appliance increases 20%, and then decreases 20%. The final price is what percent of the original price?

Every single time that question is asked as a multiple choice problem, the incorrect answer of 100% will be an answer choice, and every single time, a large portion of students who take the GRE will select it. You have a leg up if you simply recognize and remember that this is a trap.

In fact, solving this problem is just an extension of the previous item:

a 20% increase makes the multiplier = 1.20
a 20% decrease makes the multiplier = 0.80
total change = (1.20)(0.80) = 0.96

Thus, after the increase and decrease, the final price is 96% of the original price, which means it's a 4% *decrease*.

When you go up by a percent, then down by the same percent, you do *not* wind up where you started: that's the trap. In this situation, as in any situation in which you have a series of percentage changes, simply multiply the respective multipliers.

Fractions/Ratios/Percents Practice Questions

These questions should help you get an idea of what to expect from fraction, ratio, and percent questions on the GRE. Some of the following questions may be more difficult than what was covered in the previous section. But fear not! You'll learn more tricks and subtleties in the upcoming Answers and Explanations section. There are even more practice questions in the GRE practice test in chapter 6.

Question 1
Difficulty: **Easy** · Percent Correct: **78.5%*** · Type: **Multiple Choice**

After receiving a 25% discount, Sue paid $180 for a lawnmower. What is the original price of the lawnmower before the discount?

(A) $215
(B) $220
(C) $225
(D) $240
(E) $245

Question 2
Difficulty: **Easy** · Percent Correct: **77.9%** · Type: **Numeric Entry**

30% of 50 is what fraction of 75% of 80?

Enter your answer as a fraction. Fractions do not need to be in their simplest forms.

Question 3
Difficulty: **Medium** · Percent Correct: **44.0%** · Type: **Multiple Answer**

If $x > 0$, which of the following expressions are equal to 3.6 percent of $\frac{(5x)}{12}$?

Indicate <u>all</u> such expressions.

[A] 3 percent of $20x$

[B] x percent of $\frac{3}{2}$

[C] $3x$ percent of 0.2

[D] 0.05 percent of $3x$

[E] $\frac{(3x)}{200}$

*Based on thousands of students' answers in the Magoosh online premium product.

47

Question 4

Difficulty: **Medium** · Percent Correct: **74.9%** · Type: **Quantitative Comparison**

Four friends win $120,000 in the lottery, and they divide the
winnings in a 1:2:4:5 ratio.

Column A	Column B
The difference between the greatest share and the least share	$40,000

(A) The quantity in Column A is greater

(B) The quantity in Column B is greater

(C) The two quantities are equal

(D) The relationship cannot be determined from the information given

When you're ready, turn the page to see the answers.

Fractions/Ratios/Percents Answers and Explanations

Question 1

Difficulty: **Easy** · Percent Correct: **78.5%** · Type: **Multiple Choice**

Answer: **D**

After receiving a 25% discount, Sue paid $180 for a lawnmower. What is the original price of the lawnmower before the discount?

- (A) $215
- (B) $220
- (C) $225
- **(D) $240**
- (E) $245

Let x be the original price.

discounted price $= 0.75x$

$$180 = 0.75x$$

$$180 = \frac{3}{4}x$$

$$\left(\frac{4}{3}\right)180 = \left(\frac{4}{3}\right)\frac{3}{4}x$$

$$\mathbf{240 = x}$$

Question 2

Difficulty: **Easy** · Percent Correct: **77.9%** · Type: **Numeric Entry**

Answer: $\frac{1}{4}$

30% of 50 is what fraction of 75% of 80?

10% of 50 is 5, so 30% is three times this, which is 15.

75% of something is $\frac{3}{4}$ of that thing. One quarter of 80 is 20, so three quarters, or 75%, is 60.

15 is what fraction of 60?

$$\text{fraction} = \frac{15}{60} = \frac{1}{4}$$

Question 3

Difficulty: **Medium** · Percent Correct: **44.0%** · Type: **Multiple Answer**

Answer: **B E**

If $x > 0$, which of the following expressions are equal to 3.6 percent of $\frac{5x}{12}$?

Indicate all such expressions.

- [A] 3 percent of $20x = \left(\frac{3}{100}\right)20x = \frac{3x}{5}$
- [B] x percent of $\frac{3}{2} = \left(\frac{x}{100}\right)\left(\frac{3}{2}\right) = \frac{3x}{200}$
- [C] $3x$ percent of $0.2 = \left(\frac{3x}{100}\right)\left(\frac{1}{5}\right) = \frac{3x}{500}$
- [D] 0.05 percent of $3x = \left(\frac{0.05}{100}\right)(3x) = \left(\frac{5}{10,000}\right)(3x) = \frac{3x}{2000}$
- [E] $\frac{3x}{200}$

3.6% of $\frac{5x}{12} = \left(\frac{3.6}{100}\right)\left(\frac{5x}{12}\right)$

$\qquad = \left(\frac{36}{1000}\right)\left(\frac{5x}{12}\right)$ Cancel common

$\qquad = \frac{3x}{200}$ factors 3 and 5

Question 4

Difficulty: **Medium** · Percent Correct: **74.9%** · Type: Quantitative Comparison

Four friends win $120,000 in the lottery, and they divide the winnings in a 1:2:4:5 ratio.

Answer: **C**

Column A	Column B
The difference between the greatest share and the least share	$40,000
$50,000 − $10,000 = **$40,000**	**$40,000**

1:2:4:5 ⇨ 1 + 2 + 4 + 5 = 12

$120,000 ÷ 12 = $10,000

1 ⇨ $10,000   2 ⇨ $20,000   4 ⇨ $40,000   5 ⇨ $50,000

Ⓐ The quantity in Column A is greater

Ⓑ The quantity in Column B is greater

Ⓒ The two quantities are equal

Ⓓ The relationship cannot be determined from the information given

You can find even more fractions/ratios/percents questions on gre.magoosh.com!

51

Quantitative Concept #2: Integer Properties and Number Sense

"Number sense" is a good intuition for what happens to different kinds of numbers (positive, negative, fractions, etc.) when you perform various arithmetic operations on them. It's what allows some students to easily apply shortcuts such as estimation or visual solutions. When you strengthen your number sense, you'll start seeing many math problems through a whole new lens.

Now, how do you develop your number sense? Unfortunately, there isn't a simple answer to this question. That said, a key component of number sense is a solid grasp of the basic properties of numbers. For example, it's important to know how to distinguish between the general meaning of the word "number" and more specific types of numbers, such as integers. Similarly, learning how to choose numbers that are convenient for a particular problem and becoming comfortable with units are also parts of developing number sense.

With that in mind, let's get started! First, we'll look at some number properties to build your number-sense foundations. Then we'll take a look at number sense itself and specific strategies to further strengthen this type of intuition!

Numbers

Let's start with how you think about the word *number*. A narrow view of the definition would be the set $\{1, 2, 3, 4, 5, ...\}$. In reality, the word *number* is a broad category, encompassing everything on the number line: 0 is a number; $\frac{4}{7}$ is a number; -4 is a number; $-\frac{1}{5}$ is a number; π is a number; the square root of 17 is a number; and so on. All of these possibilities must leap to mind when a problem mentions the word *number*.

Integers

Integers are positive and negative whole numbers, meaning the following set:

$$\{... , -3, -2, -1, 0, 1, 2, 3, ...\}$$

Integers go on forever in the positive and negative directions. They don't include fractions, decimals, and numbers like π. One way for you to remember the definition of *integer* is by looking at its root. The word *integer* shares a root with the word *integrity*—both come from the Latin word for "whole, wholeness."

If the GRE shows a numerical statement, such as $x < 3$, don't assume that x is an integer unless that's specified. That's one of the biggest traps on the test: assuming that the only possibilities are integers when there are many more possibilities allowed.

Even and Odd

First of all, you need to be aware that even and odd numbers are all integers. After that, here are three addition rules to know when it comes to even and odd numbers:

1. (even) + (even) = (even)
2. (odd) + (odd) = (even)
3. (even) + (odd) = (odd)

These rules also work when the + is changed to a −.

Now, here are three multiplication rules:

1. (even) × (even) = (even)
2. (odd) × (odd) = (odd)
3. (even) × (odd) = (even)

These rules are *not* the same if the × is changed to ÷. If you have trouble remembering these six rules, you can always use (even) = 2 and (odd) = 3 to remind yourself. Yes, 1 is also odd, but it's good to get into the habit of not using 1 as a test number, only because 1 has so many unique properties.

Keep in mind that 0 is an even number. Also remember that negative numbers can be even and odd, just like their positive counterparts. Fractions and non-integers cannot be even or odd, as it's a property reserved for integers only.

Prime

Every number has 1 as a factor. Every number has itself as a factor. A number is *prime* if its only factors are 1 and itself. Only positive integers are said to be prime. The distinction isn't given to negative integers, 0, or non-integers.

Here is a list of the first few primes:

{2, 3, 5, 7, 11, 13, 17, 19, 23, 29, ...}

The primes go on forever in an irregular pattern. It would be good to memorize this list of the first ten prime numbers. Notice that, for a variety of reasons with which we need not concern ourselves here, **1 is not considered a prime number**. Also notice that 2 is the only even prime number; all other even numbers are divisible by 2.

Prime Factorizations

Every positive integer greater than 1 is either prime or a product of two or more primes. The numbers in the latter category—the numbers that equal a product of two or more prime numbers—are called *composite* numbers. (Notice that 1 is the only positive integer that's neither prime nor composite.) For the composite numbers, there's an important mathematical theorem that says that each composite number equals a *unique* product of prime numbers. This is called *prime factorization*: the unique product of prime numbers that equals the number. The prime factorization of a number is like the DNA of that number, meaning that from the prime factorization of a number, we

The Greek mathematician **Euclid** (fl. 300 BCE), famous for his work in geometry, was the first to prove that there are an infinite number of prime numbers.

can derive a tremendous amount of information.

First, let's explore this. Technically, even a prime number has a prime factorization, but it's not all that hard to figure out for each one. Why? Because the prime factorization of any prime number is simply that number. For example, the prime factorization of 7 is 7. It becomes much more interesting when we look at composite numbers. Here are the prime factorizations of the first eight composite numbers:

$$4 = 2 \times 2$$
$$6 = 2 \times 3$$
$$8 = 2 \times 2 \times 2$$
$$9 = 3 \times 3$$
$$10 = 2 \times 5$$
$$12 = 2 \times 2 \times 3$$
$$14 = 2 \times 7$$
$$15 = 3 \times 5$$

The numbers 6, 10, 14, and 15 each have two prime factors. How many prime factors does 9 have? Well, it has two of the same thing, so how do we answer this question? Mathematicians have developed precise language for this: they use the word *distinct* to denote items that are different. Thus, 9 has a total of two prime factors but it has only one distinct prime factor, 3. Similarly, 12 has a total of three prime factors, but it has only two distinct prime factors, 2 and 3.

The prime factorization of a number N allows us to see all the factors of the number. Any prime factor in the prime factorization is a factor of N, and the product of any combination of prime factors is also a factor of N. For example, the prime factorization of $30 = 2 \times 3 \times 5$. So what are the factors of 30? Well, first of all, 1 is a factor of every integer, and every integer is a factor of itself, so 1 and 30 are factors. Each of the three primes in the prime factorization are factors: 2, 3, and 5. Finally, here are the products of each pair of prime factors: $2 \times 3 = 6$; $2 \times 5 = 10$; and $3 \times 5 = 15$. Thus, the total factor list for 30 is as follows: {1, 2, 3, 5, 6, 10, 15, 30}.

Typically, the test won't provide the prime factorization of a number. Instead, it will give you a large number and it will be your job to find the prime factorization. Doing so would be a particularly relevant move if the question is asking about the factors or especially the prime factors of the number. How do we find the prime factorization of a number?

Let's say we have to find the prime factorization of 84. We can begin by finding any two numbers that multiply to 84. For example, suppose we notice that $84 = 7 \times 12$. We would put 84 at the top of a factor "tree" with "branches" down to these two factors, 7 and 12. The number 7 is already prime, so this will just have a single "branch" below it. The number 12 can be factored further, so we continue branching into factors until everything is prime. Here is the entire factor tree for 84:

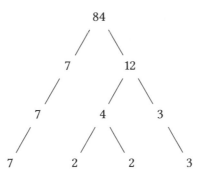

Notice that it doesn't matter where we start. If we had started with 84 = 6 × 14, the steps would have been different, but the combination of prime factors at the bottom would be the same, and that's all that matters. This combination is the prime factorization of 84. Thus,

84 = 2 × 2 × 3 × 7

As another example, let's come up with the factor tree for 120. Again, we could make many different choices in the branching patterns. All that matters is the bottom row (the combination of prime factors), and that will always be the same, no matter what branching choices we make. Here's one possible factor tree:

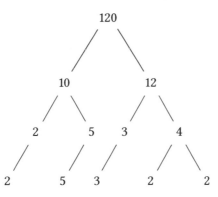

Thus, 120 = 2 × 2 × 2 × 3 × 5. The order in which we write the factors in the prime factorization doesn't matter at all because multiplication of a bunch of factors never depends on the order of the factors. Conventionally, we write the factors from smallest to biggest, to make it easier to read. Also, when there are multiple factors of the same prime numbers, mathematicians often simplify by using an exponent: $120 = 2^3 × 3 × 5$.

Here's a practice quantitative comparison question:

Column A	Column B
The number of distinct prime factors in 84	The number of distinct prime factors in 150

Ⓐ The quantity in Column A is greater
Ⓑ The quantity in Column B is greater
Ⓒ The two quantities are equal
Ⓓ The relationship cannot be determined from the information given

Of course, to solve this, we need to find the prime factorization of both numbers. We'll leave the factor trees for you, but here are the completed prime factorizations:

$$84 = 2^2 \times 3 \times 7$$
$$150 = 2 \times 3 \times 5^2$$

Thus 84 has three distinct prime factors {2, 3, 7} and 150 also has three distinct prime factors {2, 3, 5}. The columns are equal. The answer is **(C)**.

The question didn't ask about this, but 84 and 150 also have the same total numbers of prime factors: four.

Number Sense: The Lowdown

Many GRE quantitative problems test number sense. Here are a few examples of mathematical practices that people with strong number sense know:

• Making the numerator of a fraction bigger makes the whole fraction bigger.
• Making the denominator of a fraction bigger makes the whole fraction smaller.
• (big positive) + (small negative) = something positive
• (small positive) + (big negative) = something negative
• Multiplying a positive number by a positive decimal less than 1 makes that number smaller.
• Dividing a positive number by a positive decimal less than 1 makes that number bigger.

How do you get number sense?

There's no magical shortcut to number sense, but here are some ways to strengthen it.

• **Do only mental math.** You shouldn't be using a calculator to practice for the GRE because you know that you'll rarely need to use it. Try to do simpler math problems without even writing anything down. In addition, look for opportunities every day, in every situation, to do some simple math or simple estimation (e.g., There are about 20 cartons of milk on the grocery store's shelf; about how much would it cost to buy all 20?).

- **Look for patterns with numbers.** Add, subtract, multiply, and divide all kinds of numbers such as positive integers, negative integers, positive fractions, and negative fractions. Always be on the lookout for patterns.

- **Study mathematical solutions and explanations.** If a GRE practice problem seemed to demand an incredibly long calculation or took a long time for you to solve, write down what you learned about how to simplify the problem. Force yourself to study these shortcuts, and return to this solution and to your notes on it often. Over time, you should develop a great collection of problems that once seemed long and tricky, and if you study the solutions to those problems, you'll probably start to see patterns you can use in other problems.

- **Play games with numbers.** Here's one you can play alone or with others who also want practice. Pick four single digit numbers at random—some repeats are allowed. (You could even try rolling a die four times and use the results.) Now, once you have those four numbers, your job is to use all four of them and any arithmetic to generate each number from 1 to 20. "Any arithmetic" means any combination of the following:
  - addition, subtraction, multiplication, division
  - exponents
  - parentheses and fractions

For example, if the four numbers you picked were {1, 2, 3, 4}, you could get 2 from $(4 - 3) + (2 - 1)$ or $2 \times 1^{3+4}$ or $4 \times \frac{1^3}{2}$.

For any one number, you only need to come up with it in one way. The set {1, 2, 3, 4} is a very good warm-up set. When you want more of a challenge, use {2, 3, 3, 5}.

Number Sense Strategies

Estimation

There's an old saying that goes, "'Almost' only counts in horseshoes and hand grenades." In grade school and high school, you were probably taught that math had to be precise; maybe you even had that unforgivingly drilled into you. Well, now you're preparing for the GRE, and the rules are different. In the GRE Quantitative, "almost" can be good enough to count.

The GRE may give you the green light to estimate by using signal words or phrases such as "the estimated value of" or "approximately." Another clue about when it's time to estimate is the spread of the answer choices. If the answer choices are all very close together, well, then it's going to take some precision to distinguish among them. But, if the answer choices are widely spaced, estimating will get you close enough to the right answer.

Avoid picking 1

Sometimes, when you're given an abstract expression or relationship, it helps to plug numbers into the variables in order to see relationships concretely. When you do this, avoid picking the number 1 as a value for a variable. The reason is 1 has so many special properties that no other number has. For example, all powers of 1 equal 1, and 1 is the only number that has this particular property. If you come across a question asking you to distinguish choices involving different powers of that variable, picking 1 for the value would make all the powers equal the same thing, making it impossible to distinguish which answers should be eliminated. 1 is often the worst possible choice.

The only exception to this is that sometimes it's worthwhile to pick very easy numbers, like 1 and 2, just to do a very quick elimination of a couple of answers. If that's your goal, 1 can be a perfectly acceptable choice on a first pass. It will never be a choice that eliminates everything, but if your goal is to begin by eliminating low-hanging fruit, then by all means pick it.

Percentage problems

Everyone has heard the strategy of picking 100 for the starting value in a percent problem. But we're here to tell you to avoid that strategy. Yep. Forget about it! You see, if the test writers *know* that everyone uses that strategy, they'll design answer options to trip up people who make that all-too-obvious choice. Think a little out of the box here. Instead of 100, pick 500 or 1,000—you should be able to figure out round number percents with those numbers relatively quickly.

Extending that strategy even a little further is the idea that if any answer on the GRE seems like a super-obvious choice, you should probably second-guess yourself. Rather than pick that super-obvious answer, pick something a shade away from super-obvious.

Dimensional analysis

If different variables represent quantities of different units, then make sure you understand what combination of them will have the correct units for the answer choice. In physics, this thinking about the units of different quantities is called *dimensional analysis*. For example, if J is in units of miles per gallon, and M is in units of miles, then to get units of gallons, you would use $\frac{M}{J}$. If the question is asking for "how many gallons," then the correct answer would have to be a number $\times \frac{M}{J}$. Any other combinations ($\frac{J}{M}$, M × J, etc.) are automatically incorrect. This helps you eliminate answer choices, which makes the process of plugging in numbers easier.

Integer Properties and Number Sense
Practice Questions

These questions should help you get an idea of what to expect from the integer properties and number sense questions on the GRE. There are even more practice questions in the GRE practice test in chapter 6.

Question 1

Difficulty: **Easy** · Percent Correct: **83.9%** · Type: **Multiple Choice**

The greatest common factor (GCF) of 48 and 72 is

(A) 4

(B) 6

(C) 12

(D) 24

(E) 48

Question 2

Difficulty: **Medium** · Percent Correct: **72.4%** · Type: **Multiple Choice**

If k is an odd integer, which of the following must be an even integer?

(A) $k^2 - 4$

(B) $3k + 2$

(C) $2k + 1$

(D) $\frac{12k}{8}$

(E) $\frac{6k}{3}$

Question 3

Difficulty: **Medium** · Percent Correct: **70.7%** · Type: **Quantitative Comparison**

The greatest prime factor of 144 is x

The greatest prime factor of 96 is y

Column A	Column B
x	y

(A) The quantity in Column A is greater

(B) The quantity in Column B is greater

(C) The two quantities are equal

(D) The relationship cannot be determined from the information given

Question 4

Difficulty: **Medium** · Percent Correct: **63.5%** · Type: **Multiple Choice**

If k is an integer, what is the smallest possible value of k such that $1040k$ is the square of an integer?

- (A) 2
- (B) 5
- (C) 10
- (D) 15
- (E) 65

Question 5

Difficult: **Hard** · Percent Correct: **36.1%** · Type: **Numeric Entry**

The number 16,000 has how many positive divisors?

Question 6

Difficulty: **Very Hard** · Percent Correct: **25.1%** · Type: **Multiple Answer**

If x and y are integers, and $w = x^2y + x + 3y$, which of the following statements must be true?

Indicate <u>all</u> such statements.

- A If w is even, then x must be even.
- B If x is odd, then w must be odd.
- C If y is odd, then w must be odd.
- D If w is odd, then y must be odd.

Question 7

Difficulty: **Easy** · Percent Correct: **92%** · Type: **Quantitative Comparison**

Column A	Column B
43 percent of 207	85

- (A) The quantity in Column A is greater
- (B) The quantity in Column B is greater
- (C) The two quantities are equal
- (D) The relationship cannot be determined from the information given

Question 8

Difficulty: **Easy** · Percent Correct: **76.9%** · Type: Quantitative Comparison

- A certain taxi charges $0.85 for the first $\frac{1}{2}$ mile and $0.25 for every $\frac{1}{2}$ mile after that.
- The total cost of a trip was $8.85.

Column A	Column B
The trip's distance in miles	16

Ⓐ The quantity in Column A is greater

Ⓑ The quantity in Column B is greater

Ⓒ The two quantities are equal

Ⓓ The relationship cannot be determined from the information given

Question 9

Difficulty: **Easy** · Percent Correct: **78.3%** · Type: Quantitative Comparison

The average (arithmetic mean) of x, y, and 15 is 9.

Column A	Column B
Average of x and y	6

Ⓐ The quantity in Column A is greater

Ⓑ The quantity in Column B is greater

Ⓒ The two quantities are equal

Ⓓ The relationship cannot be determined from the information given

Integer Properties and Number Sense
Answers and Explanations

Question 1

Difficulty: **Easy** · Percent Correct: **83.9%** · Type: **Multiple Choice**

Answer: **D**

The greatest common factor (GCF) of 48 and 72 is

(A) 4

(B) 6

(C) 12

D 24

(E) 48

Find the prime factorizations of both numbers, and mark the factors they have in common:

$$48 = 2 \times 2 \times 2 \times 2 \times 3$$
$$72 = 2 \times 2 \times 2 \times 3 \times 3$$

They both have at least three factors of 2 and one factor of 3, and $2 \times 2 \times 2 \times 3 =$ **24**, so this is the GCF.

Question 2

Difficulty: **Medium** · Percent Correct: **72.4%** · Type: **Multiple Choice**

Answer: **E**

If k is an odd integer, which of the following must be an even integer?

(A) $k^2 - 4$ ⇨ $(1)^2 - 4 = -3$ $k = 1$

(B) $3k + 2$ ⇨ $3(1) + 2 = 5$

(C) $2k + 1$ ⇨ $2(1) + 1 = 3$

(D) $\dfrac{12k}{8}$ ⇨ $\dfrac{12(1)}{8} = \dfrac{3}{2}$

E $\dfrac{6k}{3}$ ⇨ $\dfrac{6(1)}{3} =$ **2**

Question 3

Difficulty: **Medium** · Percent Correct: **70.7%** · Type: **Quantitative Comparison**

Answer: **C**

The greatest prime factor of 144 is x

The greatest prime factor of 96 is y

Column A	Column B
x	y
$144 = 2 \times 2 \times 2 \times 2 \times 3 \times 3$ 3	$96 = 2 \times 2 \times 2 \times 2 \times 2 \times 3$ 3

GRE Quantitative Reasoning

(A) The quantity in Column A is greater
(B) The quantity in Column B is greater
(C) The two quantities are equal
(D) The relationship cannot be determined from the information given

Question 4

Difficulty: **Medium** · Percent Correct: **63.5%** · Type: **Multiple Choice**

If k is an integer, what is the smallest possible value of k such that $1040k$ is the square of an integer?

Answer: **E**

(A) 2

(B) 5

(C) 10

(D) 15

E 65

$$1040 = 2 \times 2 \times 2 \times 2 \times 5 \times 13$$

$$1040k = 2 \times 2 \times 2 \times 2 \times 5 \times 13 \times k$$

$$= (2 \times 2 \times 5 \times 13)(2 \times 2 \times k)$$

$$\Downarrow$$

$$k = 5 \times 13$$

$$= \mathbf{65}$$

Question 5

Difficult: **Hard** · Percent Correct: **36.1%** · Type: **Numeric Entry**

The number 16,000 has how many positive divisors?

Answer: **32**

If $N = p^a \times q^b \times r^c \times \cdots$, where p, q, r, etc. are prime numbers, then the total number of positive divisors of N is $(a + 1)(b + 1)(c + 1) \cdots$

$$16{,}000 = 16 \times 1000$$

$$= 2^4 \times (10)^3$$

$$= 2^4 \times (2 \times 5)^3$$

$$= 2^4 \times 2^3 \times 5^3$$

$$= 2^7 \times 5^3 \;\Rightarrow\; \text{Number of divisors} = (7 + 1)(3 + 1)$$

$$= (8)(4)$$

$$= \mathbf{32}$$

Question 6

Difficulty: **Very Hard** · Percent Correct: **25.1%** · Type: **Multiple Answer**

If x and y are integers, and $w = x^2y + x + 3y$, which of the following statements must be true?

Answers: **A** **B** **C**

Indicate _all_ such statements.

		x	y	$x^2y + x + 3y = w$		
A	If w is even, then x must be even.	E	E	$(0)^2(0) + 0 + 3(0) = 0$	$\Rightarrow$	even
B	If x is odd, then w must be odd.	E	O	$(0)^2(1) + 0 + 3(1) = 3$	$\Rightarrow$	odd
C	If y is odd, then w must be odd.	O	E	$(1)^2(0) + 1 + 3(0) = 1$	$\Rightarrow$	odd
D	If w is odd, then y must be odd.	O	O	$(1)^2(1) + 1 + 3(1) = 5$	$\Rightarrow$	odd

Question 7

Difficulty: **Easy**   ·   Percent Correct: **92%**   ·   Type: **Quantitative Comparison**

Answer: **A**

Column A	Column B
43 percent of 207	85
43% of 100 = 43 43% of 200 = 86 43% of 207 = **86⁺**	85

$43\% \text{ of } 100 = 43$, $43\% \text{ of } 200 = 86$, $43\% \text{ of } 207 = \mathbf{86^{+}}$

- **A** The quantity in Column A is greater
- (B) The quantity in Column B is greater
- (C) The two quantities are equal
- (D) The relationship cannot be determined from the information given

Question 8

Difficulty: **Easy**   ·   Percent Correct: **76.9%**   ·   Type: **Quantitative Comparison**

Answer: **A**

- A certain taxi charges \$0.85 for the first $\frac{1}{2}$ mile and \$0.25 for every $\frac{1}{2}$ mile after that.
- The total cost of a trip was \$8.85.

Column A	Column B
The trip's distance in miles	16
\$0.25 per 0.5 miles = \$0.50 per 1 mile	16
Total cost for 16-mile trip = \$0.85 + \$0.5(15.5) = **\$8.60**	

- **A** The quantity in Column A is greater
- (B) The quantity in Column B is greater
- (C) The two quantities are equal
- (D) The relationship cannot be determined from the information given

A certain taxi charges \$0.85 for the first $\frac{1}{2}$ mile and \$0.25 for every $\frac{1}{2}$ mile after that. If we assume the trip was 16 miles, the total cost is \$8.60, so the trip must have been greater than 16 miles to have totaled \$8.85.

Question 9

Difficulty: Easy · Percent Correct: 78.3% · Type: Quantitative Comparison

The average (arithmetic mean) of x, y, and 15 is 9.

Answer: **C**

Column A	Column B
Average of x and y	6
$\dfrac{x + y + 15}{3} = 9 \Rightarrow \begin{aligned} x + y + 15 &= 27 \\ x + y &= 12 \end{aligned}$ $\dfrac{x + y}{2} = \dfrac{12}{2} = \mathbf{6}$	**6**

(A) The quantity in Column A is greater

(B) The quantity in Column B is greater

(C) The two quantities are equal

(D) The relationship cannot be determined from the information given

You can find even more integer properties and number sense questions on magoosh.com!

65

Quantitative Concept #3: Algebra

After the advances of the Greeks, mathematical progress in Europe stagnated for much of the Dark Ages. During this time, though, the Muslims created one of the most scholarly civilizations ever: they developed algebra.

Algebra is a really broad and diverse topic. So we're going to break down three of the most important concepts related to algebra and then let you practice with several different algebra practice questions.

Ready to review?

Algebraic Concepts: The Lowdown

Fundamentally, algebra is a system that involves representing unknown numbers as letters. We won't spend a great deal of time talking about how to solve "3x + 5 = 11" sorts of equations, because (a) you're probably already familiar with the process, and (b) the GRE algebra tends to be a little harder than that.

Let's begin with a few suggestions on the basics. First of all, don't assume that the form in which an equation is given will automatically be the most useful form to you. If the GRE gives you the equation $7x + 14y = 84$, it likely would be easier if you began by dividing both sides by 7 and using the result, $x + 2y = 12$. If the GRE gives you the equation $x = \frac{25}{x}$, then it would be easier to multiply both sides by x to clear the fraction. This would result in $x^2 = 25$, which has solutions $x = +5$ and $x = -5$. In general, it's helpful to multiply by whatever's in the denominator, just to clear any fractions.

Notice that x is just a placeholder for a number, so we can always multiply both sides by x, just as we would for a number. Similarly, we can always add any multiple of x to both sides, or subtract any multiple of x from both sides—again, as we can do with any number on the number line.

The tricky one is division. If we're guaranteed that x cannot possibly be zero, then we can divide, but as long as zero is a possible value, it's 100 percent forbidden to divide by a variable. (Many times we're tempted to divide by a variable, we actually have to use factoring techniques, some of which are discussed below.)

Also, don't assume that the words don't matter just because there's algebra in the problem. Sometimes people want to ignore the words and jump to the equation. For example, imagine a problem that says, "*For all values of x greater than 6, if 3(x – 4) + 4y = xy, what is the value of y?*" Some people just see "*blah blah blah blah, if 3(x – 4) + 4y = xy, blah blah value of y?*" Don't be one of those people. **Success in math depends on precise attention to detail, and this attention has to extend to every single syllable in the phrasing of a math problem.**

By the way, the solution to that problem is as follows:

1. First, subtract $4y$ from both sides to get the following: $3(x – 4) = xy – 4y$
2. Then, factor out a y from the two terms on the right: $3(x – 4) = y(x – 4)$
3. At this point, it sure would be convenient if we could just divide by $(x – 4)$. Well, this is where the verbal stipulation at the beginning of the problem comes in: if $x > 6$, then $(x – 4)$ is *always positive* and there is absolutely no way this expression could have a value of zero. Since the expression can't possibly equal zero, it's 100 percent legitimate to divide by it, resulting in $3 = y$, the answer to the question.

Working with quadratics

First, let's look at terminology. In algebra, any product of numbers and variables is called a "monomial" or a "term." For example, $2x$, $5y^2$, and $-3\frac{xy}{z^7}$ are all terms. When you add terms together, you get a polynomial. A polynomial with two terms is a binomial. For example, $(x + 5)$, $(y^5 - x)$, and $(a^2 + b^2)$ are all binomials. A polynomial with three terms is a trinomial.

FOIL: simplifying and expanding

The word FOIL is an acronym that stands for First, Outer, Inner, Last. The FOIL process is used quite specifically to organize the multiplication of two binomials. The four words that make up FOIL tell you which terms of the binomial to multiply together. Suppose we want to multiply $(3x + 5) \times (2x - 7)$. Here is a step-by-step guide to the FOIL process for this:

FIRST terms: $(3x + 5) \times (2x - 7)$ $\Rightarrow$ product $= (3x) \times (2x) = 6x^2$

OUTER terms: $(3x + 5) \times (2x - 7)$ $\Rightarrow$ product $= (3x) \times (-7) = -21x$

INNER terms: $(3x + 5) \times (2x - 7)$ $\Rightarrow$ product $= 5 \times (2x) = 10x$

LAST terms: $(3x + 5) \times (2x - 7)$ $\Rightarrow$ product $= 5 \times (-7) = -35$

Those terms at the end are the individual FOIL terms. You add those together to get the product:

$$(3x + 5) \times (2x - 7) = 6x^2 - 21x + 10x - 35 = 6x^2 - 11x - 35$$

That last expression results from combining the two like terms ($-21x$ and $10x$) into a single term. That's the process of FOILing.

Factoring

A quadratic is a polynomial with three terms whose highest power is x squared. To factor a quadratic is to express it as the product of two binomials. Technically, any quadratic could be factored, but often the result would be two binomials with horribly difficult numbers—radicals or even non-real numbers. You won't have to deal with those cases on the GRE. A quadratic is "factorable" if, when you factor it, the resulting equation has only integers appearing. You'll only have to deal with "factorable" quadratics on the GRE.

The best way to understand factoring well is first to understand FOILing. Suppose you multiply two binomials:

$$(x + p)(x + q) = x^2 + qx + px + pq = x^2 + (p + q)x + pq$$

Notice that if you follow the FOIL process forward, you'll see two things. First, the middle coefficient, the coefficient of the x term, is the sum of the two numbers. Second, the final term, the constant term with no x, is a product of the two numbers. Right there, that's the key of factoring.

If you want to factor any quadratic of the form $x^2 + bx + c$, then you're looking for two numbers that have a product of c and a sum of b.

Suppose we have to factor $x^2 + 10x + 16$. It's always good to begin with c, which here equals $+16$. This is the product of $p \times q$. Since it's positive, both p and q must have the same sign, either both positive or both negative. Now, if we look at b, which equals $+10$, we see that the sum of p and q must be positive. We need two positive numbers that have a product of $+16$ and a sum of $+10$. Start going through the factor pairs of 16: the pair $\{4, 4\}$ doesn't work, but the pair $\{2, 8\}$ does. Thus, the factored form is $x^2 + 10x + 16 = (x + 2)(x + 8)$.

Suppose we have to factor $x^2 - 8x + 15$. Again, we start with c, which here equals $+15$. This is the product of $p \times q$. Since it's positive, p and q must have the same sign, either both positive or both negative. Now if we look at b, which equals -8, we see that the sum of p and q must be negative. We need two negative numbers that have a product of $+15$ and a sum of -8. These must be -3 and -5. Thus, the factored form is $x^2 - 8x + 15 = (x - 3)(x - 5)$.

Suppose we have to factor $x^2 - 5x - 24$. Again, we start with c, which here equals -24. This is the product of $p \times q$. Since it's negative, we know that of the numbers p and q, one must be positive and one must be negative. In other words, they must have opposite signs. Now, we look at b, or the sum. Here, $b = -5$, so the sum is negative. This tells us that the bigger number, the number with the larger absolute value, is the negative one, and the one with a smaller magnitude is positive. We need a pair of factors that multiplies to 24 and has a difference of 5. The pair $\{1, 24\}$ is too far apart, as is the pair $\{2, 12\}$, but the pair $\{3, 8\}$ works. We have to make the bigger number negative and the smaller number positive, so the numbers we want are $+3$ and -8. These are the numbers that have a sum of -5 and a product of -24. The factored form is $x^2 - 5x - 24 = (x + 3)(x - 8)$.

Finally, suppose we have to factor $x^2 + x - 72$. Again, we start with c, which here equals -72. This is the product of $p \times q$. Since it's negative, we know that of the numbers p and q, one must be positive and one must be negative—they must have opposite signs. Now, we look at b, the sum. Here, $b = +1$, so the sum is positive. This tells us that the bigger number, the number with the larger absolute value, is the positive one, and the one with a smaller magnitude is negative. We need a pair of factors that multiplies to 72 and has a difference of 1. The pairs $\{1, 72\}$, $\{2, 36\}$, $\{3, 24\}$, $\{4, 18\}$, and $\{6, 12\}$ are all too far apart, but the pair $\{8, 9\}$ works. We have to make the bigger number positive and the smaller number negative, so the numbers we want are $+9$ and -8. These are the numbers that have a sum of $+1$ and a product of -72. The factored form is $x^2 + x - 72 = (x + 9)(x - 8)$.

Let's generalize this logic. To figure out p and q, we start by observing the sign of c. If c is positive, then p and q have the same sign. If c is negative, then p and q have opposite signs. Everything follows from there. One way to present this information is in flowchart form.

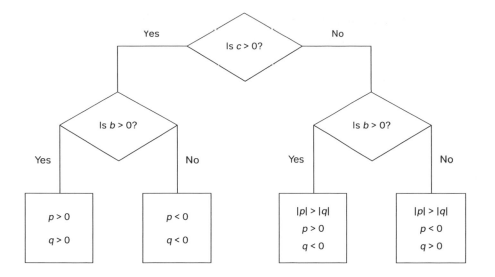

We recommend that you practice both FOILing and factoring repeatedly, especially if this is new or unfamiliar to you. This is one of these things that, as you practice it, becomes much, much easier.

Now, why is it important to know how to factor a quadratic? Factoring is one of the most important methods of solving a quadratic equation. So far, notice that the entire section above dealt with just the quadratic expressions: the quadratic wasn't equal to anything. When we take an expression and set it equal to something, we transform the expression into an equation!

Suppose we had the equation $x^2 + 10x + 16 = 0$. We already factored this above, so we know this is equivalent to the equation $(x + 2)(x + 8) = 0$. Well, if the product of two things equals zero, then at least one of the two things must equal zero. Thus, if $(x + 2)(x + 8) = 0$, then the following must be true:

$x + 2 = 0$ OR $x + 8 = 0$
$x = -2$ OR $x = -8$

Those are the two roots of the quadratic, the values that make the quadratic expression equal zero. Notice that the signs of the roots are always opposite of the signs of the p and q we get in the factoring process. Here, both p and q were positive, and both roots are negative.

Let's look at another example. Suppose we had the equation $x^2 - 5x - 24 = 0$. We already factored this above, so we know this is equivalent to the equation $(x + 3)(x - 8) = 0$. Again, the product equals zero, so one of the two factors must be zero. Thus, the following must be true:

$x + 3 = 0$ OR $x - 8 = 0$
$x = -3$ OR $x = +8$

Once again, the roots have the opposite sign from the p and q numbers produced in the factoring process. The roots -3 and $+8$ are a "small" negative number and a "big" positive number.

Notice also that setting each factor equal to zero depends on having the whole quadratic equal to zero. This is why it's crucial when solving a quadratic to begin by getting everything on one side. We need that zero on the other side of the equation before we start any factoring. Suppose we have to solve the equation $x^2 + 2x - 100 = x - 28$. It's a bad idea to start trying to factor that expression on the left side because it doesn't equal zero yet. We have to move everything from the right side first: subtract x and add 28.

$$x^2 + 2x - 100 = x - 28$$
$$x^2 + x - 100 = -28$$
$$x^2 + x - 100 + 28 = 0$$
$$x^2 + x - 72 = 0$$

Ah, we recognize this! This is one we already factored above. We know this is equivalent to the following equation:

$$(x + 9)(x - 8) = 0$$

Once again, the product equals zero, so either factor could be zero.

$$x + 9 = 0 \quad \text{OR} \quad x - 8 = 0$$
$$x = -9 \quad \text{OR} \quad x = +8$$

Those are the two roots of the original equation. If you have time, and especially when you're first learning this, it's a good exercise to go back to the starting equation, $x^2 + 2x - 100 = x - 28$, plug in the roots −9 and +8 for x on both sides, and make sure that the two sides of the equation are equal. You won't always have to time to check your answers, but when you do, understanding why each value of x works in the equation will build your number sense.

Essential Algebra Formulas

Doing math involves both following procedures and recognizing patterns. Here are three important patterns for algebra on the GRE:

Pattern #1: The Difference of Two Squares

$$A^2 - B^2 = (A + B)(A - B)$$

Pattern #2: The Square of a Sum

$$(A + B)^2 = A^2 + 2AB + B^2$$

Pattern #3: The Square of a Difference

$$(A - B)^2 = A^2 - 2AB + B^2$$

For success on the GRE Quantitative, you need to know these patterns cold. You need to know them as well as you know your own phone number or address. The GRE will throw question after question at you that will require an intimate familiarity with these patterns. When you're staring down questions and you're able to recognize the relevant formula, it will simplify the problem enormously. If you don't recognize the relevant formula, you're likely to be totally baffled by the question.

Two Equations with Two Variables

Fundamentally, a mathematical equation is a like a sentence. It contains a certain amount of mathematical information for you to read or decipher. It's easier to read when you have *one* equation with *one* variable. If we have an equation like this—as long as the one variable isn't raised to any powers or under a root—then we generally have enough mathematical information to solve for the variable. By contrast, if a single equation has *two* variables, say, $3x + 2y = 5$, then with this alone, we don't have enough information to solve definitively for the variables. Sure, we could find a pair that might work—for example, {1, 1}, {3, −2}, {−1, 4}. But there are an infinite number of points (x, y) that would work. Why is that? Because if we graph the points {x, y}, they would form a line in the coordinate plane. In other words, when we have a single equation with x and y, you can determine a line but *not* a single point.

If we want to determine unique values for both x and y, then in order to have enough mathematical information to do so, we would need to have *two* separate equations. How come? Well, if you think of an equation as a tool to determine a line, then with two equations, we would have two lines, and the intersection point of these two lines contains the values of x and y that work for *both* equations. So we need two different equations if we're going to solve for the values of two different variables. This last fact generalizes the whole concept: To solve for N variables, we would need to have N separate equations.

Don't worry: the GRE is *not* going to give you seventeen different equations and ask you to find the values of seventeen different variables. The GRE Quantitative tends to stick with the simplest case: just two equations with just two variables.

Suppose we have such a problem, involving two equations with two variables. The set of two equations is often called a "system" of equations. Here is one such system of equations:

$$3x + 2y = 5$$
$$2x - y = 8$$

The test could present this system and ask for the value of either variable, x or y.

There are two basic procedures for solving such systems: substitution and elimination.

Solving systems: substitution

This solution method depends on the magic of the equals sign. To say that two things are equal is to say that they're mathematically identical and 100 percent mathematically interchangeable. The equals sign is too often taken for granted; it's a powerful symbol with profound implications!

The steps of the substitution method are as follows:

1. We pick one equation (either one will do) and solve for one of the variables (either x or y).
2. We replace the variable in the other equation with the expression that's equal to it.

The substitution method is most appropriate when one of the variables in the equations given already appears with a coefficient of ±1. When a variable has a coefficient with an absolute value of 1, we can solve for it without creating any fractions.

In the system above, notice that in the second equation, the y has a coefficient of –1. If we add y to both sides and subtract 8 from both sides of that second equation, we get the following:

$$2x - 8 = y$$

So far, we have just rearranged this mathematical equation; we haven't changed the information it contains, and by itself, this doesn't contain enough information to solve for the values of x and y, because it's only one equation. We need to combine this information with the other equation. Think about what we have, though. We have an equation telling us that y is mathematically indistinguishable from the expression $2x - 8$. Where there's a y, whatever value that has, we could replace it with $2x - 8$, which must have the exact same value.

This gives us a way to combine the two equations. Because y is equal to $(2x - 8)$, we can go back to the first equation and replace the y in that equation with the expression $(2x - 8)$. This is called substitution. We're substituting $(2x - 8)$ for y. Here's the first equation, as it was given:

$$3x + 2y = 5$$

Here is the equation after we have substituted. Because we now have just one equation with one variable, we can solve it!

$$3x + 2(2x - 8) = 5$$
$$3x + 4x - 16 = 5$$
$$7x = 21$$
$$x = 3$$

We now have the value of x. To find y, all we have to do is plug this value of x into either equation. It's often convenient to plug it into the equation that was solved for y.

$$y = 2x - 8 = 2(3) - 8 = 6 - 8 = -2$$

So the values $x = 3$ and $y = -2$ solve this system of equations. That's a solution by the substitution method, one of the two methods for solving a system of equations.

Solving systems: elimination

The second method for solving two equations with two variables combines the equations in a completely different way. Suppose we have this new system of equations to solve:

$$4x + 3y = 1$$
$$5x + 6y = 8$$

Now, of course, we could use substitution if we wanted, but no matter which equation and which variable we chose, solving for the variable would introduce fractions. For example, if we were to solve the second equation for x, we would get the following:

$$x = -\frac{6}{5}y + \frac{8}{5}$$

Yes, we could work with this further, but fractional coefficients tend to complicate simple algebra. It would be nice to use another method, one that didn't introduce fractions.

Here's a new approach. First of all, we know that we can add the same number to both sides of any equation—any number we like. Based on that, if we have two separate equations, we're always able to add these two equations. If we know that $P = Q$ and $S = T$, then we're welcome to add them either way.

For example, we could add the two equations $P = Q$ and $S = T$ like this:

$$
\begin{aligned}
P &= Q \\
+ \; S &= T \\
\hline
P + S &= Q + T
\end{aligned}
$$

That's because S and T are mathematically identical, so we're really just adding the same thing to both sides of $P = Q$. As another example, we could turn the second equation around, to $T = S$, and add them that way:

$$
\begin{aligned}
P &= Q \\
+ \; T &= S \\
\hline
P + T &= Q + S
\end{aligned}
$$

We also could subtract $S = T$ from $P = Q$:

$$
\begin{aligned}
P &= Q \\
- \; S &= T \\
\hline
P - S &= Q - T
\end{aligned}
$$

To reiterate, we're now subtracting the same thing from both sides. These are just three examples of new equations we can create from these two starting equations. We also could swap the two equations around and subtract in reverse order, or we could multiply both sides of one equation by a number and then add or subtract. For example, we could multiply both sides of $P = Q$ by 3, and then subtract $T = S$ from this.

$$3P = 3Q$$
$$- T = S$$
$$3P - T = 3Q - S$$

Clearly, given that we can multiply either equation by any number we want, and then add or subtract the equations, we have quite a variety of possible choices open to us. So how exactly does this help us solve a system of equations?

Let's go back to our system.

$$4x + 3y = 1$$
$$5x + 6y = 8$$

We could add these two as they are, or subtract one from the other, but that would just give us another equation with both x and y.

Now, here's where strategy comes in. We have to look at the two equations and see if the two coefficients for the same variable are either the same or easy multiples of one another. In this system, the two coefficients of x are 4 and 5, which are not multiples and have no common factors larger than 1. On the other hand, the two coefficients of y are 3 and 6, and 6 is a multiple of 3. That's good!

The goal is to multiply one or both equations by numbers, so that the two coefficients for the same variable have equal absolute value and opposite signs. That way, we can add the two equations, and that variable will cancel—it will be eliminated (hence the name "elimination").

Below, we multiply the top equation by –2 and leave the bottom equation unchanged. This will give us a $-6y$ in the top equation and a $+6y$ in the bottom. When we add the two equations, these two will be eliminated.

$4x + 3y = 1$	$\Rightarrow$	multiply both sides by –2	$\Rightarrow$	$-8x - 6y = -2$
$5x + 6y = 8$	$\Rightarrow$	leave the same	$\Rightarrow$	$+ (5x + 6y = 8)$
				$-3x = 6$
				$x = -2$

That was a solution by elimination. When we added the equations, what we eliminated was the y variable, so we could solve for the x. Once we have the value of x, we can plug this into either equation to get the value of y. If you have the time, it's a good check to plug x into both equations and make sure that you get the same value for y!

$$4x + 3y = 1$$
$$4(-2) + 3y = 1$$
$$-8 + 3y = 1$$
$$3y = 9$$
$$y = 3$$

Check:

$$5x + 6y = 8$$
$$5(-2) + 6y = 8$$
$$-10 + 6y = 8$$
$$6y = 18$$
$$y = 3$$

This solution works in both equations. The solution is $x = -2$ and $y = 3$.

In the previous section, we solved another system using substitution. We also could have used elimination. Here's that system again:

$$3x + 2y = 5$$
$$2x - y = 8$$

We have a $+2y$ in the first equation and a $-y$ in the second. If we leave the first equation as is and multiply the second by 2, we can add them and eliminate the y's.

$3x + 2y = 5$	$\Rightarrow$	leave as is	$\Rightarrow$	$3x + 2y = 5$
$2x - y = 8$	$\Rightarrow$	multiply by 2	$\Rightarrow$	$+ 4x - 2y = 16$
				$7x = 21$
				$x = 3$

Once again, we can plug this value of x into either equation to find y.

$$2x - y = 8$$
$$6 - y = 8$$
$$-y = 2$$
$$y = -2$$

Using elimination, we found the same solutions that we found above using substitution.

Here's a practice problem:

$$5p - 3q = 42$$
$$5p + 3q = 18$$

Given this system of equations, what is the value of $|p| + |q|$?
(Note: the notation $|n|$ means the absolute value of n.)

(A) 2

(B) 4

(C) 6

(D) 8

(E) 10

In this system, the substitution method would result in some ugly fractions. The elimination method is a much better approach. In fact, we don't even have to multiply either equation by anything. We simply can add them together as is, and the $(-3q)$ and $(+3q)$ will cancel out. When we add the two equations, we get the following:

$$10p = 42 + 18 = 60$$
$$p = \mathbf{6}$$

We can plug this into either equation. Let's plug it into the first.

$$5(6) - 3q = 42$$
$$30 - 3q = 42$$
$$-3q = 12$$
$$q = \mathbf{-4}$$

Now that we have the values of p and q, we have to first take their absolute values, then add them.

$$|p| + |q| = |6| + |-4| = 6 + 4 = \mathbf{10}$$

The answer is **(E)**.

Inequalities

So far in this algebra section, we have been talking about equations, about mathematical statements that involve equals signs. Many important mathematical statements do involve equals signs, but some don't. Instead, these mathematical statements involve one of the following signs:

$$< \quad > \quad \leq \quad \geq \quad \neq$$

Any mathematical statement that uses one of these signs is called an *inequality*. Sometimes on the GRE, we have to do algebra with inequalities.

Many of the algebraic rules for inequalities are the same as the rules for equations. For example, just as we're always allowed to add or subtract any equal quantities on both sides of an equation, so too can we add or subtract any equal quantities on both sides of an inequality.

We know that $5 > 2$ is a true inequality. There's a fixed gap by which 5 is greater than 2. If we add the same number to both sides, say 7, then we get $12 > 9$, another true inequality.

Adding or subtracting equal quantities on both sides preserves the fixed gap between the two numbers. It's as if we found the two numbers on the number line, and just slid them up the line while preserving the gap between them.

If we add the same thing to both sides of the inequality, we slide the gap up the number line, to the right, and if we subtract the same thing from both sides, we slide the gap down the number line to the left.

Notice that we were careful to say that we could add *equal quantities* to both sides, not that we could add the *same number* to both sides. Of course, we can add the same number, but we also can add other things that are equal. For example, suppose the test gives us the following inequality:

$$x - y > 17$$

Suppose the test also tells us that $y = 5$. Then we could add the equation $y = 5$ to the inequality. On the left side, the $+y$ and the $-y$ would cancel, and the numbers would add on the right side. All this results in the following inequality:

$$x > 22$$

Notice that just as we can add or subtract any number on both sides, we also can add or subtract a variable on both sides. After all, a variable is just a holder for a number, and it doesn't matter what number the variable is a holder for, since we can add or subtract any number on the number line. For example:

$$2x - 3 \geq x + 6$$

To solve this inequality, we could add 3 to both sides:

$$2x > x + 9$$

Then, we could subtract x from both sides:

$$x \geq 9$$

That's the "solution" of the inequality, the statement of the possible range of x.

Multiplication and division aren't quite as straightforward. With *equations*, we can multiply both sides by any number on the number line, and we can divide by any number other than 0. Either of those actions would maintain the equality of the two sides. Inequalities, however, have a few more restrictions than that.

With positive numbers, everything is golden. We can multiply or divide both sides of an inequality by any positive number, and the inequality remains unchanged. For instance, we know that:

$$3 < 7$$

Multiplying or dividing produces more true inequalities:

- Multiply by 2, and we get 6 < 14.
- Multiply by 5, and we get 15 < 35.
- Divide by 3, and we get $1 < \frac{7}{3}$.
- Divide by 10, and we get $\frac{3}{10} < \frac{7}{10}$.
- **Multiplying or dividing any inequality by a *positive* number leaves the inequality true.**

Obviously, we can't divide both sides of an inequality by 0, because we never can divide by 0! Also, though, we can't multiply both sides of an inequality by 0, because then we would get 0 on both sides. That would change the inequality into an equation, so that would completely alter the nature of the mathematical situation.

What happens if we multiply or divide both sides of an inequality by a negative? Start with the perfectly true and sensible inequality 3 > –7. This is true, and in fact, **any positive number is greater than any negative number**. Now, let's just multiply both sides by –1.

$$3(-1) \ [< \text{ or } >] \ (-7)(-1)$$
$$-3 < +7$$

Again, any positive number is greater than any negative number, so the direction of the inequality has reversed. **Multiplying or dividing by a negative reverses the direction of an inequality.** A "greater than" becomes a "less than" and vice versa.

Even if both numbers in the inequality are positive, this is true. It's true that 300 > 50 and, after multiplying by –1, it's also true that –300 < –50. Think about it. If we're talking about positive amounts—the amount in your bank account, for example—then you're in better shape if you have $300 in your account than just $50 in your account. But if you're talking about negative amounts—say, credit card debt—then you're in better shape if you owe just $50 on the card than if you owe $300 on the card. Bank account "pluses" versus credit card "minuses" are a good practical way to think about positive versus negative numbers.

If we have variables in an inequality, what actions can we do with those variables? As we discussed earlier, since we can add or subtract any number on the number line to both sides of an inequality, we can also add or subtract any variable. The value of the variable doesn't matter because we can add or subtract either positives or negatives.

On the other hand, we *can't* multiply or divide an inequality by a variable because we wouldn't know whether the variable is positive or negative. Once again, multiplying or dividing by a negative would reverse the inequality, whereas doing so with a positive would not. Since we normally wouldn't know whether a number represented by a variable is positive or negative, we wouldn't know what to do with the inequality!

Here's a practice problem:

$2x + 12 > 2 - 3x$

Which values of x below satisfy this inequality?

Indicate all such values.

A −7
B −5
C −3
D −1
E 1
F 3
G 5
H 7

We can simplify the inequality by adding and subtracting. Just so we can avoid having a negative coefficient for x, we'll begin by adding $3x$ to both sides, to get all the x's on one side so their coefficient is positive.

$5x + 12 > 2$

Now, subtract 12.

$5x > -10$

Now, divide by +5.

$x > -2$

The answers that are greater than −2 are [D], [E], [F], [G], and [H]. This question was about as easy as a question will get on the GRE Quantitative section. The answers are **[D]**, **[E]**, **[F]**, **[G]**, and **[H]**.

Here's a slightly more challenging practice problem:

> If $A < 0$, $10 < B < 30$, and $50 < C < 80$, what is the relative order of the reciprocals $\frac{1}{A}$, $\frac{1}{B}$, and $\frac{1}{C}$?
>
> (A) $\frac{1}{A} < \frac{1}{B} < \frac{1}{C}$
>
> (B) $\frac{1}{A} < \frac{1}{C} < \frac{1}{B}$
>
> (C) $\frac{1}{C} < \frac{1}{A} < \frac{1}{B}$
>
> (D) $\frac{1}{C} < \frac{1}{B} < \frac{1}{A}$
>
> (E) $\frac{1}{B} < \frac{1}{C} < \frac{1}{A}$

We know that B and C are positive numbers, and that $B < C$. To get the reciprocals, we have to divide by B and by C, so simply divide both sides of that inequality by the positive number $B \times C$.

$$B < C$$

$$\frac{B}{BC} < \frac{C}{BC}$$

$$\frac{1}{C} < \frac{1}{B}$$

This determines the order of these two. On the basis of this only, we could eliminate (A) and (E).

We don't know the values of $\frac{1}{C}$ and $\frac{1}{B}$, but we know these also are positive numbers of some value. Meanwhile, A is negative, so $\frac{1}{A}$ will also be negative. As we mentioned earlier, **any negative is less than any positive**. This means that $\frac{1}{A}$ must be the least, less than the two positive numbers. Putting everything together, we get the following:

$$\frac{1}{A} < \frac{1}{C} < \frac{1}{B}$$

The answer is **(B)**.

Algebra Practice Questions

These examples should help you get an idea of what to expect from algebra questions on the GRE. There are even more practice questions in the GRE practice test in chapter 6.

Question 1

Difficulty: **Easy** · Percent Correct: **79.1%** · Type: **Multiple Choice**

If $2x - y = 10$ and $\frac{x}{y} = 3$, then $x =$

(A) −10

(B) 2

(C) 4

(D) 6

(E) 12

Question 2

Difficulty: **Easy** · Percent Correct: **74.4%** · Type: **Multiple Choice**

If $\frac{1}{x} = 0.4$, then $\frac{1}{x + 2} =$

(A) $\frac{1}{8}$

(B) $\frac{1}{5}$

(C) $\frac{2}{9}$

(D) $\frac{1}{4}$

(E) $\frac{2}{7}$

Question 3

Difficulty: **Easy** · Percent Correct: **75.9%** · Type: **Multiple Choice**

If $4x - 3y = 13$ and $5x + 2y = -1$, then $x =$

(A) −3

(B) −1

(C) 1

(D) 3

(E) 5

Question 4

Difficulty: **Medium** · Percent Correct: **54.9%** · Type: **Numeric Entry**

If $x > 0$ and $\frac{4x}{x^2 - 3x} - \frac{2}{7} = 0$ what is the value of x?

Question 5

Difficulty: **Medium** · Percent Correct: **64.6%** · Type: **Multiple Choice**

If $2x - 3y = 6$, then $6y - 4x =$

Ⓐ −12

Ⓑ −6

Ⓒ 6

Ⓓ 12

Ⓔ Cannot be determined

Question 6

Difficulty: **Hard** · Percent Correct: **40%** · Type: **Multiple Answer**

If $y - 3x > 12$ and $x - y > 38$, which of the following are possible values of x?

Indicate <u>all</u> such values.

A −60

B −30

C −6

D 4

E 20

F 40

G 80

Question 7

Difficulty: **Hard** · Percent Correct: **26%** · Type: **Multiple Answer**

If $\dfrac{5x^2 + 65x + 60}{x^2 + 10x - 24} = \dfrac{5x + 5}{x - 2}$, then which of the following are possible values of x?

Indicate <u>all</u> such values.

A −60

B −12

C −1

D 1

E 2

F 5

When you're ready, turn the page to see the answers.

Algebra Answers and Explanations

Question 1

Difficulty: **Easy** · Percent Correct: **79.1%** · Type: **Multiple Choice**

Answer: **D**

If $2x - y = 10$ and $\frac{x}{y} = 3$, then $x =$

(A) -10

(B) 2

(C) 4

D 6

(E) 12

$$\frac{x}{y} = 3$$
$$3y = x \quad \Rightarrow \quad 2x - y = 10$$
$$2(3y) - y = 10$$
$$6y - y = 10$$
$$5y = 10$$
$$y = 2 \quad \Rightarrow \quad \frac{x}{y} = 3$$
$$\frac{x}{2} = 3$$
$$x = 6$$

Question 2

Difficulty: **Easy** · Percent Correct: **74.4%** · Type: **Multiple Choice**

Answer: **C**

If $\frac{1}{x} = 0.4$, then $\frac{1}{x+2} =$

(A) $\frac{1}{8}$

(B) $\frac{1}{5}$

C $\frac{2}{9}$

(D) $\frac{1}{4}$

(E) $\frac{2}{7}$

$$\frac{1}{x} = 0.4 \qquad \frac{1}{x+2} = \frac{1}{\frac{5}{2}+2}$$
$$\frac{1}{x} = \frac{2}{5} \qquad = \frac{1}{\frac{5}{2}+\frac{4}{2}}$$
$$\frac{x}{1} = \frac{5}{2} \qquad = \frac{1}{\frac{9}{2}}$$
$$x = \frac{5}{2} \qquad = \frac{2}{9}$$

Question 3

Difficulty: **Easy** · Percent Correct: **75.9%** · Type: **Multiple Choice**

Answer: **C**

If $4x - 3y = 13$ and $5x + 2y = -1$, then $x =$

(A) -3

(B) -1

C 1

(D) 3

(E) 5

$$4x - 3y = 13 \quad \overset{\times 2}{\Rightarrow} \quad 8x - 6y = 26$$
$$5x + 2y = -1 \quad \underset{\times 3}{\Rightarrow} \quad + 15x + 6y = -3$$
$$\overline{23x \qquad = 23}$$
$$x = 1$$

Question 4

Difficulty: **Medium** · Percent Correct: **54.9%** · Type: Numeric Entry

Answer: **17**

If $x > 0$ and $\frac{4x}{x^2 - 3x} - \frac{2}{7} = 0$ what is the value of x?

First, create equivalent fractions.

$$\frac{4x}{x^2 - 3x} - \frac{2}{7} = 0 \qquad \frac{4x}{x^2 - 3x} = \frac{2}{7}$$

Now cross-multiply.

$$7(4x) = 2(x^2 - 3x)$$
$$28x = 2x^2 - 6x$$
$$34x = 2x^2$$
$$17x = x^2$$

Because $x > 0$, it cannot equal 0, so you can divide by x.

$$x = \mathbf{17}$$

Question 5

Difficulty: Medium · Percent Correct: 64.6% · Type: **Multiple Choice**

If $2x - 3y = 6$, then $6y - 4x =$

Answer: Ⓐ

Ⓐ −12

Ⓑ −6

Ⓒ 6

Ⓓ 12

Ⓔ Cannot be determined

$$2x - 3y = 6$$
$$4x - 6y = 12$$
$$-4x + 6y = -12$$
$$6y - 4x = \mathbf{-12}$$

If $a - b = c$ then $b - a = -c$

Question 6

Difficulty: Hard · Percent Correct: 40% · Type: Multiple Answer

If $y - 3x > 12$ and $x - y > 38$, which of the following are possible values of x?

Answers: Ⓐ Ⓑ

Indicate <u>all</u> such values.

A −60

B −30

C −6

D 4

E 20

F 40

G 80

$$y - 3x > 12 \quad \Rightarrow \quad y - 3x > 12$$
$$x - y > 38 \quad \Rightarrow \quad \underline{+ \; -y + x > 38}$$
$$-2x > 50$$
$$x < \mathbf{-25}$$

Question 7

Difficulty: Hard · Percent Correct: 26% · Type: Multiple Answer

If $\dfrac{5x^2 + 65x + 60}{x^2 + 10x - 24} = \dfrac{5x + 5}{x - 2}$, then which of the following are possible values of x?

Answers:

Indicate <u>all</u> such values.

A −60

B −12

C −1

D 1

E 2

F 5

This question is about **factoring**, which is a very important skill to master for the GRE Quantitative.

The first thing you have to do is factor both the numerator and denominator of the fraction on the left. To factor the quadratic in the numerator, the easiest first step is to factor out the GCF of 5.

$$\frac{5x^2 + 65x + 60}{x^2 + 10x - 24} = \frac{5(x^2 + 13x + 12)}{x^2 + 10x - 24}$$

$$= \frac{5(x + 12)(x + 1)}{(x + 12)(x - 2)}$$

Now, set this equal to the equation on the other side, and factor out the 5 in the numerator of that fraction as well.

$$= \frac{5(x + 12)(x + 1)}{(x + 12)(x - 2)} = \frac{5(x + 1)}{x - 2}$$

Now, here comes a crucial question. Can you cancel the factor of $(x + 12)$ in the numerator and the denominator? Well, canceling is division, so the underlying question is, Can you divide by a variable or by a variable expression? The answer is "no," because you may be dividing by 0. And don't forget to consider two cases, one in which the variable expression equals 0 and one in which it doesn't equal 0, and find the consequences in either case.

Here, if $x = -12$, which would make $(x + 12) = 0$, the fraction on the left becomes $\frac{0}{0}$, which is a mathematical obscenity. That's absolutely not allowed. Therefore, you have determined that $x = -12$ is a totally illegal value of x.

If $x \neq -12$, then $(x + 12) \neq 0$, which would mean you could divide by it and cancel. That would lead you to

$$= \frac{5(x + 1)}{x - 2} = \frac{5(x + 1)}{x - 2}$$

Here, you have the exact same expression on both sides. These two expressions would be equal for every value of x for which they're defined. The only other value that's problematic is $x - 2$, which makes both denominators equal 0. Dividing by 0 is one of the all-time big no-no's in mathematics, so $x = 2$ is an absolutely illegal value. Notice, though, if x equals anything other than 2 or -12, those two expressions would be equal to each other for the whole continuous infinity of real numbers.

Thus, the possible values of x are **absolutely everything except** $x = 2$ and $x = -12$. Here, that would be choices (A) -60, (C) -1, (D) 1, (F) 5.

Does the GRE test my ability to recognize where rational expressions aren't defined? Yes, this is something relatively rare, but the GRE could ask a question in which this was important. You should know that an algebraic rational expression could be undefined and that values that would make it undefined cannot be solutions.

What is an undefined value? Any fraction that has 0 as the denominator (on the bottom) creates a number with an undefined value. You cannot divide any number by 0.

GRE Quantitative
Reasoning

86   You can find even more algebra questions on gre.magoosh.com!

Quantitative Concept #4: Exponents and Roots

If math isn't your thing, then it's possible that the last time you gave any thought to exponents and roots was back in high school. But take heart! Exponents and roots are *fun*, and if you can multiply and divide, you can definitely figure out questions with exponents.

The Lowdown on Exponents

Fundamentally, an exponent is how many times you multiply a number, that is, how many factors of a number you have. The expression 5^4 means multiply four 5s together. The expression 2^3 means multiply three 2s together, which gives an answer of 8, so $2^3 = 8$. To get into the actual terminology, 2 is the *base*, 3 is the *exponent*, and 8 is the *power*. The action of raising something to an exponent is called *exponentiation*.

Distribution

Just as multiplication distributes over addition and subtraction, exponentiation distributes over multiplication and division. Why is that? Well, consider $(x \times y)^3$. This means to multiply the mathematical statement in parentheses three times: $(x \times y)^3 = (x \times y) \times (x \times y) \times (x \times y)$. Well, when there are a bunch of factors, they can be rearranged in any order, because order doesn't matter in multiplication. So you could rearrange them as follows:

$$(x \times y)^3 =$$
$$(x \times y) \times (x \times y) \times (x \times y) =$$
$$x \times x \times x \times y \times y \times y =$$
$$(x \times x \times x) \times (y \times y \times y) =$$
$$(x^3) \times (y^3)$$

All the laws of exponents make sense if you just go back to the fundamental definition. One thing to keep in mind, though, is that exponentiation does **not** distribute over addition.

$$(a + b)^n \neq a^n + b^n$$

Beware. Even when you know this is wrong, even when you make an effort to remember that it's wrong, the inherent pattern-matching machinery of your brain will automatically pull your mind back in the direction of making this mistake.

Multiplying powers

What happens when you multiply two unequal powers of the same base?

$$(x^r) \times (x^s) = ?$$

The brilliant Greek mathematician **Archimedes** (287–212 BCE) is widely considered one of the three greatest mathematicians of all times: the other two are **Sir Isaac Newton** (1642–1727) and **Leonard Euler** (1707–1783). Archimedes was the first to discover and prove the laws of exponents.

Let's think about a concrete example. Suppose you're multiplying $(x^5) \times (x^3)$. Using the fundamental definition, the problem works out to $x^5 = x \times x \times x \times x \times x$ and $x^3 = x \times x \times x$, so ...

$$(x^5) \times (x^3) = (x \times x \times x \times x \times x) \times (x \times x \times x) = x \times x \times x \times x \times x \times x \times x \times x = x^8$$

You can see that when you start with five factors of x, and add three more factors of x, you'll wind up with a total of eight factors. All you have to do is add the exponents. The pattern of multiplying numbers with exponents can be summed up by this formula:

$$(x^r) \times (x^s) = x^{r+s}$$

Remember, don't just memorize this formula; instead make sure you understand the logic that leads to it.

Dividing powers

What happens when you divide two unequal powers of the same base?

$$\frac{x^r}{x^s} = ?$$

As with the previous example, a concrete problem will illuminate the question. Suppose you divide $\frac{(x^7)}{(x^3)}$. Using the fundamental definition, the problem works out to the following: $x^7 = x \times x \times x \times x \times x \times x \times x$ and $x^3 = x \times x \times x$, so ...

$$\frac{x^7}{x^3} = \frac{x \times x \times x \times x \times x \times x \times x}{x \times x \times x} = \frac{x \times x \times x \times x \times x \times \cancel{x} \times \cancel{x} \times \cancel{x}}{\cancel{x} \times \cancel{x} \times \cancel{x}} = x \times x \times x \times x = x^4$$

If you start out with seven factors, and then cancel away three of them, you're left with four. You just subtract the exponents. The pattern of dividing numbers with exponents is written as the following:

$$\frac{x^r}{x^s} = x^{r-s}$$

An exponent of 0

Mathematicians love to extend patterns. One example of this is the 0 exponent. Do you wonder what it means for a number to have a 0 as an exponent? The fundamental definition of exponentiation won't help you with this one. So let's take a closer look.

One clever trick you can use is to employ the pattern found in division of powers. Suppose you have $\frac{(x^4)}{(x^4)}$. You'd solve this by subtracting the exponents.

$$\frac{x^4}{x^4} = x^{4-4} = x^0$$

But, when you think about it logically, you know that anything divided by itself is equal to one. Therefore, the expression $\frac{(x^4)}{(x^4)}$ must have a value of one. That, in turn, tells us the value of $x^0 = 1$.

Negative exponents

Here, we'll extend the patterns even further. Consider this chart, for a base of 2:

Exponent	2^0	2^1	2^2	2^3	2^4
Power	1	2	4	8	16

Each time you move one cell to the right, the power gets multiplied by 2, and each time you move one cell to the left, the power gets divided by 2. That's a very easy pattern to continue extending to the left into negative numbers, as shown here:

Exponent	2^{-4}	2^{-3}	2^{-2}	2^{-1}	2^0	2^1	2^2	2^3	2^4
Power	$\frac{1}{16}$	$\frac{1}{8}$	$\frac{1}{4}$	$\frac{1}{2}$	1	2	4	8	16

The result, you see, is that negative powers are reciprocals of their corresponding positive powers. This is consistent with the division of powers rule: if dividing means subtracting the exponents, then an exponent of −3 means we're dividing by three factors of the number. Therefore, the general rule is:

$$x^{-r} = \frac{1}{x^r}$$

The Lowdown on Roots

Square roots

When you square a number, you multiply it by itself, e.g., $6 \times 6 = 36$. When you take the square root of a number, you're undoing the square, going backwards from the result of squaring to the input that was originally squared: $\sqrt{36} = 6$. Similarly, $8 \times 8 = 64$, so $\sqrt{64} = 8$. As long as all the numbers are positive, everything with square roots is straightforward.

It's easy to find the square root of a number that's a perfect square. All other square roots are ugly decimals. For estimation purposes on the very hardest GRE questions, it might be useful to memorize that $\sqrt{2} \approx 1.4$ and $\sqrt{3} \approx 1.7$, but without a calculator, no one is going to ask you to calculate the values of any decimal square roots bigger than that. If something like $\sqrt{52}$ shows up, all you have to figure out is which integers you would find that decimal between. For example,

$$49 < 52 < 64$$

Therefore,

$$\sqrt{49} < \sqrt{52} < \sqrt{64}$$

Therefore,

$$7 < \sqrt{52} < 8$$

Numbers are called "irrational" not because they're crazy or because we're crazy for using them, but simply because they cannot be written as ratios, that is, as a fraction of two positive integers.

The symbol: positive or negative?

Most simply people call it the "square root symbol," but that's not the full story. The technical name is the "*principal* square root symbol." In this definition, *principal* means "take the positive root only."

That definition changes things because, technically, the equation $x^2 = 16$ has two solutions, $x = +4$ and $x = -4$, because $4^2 = 16$ and $(-4)^2 = 16$, and the GRE requires you to know both of those solutions. At the same time, $\sqrt{16}$ has only one output: $\sqrt{16} = +4$. When you undo a square by taking a square root, that's a process that results in two possibilities, but when you see this symbol as such, printed as part of the problem, it means **find the positive square root only**.

Notice that you can take the square root of 0: $0^2 = 0$, so $\sqrt{0} = 0$. Also notice, though, that you **cannot** take the square root of a negative, such as $\sqrt{-1}$, because that involves leaving the real number line. There are branches of math that do this, but it's well beyond the scope of the GRE, so don't worry about it!

Cubes and cube roots

When you raise a number to the third power, you're "cubing" it. This name comes from the idea that when you have a cube, you multiply all three equal dimensions ($l \times w \times h$) to find the volume. Here, $2^3 = 8$. A cube root simply undoes this process: $\sqrt[3]{8} = 2$. As with a square root, it's easy to find the cube roots of perfect cubes, and on the GRE you would never be expected to find an ugly decimal cube root.

Cubes and cube roots with negatives get interesting. While $2^3 = 8$, it turns out that $(-2)^3 = -8$. When you multiply two negatives, you get a positive; but when you multiply three negatives, you get a negative. More generally, when you multiply any even number of negatives, you get a positive, but when you multiply any odd number of negatives, you get a negative. Therefore, when you cube a positive, you get a positive, but if you cube a negative, you get a negative.

This means that while you can't take the square root of a negative, you certainly can take the cube root of a negative. Undoing the equation $(-2)^3 = -8$, we get $\sqrt[3]{-8} = -2$. In general, the cube root of a positive will be positive, and the cube root of a negative will be negative.

It can also be a time-saver to remember the first five cubes:

$$1^3 = 1 \quad 2^3 = 8 \quad 3^3 = 27 \quad 4^3 = 64 \quad 5^3 = 125$$

You generally won't be expected to recognize cubes of larger numbers. Knowing just these will translate handily into all sorts of related facts: for example, $\sqrt[3]{125} = 5$ and $\sqrt[3]{-125} = -5$.

Exponents and Roots Practice Questions

These questions should give you an idea of what to expect from any exponent or root questions you may face on the GRE. There are even more practice questions in the GRE practice test in chapter 6.

Question 1

Difficulty: **Easy** · Percent Correct: **80.5%** · Type: **Multiple choice**

$(3 \times 10^{20}) \times (8 \times 10^{30}) =$

(A) 2.4×10^{50}

(B) 2.4×10^{51}

(C) 2.4×10^{60}

(D) 2.4×10^{61}

(E) 2.4×10^{301}

Question 2

Difficulty: **Easy** · Percent Correct: **87.1%** · Type: **Quantitative Comparison**

1. The population of bacteria doubles every 30 minutes.
2. At 3:30 p.m. on Monday, the population was 240.

Column A	Column B
The bacteria population at 2 p.m. on Monday	40

(A) The quantity in Column A is greater

(B) The quantity in Column B is greater

(C) The two quantities are equal

(D) The relationship cannot be determined from the information given

Question 3

Difficulty: **Easy** · Percent Correct: **80.5%** · Type: **Multiple Choice**

If $9^{2x+5} = 27^{3x-10}$, then $x =$

(A) 3

(B) 6

(C) 8

(D) 12

(E) 15

Question 4

Difficulty: Medium · Percent Correct: 68.2% · Type: Multiple Choice

The microcurrent through the electrode in a delicate circuit is usually held constant at 3.6×10^{-8} amps. Because of a defect in another part of the circuit, the current was 1,000 times smaller. What was the current, in amps, caused by this defect?

(A) $3.6 \times 10^{(-8000)}$

(B) $3.6 \times 10^{(-24)}$

(C) $3.6 \times 10^{(-11)}$

(D) $3.6 \times 10^{(-5)}$

(E) $3.6 \times 10^{(\frac{-8}{3})}$

Question 5

Difficulty: Hard · Percent Correct: 34.4% · Type: Multiple Answer

Which of the following are equal to $\left(\frac{1}{560}\right)^{-4}$?

Indicate all correct answers.

A $\dfrac{560^5 - 560^4}{559}$

B $\dfrac{560^{-8}}{560^2}$

C $70^4 \left(\dfrac{1}{8}\right)^{-4}$

D $\sqrt{560^{16}}$

Question 6

Difficulty: Hard · Percent Correct: 36.9% · Type: Numeric Entry

If $\sqrt{\sqrt{\sqrt{3x}}} = \sqrt[4]{2x}$, what is the greatest possible value of x?

Question 7

Difficulty: Very Hard · Percent Correct: 35.3% · Question Type: Multiple Choice

If a and b are integers and $\left(\sqrt[3]{a} \times \sqrt{b}\right)^6 = 500$, then $a + b$ could equal

(A) 2

(B) 3

(C) 4

(D) 5

(E) 6

When you're ready, turn the page to see the answers.

Exponents and Roots Answers and Explanations

Question 1

Difficulty: **Easy** · Percent Correct: **80.5%** · Type: **Multiple choice**

Answer: **Ⓑ**

$(3 \times 10^{20}) \times (8 \times 10^{30}) =$

Ⓐ 2.4×10^{50}
Ⓑ 2.4×10^{51}
Ⓒ 2.4×10^{60}
Ⓓ 2.4×10^{61}
Ⓔ 2.4×10^{301}

You can rearrange the factors in multiplication in any order you like, so you'll group the ordinary numbers together and group the powers of ten together. You have to remember the exponent rule: multiplying powers means adding the exponents.

$$(3 \times 10^{20}) \times (8 \times 10^{30}) = (3 \times 8) \times (10^{20} \times 10^{30}) = 24 \times (10^{20+30}) = 24 \times (10^{50})$$

That final expression is correct, but all of the answers are listed in terms of 2.4 (they're listed in proper scientific notation).

$$24 \times (10^{50}) = (2.4 \times 10^{1}) \times (10^{50}) = 2.4 \times (10^{1} \times 10^{50}) = 2.4 \times (10^{1+50}) = \mathbf{2.4 \times 10^{51}}$$

Question 2

Difficulty: **Easy** · Percent Correct: **87.1%** · Type: **Quantitative Comparison**

Answer: **Ⓑ**

The population of bacteria doubles every 30 minutes. At 3:30 p.m. on Monday, the population was 240.

Column A	Column B
The bacteria population at 2 p.m. on Monday	40

Time	Population	
2 p.m.	30	**40**
2:30 p.m.	60	
3 p.m.	120	
3:30 p.m.	240	

Ⓐ The quantity in Column A is greater
Ⓑ The quantity in Column B is greater
Ⓒ The two quantities are equal
Ⓓ The relationship cannot be determined from the information given

Question 3

Difficulty: **Easy** · Percent Correct: **80.5%** · Type: **Multiple Choice**

If $9^{2x+5} = 27^{3x-10}$, then $x =$

Answer: **C**

(A) 3

(B) 6

(C) 8

(D) 12

(E) 15

$$9^{2x+5} = 27^{3x-10}$$
$$(3^2)^{2x+5} = (3^3)^{3x-10}$$
$$3^{4x+10} = 3^{9x-30}$$
$$4x + 10 = 9x - 30$$
$$10 = 5x - 30$$
$$40 = 5x$$
$$\mathbf{8 = x}$$

$$x^a = x^b \implies a = b$$

Question 4

Difficulty: **Medium** · Percent Correct: **68.2%** · Type: **Multiple Choice**

The microcurrent through the electrode in a delicate circuit is usually held constant at 3.6×10^{-8} amps. Because of a defect in another part of the circuit, the current was 1,000 times smaller. What was the current, in amps, caused by this defect?

Answer: **C**

(A) $3.6 \times 10^{(-8000)}$

(B) $3.6 \times 10^{(-24)}$

(C) $3.6 \times 10^{(-11)}$

(D) $3.6 \times 10^{(-5)}$

(E) $3.6 \times 10^{(\frac{-8}{3})}$

If the normal current $= 3.6 \times 10^{-8}$ amp and the "defect current" is a 1000 times smaller, then you need to divide the number above by 1000.

$$\text{defect current} = \frac{3.6 \times 10^{-8}}{1000} = \frac{3.6 \times 10^{-8}}{10^3}$$

$$= 3.6 \times 10^{-8-3} = \mathbf{3.6 \times 10^{-11}}$$

Question 5

Difficulty: **Hard** · Percent Correct: **34.4%** · Type: **Multiple Answer**

Which of the following are equal to $\left(\frac{1}{560}\right)^{-4}$? $= \mathbf{560^4}$

Answers: **A** **C**

Indicate __all__ correct answers.

A $\dfrac{560^5 - 560^4}{559} = \dfrac{560^4(560^1 - 1)}{559} = \dfrac{560^4(559)}{559}$ $= \mathbf{560^4}$

B $\dfrac{560^{-8}}{560^2} = 560^{-8-2} = 560^{-10}$

C $70^4\left(\dfrac{1}{8}\right)^{-4} = 70^4\left(\dfrac{8}{1}\right)^4 = 70^4 \times 8^4 = (70 \times 8)^4$ $= \mathbf{560^4}$

D $\sqrt{560^{16}} = (560^{16})^{\frac{1}{2}} = 560^8$

Question 6

Difficulty: **Hard** · Percent Correct: **36.9%** · Type: **Numeric Entry**

Answer: 0.75

If $\sqrt{\sqrt{\sqrt{\sqrt{3x}}}} = \sqrt[4]{2x}$, what is the greatest possible value of x?

$$\sqrt{\sqrt{\sqrt{\sqrt{3x}}}} = \sqrt[4]{2x}$$

$$\left(\left[(3x)^{\frac{1}{2}}\right]^{\frac{1}{2}}\right)^{\frac{1}{2}} = (2x)^{\frac{1}{4}}$$

$$(3x)^{\frac{1}{8}} = (2x)^{\frac{1}{4}}$$

$$\left[(3x)^{\frac{1}{8}}\right]^{8} = \left[(2x)^{\frac{1}{4}}\right]^{8}$$

$$(3x)^{1} = (2x)^{2}$$

$$3x = 4x^2$$

$$3x = 4x^2$$

$$4x^2 - 3x = 0$$

$$x(4x - 3) = 0$$

$$\Rightarrow \quad x = \mathbf{0}$$

$$\Rightarrow \quad 4x - 3 = 0$$

$$4x = 3$$

$$x = \frac{3}{4} = \mathbf{0.75}$$

Question 7

Difficulty: **Very Hard** · Percent Correct: **35.3%** · Question Type: **Multiple Choice**

Answer: B

If a and b are integers and $\left(\sqrt[3]{a} \times \sqrt{b}\right)^6 = 500$, then $a + b$ could equal

(A) 2

(B) 3

(C) 4

(D) 5

(E) 6

$\sqrt[n]{x} = x^{\frac{1}{n}}$

$$\left(\sqrt[3]{a} \times \sqrt{b}\right)^6 = 500$$

$$\left(a^{\frac{1}{3}} \times b^{\frac{1}{2}}\right)^6 = 500$$

$$a^2 \times b^3 = 500 \qquad (x^a y^b)^c = x^{ac} y^{bc}$$

$$a^2 \times b^3 = 2 \times 2 \times 5 \times 5 \times 5$$

$$a^2 \times b^3 = 2^2 \times 5^3$$

$$\Rightarrow \quad \begin{array}{l} b = 5 \\ a = \pm 2 \end{array} \qquad \begin{array}{l} a + b = 5 + 2 = 7 \\ a + b = 5 + (-2) = \mathbf{3} \end{array}$$

You can find even more exponents and roots questions on gre.magoosh.com!

Need a study break? Color in the shapes below to make whatever pattern you'd like. Have fun!

Quantitative Concept #5: Word Problems and Statistics

Now that you have read all about algebra, it's time to think about what its purpose is in the first place. The reason human beings created algebra was to solve problems about real world situations, and the GRE loves asking math problems about real world situations, a.k.a. word problems! Even students who can do algebra in the abstract sometimes find word problems challenging. Here's a rough-and-ready guide to what you need to know about word problems.

Translating from Words to Math

Suppose you have the following sentence in a word problem:

> Three-fifths of x is 14 less than twice y squared.

First, here's a quick guide to changing words to math:

1. The verbs *is* and *are* are the equivalent of an equals sign; the equals sign in an equation is, in terms of "mathematical grammar," the equivalent of a verb in a sentence. Every sentence has a verb and every equation has an equals sign.
2. The word *of* means multiply (often used with fractions and percents). For example, "26% of x" means $(0.26x)$.
3. The phrases *more than* or *greater than* mean addition. For example, "5 greater than x" means $(x + 5)$ and "7 more than y" means $(y + 7)$.
4. The phrase *less than* means subtraction. For example, "8 less than Q" means $(Q - 8)$.

With that in mind, let's go back to the sentence above.

- "three fifths of x" means $\left[\left(\frac{3}{5}\right) \times x\right]$
- "is" marks the location of the equals sign
- "twice y squared" means $2y^2$
- "14 less than twice y squared" means $2y^2 - 14$

Altogether, the equation you get is:

$$\frac{3}{5}x = 2y^2 - 14$$

Assigning Variables

Occasionally, the GRE will give you a word problem about variables, and then a sentence about variables, similar to the one we just worked through. Even more frequently, the problems concern real-world quantities, and you need to assign algebraic variables to these real-world quantities.

Sometimes, one quantity is directly related to every other quantity in the problem. For example:

Sarah spends $\frac{2}{5}$ of her monthly salary on rent; spends $\frac{1}{12}$ of her monthly salary on auto costs, including gas and insurance; and puts $\frac{1}{10}$ of her monthly salary into savings each month. With what she has left each month, she spends $800 on groceries and …

In that problem, everything is related to "monthly salary," so it would make a lot of sense to introduce just one variable for that and express everything else in terms of that variable. Note that you don't always have to use the boring choice of x for a variable! If you want a variable for salary, you might use the letter s, which will help you remember what the variable means!

If there are two or more quantities that don't depend directly on each other, then you may have to introduce a different variable for each. Just remember that it's mathematically problematic to litter a problem with a whole slew of different variables. You see, for each variable, you need an equation to solve it. If you want to solve for two different variables, you need two different equations—a common scenario with word problems. If you want to solve for three different variables, you need three different equations—a considerably less common scenario. And while the mathematical pattern continues upward from there, having more than three completely separate variables is almost unheard of in GRE math problems.

When you assign variables, always be hyper-vigilant and over-the-top explicit about exactly what each variable means. Write a quick note to yourself on the scratch paper, such as "t = the price of one box of tissue," or whatever the problem wants. You want to avoid the undesirable situation of solving for a number and not knowing what that number means in the problem!

As an example, here's a word problem that's easier than what you'll find on the GRE:

Andrew and Beatrice each have their own savings account. Beatrice's account has $600 less than three times what Andrew's account has. If Andrew had $300 more dollars, then he would have exactly half what is currently in Beatrice's account. How much does Beatrice have?

The obvious choices for variables are a = *the amount in Andrew's account* and b = *the amount in Beatrice's account.* The GRE will be good about giving you word problems involving people whose names start with different letters, so that it's easier to assign variables. You can turn the second and third sentences into equations.

second sentence: $b = 3a - 600$

third sentence: $(a + 300) = \frac{b}{2}$ or $2(a + 300) = b$

Both equations are solved for b, so simply set them equal.

$3a - 600 = 2(a + 300)$

$3a - 600 = 2a + 600$

$a - 600 = 600$

$a = 1200$

You can plug this into either equation to find b. And, if you're feeling like you're good on time, plug it into **both** equations, and make sure the value of b you get is the same!

$b = 3000$

Alternative Solutions: Backsolving

If the GRE hands you a word problem, one possible solution is the "algebraic solution," in which you assign variables to words and perform algebra to answer the question. We walked through that approach above. The benefit of the algebraic solution is that it always works, on all kinds of word problems.

The disadvantages of the algebraic solution include the fact that many students aren't particularly thrilled with doing algebra and that sometimes doing all the algebra takes a really, really long time. It's important to realize that the algebraic solution is one possible solution, but not the *only* one. Another big strategy is backsolving.

Suppose the word problem is a multiple choice problem with five numerical answer choices. Let's look at an example problem:

The original cost of a coat was increased by 40% at the beginning of 2015. In March 2015, the new price was reduced by 20%, and the cost remained at this new reduced price. Chris had a coupon for a $50 discount and, in April, used the coupon to buy the coat at the further reduced price. There was no tax or additional fee on the purchase. If Chris paid $95.60 for the coat, which would be the original price of the coat?

Ⓐ $92.50

Ⓑ $100

Ⓒ $104.83

Ⓓ $120

Ⓔ $130

Now, we *could* assign a variable to the original price of the coat and do all the algebra, but let's explore the other method we just mentioned: backsolving. When the answers to a word problem are all numbers (as they are in this question), we can use backsolving—working backward from the answers. If we pick one answer choice as if it is the correct price of the coat, we can do all the calculations with numbers, including use of the calculator if needed. If we happened to pick the right answer the first time, then great: we know the answer. Of course, our chances of picking the right answer on the first pick is only 20%, but even if the number we pick isn't the right answer, it still helps us!

Suppose one answer choice is $200, and I pick that first: up 40% to $280, down 20% to $224, then down $50 to $174. This, of course, isn't the answer, but here's the first **big idea**: if I pick $200 as a starting value and get a value that's too big, that means that any starting value bigger than $200 is also going to be too big. On the other hand, if I pick some starting value and get a value that's too small, then any other starting value smaller than what I chose isn't going to work either.

This leads directly to a second **big idea**: since the GRE typically lists numerical answers in numerical order, in general you should start backsolving with answer choice (C), which is typically the middle value. If picking the starting value (C) leads to a final value that's too big, we can eliminate not only (C) but also (D) and (E); if picking the starting value (C) leads to a final value that's too small, we can eliminate not only (C) but also (A) and (B). In that way, usually we can eliminate three answers with one guess, and of course, once in a while, (C) itself will be the answer. This makes backsolving an incredibly efficient strategy when the multiple-choice answers are all number choices.

A couple caveats about backsolving:

1. In the example we just gave you, and in many word problems, there's a very simple relationship between the starting value and the ending value: if one goes up, the other goes up, and vice versa. In some harder word problems, it may not be clear whether increasing or decreasing the starting value would increase or decrease the ending value. In such cases, we can't necessarily eliminate other answer choices when one choice doesn't work. Depending on the nature of the scenario, there may be other ways to eliminate answers.

2. Suppose in some word problem with numerical choices, the choices are as follows:

    (A) $48.19
    (B) $50
    (C) $56.72
    (D) $60
    (E) $63.34

    Notice that a couple choices are clear-cut and straightforward and others are ... not so much. Instead of starting with (C), which isn't as clear-cut, start with one of the choices without a "cents" value. Suppose we start backsolving with the value in (B). If this works, (B) is the answer, and if it's too big, (A) is the answer; but if it's too small, I eliminate (A) and (B). Now, use the other clear-cut choice, (D), and the result of this will determine a unique answer.

Let's go back to the problem about the coat Chris bought. Normally, we would start with (C), but $104.83 isn't as clear-cut. Instead, choice (B), $100, is a very nice round number, so we should start there. Original price = $100, up 40% to $140. We know 10% of $140 is $14, so 20% is $28: down 20% would be $140 − $28 = $112. Down $50 would give us a sale price of $62. That's way too low. You can eliminate (A) and (B).

Now, to decide between the three choices remaining. We'll choose (D), original price = $120, because that will definitely decide the answer. We can use a calculator for this. Original price = $120. Up 40%, to ($120) × 1.4 = $168. Down 20% to ($168) × 0.8 = $134.40. Now, subtract $50, and we get $84.40. This is still too low, so the original price must be higher than $120. The only possible choice is $130, so the answer is **(E)**.

Distance, Rate, and Time

The fastest land animal is a **cheetah**, which can top out at about 112 mph in a short burst of speed. The fastest of all animals in the natural state is the **peregrine falcon**, which can reach speeds up to about 200 mph on a dive. As of 2015, the fastest land speed record was set by British RAF pilot **Andy Green**, who in October 1997 achieved a speed just over 763 mph in a jet-powered supersonic car. Experts and enthusiasts apparently are trying to break the 1000 mph level for land-based crafts.

You've already seen the $d = rt$ formula a few times in this book. And now here it is again! But we want you to know a few more things about this formula, because it's fantastically useful.

One point we want to make painstakingly clear: absolutely no problem on the GRE will be about only one distance, only one rate, and only one amount of time. You will never, never, never have a problem that gives you two of those three numbers and simply asks for the third. Instead, the distance/rate problems on the GRE will make you think. Maybe there will be two or more travelers. Maybe there will be a single traveler, moving differently in separate legs of her trip. You'll have to analyze the problem, breaking it into different pieces—separate travelers or separate legs—and each one will have its own distance, its own rate, and its own time, so you'll use a different $d = rt$ separately for each piece. Often, you have to combine results from individual uses of the $d = rt$ formula to find the answer to the question.

One technique that helps many people think about these problems is to sketch a diagram, just to get a sense of directions and which distances are getting larger or smaller at any given point in the problem. Motion, by its very nature, is spatial, so it's necessary to engage your spatial/visual reasoning in some way. Drawing a diagram does that for many test takers.

Here are a few things to keep in mind, some of which are repetitions from the previous paragraphs:

1. If the problem has two different travelers, each one gets a $d = rt$ formula.
2. If the trip has two or more "legs," then each "leg" of the trip gets its own $d = rt$.
3. You *cannot* find the average velocity of two different segments by finding the numerical mean of the velocities of the individual segments. Instead, you have to find the individual distances and times—**average velocity of a trip = (total distance)/(total time)**.

4. If two cars are traveling in opposite directions (toward or away from each other), you can add the velocities.
5. If two cars are traveling in the same direction, you can subtract the velocities.

Point number three is important to remember, because it's a common GRE trap answer. Some test takers find the numerical mean of two given velocities and mistakenly think that this mean is the average velocity—it's not!

Here's an example problem:

A car travels 120 miles at 40 mph and then another 120 miles at 60 mph. What is the car's average velocity during the entire trip?

The trap answer is 50 mph, the numerical mean of 40 and 60. This isn't the correct answer, but you're nearly guaranteed it would appear in the answer choices of a GRE question.

Average velocity is the total distance of the trip divided by the total time of the trip. From the prompt, we know that the total distance is 120 + 120 = 240 miles. Somehow, it's up to us to figure out the total time of the trip so that we can answer the question.

Notice that the trip has two parts (two "legs"), each of which happen at a different speed. Whenever different speeds are happening in different "legs" of the trip, we have to use a different $d = rt$ separately for each leg.

Again, in this problem, we know the total distance is 120 + 120 = 240 miles, but we still need the total time. So what we need to do now is find the individual times for each leg.

First leg: $t = \frac{d}{r} = \frac{120}{40} = 3$ hours

Second leg: $t = \frac{d}{r} = \frac{120}{60} = 2$ hours

Now that we have the time for each leg, we simply can add these to get the total time, because here the two legs happen one after the other.

Total time = 3 + 2 = 5 hours

Now we know the total distance and the total time, so we can calculate average velocity directly.

$$average\ velocity = \frac{(total\ distance)}{(total\ time)} = \frac{240\,mi}{5\,hours} = \textbf{48 mph}$$

Once again, the key to this problem, and to most $d = rt$ problems on the GRE, is that we didn't just jump in formula-happy. Jumping in formula-happy to any problem is the wrong approach. Instead, we stopped and took stock first. Critical thinking should always be the first step! Realizing that there were two different legs to the trip, we broke the problem into pieces and *then* applied the formula separately in each leg. Once we had figured out what we needed in each leg—the times—we could combine that information to answer the question.

Work Rate

Some problems concern how fast different people accomplish different tasks, and the GRE likes to ask about what would happen if the two people worked together or apart. For example:

> When Dan and Stan work together, they can wash a car in 4 minutes. When Dan works alone, he can wash a car in 5 minutes. How long does it take Stan to wash a car?

The first big idea in problems of this sort is that you can't add or subtract or do anything else with the times as given. You can't add or subtract *times*, but you can and should add or subtract *rates*.

In this problem, you could say that Dan has a rate of 1 car per 5 minutes, or $\frac{1}{5}$ in units of "cars per minute." It doesn't matter that the rate unit is a bit unconventional, as long as time is in the denominator and we're consistent throughout the problem.

You don't know Stan's solo rate, but you do know that the combined rate is $\frac{1}{4}$.

The second big idea is that you can add individual rates to get a combined rate.

$$(\textit{Stan's rate}) + (\textit{Dan's rate}) = (\textit{combined rate})$$

$$(\textit{Stan's rate}) + \frac{1}{5} = \frac{1}{4}$$

$$(\textit{Stan's rate}) = \frac{1}{4} - \frac{1}{5} = \frac{5}{20} - \frac{4}{20} = \frac{1}{20}$$

So Stan, working at a rate of 1 car in 20 minutes, would take 20 minutes to wash one car. Basically, you want Dan to wash your car if you're in a hurry.

Mean and Median

The **mean** is just the ordinary average—add up all the items on the list and divide by the number of items. As a formula, that looks like this:

$$average = \frac{sum\ of\ items}{number\ of\ items}$$

Notice that you can also write it as this:

$$sum\ of\ items = (average) \times (number\ of\ items)$$

This latter form can be powerful. For example, if you add or subtract one item from a set, you can easily figure out how that changes the sum, and that can allow you to calculate the new average. Also, if you're combining two groups of different sizes, you can't add averages, but you can add sums.

When you put the list in ascending order, the **median** is the middle. If there are an odd number of items on the list, the middle item equals the median; for example, in the seven-element set {3, 5, 7, 9, 13, 15, 17}, the median is the fourth number, 9. If there are an even number of items on the list, then the median is the average of the two middle numbers; for example, in the eight-element set {3, 5, 7, 9, 13, 15, 17, 17}, the median is 11 (the average of the fourth and fifth entries, 9 and 13). Notice that when the number of items on the list is even, the median can equal a number not on the list. Numbers above and below the median can be equal to the median, and that doesn't change the fact that it's a median; for example, the median of the set {1, 3, 3, 3, 3, 3, 74, 89, 312} is just 3, the fifth number of that nine-element set.

Notice that making the largest number on the list larger or making the smallest number smaller would not affect the median at all, although it would substantially change the mean. The mean is affected by outliers, but the median is not.

Weighted Average

On the GRE, weighted average situations occur when you combine groups of different sizes and different averages. Supposed, for example, the male employees of a company have one average score on some random assessment, and the females have another average score. If there were an equal number of males and females, you could just average the two separate gender averages. Of course, a problem like that's too easy and the GRE will never present you with two groups of equal size in such a question. Instead, the number of male employees and number of female employees will be profoundly different, one significantly outnumbering the other, and then you'll have to combine the individual gender averages to produce a total average for all employees. That's a weighted average. Consider the following problem:

> In Cytherea Corporation, each employee was given an interpersonal assessment with a score from 0 to 60. The average score among all male employees was 35, and the average score for all employees was 39. If Cytherea Corporation has 40 male employees and 10 female employees, what was the average score among all female employees?

Don't worry about trying to solve the problem at this point. Right now, we're stating this problem simply to give you a sense of how a weighted average question might be phrased.

The example we just gave includes just two groups, which is common, but sometimes there are three. Conceivably, on a very hard problem, there could even be four groups. Regardless, in weighted average problems, each group will be a different size and each will have its own average. Sometimes your job will be to find the average of everyone all together. Sometimes the question will give you most of the information for the individual groups, give you the total average for everyone, and then ask you to find the size or average of one particular group—as our example question does.

In this particular question, the trap approach would be to assume that 39 is simply the average of the male score and the female score. In other words, you'd fall for the trap by mistakenly thinking that $(F + 35)/2 = 39$, and arriving at the wrong answer of $F = 43$. The analogous trap answer will always be listed and will *always* be wrong. Remember, we can't add or subtract or average the individual group averages.

Remember also that, even with ordinary average questions, thinking in terms of the sum can often be helpful. You *can't* add or subtract averages, but you *can* add or subtract sums! That's the key to the weighted average situation. If you calculate the sums for each separate group, you can simply add these sums to get the sum of the whole group. Alternately, if you know the size of most of the individual groups and the total average for everyone, you can figure out the total sum for everyone and simply subtract the sums of the individual groups in order to find what you need.

Now, let's look at the practice problem again (with answer choices this time):

In Cytherea Corporation, each employee was given an interpersonal assessment with a score from 0 to 60. The average score among all male employees was 35, and the average score for all employees was 39. If Cytherea Corporation has 40 male employees and 10 female employees, what was the average score among all female employees?

(A) 40
(B) 43
(C) 47
(D) 51
(E) 55

First, we have to think about sums. Remember that **sum = (average) × (number of participants)**.

Sum for the males = $35 \times 40 = 70 \times 20 = 1400$

Notice that we used the "doubling and halving" trick there, taking half of 40 to get 20, and doubling 35 to get 70: this made the multiplication much easier to do in our heads.

Sum for everyone = $39 \times 50 = hmm\ldots$

We can do this, too, without a calculator! We know $40 \times 50 = 2000$. That's 40 different groups of size 50, so 39×50 should be one group of 50 less than 2000. Thus, $39 \times 50 = 2000 - 50 = 1950$. That's the sum for everyone. Now, subtract the sums:

(sum for females) = (sum for everyone) − (sum for males)
(sum for females) = $1950 - 1400 = 550$

Let F be the average female score, the quantity the question is seeking.

$$\text{(sum for females)} = F \times \text{(number of females)}$$
$$550 = F \times 10$$
$$55 = F$$

The average for the females was 55, so the correct answer choice is **(E)**.

Some weighted average problems give percents, not actual counts, of individual groups. In that case, you could simply pick a convenient number for the size of the population and use the sums method from there.

For example, if group A is 20% of the population, group B is 40% of the population, and group C is the last 40% of the population, you could just pretend that group A has one person, groups B and C each have two people, and total population equals five people. From this, you could calculate all your sums.

Here's a slightly harder practice problem, with three groups:

In Dives Corporation, 75% of the employees are customer service representatives, 15% are programmers, and 10% are managers. The customer service representatives have an average salary of $60,000, and the programmers have an average salary of $100,000. If the average salary of all employees is also $100,000, what is the average salary of the managers?

(A) $140,000
(B) $180,000
(C) $260,000
(D) $400,000
(E) $560,000

For simplicity, let's assume the company has 100 employees: 75 CSRs, 15 programmers, and 10 managers. Also, all the numbers are in the thousands, so let's drop three zeros from all the dollar amounts and add them in later. The customer service representatives average is $60, programmer average is $100, and the company-wide average is also $100.

Finally, just to show another solution method, we'll use backsolving. Backsolving was already introduced on page 100. Let's start by assuming that (C) is the answer, that managers make an average of $260. Does this lead to the correct company-wide average? Calculate the sums.

$$\text{sum} = \text{(average)} \times \text{(number of members)}$$
customer service representative sum = $60 \times 75 = \$4{,}500$
programmer sum = $100 \times 15 = \$1{,}500$
manager sum = $260 \times 10 = \$2{,}600$

For the first, you can use a calculator, but you shouldn't have needed one for the other two!

Add those up for the total sum.

total sum = 4500 + 1500 + 2600 = $8600

When we divide that total sum by 100 employees, we get a company-wide average of $86. That's too small! The manager average must be higher than $260. Immediately, we can eliminate answers (A), (B), and (C). If you were running out of time at this point, you would have excellent chances of guessing from the remaining answers.

Let's assume we still have time for this problem. (D) is a better-looking number than (E), so I will choose to work with (D). Assume the manager salary is $400. We have the same individual sums from above for the first two:

customer service representatives sum = $4,500
programmer sum = $1,500
manager sum = 400 × 10 = $4,000
total sum = 4,500 + 1,500 + 4,000 = $10,000

Divide that total sum by 100 employees, and we get a company-wide average of $100. Bingo! That works! The managers must have an average of $400, or $400,000 when we put the thousands back in. The answer must be **(D)**.

Range and Standard Deviation

The GRE loves this topic, because it's so simple. The *range* is the difference between the maximum value and the minimum value. In the set {3, 5, 7, 9, 13, 15, 17}, the range = 17 − 3 = 14. In the set {1, 3, 3, 3, 3, 3, 74, 89, 312}, the range = 312 − 1 = 311.

The range is a measure of the spread from the highest to the lowest value, but it doesn't account for any of the numbers in between. The *standard deviation* is also a measure of spread, that is to say, an indication of how far apart the numbers on the list are from each other. Like the mean and unlike the range, the standard deviation takes every number on the list into consideration.

Here's what you need to know about standard deviation:

- If all the entries of the list are equal, the standard deviation = 0. In other words, they don't deviate at all, because they're all the same.

- If you add/subtract a constant to/from every number on a list, that doesn't change the standard deviation at all. It's just like taking the batch of data points and sliding them up or down the number line: that process doesn't change how far apart they are from each other.

- If you multiply/divide a list by a constant, then you also multiply/divide the standard deviation by this constant.

- If all the entries are the same distance from the mean, that distance is the standard deviation. For example, in the set {3, 3, 3, 7, 7, 7}, the mean = 5, and every number "deviates" from the mean by exactly two units, so the standard deviation = 2.

Here's a practice problem with standard deviation.

The following sets each have a mean of 10 and the standard deviations are given as variables.

Set I = {7, 8, 9, 11, 12, 13}, standard deviation = P
Set II = {10, 10, 10, 10, 10, 10}, standard deviation = Q
Set III = {6, 6, 6, 14, 14, 14}, standard deviation = R

Rank these three standard deviations from least to greatest.

    (A) P, Q, R
    (B) P, R, Q
    (C) Q, P, R
    (D) Q, R, P
    (E) R, Q, P

As with many GRE problems about standard deviation, this problem is conceptual: we don't have to do a complicated calculation to get the exact standard deviations of each set.

For Set II, however, we *can* actually calculate the exact standard deviation—and without a calculator—only because all the elements are equal. No element deviates at all from the mean. In this case, the standard deviation is zero, so $Q = 0$, the smallest possible standard deviation. This insight alone means that either (C) or (D) must be the answer.

We don't know the standard deviation of Set I. Different numbers have different distances from the mean, and those distances are between 1 and 3, so we know that the standard deviation is between 1 and 3. We can tell $1 \le P \le 3$. That's all we know about P.

That brings us to Set III. And, what do you know, we can also figure out the standard deviation of this set without a calculator. Each member of the set is a distance of 4 from the mean. Since each individual deviation equals 4, the standard deviation also must be 4. $R = 4$, so it's clear that $R > P$.

Thus, the correct order is Q, P, R. The answer is (C).

The fact that all the elements in Set II were the same number made this problem a little easier than what the GRE would probably give you. It's important to realize that standard deviation is about how far apart numbers are, so {2, 4, 6, 8, 10} and {302, 304, 306, 308, 310} have identical standard deviations; adding 300 to each number doesn't change the spacing between the numbers at all. Similarly, the set {50, 55, 60, 65, 70} would have a higher standard deviation than the set {302, 304, 306, 308, 310}, because in the former, the numbers are spaced by 5s rather than by 2s. It doesn't matter that all the numbers in that second set are located further to the right on the number line. Once again, these conceptual ideas about standard deviation will be what the GRE wants you to know. You won't have to perform complicated calculations to find numerical values of the standard deviations for sets like the ones mentioned in this paragraph.

In addition to its use as a general measure of spread, standard deviation is used as a kind of "yardstick" in large distributions, especially in populations that follow the normal distribution for some variable.

Let's say that the mean for all SAT math scores is 500 and the standard deviation is 100 (that's not exactly true, but something along those lines was the initial motivation for the 200–800 scoring scale). If we assume these nice neat values, then we could say that an SAT math score of 700 is two standard deviations above the mean and that a score of 450 is half a standard deviation below the mean.

We can specify the value of any score by indicating how many standard deviations above or below the mean. For example, the GRE could tell you that, for some fictional test, 80 is two standard deviations above the mean and 65 is one standard deviation below the mean, and then ask you to find either the mean or the standard deviation of this fictional test.

From one standard deviation *below* the mean to two standard deviations *above* the mean (−1 to +2) is a distance of three standard deviation units. Since this is a score difference of 80 − 65 = 15, each standard deviation length has a score value of 15/3 = 5. Then we can tell that the mean = 70 and the standard deviation = 5: two 5s above 70 gives us 80, and one 5 below 70 lands us at 65—this works! Those were relatively simple numbers, but that will give you the idea of the context in which units of standard deviation might appear on the GRE.

Consecutive Integers

Any sequence of consecutive integers has a few interesting properties. The mean and median of such a sequence are always equal. If the number of terms in the sequence is odd, then the median is simply the middle integer on the list; if the number of terms is even, then the median is the average of the two middle integers.

If you have to count all the terms in a sequence, you use inclusive counting. For this, you subtract and then add one. Thus, the number of terms from 25 to 60 would be 60 − 25 + 1 = 36.

It's also easy to find the sum of any set of consecutive integer or consecutive multiples of the same factor. Suppose you had to find the sum of all the positive integers from 25 to 60. Think about this sum:

$$25 + 26 + 27 + 28 + \cdots + 57 + 58 + 59 + 60$$

Break it up as follows: Pair the first number with the last number and find that sum. Then pair the second number with the second-to-last number, find that sum, and repeat.

First pair = 25 + 60 = 85
Second pair = 26 + 59 = 85
Third pair = 27 + 58 = 85
Fourth pair = 28 + 57 = 85, etc.

Each pair will have the same sum, 85. But how many pairs do we have? Well, above you found that there were 36 numbers on the list, so that would be 18 pairs.

sum = (*sum of each pair*) × (*# of pairs*) = 85 × 18 = 1530

It doesn't matter if the number of terms in the sequence is odd, making the number of pairs a half-integer value—this approach still works. For example, suppose you had to find the sum of the numbers from 1 to 25. Obviously, you have 25 terms, an odd number. The sum of each pair will be 1 + 25 = 26. The number of pairs would be $\frac{25}{2}$ = 12.5. What this really means is 12 full pairs, and then the single middle number 13, which is a "half pair" that has a value equal to exactly half the sum of all the other pairs. So, basically, you can still just multiply.

sum = (*sum of each pair*) × (*# of pairs*) = (26)(12.5) = 325

You can use this approach to find the sum of any equally spaced sequence of integers. This would include:

- consecutive integers: {37, 38, 39, 40, 41, ...}
- consecutive multiples of any integer: {28, 35, 42, 49, 56, ...}
- any sequence in which each new term is the previous term plus a fixed constant: {19, 27, 35, 43, 51, ...}

Algebraic Sequences

The previous section had examples of sequences that were specified simply as lists of numbers. For some more complicated sequences on the GRE, the test will specify the sequence using algebra. The standard notation is to use subscripts to denote the term number: for example, a_1 is the first term, a_2 is the second term, and so forth. A general term, the nth term, would be denoted by a_n, and the single equation for a_n can define the entire sequence in one fell swoop.

An algebraically defined sequence may either have explicitly defined terms or be recursively defined.

An *explicit series* is one in which the general rule for finding each term can be stated, either verbally or mathematically. Sometimes the GRE will give you the general rule for a sequence in algebraic form.

Leonardo Fibonacci (ca. 1170–ca. 1250) popularized the use of the Hindu-Arabic digit, that is, the modern positional decimal system using the 0 through 9 digits we use today. Before Fibonacci, it might take several letters to write a number in Roman numerals (e.g., CDXLIV), whereas with Fibonacci's system, we could simply write 444.

For example:

> If a sequence is defined by $a_n = n^2 - n$ for $n \geq 1$, what is the difference between the fourth and third terms?

If the rule is given algebraically, all you have to do is plug in the index number to find the value of each term. Here, you plug in $n = 3$ to find the third term, and plug in $n = 4$ to find the fourth term. The third and fourth terms are:

$$a_3 = 3^2 - 3 = 9 - 3 = 6$$
$$a_4 = 4^2 - 4 = 16 - 4 = 12$$

So the difference between them is $12 - 6 = 6$.

In mathematics, a *recursive* definition is one where you need the result at the end of each step in order to proceed to the next step. A sequence has a recursive definition if the only way to calculate the third term is first to calculate the second term, the only way to calculate the fourth term is first to calculate the third term, etc. Clearly, if you were asked for, say, the sixth term of a recursive sequence, you would have to calculate each and every term along the way: there's no "shortcut" we can use to solve directly for the sixth term.

Here's an example of a question that includes a recursive definition.

> If a sequence is defined by $a_n = (a_{n-1})^2 - 5$ for all $n \geq 1$, and if $a_2 = 3$, then what is the fifth term?

Whenever you see the nth term equal to some expression involving an $(n - 1)$th term, that's a recursively defined sequence. The idea can be described as follows: to find the $n =$ third term, you would have to plug the $n - 1 =$ second term into the formula; to find the $n =$ fourth term, you would have to plug the $n - 1 =$ third term into the formula; etc. You always will be given a "starter" term for such a sequence.

For the sequence in this problem, you already know a_2, so you can use that to find a_3, and work from there:

$$a_n = (a_n - 1)^2 - 5$$
$$a_3 = (a_2)^2 - 5 = 3^2 - 5 = 9 - 5 = 4$$
$$a_4 = (a_3)^2 - 5 = 4^2 - 5 = 16 - 5 = 11$$
$$a_5 = (a_4)^2 - 5 = 11^2 - 5 = 121 - 5 = 116$$

Thus, the fifth term is $a_5 = 116$.

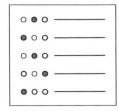

Word Problems and Statistics Practice Questions

These examples should help you get an idea of what to expect from word problems and statistics questions on the GRE. There are even more practice questions in the GRE practice test in chapter 6.

Word problems

Question 1

Difficulty: **Easy**   ·   Percent Correct: **79.5%**   ·   Type: **Numeric Entry**

Luke drives the first 300 miles of a trip at 60 miles an hour. How fast does he have to drive, in miles per hour, on the final 200 miles of the trip if the total time of the trip is to equal 7 hours?

Question 2

Difficulty: **Easy**   ·   Percent Correct: **78.2%**   ·   Type: **Quantitative Comparison**

Column A	Column B
Sum of the integers from 1 to 40 inclusive	800

Ⓐ The quantity in Column A is greater

Ⓑ The quantity in Column B is greater

Ⓒ The two quantities are equal

Ⓓ The relationship cannot be determined from the information given

Question 3

Difficulty: **Easy**   ·   Percent Correct: **65.5%**   ·   Type: **Numeric Entry**

If Michael can shovel all the snow off a standard driveway in 12 minutes, and Eamon can shovel all the snow off a standard driveway in 36 minutes, then working together, how many minutes would it take for them both to shovel all the snow off a standard driveway?

Question 4

Difficulty: **Medium** · Percent Correct: **63.4%** · Type: **Multiple Choice**

Sue planted 4 times as many apple seeds as she planted orange seeds. 15% of the apple seeds grew into trees, and 10% of the orange seeds grew into trees. If a total of 420 apple trees and orange trees grew from the seeds, how many orange seeds did Sue plant?

(A) 540

(B) 600

(C) 660

(D) 720

(E) 760

Question 5

Difficulty: **Hard** · Percent Correct: **55.8%** · Type: **Multiple Choice**

A container holds 4 quarts of alcohol and 4 quarts of water. How many quarts of water must be added to the container to create a mixture that is 3 parts alcohol to 5 parts water by volume?

(A) $\frac{4}{3}$

(B) $\frac{5}{3}$

(C) $\frac{7}{3}$

(D) $\frac{8}{3}$

(E) $\frac{10}{3}$

Question 6

Difficulty: **Hard** · Percent Correct: **38.2%** · Type: **Numeric Entry**

The sum of the pre-tax costs of Item A and Item B is $300. In Alumba, each item would be charged a flat 7%. In Aplandia, Item A is subject to 5% tax and Item B is subject to 10% tax. If the tax in Aplandia on the purchase of both items is exactly $3 more than it is in Alumba, then what is the pre-tax price of Item A?

Question 7

Difficulty: **Hard** · Percent Correct: **54.2%** · Type: **Multiple Choice**

The nth term (t_n) of a certain sequence is defined as $t_n = t_{n-1} + 4$.
If $t_1 = -7$ then $t_{71} =$

(A) 273

(B) 277

(C) 281

(D) 283

(E) 287

Question 8

Difficulty: **Medium** · Percent Correct: **49.7%** · Type: **Multiple Answer**

a, b and c are positive integers. If b equals the square root of a, and if c equals the sum of a and b, which of the following could be the value of c?

Indicate <u>all</u> such values.

A 21

B 30

C 45

D 72

E 100

F 331

Question 9

Difficulty: **Easy** · Percent Correct: **62.3%** · Type: **Multiple Answer**

In set s, there are four numbers. Three of the numbers are 13, 29, and 41, and the fourth number is x. If the mean of the set is less than 25, what could be the value of x?

Indicate <u>all</u> possible values of x.

A 13

B 15

C 17

D 19

E 21

F 23

G 25

H 27

Question 10

Difficulty: **Easy** · Percent Correct: **69.2%** · Type: **Numeric Entry**

In Alioth Industries, 20% of the employees have advanced degrees and the others have bachelor's degrees. The average salary for the employees with an advanced degree is $350,000, and the average salary for employees with a bachelor's degree is $100,000. What is the average salary, in dollars, for all the employees at Alioth Industries?

Question 11

Difficulty: **Medium** · Percent Correct: **71.1%** · Type: **Quantitative Comparison**

The average (arithmetic mean) of 7 different numbers is 5

Column A	Column B
Median of the 7 numbers	5

(A) The quantity in Column A is greater

(B) The quantity in Column B is greater

(C) The two quantities are equal

(D) The relationship cannot be determined from the information given

Question 12

Difficulty: **Hard** · Percent Correct: **39.2%** · Type: **Multiple Answer**

Marcia has 2 liters (L) of a 60% concentrated solution of phosphoric acid. She wants to add 3L of less concentrated phosphoric acid solutions, so that she has 5L of a solution with a concentration less than 50%. Which could she add?

Indicate all possible combinations of solutions.

[A] 3L of a **40%** concentrated solution

[B] 3L of a **42%** concentrated solution

[C] 3L of a **44%** concentrated solution

[D] 3L of a **46%** concentrated solution

[E] 3L of a **48%** concentrated solution

[F] 2L of a **40%** solution and 1L of a **45%** solution

[G] 1L of a **40%** solution and 2L of a **45%** solution

Question 13

Difficulty: **Hard** · Percent Correct: **36.5%** · Type: **Numeric Entry**

In a certain set of numbers, 12.5 is 1.5 units of standard deviation above the mean, and 8.9 is 0.5 units of standard deviation below the mean. What is the mean of the set?

Give your answer to the <u>nearest 0.1</u>.

Word Problems and Statistics Answers and Explanations

Answer: 100

Question 1

Difficulty: **Easy** · Percent Correct: **79.5%** · Type: **Numeric Entry**

Luke drives the first 300 miles of a trip at 60 miles an hour. How fast does he have to drive, in miles per hour, on the final 200 miles of the trip if the total time of the trip is to equal 7 hours?

On the first leg of the trip, he travels 300 miles at 60 mph. You can find the time by using the following formula:

$$T = \frac{D}{V} = \frac{300}{60} = 5 \text{ hr}$$

If the first leg takes 5 hours, and if Luke wants to complete the trip in 7 hours, then he will have to complete the second leg in just 2 hours. This second leg has a distance of 200 miles. This would require a speed of

$$V = \frac{D}{T} = \frac{200}{2} = \textbf{100 mph}$$

Question 2

Difficulty: **Easy** · Percent Correct: **78.2%** · Type: **Quantitative Comparison**

Answer:

Column A	Column B
Sum of integers from 1 to 40 inclusive	800

To evaluate column A, look at pairs of integers, starting with the greatest and least in the list. The sum of 1 and 40 is 41. Similarly, the sum of 2 and 39 is 41. If you continue in that pattern, you can create 20 pairs of numbers that add to 41:

1 + 40
2 + 39
3 + 38
⋮
19 + 22
20 + 21

Since each pair sums to 41, and there are 20 pairs, the total sum described in column A is 41 × 20 = 820. Since 820 is greater than 800, the answer is choice **(A)**.

Ⓐ The quantity in Column A is greater
Ⓑ The quantity in Column B is greater
Ⓒ The two quantities are equal
Ⓓ The relationship cannot be determined from the information given

Question 3

Difficulty: **Easy**   ·   Percent Correct: **65.5%**   ·   Type: **Numeric Entry**

If Michael can shovel all the snow off a standard driveway in 12 minutes, and Eamon can shovel all the snow off a standard driveway in 36 minutes, then working together, how many minutes would it take for them both to shovel all the snow off a standard driveway?

Answer: **9**

You can't add or subtract times to complete the driveway, but the big idea is that you can add rates.

(Michael's rate) + (Eamon's rate) = (their combined rate)

Michael's rate = $\frac{1}{12}$ (1 driveway / 12 minutes)

Eamon's rate = $\frac{1}{36}$ (1 driveway / 12 minutes)

These rates are in the unlikely units of "driveways per minute." You add these to get the combined rate.

combined rate = $\frac{1}{12} + \frac{1}{36} = \frac{3}{36} + \frac{1}{36} = \frac{4}{36} = \frac{1}{9}$

Combined, they would complete one driveway every **9** minutes.

Question 4

Difficulty: **Medium**   ·   Percent Correct: **63.4%**   ·   Type: **Multiple Choice**

Sue planted 4 times as many apple seeds as she planted orange seeds. 15% of the apple seeds grew into trees, and 10% of the orange seeds grew into trees. If a total of 420 apple trees and orange trees grew from the seeds, how many orange seeds did Sue plant?

Answer: **B**

(A) 540

(B) 600

(C) 660

(D) 720

(E) 760

Let A = number of apple seeds

Let O = number of orange seeds

$A = 4O$

\# of apple trees = 0.15A

\# of orange trees = 0.10O

$0.15_{(\times 100)}A + 0.1_{(\times 100)}O = 420_{(\times 100)}$

$\Rightarrow$ $15A + 10O = 42{,}000$

Shouldn't the ratio of apple:orange be 4:1 or 4A=O? You know there are 4 times as many apple seeds as there are orange seeds. So if there are 4 apple seeds, then there is 1 orange seed. When setting up the equation, you need to multiply orange seeds by 4 to make the number equal to apple seeds.

If you tried $4A = 1O$, then with our example you would get 16 = 1. So you need to flip it to be $1A = 4O$, and then you get 4 = 4.

Alternatively, you might rephrase the statement in your own words or draw a small picture before writing an equation. A group of apples is 4 times the size of a group of oranges, i.e., $A = 4 \times O$.

Or, visually,

AAAA:O

Notice that those aren't set equal to each other—it's a ratio. If you want to set these equal to each other, you have to make the oranges side 4 times the size.

$(AAAA) = (O) \times 4$

Question 5

Difficulty: **Hard** · Percent Correct: **55.8%** · Type: **Multiple Choice**

Answer: **D**

A container holds 4 quarts of alcohol and 4 quarts of water. How many quarts of water must be added to the container to create a mixture that is 3 parts alcohol to 5 parts water by volume?

(A) $\frac{4}{3}$

(B) $\frac{5}{3}$

(C) $\frac{7}{3}$

D $\frac{8}{3}$

(E) $\frac{10}{3}$

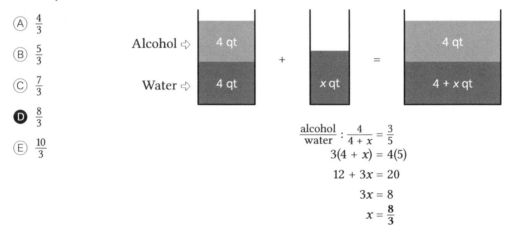

$$\frac{\text{alcohol}}{\text{water}} : \frac{4}{4+x} = \frac{3}{5}$$
$$3(4 + x) = 4(5)$$
$$12 + 3x = 20$$
$$3x = 8$$
$$x = \frac{8}{3}$$

Question 6

Difficulty: **Hard** · Percent Correct: **38.2%** · Type: **Numeric Entry**

Answer: **$120**

The sum of the pre-tax costs of Item A and Item B is $300. In Alumba, each item would be charged a flat 7%. In Aplandia, Item A is subject to 5% tax and Item B is subject to 10% tax. If the tax in Aplandia on the purchase of both items is exactly $3 more than it is in Alumba, then what is the pre-tax price of Item A?

In Alumba, the flat tax would be 7% of $300, or $21.

In Aplandia, A is subject to 5% tax, B subject to 10%, and the total tax comes to $24.

Let A be the price of Item A. Then the price of Item B is (300 − A).

$$0.05A + 0.10(300 - A) = 24$$
$$0.05A + 30 - 0.1A = 24$$
$$-0.05A = -6$$
$$0.05A = 6$$
$$0.1A = 12$$
$$A = \textbf{120}$$

Shouldn't you calculate the tax rate in Alumba as (7% *A*) + (7% *B*) instead of 7% of the total? Would using (7% *A*) + (7% *B*) mean that you have a 14% total tax rate? The individual price of the items doesn't matter for determining the total tax rate in Alumba. Assessing a tax of 7% individually (on each item) or on the entire purchase will give you the same tax amount, which is $21 for Alumba.

Think of the flat 7% tax as something you could distribute. Let's say the two items cost *X* and *Y*. You can express this 7% tax as a tax on the entire purchase:

$$0.07(X + Y)$$

Or you can express this tax, by distributing the multiplication, as a tax on each part of the purchase:

$$0.07X + 0.07Y$$

The tax rate remains at 7% for the overall purchase, but it turns out that when you tax something as a group, each part of the group is also taxed at 7%.

You can also prove this using real numbers. Let's say Item A costs $10 and item B costs $20. First let's evaluate the tax if it were applied to the whole purchase:

$10 + $20 = $30
$0.07 \times $30 = 2.10
Total Tax: $2.10

Now let's evaluate the tax on each item individually and compare this to our first answer.

Item A: $10 \times 0.07 = 0.70
Item B: $20 \times 0.07 = 1.40
Total Tax: $1.40 + $0.70 = $2.10

As you can see, both methods arrive at the same answer, so you can definitely conclude that the tax doesn't become 14% just because you tax two items in a purchase at 7%.

Question 7

Difficulty: **Hard** · Percent Correct: **54.2%** · Type: **Multiple Choice**

The *n*th term $\left(t_n\right)$ of a certain sequence is defined as $t_n = t_{n-1} + 4$. If $t_1 = -7$ then $t_{71} =$

Answer: **A**

Ⓐ 273
Ⓑ 277
Ⓒ 281
Ⓓ 283
Ⓔ 287

The first thing to realize is that this formula:

$$t_n = t_{n-1} + 4$$

would imply that:

$$t_2 = t_1 + 4$$
$$t_3 = t_2 + 4, \text{ etc.}$$

In other words, to get each new term, we're simply adding 4 to the previous term.

We start with the first term of –7, and then we add a bunch of 4s. How many 4s do we add? Well, for the second term, we add 4 once; for the third term, we add 4 twice from the start. Hence, for the nth term, we add 4 a total of $(n – 1)$ times from the start.

Thus, for the 71st term, we would start with the first term of –7 and add 4 a total of seventy times.

$$t_{71} = -7 + (4 \times 70) = 280 - 7 = 273$$

The answer is **(A)**.

Question 8

Difficulty: **Medium** · Percent Correct: **49.7%** · Type: **Multiple Answer**

Answer: **B** **D**

a, b, and c are positive integers. If b equals the square root of a, and if c equals the sum of a and b, which of the following could be the value of c?

Indicate <u>all</u> such values.

~~A~~	21	$b = \sqrt{a} \Rightarrow b^2 = a$
B	30	$c = a + b$
~~C~~	45	$= b^2 + b$
D	72	$= b(b + 1) = $ even number
E	100	
~~F~~	331	

Because b is an integer, we know that b and $(b + 1)$ are consecutive integers. In other words, c is the product of two consecutive integers. Knowing that, we can reword the original question prompt—"Which of the following can be written as the product of two consecutive integers?"—and find the possible values of c.

GRE Quantitative
Reasoning

122

Question 9

In set *s*, there are four numbers. Three of the numbers are 13, 29, and 41, and the fourth number is *x*. If the mean of the set is less than 25, what could be the value of *x*?

Indicate <u>all</u> possible values of *x*.

- **A** 13
- **B** 15
- C 17
- D 19
- E 21
- F 23
- G 25
- H 27

Answer: **A B**

The easiest way to approach this problem is to think about the sum.

$$\text{average} = \frac{\text{sum of list}}{N} \quad \Rightarrow \quad \text{sum of list} = N \times (\text{average})$$

The second, rewritten form is useful to you.

average < 25
sum = 4 × (average) < 100
13 + 29 + 41 + *x* < 100
83 + *x* < 100
***x* < 17**

The missing number must be less than 17, so it could be 13 or 15.

Question 10

Statistics

In Alioth Industries, 20% of the employees have advanced degrees and the others have bachelor's degrees. The average salary for an employee with an advanced degree is $350,000, and the average salary for an employee with a bachelor's degree is $100,000. What is the average salary, in dollars, for all the employees at Alioth Industries?

Answer: **$150,000**

This is a weighted average. Let's make all the salaries 1,000 times smaller, just to simplify calculations. This would give us the problem:

$$0.2 \times (350) + 0.8 \times (100) = 70 + 80 = 150$$

The average for all employees is $150,000.

Question 11

Difficulty: **Medium** · Percent Correct: **71.1%** · Type: **Quantitative Comparison**

The average (arithmetic mean) of 7 different numbers is 5

Column A	Column B
Median of the 7 numbers	5

(A) The quantity in Column A is greater

(B) The quantity in Column B is greater

(C) The two quantities are equal

D The relationship cannot be determined from the information given

We know that the average of seven different numbers is 5. The word "different" implies that no number appears twice on the list. For example, having a set in which all the entries equal 5 would be excluded by this restriction.

Certainly, we could have a symmetrical set of consecutive integers centered on 5. This would be the set {2, 3, 4, 5, 6, 7, 8}. Both the mean and the median of this set are 5. This choice for the set makes the columns equal, suggesting the answer (C) for at least this choice.

If we can select another set that fits the criteria, mean = 5, and makes one column bigger than the other, then we will have chosen two different possibilities that give two different relationships, and *bam!* right away we would know that (D) would be the answer. Can we find another set that fits the requirements?

Well, we could subtract one from each of the first six numbers to get the consecutive integers 1 through 6. To keep the same average and same sum, we would have to add six to the highest number giving us 8 + 6 = 14. This gives us another set with an average of 5, the set {1, 2, 3, 4, 5, 6, 14}. This set has a median of 4, which is less than the 5.

This is an idea we discuss in depth in the "picking numbers" section of the quantitative comparison strategies chapter starting on page 196, but here we'll simply point out that if we can make different choices that indicate different relationships, this automatically means that a single relationship between the columns is not uniquely determined by the situation, and that necessitates an answer of **(D)**.

Question 12

Difficulty: **Hard** · Percent Correct: **39.2%** · Type: **Multiple Answer**

Marcia has 2 liters (L) of a 60% concentrated solution of phosphoric acid. She wants to add 3L of less concentrated phosphoric acid solutions, so that she has 5L of a solution with a concentration less than 50%. Which could she add?

Answers: **A** **B** **F**

Indicate <u>all</u> possible combinations of solutions.

A 3L of a **40%** concentrated solution
B 3L of a **42%** concentrated solution
C 3L of a **44%** concentrated solution
D 3L of a **46%** concentrated solution
E 3L of a **48%** concentrated solution
F 2L of a **40%** solution and 1L of a **45%** solution
G 1L of a **40%** solution and 2L of a **45%** solution

Subtract 50 from all the concentration numbers, just to make the calculations easier to handle. In this view, she has 2L of a concentration 10, and wants to add 3L of Concentration X to get 5L of concentration less than 0. First, let's focus on getting 5L of concentration exactly 0.

$$10 + 10 + X + X + X = 0$$
$$20 + 3X = 0$$
$$3X = -20$$
$$X = \frac{-20}{3} = -6.67$$

Now, change back to real concentrations. This X would have concentration of

$$50 - 6.67 = 43.33\%$$

Three liters of a solution with concentration 43.33% would produce 5L of exactly 50% concentration. You want a concentration less than 50%, so you need to add 3L of a solution that has a concentration lower than 43.33%.

(A) and (B) work.

(C) and (D) and (E) don't work.

Now, the last two choices are tricky. For these two, subtract 40 from all the concentration values, to make the calculations easier.

For (F), you want to combine 2L of concentration 0 with 1L of concentration 5. That's an average of (0 + 0 + 5)/3 = 1.67. In other words, in real concentrations, mixing these would be equivalent to 3L of solution with concentration 41.67%. This is less than 43.33%, so (F) works.

For (G), you want to combine 1L of concentration 0 with 2L of concentration 5. That's an average of (0 + 5 + 5)/3 = 3.33. In other words, in real concentrations, mixing these would be equivalent to 3L of solution with concentration 43.33%. This is exactly the concentration of the 3L that would produce a resultant solution of exactly 50% concentration, but you want a concentration less than 50% in the final solution, so (G) doesn't work.

Why did we subtract 50? What we're doing here is comparing the percentages to 50%. So, in other words, we're setting 50% to 0. The reason for doing this is that the question asks for a final solution of less than 50%.

So you write each 60% as "+10" because it's 10 more than 50%. And you have 2L of "+ 10" and you want to add 3L of X to get something less than 0 (which you mean to represent less than 50%).

$$10 + 10 + x + x + x < 0$$
$$x < -\frac{20}{3}$$
$$x < -6$$

The concentration you want should be 6.67 less than 50%, or 43.33% phosphoric acid.

This means that the average concentration of the 3L solution should be less than 43.33% phosphoric acid.

If that's confusing, here is another way to do the problem:

$$2L \times 60\% \text{ phosphoric acid} = 2 \times 0.6 = 1.2L \text{ of pure phosphoric acid}$$

Now you're adding 3L to get less than 50% of a 5L solution. 50% of 5 is 2.5L of pure phosphoric acid.

So if you're starting with 1.2L of the acid and you must have less than 2.5L in our final solution, then you must add less than

$$2.5 - 1.2 = 1.3L \text{ of pure phosphoric acid}$$

In other words, the 3L added must contain less than a total of 1.3L pure phosphoric acid.

So you look at the answer choices and multiply the liters by the percents to see which are less than 1.3L of pure acid. For example, 3L of 42% is okay because you get the following:

$$3 \times 0.42 = 1.26L \text{ of acid, which is less than 1.3}$$

Question 13

Difficulty: **Hard** · Percent Correct: **36.5%** · Type: **Numeric Entry**

Answer: **9.8**

In a certain set of numbers, 12.5 is 1.5 units of standard deviation above the mean, and 8.9 is 0.5 units of standard deviation below the mean. What is the mean of the set?

Give your answer to the <u>nearest 0.1</u>.

Both the mean and the standard deviation are unknown, so we have two unknowns. If we assign a variable to each, then each statement in the prompt allows us to set up an equation, and we would have two equations with two unknowns. Let mean = M and standard deviation = S. Then,

"12.5 is 1.5 units of *SD* above the mean" ⇨ $12.5 = M + 1.5S$
"8.9 is 0.5 units of *SD* below the mean" ⇨ $8.9 = M - 0.5S$

We discussed two equations with two unknowns in the algebra section on page 451.

Since M appears with a coefficient of 1 in both equations, we could eliminate M and find S by subtracting the equations.

$$12.5 = M + 1.5S$$
$$- [8.9 = M - 0.5S]$$
$$12.5 - 8.9 = 1.5S - (-0.5S) = 1.5S + 0.5S$$
$$3.6 = 2S$$
$$1.8 = S$$

Now that we have a value for S, we can plug this into either equation to find the M.

$$M + (1.5)(1.8) = 12.5$$
$$M + 2.7 = 12.5$$
$$M = 12.5 - 2.7 = \mathbf{9.8}$$

This value is already rounded to the nearest 0.1, so we can enter this as is.

The answer is 9.8.

You can find even more word problems and statistics questions on gre.magoosh.com!

127

Quantitative Concept #6: Geometry

Geometry questions on the GRE cover a wide range of topics. You probably took a geometry class in high school and remember that you learned about shapes, sizes, measurements, and positions of objects. From lines to circles to coordinate places, a solid understanding of geometry gives us a fascinating look at the world.

Geometric Concepts: The Lowdown

Lines and angles

Some of the most fundamental geometry facts have to do with the special properties of parallel lines.

But while there are a number of special geometry facts that are true for parallel lines, absolutely none of them are true for lines that are *almost* parallel. This is important to remember when you're looking at diagrams. Unless otherwise specified, all diagrams on the GRE are drawn as accurately as possible. That said, if two lines *look* parallel, you cannot assume they *are* parallel. Two lines that *look* parallel could be half a degree off from being truly parallel—that difference wouldn't be visually apparent, but none of the special parallel-line facts would be true if the two lines aren't exactly parallel. Your eyes can deceive you, so until you see "the lines are parallel" printed in black and white, assume that they are not.

If two lines are parallel

When we're guaranteed that the lines are parallel, and another line intersects these parallel lines, what do we know? The following diagram summarizes everything you'll need to know about the relationships between parallel and intersecting lines.

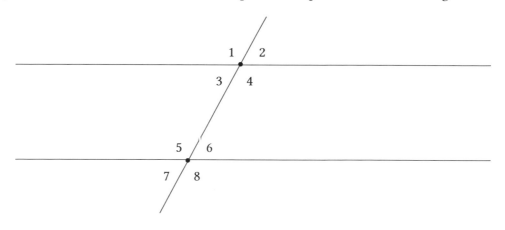

Notice that we could categorize these eight angles by size into big angles (angles 1, 4, 5, and 8) and small angles (angles 2, 3, 6, 7). Here's what's true:

1. All the big angles are equal.
2. All the small angles are equal.
3. Any big angle plus any small angle equals 180°.

There are all kinds of fancy geometry names for these angles—for example, angles 3 and 6 are "alternate interior angles"—but for the purpose of the GRE, you don't need to know any terms more technical than "big angles" and "small angles." Let's keep it simple.

Triangles

Ordinary triangles

The sum of the three angles of any triangle is 180°, a fact that you probably already know. As a result of that rule, if all three angles are equal (an equiangular, equilateral triangle), then all three angles must be $\frac{180°}{3} = 60°$. In addition, in a right triangle, the sum of the two acute angles must be 90°. Both are good facts to have at your fingertips on the GRE.

The triangle inequality theorem
That has a scary-sounding name, doesn't it? It sounds really sophisticated. In reality, though, it's a pretty simple idea. What is means is that the sum of any two sides of a triangle must be greater than the third. In picture form:

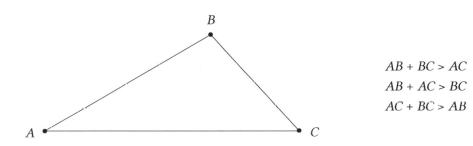

$$AB + BC > AC$$
$$AB + AC > BC$$
$$AC + BC > AB$$

The triangle inequality rule produces three inequalities for any triangle. Now, think about why this has to be true. The shortest distance between point *A* and point *C* has to be the straight line. If you take an indirect or crooked path from *A* to *C* (via point *B*), that has to be longer than taking the straight-line distance, represented by *AC*. That's the simple idea at the heart of the triangle inequality rule.

The side-angle inequalities theorem
The side-angle inequalities rule states that measures of the three angles of a triangle are unequal in the same order as the lengths of their opposite sides. That's certainly a mouthful. Let's look at that in picture form to see if it makes better sense:

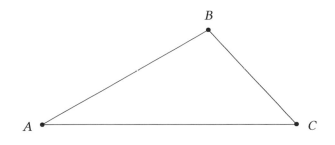

$$BC < AB < AC$$
if and only if
$$(\angle A) < (\angle C) < (\angle B)$$

The astronomer **Johannes Kepler** (1571–1630), who formulated the three laws of planetary motion, was a huge fan of geometry. He wrote: "Geometry has two great treasures: one is the Theorem of Pythagoras; the other, the division of a line into extreme and mean ratio [i.e., the Golden Ratio]. The first we may compare to a measure of gold, the second we may name a precious jewel."

Aha! So what it really means is the biggest side is opposite the biggest angle and the smallest side is opposite the smallest angle.

True for all

These two mathematical patterns, the triangle inequality theorem and the side-angle inequalities theorem, are true for all triangles, so knowing them will come in handy during the GRE.

Isosceles triangles

An isosceles triangle has two congruent sides, meaning they're equal in length.

Euclid's theorem

Euclid's theorem, proved over 2,200 years ago, applies directly to isosceles triangles. The theorem states the following:

If the two sides are equal, then the opposite angles are equal.

and

If the two angles are equal, then the opposite sides are equal.

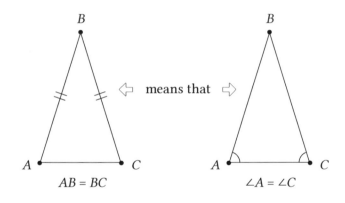

Isosceles triangles and the 180°-Triangle Theorem

If you're told that triangle ABC is isosceles, and one of the bottom equal angles (called a "base angle") is 50°, then you'll know that the measure of the other base angle is also 50°, and that means the top angle, or the vertex angle, must be 80°. Knowing the measure of one base angle of an isosceles triangle is sufficient to find the measures of all three angles.

Suppose you're told that triangle ABC is isosceles, and the vertex angle is 50°. Well, you don't know the measures of the base angle, but you know they're equal. Let x be the degrees of the base angle; then $x + x + 50° = 180°$ ⇨ $2x = 130°$ ⇨ $x = 65°$. So each base angle is 65°. Knowing the measure of the vertex angle of an isosceles triangle is sufficient to finding the measures of all three angles.

However, if you're told that triangle ABC is isosceles, and one of the angles is 50°, but you don't know whether that 50° is a base angle or a vertex angle, then you cannot conclude anything about the other angles in the isosceles triangle without more information.

Pythagorean theorem

Excuse us while we geek out a bit, but there's a reason the Pythagorean theorem is the most famous theorem in mathematics! This remarkable theorem is one of the most versatile and highly adaptable formulas in existence. It states the following: for any right triangle, *a*-squared plus *b*-squared equals *c*-squared.

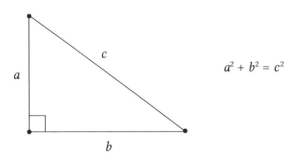

$$a^2 + b^2 = c^2$$

You can use this formula when a question on the GRE gives you two sides of a right triangle and asks you to find the third. Remember that *c* has to be the hypotenuse, the longest side.

Special right triangles

These two special triangles are right triangles with special angles and sides. Like all right triangles, they satisfy the Pythagorean theorem. These two triangles are special because, with just a few pieces of information, we can figure out all their properties. The GRE writers love that about these two triangles, so they're all over the GRE Quantitative.

The 45-45-90 triangle

Let's start with the square, that magically symmetrical shape. Assume the square has a side of 1. Cut the square in half along a diagonal, and look at the triangle that results.

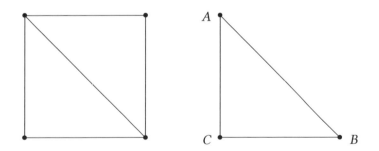

We know $\angle C = 90°$, because it was an angle from the square. We know $AC = BC = 1$, which means the triangle is isosceles, so $\angle A = \angle B = 45°$. Let's call hypotenuse $AB = x$. By the Pythagorean theorem,

$$(AC)^2 + (BC)^2 = (AB)^2$$
$$1 + 1 = x^2$$
$$x^2 = 2$$
$$x^2 = \sqrt{2}$$

The sides have the ratios $1{:}1{:}\sqrt{2}$. We can scale this up simply by multiplying all three of those by any number we like: $a : a : (a \times \sqrt{2})$.

Here are the three names for this triangle, which are useful to remember because they summarize all its properties:

- The Isosceles Right Triangle
- The 45-45-90 Triangle
- The 1:1:$\sqrt{2}$ Triangle

The 30-60-90 triangle

Let's start with an equilateral triangle, another magically symmetrical shape. Of course, by itself, the equilateral triangle isn't a right triangle, but we can cut it in half and get a right triangle.

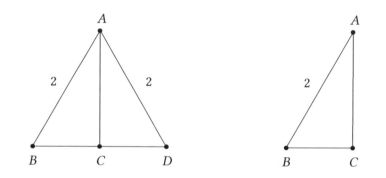

Let's assume *ABD* is an equilateral triangle with each side = 2. We draw a perpendicular line from *A* down to *BD*, which intersects at point *C*. Because of the highly symmetrical properties of the equilateral triangle, the segment *AC* (a) forms a right angle at the base, (b) bisects the angle at *A*, and (c) bisects the base *BD*.

So in the triangle *ABC*, we know ∠*B* = 60°, because that's the old angle of the original equilateral triangle. We know ∠*C* = 90°, because *AC* is perpendicular to the base. We know ∠*A* = 30°, because *AC* bisects the original 60° angle at A in the equilateral triangle. Thus, the angles are 30-60-90. We know *AB* = 2, because that's a side from the original equilateral triangle. We know *BC* = 1, because *AC* bisects the base *BD*. Call *AC* = *x*: we can find it from the Pythagorean theorem.

$$(AC)^2 + (BC)^2 = (AB)^2$$
$$x^2 + 1^2 = 2^2$$
$$x^2 = 4 - 1 = 3$$
$$x = \sqrt{3}$$

The sides are in the ratio of 1:$\sqrt{3}$:2. This can be scaled up by multiplying by any number, which gives the following general form of $a : a \times \sqrt{3} : 2a$.

Here are the three names for this triangle, which are useful to remember, because they summarize all its properties:

1. The Half-Equilateral Triangle
2. The 30-60-90 Triangle
3. The 1:$\sqrt{3}$:2 Triangle

Circles

Here is a rundown of geometry facts you might need to know about circles for the GRE.

Basic circle terminology

A circle is the set of all points equidistant from a fixed point. That means a circle is this:

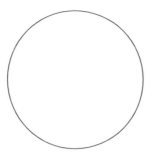

and not this:

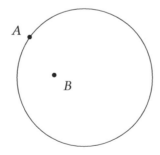

In other words, the circle is only the curved round edge, not the filled-in middle part. A point on the edge is *on* the circle, but a point in the middle part is *in* or *inside* the circle. In the diagram below, point A is *on* the circle, but point B is *in* the circle.

By far, the most important point in the circle is the center of the circle, the point equidistant from all points on the circle.

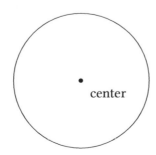

The circle is by far the most symmetrical geometric shape. For this reason, it appears in many religious symbols and designs (e.g., yin-yang, Zen ensō, rose windows, etc.). The Christian mystic **Nicholas of Cusa** (1401–1464) said, "God is an infinite circle whose center is everywhere and whose circumference is nowhere." No other geometric shape inspires comments such as that!

Chords

Any line segment that has both endpoints on the circle is a *chord*.

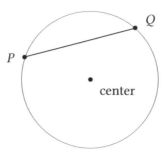

If the chord passes through the center, this chord is called a *diameter*. The diameter is the longest possible chord. Among chords, only a diameter includes the center of the circle. The diameter is an important length associated with a circle, because it tells you the maximum length across the circle in any direction.

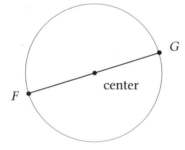

An even more important length is the *radius*. A radius is any line segment with one endpoint at the center and the other on the circle.

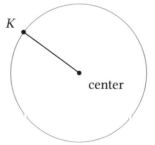

As you can see, the radius is exactly half the diameter, because a diameter can be divided into two radii. The radius is crucially important because if you know the radius, it's easy to calculate not only the diameter but also the other two important measurements associated with a circle: the circumference and the area.

Circle formulas

The circumference of a circle is the length of the circle itself. This is a curve, so you would have to imagine cutting the circle and laying it flat against a ruler. As it turns out, there's a magical constant that relates the diameter (*d*) and radius (*r*) to the circumference. Of course, that magical constant is π. Using π itself gives you two equations for the circumference, *c*.

$$c = \pi d \qquad c = 2\pi r$$

If you remember the second, more common form, you don't need to know the first. The number π is slightly larger than 3. This means that three pieces of string, each as long as the diameter, wouldn't be quite long enough to make it all the way around the circle. The number π can be approximated by 3.14 or by the fraction $\frac{22}{7}$. Technically, though, it's an irrational number that goes on forever in a non-repeating pattern.

The brilliant mathematician Archimedes discovered another important formula, the area of a circle. Here is Archimedes' amazing formula:

$$A = \pi r^2$$

For example, if the radius of a circle is $r = 6$, then the area is $A = \pi r^2 = \pi(6)^2 = \mathbf{36\ \pi}$. If the area of another circle is $400\ \pi$, then $r^2 = 400$ and $r = 20$. If we're given the diameter, we would divide that in half to find the radius, and then find the area from the radius. Since we can find both the circumference and the area from the radius, it's a good strategy in circle problems to find the radius first and then use the radius to find whatever else you need.

For most math formulas on the test, we strongly discourage rote memorization. When you avoid memorization and force yourself to understand the *logic* behind math formulas, you're much better off on test day. However, this formula, $A = \pi r^2$, is one of the few formulas we'll let slide. Archimedes had a brilliant argument about why this formula is true, but that's far more advanced than you need to know. For this one, we'll simply say, *just memorize it!*

Slope and the Equations of Lines

Slope is a measure of how steep a line is. There's a very algebraic formula for the slope, and if you know that, hurray! If you don't know that formula or used to know it and can't remember it, we'll say, "*fuhgeddaboudit!*" and offer you a much simpler way of thinking about slope. Slope is **rise over run**.

To calculate rise and run, first you have to put the two points in order. It actually doesn't matter which one we say is the first and which one the second; all that matters is that we're consistent.

The *rise* is the vertical change—the change in y-coordinate, which is calculated by subtracting the first point from the second. The *run* is the horizontal change—the change in the *x*-coordinate, which is also calculated by subtracting the first point from the second. Once you have the rise and run quantities, divide them. Rise divided by run will give you the slope of a line.

Remember that there are several ways to think about a slope you're given. A slope of $m = 2$ means (right 1, up 2), but it also means any multiple of that, such as (right 3, up 6) or (right 12, up 24). It also means the same in the opposite direction: (left 1, down 2), (left 3, down 6), etc. A slope of $-\frac{2}{3}$ can mean all of the following:

- right 1, down $\frac{2}{3}$
- right 3, down 2
- any multiple of the above (e.g., right 12, down 8)
- left 1, up $\frac{2}{3}$
- left 3, up 2
- any multiple of the above (e.g., left 12, up 8)

If you have to think in terms of a distance of several integer units, then one of the larger multiples would be appropriate. If you have to think about the changes over some small distance, one of the fractional values would be more appropriate. Just remember that there are many different ways to think about the same slope!

Looking at an example

Suppose our points are (−2, 4) and (5, 1). For the sake of argument, we'll say that's the order and that (−2, 4) is the first set and (5, 1) the second. The rise is the change in height, the change in y-coordinate: 1 − 4 = −3. Notice that we had to put the 1 first, which gave us a negative here! The run is the horizontal change, the change in x-coordinate, which is 5 − (−2) = 5 + 2 = 7. Remember, subtracting a negative is the same as adding a positive. Now, rise/run = $-\frac{3}{7}$. That's the slope. The fact that it's negative points to a basic but important feature of this line—it slopes downward when followed from left to right.

Whenever you find a slope, try doing a rough sketch just to verify that the sign of the slope (positive or negative) and the value of the slope are approximately correct. Here's a sketch of this particular calculation:

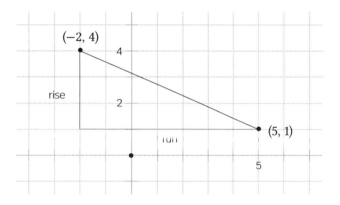

Your sketch, of course, doesn't need to be this precise. Even a rough sketch would verify that, yes, the slope should at least be negative.

Equations in the *xy*-plane

The technical name of the *xy*-plane is the Cartesian plane, named after its inventor, Mr. René Descartes. The *xy*-plane is a brilliant mathematical device. Its creation allowed for the unification of two ancient branches of mathematics—algebra and geometry. In more practical terms, every equation (an algebraic object) corresponds to a picture (a geometric object). Call us crazy, but we think that's a very deep idea.

Equations of lines

A straight line is a very simple picture and, not surprisingly, has a very simple equation. There are a few different ways to write a line, but the most popular and easiest to understand is $y = mx + b$. The m is the slope of the line. The b is the y-intercept, or where the line crosses the y-axis. For any given line, m and b are constants, meaning that no matter which point on the line we're looking at, both m and b equal a fixed number. By contrast, x and y, sometimes call the *graphing variables*, do not equal specific numbers. Instead, in order to describe the line, they will stay in variable form. This isn't the same x as used in solve-for-x algebra. This is a very powerful mathematical idea: x and y don't equal any one pair of values; **rather, every single point (x, y) on the line—the entire continuous infinity of points that make up that line—satisfies the equation of the line.**

Finding the equation of a line

Sometimes the GRE will give you the equation of a line already in $y = mx + b$ form. Sometimes the GRE gives you the line in another form (e.g., $3x + 7y = 22$) and you'll have to do a little algebraic rearranging to bring the equation into $y = mx + b$ form. Sometimes, though, you'll be given the x and y values of two points and be asked to find the equation of the line.

For those questions, here's the procedure: First, find the slope following the procedures previously discussed. Then, plug the slope in for m in the $y = mx + b$ equation, and pick either point (it doesn't matter which one) and plug those coordinates in for x and y in this equation. This will produce an equation in which everything has a numerical value except for "b"; that means you can solve this equation for the value of b. Once you know m and b, you know the equation of the line.

René Descartes (1596–1650) was a polymath, making valuable contributions to mathematics, science, and philosophy. His philosophy began with the famous statement, "I think, therefore I am": this was revolutionary, because for the first time since the ancient Greeks, it put human experience at the center of Western philosophy.

Geometry Practice Questions

These questions should help you get an idea of what to expect from the geometry questions on the GRE. There are even more practice questions in the GRE practice test in chapter 6.

Question 1

Difficulty: **Easy** · Percent Correct: **69.5%** · Type: **Multiple Answer**

Square *ABCD* has a side of 20. Circle *O* has a radius of *r*. If the circle has more area than does the square, then which of the following could be the value of *r*?

Indicate <u>all</u> possible values of the radius.

- A 8
- B 9
- C 10
- D 11
- E 12
- F 13
- G 14
- H 15

Question 2

Difficulty: **Easy** · Percent correct: **86.2%** · Type: **Quantitative Comparison**

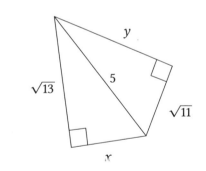

Column A	Column B
x	*y*

Ⓐ The quantity in Column A is greater

Ⓑ The quantity in Column B is greater

Ⓒ The two quantities are equal

Ⓓ The relationship cannot be determined from the information given

Question 3

Difficulty: **Medium** · Percent Correct: **52.5%** · Type: **Numeric Entry**

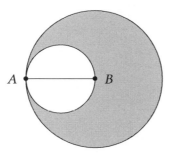

In the diagram above, *B* is the center of the larger circle. *AB* is the radius of the larger circle and the diameter of the smaller circle. The shaded area is what fraction of the larger circle?

Enter your answer as a fraction. Fractions do not need to be in their simplest forms.

```
┌─────────────┐
│             │
└─────────────┘
┌─────────────┐
│             │
└─────────────┘
```

Question 4

Difficulty: **Hard** · Percent Correct: **36.4%** · Type: **Multiple Answer**

The sides of a triangle are 1, x, and x^2. What are possible values of x?

Indicate <u>all</u> possible values.

- A 0.5
- B 1
- C 1.5
- D 2
- E 2.5
- F 3
- G 3.5

Question 5

Difficulty: **Hard** · Percent Correct: **61.5%** · Type: **Quantitative Comparison**

In this diagram, the circle is inscribed in the square.

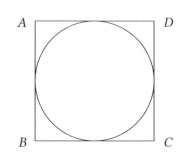

Column A	Column B
Length of diagonal AC	$\frac{5r}{2}$

Ⓐ The quantity in Column A is greater

Ⓑ The quantity in Column B is greater

Ⓒ The two quantities are equal

Ⓓ The relationship cannot be determined from the information given

Question 6

Difficulty: **Hard** · Percent Correct: **59%** · Type: **Multiple Choice**

Point O is the center of the semicircle. If $\angle BCO = 30°$ and $BC = 6\sqrt{3}$, what is the area of triangle ABO?

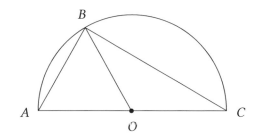

Ⓐ $4\sqrt{3}$

Ⓑ $6\sqrt{3}$

Ⓒ $9\sqrt{3}$

Ⓓ $12\sqrt{3}$

Ⓔ $24\sqrt{3}$

Question 7

Difficulty: **Very Hard** · Percent Correct: **30.4%** · Type: **Multiple Choice**

Two sides of a triangle have lengths 6 and 8. Which of the following are possible areas of the triangle?

I. 2
II. 12
III. 24

(A) I only
(B) I and II only
(C) II and III only
(D) I and III only
(E) I, II, and III

Question 8

Coordinate geometry

Difficulty: **Hard** · Percent Correct: **40.4%** · Type: **Multiple Answer**

Which of the following lines intersects the vertical line $x = 3$ between $(3, 1)$ and $(3, 2)$?

Indicate <u>all</u> possible lines.

- [A] $y = \left(\frac{3}{5}\right)x$
- [B] $y = \left(\frac{3}{7}\right)x + 1$
- [C] $y = \left(\frac{1}{5}\right)x + \frac{6}{5}$
- [D] $y = -\left(\frac{3}{2}\right)x + 5$
- [E] $y = -\left(\frac{1}{4}\right)x + 3$

Question 9

Difficulty: **Medium** · Percent Correct: **48.4%** · Type: **Multiple Answer**

Which of the following lines are perpendicular to the line $3x + 2y = 7$?

Indicate <u>all</u> possible values lines.

- [A] $y = \left(\frac{2}{3}\right)x + 8$
- [B] $y = -\left(\frac{2}{3}\right)x - 6$
- [C] $y = \left(\frac{3}{2}\right)x + 5$
- [D] $y = -\left(\frac{3}{2}\right)x - \left(\frac{4}{7}\right)$
- [E] $2x + 3y = 19$
- [F] $2x - 3y = -2$

Question 10

Difficulty: **Medium** · Percent Correct: **62.6%** · Type: **Multiple Choice**

If a triangle in the xy-coordinate system has vertices at $(-2, -3)$, $(4, -3)$ and $(28, 7)$, what is the area of the triangle?

(A) 30

(B) 36

(C) 48

(D) 60

(E) 65

Question 11

Difficulty: **Medium** · Percent Correct: **68.3%** · Type: **Multiple Choice**

In the xy-coordinate system, the distance between the point $(0, 0)$ and point P is $\sqrt{40}$. Which of the following could be the coordinates of point P?

(A) $(4, 7)$

(B) $(4, 10)$

(C) $(5, 6)$

(D) $(6, 2)$

(E) $(20, 20)$

Question 12

Difficulty: **Hard** · Correct: **59.8%** · Type: **Multiple Choice**

If $ABCD$ is a square, what are the coordinates of C?

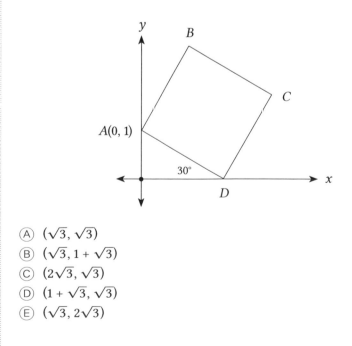

(A) $(\sqrt{3}, \sqrt{3})$

(B) $(\sqrt{3}, 1 + \sqrt{3})$

(C) $(2\sqrt{3}, \sqrt{3})$

(D) $(1 + \sqrt{3}, \sqrt{3})$

(E) $(\sqrt{3}, 2\sqrt{3})$

Question 13

Difficulty: **Very Hard** · Percent Correct: **43.2%** · Type: **Multiple Choice**

The points $A(0, 0)$, $B(0, 4a - 5)$, and $C(2a + 1, 2a + 6)$ form a triangle. If $\angle ABC = 90°$, what is the area of triangle ABC?

(A) 102

(B) 120

(C) 132

(D) 144

(E) 156

Question 14

Difficulty: **Very hard** · Percent Correct: **29.4%** · Type: **Multiple Answer**

Point A (−4, 2) and Point B (2, 4) lie in the xy-coordinate plane. If point C lies in the first quadrant and contains the coordinates (p, q), where $p < 2$ and $q < 4$, which of the following could be the area of triangle ABC?

Indicate <u>all</u> such numbers.

A 1.1

B 3.9

C 11.9

Geometry Answers and Explanations

Question 1

Difficulty: **Easy** · Percent Correct: **69.5%** · Type: **Multiple Answer**

Square *ABCD* has a side of 20. Circle *O* has a radius of *r*. If the circle has more area than does the square, then which of the following could be the value of *r*?

Indicate <u>all</u> possible values of the radius.

- [A] 8
- [B] 9
- [C] 10
- [D] 11
- **[E]** 12
- **[F]** 13
- **[G]** 14
- **[H]** 15

The area of the square is 400. The area of a circle, according to Archimedes' amazing formula, is this:

$$A = \pi r^2$$

This has to be bigger than 400. Recall that you can approximate π by 3.14. Let's start with the nice round number of 10 in (C).

$$A = 100\pi \approx 314 < 400$$

So this one doesn't work, and you know that the two smaller radius values, 8 and 9, can't work either. You can eliminate choices (A), (B), and (C). Now, let's look at *r* = 11.

$$A = \pi(11)^2 \approx 121\pi$$

You know that 3 times 121 is 363, which is less than 400. The next digit in π after the 3 is the 0.1, and 0.1 × 121 = 12.1. If you add that to 363, you're still much less than 400. The contributions from 0.04 and the other digits will be small, so this isn't going to get above 400. Choice (D) doesn't work either. Now, look at *r* = 12.

$$A = \pi(12)^2 = 144\pi > 144 \times 3 = 432 > 400$$

So choice (E) works. This means that all the bigger radii must work as well. The answers are **(E)**, **(F)**, **(G)**, and **(H)**.

Question 2

Difficulty: Easy · Percent correct: 86.2% · Type: Quantitative Comparison

Answer: **B**

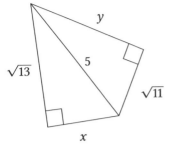

Column A	Column B
x	y

A) The quantity in Column A is greater
B) The quantity in Column B is greater
C) The two quantities are equal
D) The relationship cannot be determined from the information given

First of all, if you got this question right simply by estimating lengths on the diagram, then you have fallen into a trap that will get you into big trouble on the real GRE. Don't assume the pictures represent proper scale. The diagram isn't a sound basis for deciding anything.

You must use that most extraordinary theorem of geometry, the **Pythagorean theorem**. Notice that the length of 5 is the hypotenuse in each of the two triangles.

In the triangle on the left, the Pythagorean theorem tells you the following:

$$(\sqrt{13})^2 + (x)^2 = (5)^2$$
$$13 + (x)^2 = 25$$
$$x^2 = 25 - 13 = 12$$
$$x = \sqrt{12}$$

You could simplify that square root, and in other contexts that would be an important thing to do, but for this question, you should leave it in this form because you want to compare it directly to another square root.

In the triangle on the right, the Pythagorean theorem tells you the following:

$$(\sqrt{11})^2 + (y)^2 = (5)^2$$
$$11 + (y)^2 = 25$$
$$y^2 = 25 - 11 = 14$$
$$= \sqrt{14}$$

As long as you're dealing with positive numbers only, both squaring and taking the square root preserve the order of inequality. Because you know that 12 < 14 you automatically know that $\sqrt{12} < \sqrt{14}$ and hence $x < y$.

Question 3

Difficulty: **Medium** · Percent Correct: **52.5%** · Type: **Numeric Entry**

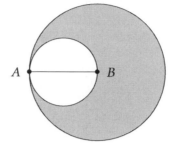

In the diagram above, *B* is the center of the larger circle. *AB* is the radius of the larger circle and the diameter of the smaller circle. The shaded area is what fraction of the larger circle?

Let *AB* = 2*r*, so that the radius of the smaller circle is *r*. Then, we'll use this outstanding formula:

$$A = \pi r^2$$

You know that *AB* is the radius of the larger circle, so it has a radius of 2*r*. The entire area of the larger circle would be this:

$$A = \pi(2r)^2 = 4\pi r^2$$

The area of the shaded region would be entire area of the larger circle minus the area of the smaller circle.

$$\text{shaded region} = (4\pi r^2) - (\pi r^2) = 3\pi r^2$$

$$\text{fraction} = \frac{3\pi r^2}{4\pi r^2} = \frac{3}{4}$$

MANTRA

I've become so much better at math. Many students persistently tell themselves, "I'm no good at math." In fact, it only takes a slight difficulty in a question to have a student throw up his or her hands and utter this phrase. Almost all of us struggle to unwrap what the question is asking. Those students who remain positive will be able to get through the initial confusion and see the mathematical light at the end of the tunnel. The truth is that no matter who you are, you've probably improved quite a bit at math since starting to prep for your test.

Question 4

Difficulty: **Hard** · Percent Correct: **36.4%** · Type: **Multiple Answer**

The sides of a triangle are 1, x, and x^2. What are possible values of x?

Answers: **B** **C**

Indicate <u>all</u> possible values.

- [A] 0.5
- **[B] 1**
- **[C] 1.5**
- [D] 2
- [E] 2.5
- [F] 3
- [G] 3.5

The triangle inequality theorum states that the sum of any two sides of a triangle must be bigger than the third side. If you can identify which side is the largest, then the other two sides must have a sum larger than that largest side in order for the triangle to be possible.

Consider the first option:

$$x = 0.5 = \frac{1}{2} \ \Rightarrow \ x^2 = \frac{1}{4}$$

The longest side is 1, and the sum of these two fractions is $\frac{3}{4}$, less than 1. This doesn't satisfy the triangle inequality, so this isn't a possible triangle.

The next option, $x = 1$, produces a triangle with three sides equal to 1. In other words, an equilateral triangle. This, of course, is possible.

Consider the next option:

$$x = 1.5 = \frac{3}{2} \ \Rightarrow \ x^2 = \frac{9}{4}$$

The longest side is $\frac{9}{4}$ = 2.25. The sum of the other two sides is 1 + 1.5 = 2.5, and this is bigger than the longest side. This is a possible triangle, so this works.

Consider the next option, $x = 2$, a triangle with sides {1, 2, 4}. Of course 1 + 2 = 3 < 4, so this doesn't satisfy the triangle inequality, and therefore this isn't a possible triangle.

The problem with $x = 2$ is that, by this point, the squared term has increased enough that it's larger than the sum of the other two terms. Exponents grow very quickly; if we use a larger value for x, the square will continue to increase more and more, totally outracing the sum of the other two terms.

$$x = 2.5 = \frac{5}{2} \ \Rightarrow \ x^2 = \frac{25}{4} = 6.25 \ \Rightarrow \ 1 + 2.5 = 3.5 < 6.25$$

$$x = 3 \ \Rightarrow \ x^2 = 9 \ \Rightarrow \ 1 + 3 = 4 < 9$$

$$x = 3.5 = \frac{7}{2} \ \Rightarrow \ x^2 = \frac{49}{4} = 12.5 \ \Rightarrow \ 1 + 3.5 = 4.5 < 12.25$$

Notice that the squared term is not only bigger than the sum of the other two terms but is also getting further and further away in each case as x increases. The only two cases that work as triangles are $x = \mathbf{1}$ and $x = \mathbf{1.5}$.

Question 5

Difficulty: **Hard** · Percent Correct: **61.5%** · Type: **Quantitative Comparison**

In this diagram, the circle is inscribed in the square.

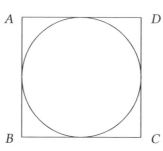

Column A	Column B
Length of diagonal AC	$\frac{5r}{2}$
$2\sqrt{2}\,r$	⇩
$4\sqrt{2}\,r$	$5r$
$4\sqrt{2}$	5
$\sqrt{2}$	$\frac{5}{4} = 1.25$

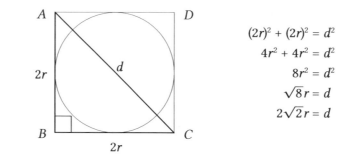

$$(2r)^2 + (2r)^2 = d^2$$
$$4r^2 + 4r^2 = d^2$$
$$8r^2 = d^2$$
$$\sqrt{8}\,r = d$$
$$2\sqrt{2}\,r = d$$

ABCD is a square. The circle has radius *r*. When a circle is inscribed in a square, the diameter of the circle is equal to each side length of the square.

Ⓐ The quantity in Column A is greater
Ⓑ The quantity in Column B is greater
Ⓒ The two quantities are equal
Ⓓ The relationship cannot be determined from the information given

Answer: **C**

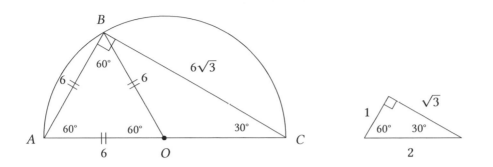

Point O is the center of the semicircle. If $\angle BCO = 30°$ and $BC = 6\sqrt{3}$, what is the area of triangle ABO?

(A) $4\sqrt{3}$

(B) $6\sqrt{3}$

(C) $9\sqrt{3}$

(D) $12\sqrt{3}$

(E) $24\sqrt{3}$

$$\text{Area} = \frac{\sqrt{3}}{4}(6^2)$$

$$= \frac{\sqrt{3}}{4}(36)$$

$$= 9\sqrt{3}$$

Whenever a triangle is inscribed in a circle such that the longest side of the triangle is also the diameter of the circle, that triangle is a right triangle. Therefore, we know that angle $ABC = 90°$. Given that angle $BCO = 30°$, angle BAO is 60°. (This makes triangle ABC a 30:60:90 triangle).

The question asks us to find the area of triangle ABO, meaning we need to figure out the angles of this triangle and then figure out the lengths of this triangle, working backward from the fact that ABC is a 30:60:90 triangle and $BC = 6\sqrt{3}$.

Given that the two sides of triangle ABO—AO and BO—are radii, the angles opposite them must be equal: angle ABO (which is opposite side AO) equals angle BAO (which is opposite BO). Since we already know that angle BAO is 60°, angle ABO is also 60°, leaving us with 60° for the final angle: BOA. Therefore, triangle ABO is an equilateral.

Given that triangle ABC is a 30:60:90 triangle, length BC corresponds to $x\sqrt{3}$ since it's the medium leg of the triangle. The shortest leg—AB—corresponds to x. Therefore, if we solve for x, we get $x\sqrt{3} = 6\sqrt{3}$, and $x = 6$. Since ABO is an equilateral triangle, we can use the formula $s^2\frac{\sqrt{3}}{4}$, where s is any side of the equilateral triangle. Since we just found out that AB is 6, we can plug that into the equilateral formula, giving us $6^2\frac{\sqrt{3}}{4} = 9\sqrt{3}$.

Question 7

Difficulty: **Very Hard** · Percent Correct: **30.4%** · Type: **Multiple Choice**

Two sides of a triangle have lengths 6 and 8. Which of the following are possible areas of the triangle?

I. 2

II. 12

III. 24

Ⓐ I only

Ⓑ I and II only

Ⓒ II and III only

Ⓓ I and III only

Ⓔ I, II, and III

This requires a picture explanation. Consider the leg of 6 and the leg of 8 attached at a "hinged" joint at *B*.

m ∠ABC = 0.01°

m $\overline{BC}$ = 8 cm

m $\overline{AB}$ = 6 cm

Here, the angle is made very narrow, only $\frac{1}{100}$ of a degree. The area of this triangle would be 0.00419—you don't need to be able to calculate something like this for the test. The point is, if the angle were one millionth, or one billionth, the area could be very small—greater than 0—but a really tiny decimal. So, clearly, the area can be less than 2.

Here, if you moved the legs of 6 and 8 apart a little and produced a triangle with an area of exactly two, you'd get the following:

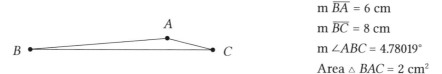

m $\overline{BA}$ = 6 cm

m $\overline{BC}$ = 8 cm

m ∠ABC = 4.78019°

Area △ BAC = 2 cm²

Again, you don't have to know how to build a triangle like this: this is just to show you that it is actually possible.

As you increase the angle *ABC*, you get triangles with more and more area. You don't need to know how to find these areas—this is just to demonstrate that the area would increase.

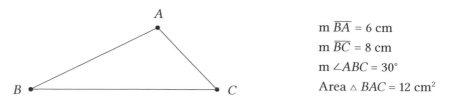

m $\overline{BA}$ = 6 cm

m $\overline{BC}$ = 8 cm

m ∠ABC = 30°

Area △ BAC = 12 cm²

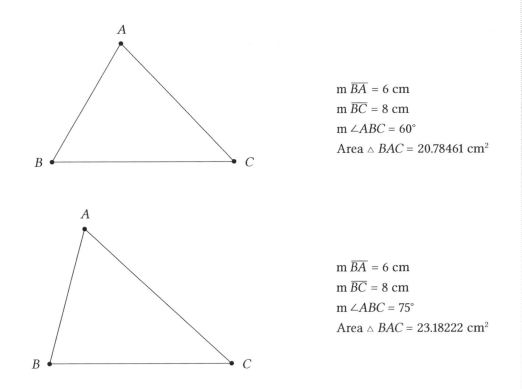

m $\overline{BA}$ = 6 cm
m $\overline{BC}$ = 8 cm
m $\angle ABC$ = 60°
Area $\triangle BAC$ = 20.78461 cm²

m $\overline{BA}$ = 6 cm
m $\overline{BC}$ = 8 cm
m $\angle ABC$ = 75°
Area $\triangle BAC$ = 23.18222 cm²

There's a geometry theorem that states that when the angle is 90°, the area of the triangle will be at its maximum. At that point, the length of 8 will be the base, and the length of 6 will be the height, so the area = 0.5 × bh = 24, the maximum possible area.

If the shortest side of the triangle must be greater than 2, how is it possible to have a height that's so close to 0? Think of it this way:

Side 1 = 2.01
Side 2 = 6.00
Side 3 = 8.00

Side 1 and side 2 have a total length of 8.01 (2.01 + 6.00). So the two sides combined are just slightly longer than side 3. If you try to draw a triangle like this, you'll notice that the height has to be very small because the sides 1 and 2 are only 0.01 longer than side 3. Now imagine a triangle that has sides (2.000001, 6, and 8). The height would be even smaller. Ultimately, you can keep shrinking the third side until the height is almost 0.

Why choose 8 for the base rather than 6? The side of the triangle you choose for the base is arbitrary—it doesn't change the area of the triangle. You could follow the same process with 6 as the base, and you would get the same result for both the minimum and maximum areas of the triangle. For instance, as long as you know that a right triangle would give you the maximum area, you find the same answer: 8 × 6 ÷ 2 and 6 × 8 ÷ 2 are both 24, and that's as big as the triangle can get.

Question 8

Difficulty: **Hard** · Percent Correct: **40.4%** · Type: **Multiple Answer**

Which of the following lines intersects the vertical line $x = 3$ between (3, 1) and (3, 2)?

Indicate <u>all</u> possible lines.

Every point on the line $x = 3$ has an x-coordinate of 3, so to figure out an intersection with that line, we merely have to plug in $x = 3$. We can plug in $x = 3$ and calculate.

A $y = \frac{9}{5}$, which is between 1 and 2, so that works.

B $y = \frac{9}{7} + 1$ ⇨ Well, $\frac{9}{7}$ is already greater than 1, so adding 1 would make this greater than 2. This doesn't work.

C $y = \frac{3}{5} + \frac{6}{5} = \frac{9}{5}$, which is between 1 and 2, so this works.

D $y = -\frac{9}{2} + 5 = -4.5 + 5 = 0.5 < 1$, so this doesn't work.

E $y = -\frac{3}{4} + 3 = 2\frac{1}{4} > 2$, so this doesn't work.

Question 9

Difficulty: **Medium** · Percent Correct: **48.4%** · Type: **Multiple Answer**

The line $3x + 2y = 7$ can be rewritten in slope-intercept form ($y = mx + b$) as the following:

$$y = -\frac{3}{2}x + \frac{7}{2}$$

So this line has a slope of m = $-\frac{3}{2}$. A line perpendicular to it must have a slope of the opposite-signed reciprocal. Thus, the perpendicular line has a slope of $m = +\frac{2}{3}$.

Of the first four, which are also written in slope-intercept form, [A] has the correct slope, whereas [B] and [C] and [D] do not.

Write [E] in slope-intercept form:

$$y = -\frac{2}{3}x + \frac{19}{3}$$

This has the wrong sign, so this isn't perpendicular. This doesn't work.

Now, write [F] in slope-intercept form:

$$y = \frac{2}{3}x + \frac{2}{3}$$

This has the correct slope, so this is perpendicular.

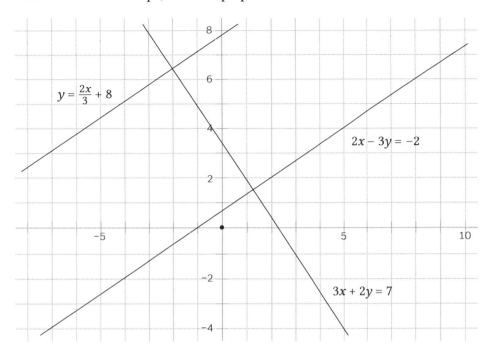

$$y = \frac{2x}{3} + 8$$

$$2x - 3y = -2$$

$$3x + 2y = 7$$

Question 10

Difficulty: **Medium** · Percent Correct: **62.6%** · Type: **Multiple Choice**

If a triangle in the xy-coordinate system has vertices at $(-2, -3)$, $(4, -3)$ and $(28, 7)$, what is the area of the triangle?

Answer: **Ⓐ**

Ⓐ 30
Ⓑ 36
Ⓒ 48
Ⓓ 60
Ⓔ 65

Area = $\frac{1}{2}$(base) × (height)

= $\frac{1}{2}$(6) × (10)

= **30**

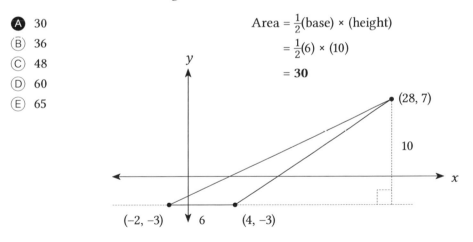

How can the base be calculated? You need to find the distance between $(-2, -3)$ and $(4, -3)$. Luckily, both points lie on the same y-coordinate. The segment between them is therefore a horizontal line. That length can be the base. The distance between $(-2, -3)$ and $(4, -3)$ is a horizontal distance of 6. You can ignore the y-coordinates since they're the same.

$$4 - (-2) = 6$$

So the base is 6.

How can the height be calculated? You have to determine the vertical distance from the base to the third vertex (28, 7). Well, the base is on the horizontal line $y = -3$. The point (28, 7) is shifted way over to the right, but that doesn't matter: a point with $y = 7$ is 10 above the line $y = -3$, because:

$$7 - (-3) = 10$$

Therefore, the height is 10.

Question 11

Difficulty: **Medium** · Percent Correct: **68.3%** · Type: **Multiple Choice**

Answer: **D**

In the xy-coordinate system, the distance between the point (0, 0) and point P is $\sqrt{40}$. Which of the following could be the coordinates of point P?

(A) (4, 7)
(B) (4, 10)
(C) (5, 6)
(D) (6, 2)
(E) (20, 20)

Some books recommend something called the distance formula—again, we're going to say "*fuhgeddaboudit!*" **Big idea**: When you need to find the distance between two points in the Cartesian plane, simply draw the slope triangle and use the Pythagorean theorem. In this instance we get the following:

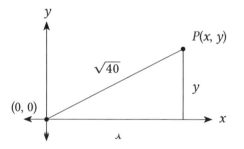

Notice that x and y are the legs, so the Pythagorean theorem gives us this:

$$x^2 + y^2 = 40$$

We simply have to plug the coordinates into this to see which one works:

(A) $4^2 + 7^2 = 16 + 49 \neq 40$
(B) $4^2 + 10^2 = 16 + 100 \neq 40$
(C) $5^2 + 6^2 = 25 + 36 \neq 40$
(D) $6^2 + 2^2 = 36 + 4 = \mathbf{40}$
(E) $20^2 + 20^2 = 400 + 400 \neq 40$

If *ABCD* is a square, what are the coordinates of *C*?

Answer: **D**

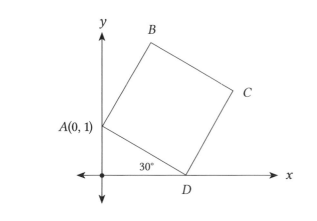

Ⓐ $(\sqrt{3}, \sqrt{3})$

Ⓑ $(\sqrt{3}, 1 + \sqrt{3})$

Ⓒ $(2\sqrt{3}, \sqrt{3})$

Ⓓ $(1 + \sqrt{3}, \sqrt{3})$

Ⓔ $(\sqrt{3}, 2\sqrt{3})$

Let's label a couple more points in the diagram. Call the origin *O*. Let *CE* be parallel to the *y*-axis, perpendicular to the *x*-axis.

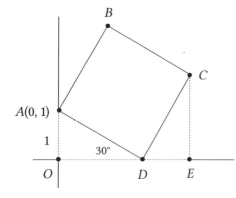

Notice that *AOD* is a 30-60-90 triangle: see a discussion of this special triangle on page 132. We know that *AO* = 1, so the other sides look like this:

hypotenuse $AD = 2$

longer leg $OD = \sqrt{3}$

Notice that, since *AD* = 2, this means that each side of the square is equal to 2. Now, look at *DCE*, which must be another 30-60-90 triangle. In fact, because it has the same hypotenuse as *AOD*, all the sides must have the same lengths. Thus,

$$DE = AO = 1$$
$$CE = OD = \sqrt{3}$$

We want the coordinates of point C. The x-coordinate of point C is the distance to the right from the y-axis, and this equals $OD + DE$:

$$x\text{-coordinate} = OD + DE = 1 + \sqrt{3}$$

The y-coordinate of point C is its height above the y-axis, and this equals CE:

$$y\text{-coordinate} = CE = \sqrt{3}$$

Thus, the coordinates should be this:

$$\text{point } C = (1 + \sqrt{3}, \sqrt{3})$$

Question 13

Difficulty: **Very Hard** · Percent Correct: **43.2%** · Type: **Multiple Choice**

Answer: **A**

The points $A(0, 0)$, $B(0, 4a - 5)$, and $C(2a + 1, 2a + 6)$ form a triangle. If $\angle ABC = 90°$, what is the area of triangle ABC?

A 102
Ⓑ 120
Ⓒ 132
Ⓓ 144
Ⓔ 156

First, we need to think about this geometric situation. Point A is at the origin. Point B is somewhere on the y-axis, so AB is a vertical line in the xy-plane. If $\angle ABC = 90°$, the only way a line can be perpendicular to a vertical line is by being horizontal. Segment BC must be horizontal.

If BC is horizontal, this means that point B and point C must have the same y-coordinate, because any two points on the same horizontal line in the coordinate plane have the same y-coordinate. This fact allows us to set up an equation:

$$4a - 5 = 2a + 6$$
$$2a = 11$$

We can leave this in terms of $2a$, because all the expressions have either $2a$ or $4a$ in them. Thus, we know the three points:

$$A = (0, 0)$$
$$B = (0, 2(2a) - 5) = (0, 22 - 5) = (0, 17)$$
$$C = (2a + 1, 2a + 6) = (11 + 1, 11 + 6) = (12, 17)$$

Here's a scaled diagram:

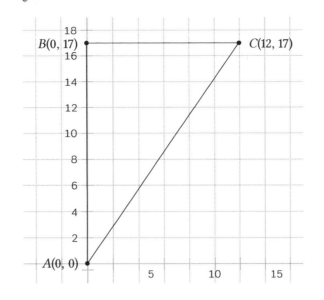

Even a rough sketch would be enough: we know that leg $AB = 17$ and leg $BC = 12$, and these can be considered the base and the height. (It actually doesn't matter which we call the base and which we call the height.)

$$area = \tfrac{1}{2}bh = \tfrac{1}{2}(12)(17) = 6 \times 17 = \mathbf{102}$$

Question 14

Difficulty: **Very hard** · Percent Correct: **29.4%** · Type: **Multiple answer**

Point A (-4, 2) and Point B (2, 4) lie in the xy-coordinate plane. If point C lies in the first quadrant and contains the coordinates (p, q), where $p < 2$ and $q < 4$, which of the following could be the area of triangle ABC?

Indicate <u>all</u> such numbers.

Answers: A B C

- A 1.1
- B 3.9
- C 11.9

Here's the situation in the coordinate plane:

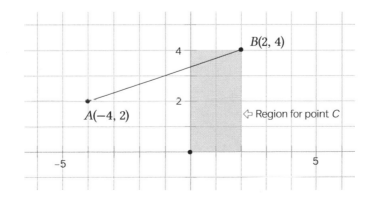

We can maximize the area by getting point C as far away from segment AB as possible. This means we would get it as close as possible to (2, 0):

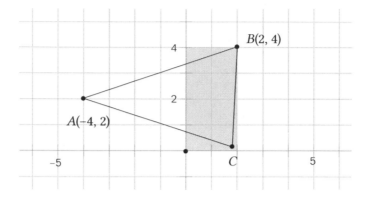

If we could put C right at (2, 0), then the triangle would have a base of $BC = 4$ and it's altitude would run from $(-4, 2)$ to $(2, 2)$: that is, it would have $h = 6$. This would give it an area of $\frac{1}{2}bh = \frac{1}{2}(4)(6) = 12$. Since C is in the first quadrant, it can't be on the x-axis, so it can't land exactly on (2, 0), but it could be infinitely close to it. Thus, the triangle couldn't have an area of exactly 12, but it could have an area of anything less than 12. By moving C slightly further away from (2, 0), we could reduce the area slightly, adjusting it to whatever we want. Thus, 11.9 certainly would be possible.

As we move C closer to the segment AB, the triangle area would become less and less. Of course, point C can't be on segment AB, because then we would have three points all on a single segment and that wouldn't be a triangle at all. A triangle has to have at least some area. We could, though, bring point C within a hair's breadth of line BC:

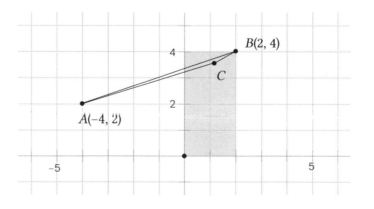

Since point C could come infinitely close to line AB, the area could go down to a value infinitely close to zero. Again, it can't equal zero, because a triangle has to have at least some area, no matter how small. Thus we can say, at the lower end, $0 <$ area.

Putting these ideas together, we see that $0 <$ area < 12. The area can take on any value greater than zero and less than 12. Thus, all three values given are correct.

The good news is we never have to find a specific point on the coordinate plane that actually yields the values in [A], [B], and [C]. We just have to know that the areas are possible, given the constraints of the problems.

Why is the area of the triangle maximized when point C is at (2, 0)? First, think about the formula for the area of a triangle:

$$base \times height \times \frac{1}{2}$$

If you can maximize the base and the height, you can maximize the area of the triangle.

If you're given just the base, then you maximize the area by maximizing the height. In doing so, you find the largest height possible given the restrictions of the problem.

This problem tells you the points must be within a certain area of the graph, so you need to work with these restrictions.

You're told (p, q) must be in the first quadrant, and $p < 2$ and $q < 4$. So you get the maximum height and base at $(< 2, 0)$, meaning by "<2," a value less than, but as close as possible to, 2.

The height is the horizontal distance from A to C. You maximize this by making the x-coordinate of C as large as possible, so < 2. And the height is then < 6.

The base is the vertical distance from B to C. B is fixed at $(2, 4)$, so, obeying the restrictions, you maximize the vertical distance from C at a y-coordinate of 0. And the base is then 4.

The height here would be (height < 6) $\times$ (base $= 4$) $\times \frac{1}{2} = (< \frac{24}{2})$ = area < 12.

Why is it certain that 0 is the lower bound for the area of the triangle? Why is a number just greater than 0 the lowest possible area? If you're given two sides of a triangle, the minimum area is *always* infinitely close to 0. Think of taking those two sides and making the triangle so skinny it looks like a line. The area is close to 0, and though it will get infinitely close to 0, it will never actually *be* 0. The maximum area is always the case when those two sides are perpendicular—when it's a right triangle. The maximum area given two sides A and B is $A \times B \times \frac{1}{2}$.

You can find even more geometry questions on gre.magoosh.com!

159

Quantitative Concept #7: Counting and Probability

Even people who consider themselves allergic to math know how to count. This basic skill lays the foundation for all sorts of fun combination and probability problems. Though you'll be asked to do a little more than just reciting numbers in order, you're more than capable of mastering the GRE counting and probability questions.

The Lowdown on Counting

The *fundamental counting principle* (FCP) is a big idea that will give you a lot of mileage on the GRE counting problems, so let's start there. It helps you figure out how many ways an event can occur.

If category one has *P* alternatives and category two has *Q* alternatives, assuming that the two sets of alternatives have no overlap, then the total number of different pairs we can form is *P* × *Q*. For example, Shakespeare wrote 15 comedies and 10 histories. If you want to know how many unique ways there are to combine one comedy and one history, you'll multiply 15 × 10 to find that there are 150 possible pairs.

The FCP easily extends from two choices to three or any higher number. However many collections of alternatives there are, you simply multiple the number of alternatives in each set to produce the total number of combinations. For example, Shakespeare wrote 15 comedies, 10 histories, and 12 tragedies. If we're going to pick one of each kind, and ask how many different trios of plays we can create, the total number is simply 15 × 10 × 12, or 1,800 trios.

Permutations and combinations

A *permutation* is a set in which order matters. For example, *AABC* is a different permutation from *BACA*. A *combination* is a set in which order doesn't matter. *AABC* and *BACA* are the same combination of four letters.

This distinction is important in counting because you have to know whether to include the sets that repeat elements in different orders.

A permutation question usually asks about the possible order in which to put a set of objects. Suppose you had a shelf of 5 different books, and you wanted to know in how many different ways you could order those 5 books. Another way to say that is "5 books have how many different permutations?"

In order to answer this question, you need an odd math symbol: the factorial. It's written as an exclamation sign, and it represents the product of that number and all the positive integers before it, down to one. For example, 4! (read "four factorial") looks like this:

$$4! = (4)(3)(2)(1) = 24$$

Here's the permutation formula:

# of permutations of *n* objects = *n*!

Using this to answer the question about how many ways to order your 5 books would look like this:

$$5! = (5)(4)(3)(2)(1) = 120$$

Combinations

A combination question requires using selections from a larger set. Suppose there's a class of 20 students and you're going to pick a team of 3 people at random. How many different possible three-person teams could you pick? Another way to say that is this: How many different combinations of 3 can be taken from a set of 20?

This formula is scary-looking but really not that bad at all. If n is the size of the larger collection, and r is the number of elements that will be selected, then the number of combinations is given by the following formula:

$$\text{\# of combinations} = \frac{n!}{r!(n-r)!}$$

Again, this looks complicated, but it gets simple very fast. In the question just posed, $n = 20$, $r = 3$, and $n - r = 17$. Therefore,

$$\text{\# of combinations} = \frac{20!}{3!(17)!}$$

To simplify the math, consider this:

$$20! = (20)(19)(18)(17)(\text{the product of all the numbers less than 17})$$

Or, in other words,

$$20! = (20)(19)(18)(17!)$$

That neat little trick allows us to enormously simplify the combinations formula:

$$\text{\# of combinations} = \frac{(20)(19)(18)(17!)}{3!(17)!} = \frac{(20)(19)(18)}{3!} = \frac{(20)(19)(18)}{(3)(2)(1)} = 1,140$$

That example is most likely harder than anything you'll see on the GRE, but you may be asked to find combinations with smaller numbers.

Probability

Simplistic probability rules

The absolute bare minimum you'll need to know for probability calculations on the GRE is as follows:

And means multiply
Or means add

The field of mathematics we now know as probability arose from letters between two mathematical thinkers, **Pierre de Fermat** (1601–1665) and **Blaise Pascal** (1623–1662). Both were avid gamblers, and because they were mathematically inclined, they wrote letters back and forth discussing how to calculate the odds of winning: the mathematics of probability was born from this correspondence.

Is that all you need to know about probability? No, not exactly. But if you remember nothing else, at least know these two bare-bones rules, because just they will put you ahead of many other students taking the GRE. Before we qualify these simplistic rules, though, we need to make two things clear.

Disjoint

Two events are *disjoint* if they're mutually exclusive. In other words, two events are disjoint if the probability of their simultaneous occurrence is 0, meaning it's absolutely impossible to have them both happen at the same time. For example, different faces of a single die are disjoint. Under ordinary circumstances, if you roll one die once, you can't simultaneously get both a 3 and a 5. Those two events are disjoint. Suppose we're picking random people and classifying them by their current age. In this process, being in the category "teenager" and being in the category "senior citizen" are disjoint because there's no one we could pick who is simultaneously in both categories.

If events **A** and **B** are **disjoint**, then we can use the **simplified OR rule**:

$$P(A \text{ or } B) = P(A) + P(B)$$

Or, to put that into words, the probability of either A or B happening is equal to the probability of A happening plus the probability of event B. That's the case in which the simplified rule, OR means ADD, works perfectly. If events A and B are **not disjoint**, then we have to use the **generalized OR rule**:

$$P(A \text{ or } B) = P(A) + P(B) - P(A \text{ and } B)$$

The reason for that final term – **P(A and B)** is that the possibility of both A and B happening—P(A and B)—is included in both P(A) and P(B). We don't want the overlap to get counted twice, so we need to subtract it; as a result, it's only counted once, like everything else.

Independent

Two events are independent if the occurrence of one has absolutely no influence on the occurrence of the other. In other words, knowing about the outcome of one event gives absolutely no information about how the other event will turn out. For example, if you roll two ordinary dice, the outcome of each die is independent of the other die. Knowing what the first die roll resulted in doesn't give you any clue into what the second die roll will be.

If you shuffle a deck of cards, draw one, replace it, reshuffle, and draw another, the two cards are independent. But if you shuffle the deck, draw the seven of hearts card, and then draw a second card without replacing the first, they aren't independent because there are fewer options among the remaining fifty-one cards. So your second draw is less likely to be a seven or a heart.

If events **A** and **B** are **independent**, then we can use the **simplified AND rule**:

$$P(A \text{ and } B) = P(A) \times P(B)$$

That's the case in which the simplified rule, "*and* means multiply," works perfectly. If events A and B are **not independent**, then things get complicated. Technically, the generalized *and* rule formula would involve a concept known as *conditional probability*, which would lead into realms of probability theory that are rarely tested on the GRE.

The Complement Rule

Just like the words *and* and *or* have their places in probability formulas, so too does the phrase *at least*. There's a very simple and very important rule relating P(A) and P(not A), linking the probability of any event happening with the probability of that same event not happening. For any well-defined event, it's 100% true that either the event happens or it doesn't happen. The GRE won't ask you a probability question about bizarre events in which, for example, you can't tell whether or not the event happened or complex events which could, in some sense, both happen and not happen.

For any event A in a probability question on the GRE, the two scenarios "A happens" and "A doesn't happen" exhaust the possibilities that could take place. With certainty, we can say that one of those two will occur. In other words,

$$P(A \text{ OR not } A) = 1$$

Having a probability of 1 means guaranteed certainty. Obviously, for a variety of deep logical reasons, the events "A" and "not A" are disjoint and have no overlap. The OR rule, discussed earlier, implies the following:

$$P(A) + P(\text{not } A) = 1$$

Subtract the first term to isolate P(not A).

$$P(\text{not } A) = 1 - P(A)$$

That's known in probability as the *complement rule*, because the probabilistic region in which an event doesn't occur complements the region in which it does occur. This is a crucial idea in general, for all GRE probability questions, and one that will be very important in solving "at least" questions in particular.

The complement of "at least" statements

Suppose event A is a statement involving the words "at least." How would you state what constituted "not A"? In other words, how do you negate an "at least" statement? Let's look at a concrete example. Suppose there's some event that involves just two outcomes: success and failure. The event could be, for example, making a basketball free throw, or flipping a coin and getting heads.

Now, suppose we have a contest involving 10 of these events in a row, and we're counting the number of successes in these 10 trials. Let A be the event defined as A = there's at least 1 success in these 10 trials. What outcomes would constitute "not A"? Well, let's think about it. In 10 trials, one could get 0 successes, exactly 1 success, exactly 2 successes, all the way up to 10 successes. There are 11 possible outcomes, the numbers from 0–10, for the number of successes one could get in 10 trials. Consider the following diagram of the number of possible successes in 10 trials:

0 <u>1 2 3 4 5 6 7 8 9 10</u>

The underlined numbers are the 10 members of A, the members of "at least 1 success" in 10 trials. Therefore, the non-underlined numbers are the complement space, the region of "not A." In words, how would we describe the conditions that land you in the non-underlined region? We would say, "not A" = "0 successes" in 10 trials. The negation, the opposite, of "at least 1" is "0."

Abstracting from this, the negation or opposite of "at least n" is the condition "$(n - 1)$ or fewer." The most common case of this on the GRE is what we have shown here, $n = 1$: **the negation or opposite of "at least one" is "none."** That last statement is a hugely important idea, arguably the key to solving almost every "at least" question you'll see on the GRE.

Solving an "at least" question

The big idea for any "at least" question on the GRE is that it's always easier to figure out the complement probability. For example, in the above scenario of 10 trials of some sort, calculating "at least 1" directly would involve 10 different calculations, 1 for each of the 10 underlined numbers above; whereas the calculation of "none" would involve only a single calculation, for $n = 0$. Once we figure out that complement probability, then we subtract from 1.

P(not A) = 1 − P(A)
P(at least one success) = 1 − P(no successes)

This is one of the most powerful time-saving shortcuts on the entire GRE.

An example calculation

Consider the following question.

> Two dice are rolled. What is the probability of rolling a 6 on at least one of them?

It turns out that calculating that directly would involve a relatively long calculation—the probability of exactly one 6, on either die, along with the rare probability of both coming up 6s. That calculation easily could take several minutes.

Instead, we'll use the shortcut defined above:

P(not A) = 1 − P(A)
P(at least one 6) = 1 − P(no 6s)

What's the probability of both dice coming up numbers other than 6? Well, first, let's consider one die. The probability of rolling a 6 is $\frac{1}{6}$, so the probability of rolling something other than 6 ("not 6") is $\frac{5}{6}$.

P(two rolls, no 6s) = P("not 6" on die #1 AND "not 6" on die #2)

As discussed previously, the word *and* means multiply. Thus,

P(two rolls, no 6s) = $\left(\frac{5}{6}\right) \times \left(\frac{5}{6}\right) = \frac{25}{36}$

P(at least one 6) = 1 − P(no 6s) = $1 - \frac{25}{36} = \frac{11}{36}$

What could have been a long calculation becomes remarkably straightforward by means of this shortcut. This can be an enormous time-saver on the GRE!

In Short

Fundamentally, the definition of probability is this:

$$probability\ of\ a\ desired\ outcome = \frac{number\ of\ desired\ outcomes}{total\ number\ of\ outcomes}$$

We've previously discussed various tricks for calculating probabilities in different scenarios, but in some problems, we just have to count the numbers in the numerator and the denominator. Any probability problem involving counting is really two counting problems in one—calculating the denominator, the number of all possible cases, and calculating the numerator, the number of only those cases that meet the condition specified. Remember to read the problems carefully. Usually you can figure out how to set up your calculations by noticing how the problem is framed.

Counting and Probability Practice Questions

These questions should help you get an idea of what to expect from counting and probability questions on the GRE. There are even more practice questions in the GRE practice test at the end of this book.

Question 1

Difficulty: **Medium** · Percent Correct: **66.9%** · Type: **Multiple Choice**

The probability that event A occurs is 0.4, and the probability that events A and B both occur is 0.25. If the probability that either event A or event B occurs is 0.6, what is the probability that event B will occur?

- (A) 0.05
- (B) 0.15
- (C) 0.45
- (D) 0.50
- (E) 0.55

Question 2

Difficulty: **Medium** · Percent Correct: **74.9%** · Type: **Quantitative Comparison**

A number, x, is randomly selected from the integers from 42 to 92 inclusive.

Column A	Column B
The probability that x is odd.	The probability that x is even.

- (A) The quantity in Column A is greater
- (B) The quantity in Column B is greater
- (C) The two quantities are equal
- (D) The relationship cannot be determined from the information given

Question 3

Difficulty: **Medium** · Percent Correct: **74.9%** · Type: **Quantitative Comparison**

An office has 6 employees. The manager must create a committee consisting of 3 employees.

Column A	Column B
Number of different committees possible.	40

- (A) The quantity in Column A is greater
- (B) The quantity in Column B is greater
- (C) The two quantities are equal
- (D) The relationship cannot be determined from the information given

Question 4

Difficulty: **Hard** · Percent Correct: **35%** · Type: **Multiple Answer**

A weighted coin has a probability p of showing heads. If successive flips are independent, and the probability of getting at least one head in two flips is greater than 0.5, then what could p be?

Indicate <u>all</u> possible values.

- [A] 0.1
- [B] 0.2
- [C] 0.3
- [D] 0.4
- [E] 0.6
- [F] 0.7

Question 5

Difficulty: **Hard** · Percent Correct: **38.1%** · Type: **Numeric Entry**

The diagonal of a polygon is a line segment from any vertex to any non-adjacent vertex. The diagram below shows a regular decagon, a 10-sided polygon, with two diagonals drawn. How many possible diagonals does the regular decagon have?

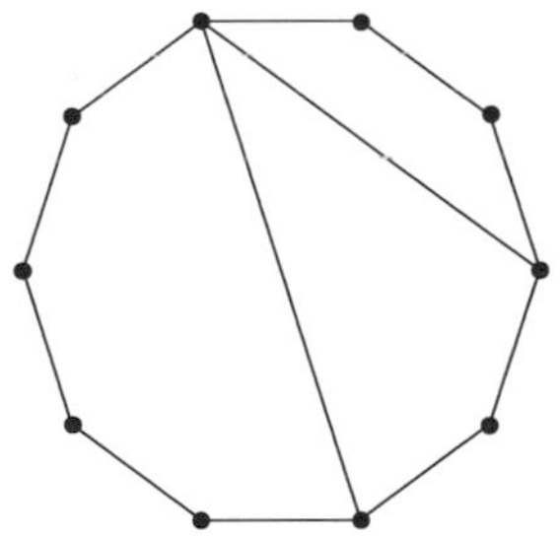

Question 6

Difficulty: **Very Hard** · Percent Correct: **39.5%** · Type: **Multiple Choice**

If points A and B are randomly placed on the circumference of a circle with a radius of 2 cm, what is the probability that the length of chord AB is greater than 2 cm?

- (A) $\frac{1}{4}$
- (B) $\frac{1}{3}$
- (C) $\frac{1}{2}$
- (D) $\frac{2}{3}$
- (E) $\frac{3}{4}$

Counting and Probability Answers and Explanations

Question 1

Difficulty: **Medium** · Percent Correct: **66.9%** · Type: **Multiple Choice**

Answer: **C**

The probability that event A occurs is 0.4, and the probability that events A and B both occur is 0.25. If the probability that either event A or event B occurs is 0.6, what is the probability that event B will occur?

(A) 0.05

(B) 0.15

(C) 0.45

(D) 0.50

(E) 0.55

$$P(A \text{ or } B) = P(A) + P(B) - P(A \text{ and } B)$$
$$0.6 = 0.4 + P(B) - 0.25$$
$$0.6 = 0.15 + P(B)$$
$$0.45 = P(B)$$

Question 2

Difficulty: **Medium** · Percent Correct: **74.9%** · Type: **Quantitative Comparison**

Answer: **B**

A number, x, is randomly selected from the integers from 42 to 92 inclusive.

Column A	Column B
The probability that x is odd.	The probability that x is even.
$\dfrac{25}{51}$	$\dfrac{26}{51}$

Because 42 and 92 are both included in the count, there's one more even integer than odd integer.

The number of integers from x to y <u>inclusive</u> is equal to $y - x + 1$.

$92 - 42 + 1 = 51$ ⇨ 51 integers altogether

26 even integers

25 odd integers

(A) The quantity in Column A is greater

(B) The quantity in Column B is greater

(C) The two quantities are equal

(D) The relationship cannot be determined from the information given

Question 3

Difficulty: **Medium** · Percent Correct: **74.9%** · Type: Quantitative Comparison

An office has 6 employees. The manager must create a committee consisting of 3 employees.

Answer: **B**

This is a combinations problem because it doesn't matter in which order we choose the three employees.

Column A	Column B
Number of different committees possible.	40
$_6C_3 = \dfrac{6!}{3!(6-3)!}$ $\quad _nC_r = \dfrac{n!}{r!(n-r)!}$ $= 20$	**40**

(A) The quantity in Column A is greater

(B) The quantity in Column B is greater

(C) The two quantities are equal

(D) The relationship cannot be determined from the information given

Question 4

Difficulty: **Hard** · Percent Correct: **35%** · Type: **Multiple Answer**

A weighted coin has a probability p of showing heads. If successive flips are independent, and the probability of getting at least one head in two flips is greater than 0.5, then what could p be?

Answers:
C **D** **E** **F**

Indicate <u>all</u> possible values.

- [ ] A 0.1
- [ ] B 0.2
- [x] C 0.3
- [x] D 0.4
- [x] E 0.6
- [x] F 0.7

Remember that to calculate the probability of an "at least" scenario, you use the complement rule. The case you want is *at least one H in two flips*. The complement of that is *no H in two flips*. If p is the probability of H, then $(1 - p)$ is the probability of T. The probably of two T in two flips would be that squared. Then you would subtract from 1 to find the "at least" probability.

   On the table below, the first column shows possible values of p, the probability of getting H on a single flip. The second column is the probability of getting T on a single flip. The third column is the probability of getting two Ts in a row, i.e., no H in two flips. The final column is the probability of at least one H in two flips.

p	$1 - p$	$(1 - p)^2$	$1 - (1 - p)^2$
0.10	0.9	0.81	~~0.19~~
0.2	0.8	0.64	~~0.36~~
0.3	0.7	0.49	**0.51**
0.4	0.6	0.36	**0.64**
0.5	0.5	0.25	**0.75**
0.6	0.4	0.16	**0.84**
0.7	0.3	0.09	**0.91**

You see that for all value of $p \geq 0.3$, the "at least" probability is greater than 0.5.

Question 5

Difficulty: **Hard** · Percent Correct: **38.1%** · Type: **Numeric Entry**

Answer: **35**

The diagonal of a polygon is a line segment from any vertex to any non-adjacent vertex. The diagram below shows a regular decagon, a 10-sided polygon, with two diagonals drawn. How many possible diagonals does the regular decagon have?

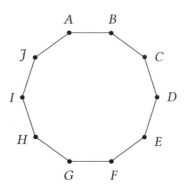

Let's pick any vertex as the starting point of the diagonal. Say you pick point A. Now, how many possible ending points would there be? Well, if A is the starting point, it can't also be the ending point. Also, neither J nor B could be the ending point, because a diagonal must go from a vertex to another **non-adjacent** vertex. That leaves seven vertices, C through I, that could be the ending point of a diagonal starting from A.

Each of the 10 vertices could be a starting point, and each has 7 other ending points, so that's a total of 70 possible diagonals.

The only problem with that method is that you have double-counted, because for, say, the diagonal DH, that gets counted both with a starting point of D and with a starting point of H. Each diagonal is counted twice.

Thus, you divide by 2 to get the correct answer.

Question 6

Difficulty: **Very Hard** · Percent Correct: **39.5%** · Type: **Multiple Choice**

If points *A* and *B* are randomly placed on the circumference of a circle with a radius of 2 cm, what is the probability that the length of chord *AB* is greater than 2 cm?

Answer: **D**

(A) $\frac{1}{4}$

(B) $\frac{1}{3}$

(C) $\frac{1}{2}$

D $\frac{2}{3}$

(E) $\frac{3}{4}$

First of all, the circle has what is called rotational symmetry. Because of rotational symmetry, you can pick, at random, any location you want for point *A*. Then you just need to consider how far away randomly chosen point *B* locations would be. If the locations of points *A* and *B* are, say, 3 cm apart, it won't make any difference to the problem where *A* and *B* are individually on the circle—the only thing that matters to the problem is the **distance between them**. That's why you can simply select an arbitrary location for point *A* and consider only the random possibilities for the location of point *B*.

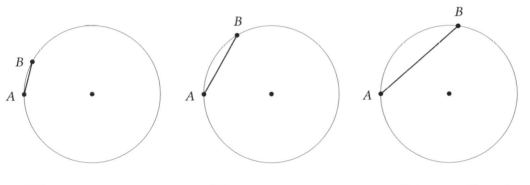

m $\overline{AB}$ = 1 cm not allowed   m $\overline{AB}$ = 2 cm not allowed   m $\overline{AB}$ = 3 cm allowed

Because you're interested in an inequality (chord > 2 cm), you should employ a standard mathematical strategy of **solving the equation** first (chord = 2 cm). Even though this particular chord wouldn't satisfy the condition, this chord or location on the circle will form a "boundary" between the "allowed" region and the "not allowed" region. Again, this is a standard mathematical strategy, often used in algebraic inequalities.

Also, keep in mind that because point *B* could be randomly located anywhere on the circle, it could be on either clockwise from point *A* or counterclockwise from point *A*. Therefore, you have to consider the (chord = 2) case on both sides of the circle.

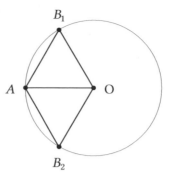

In that diagram, chords AB_1 and AB_2 both have a length of exactly 2 cm, so those points, and anything closer to point A than those points, would be a "not allowed" location, a place with a chord less than or equal to 2 cm. That's the arc on the left side of the circle, clockwise from B_2 through A to B_1, the "not allowed" region. The place where the chord would be greater than 2 would be the whole rest of the circle, starting from B_1 clockwise all the way around to B_2: this is the "allowed" region of the circle. The probability question reduces to a geometric question: what percent of the whole circle is this "allowed" region?

Notice the set of connections in that diagram. There are five line segments, all of which with a length of 2 cm: AO, AB_1, AB_2, OB_1, and OB_2. The segments AB_1 and AB_2 were chosen to have this length, and the other three are all radii of the circle, and you're told that the length of a radius is 2 cm.

This means that triangles OAB_1 and triangle OAB_2 are both equilateral triangles. In fact, any time you have chord = radius, and you connect radii to the endpoints of the chord, you get an equilateral triangle. This means that each of the angles is 60°. Since angle AOB_1 = 60° and angle AOB_2 = 60°, you know that angle B_1OB_2 = 120°. This is the central angle of the "not allowed" arc, so this "not allowed" arc must have a measure of 120°.

There are 360° in a circle altogether. Since there are 120° in the "not allowed" arc, the "allowed" arc must have a measure of 360° − 120° = 240°.

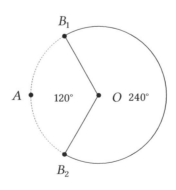

If point B lands anywhere on the solid "allowed" arc on the right, it meets the condition (chord > 2 cm), and if point B lands anywhere on the dotted "not allowed" arc on the left, it fails to meet the specified condition (because chord < 2 cm). The "allowed" arc takes up 240° of the full 360° of the circle. 240 out of 360 is $\frac{2}{3}$.

You can find even more counting and probability questions on gre.magoosh.com!

Need a study break? Have fun with this word search.
Words can go in any direction, including the four diagonals.

```
S  R  P  A  O  G  N  O  I  T  C  A  R  F  Q  T  N  V  Y  T
F  R  L  U  F  I  R  T  T  N  I  O  J  S  I  D  E  L  X  N
N  R  E  M  C  S  L  I  R  E  C  U  R  S  I  V  E  U  C  A
O  T  L  C  Y  O  A  I  V  N  S  E  D  N  E  U  I  U  P  H
E  E  L  B  I  S  I  V  I  D  L  A  A  B  Q  N  U  R  T  T
Z  R  A  R  D  C  M  M  J  Q  J  E  Y  H  T  F  A  M  A  S
A  H  R  Y  O  E  O  E  N  V  R  J  M  E  C  C  I  E  Q  S
C  B  A  W  Q  L  N  D  J  O  D  K  G  O  T  H  A  X  T  E
S  I  P  Y  U  E  I  I  G  N  F  E  M  I  F  C  G  O  B  L
U  P  T  H  E  S  B  A  D  U  R  P  C  N  E  E  K  T  H  N
A  W  T  A  O  S  H  N  P  Z  L  E  V  I  G  Z  X  R  Z  O
S  Z  D  N  R  T  W  I  C  E  Y  S  Q  U  A  R  E  D  H  I
L  F  G  O  Y  D  B  V  M  G  T  R  P  R  I  M  E  R  E  T
R  J  N  P  I  W  A  E  L  S  Q  U  A  R  E  R  O  O  T  A
O  A  U  K  F  T  N  U  Q  B  J  A  R  Y  U  K  Z  D  U  T
E  R  R  D  F  T  A  M  Q  H  I  Q  D  L  G  V  G  Y  G  U
Q  E  R  T  Q  M  C  R  Q  L  Z  O  Z  E  B  B  I  V  R  M
D  A  E  D  H  A  D  C  M  M  T  N  E  N  O  P  X  E  M  R
F  Q  V  H  L  G  R  L  A  C  O  R  P  I  C  E  R  Y  X  E
I  R  O  A  L  O  W  H  A  N  G  I  N  G  F  R  U  I  T  P
U  X  E  T  G  O  O  S  U  I  D  A  R  D  I  L  C  U  E  E
N  Y  S  D  E  S  I  E  C  P  C  H  T  W  O  R  G  S  E  E
S  X  I  W  B  H  W  E  V  T  S  E  R  E  T  N  I  T  F  V
C  T  R  G  E  L  B  I  X  E  L  F  E  B  C  X  U  I  W  U
```

FRACTION	DISJOINT	PYTHAGOREAN	RECURSIVE
RATIO	AREA	RADIUS	TWICE Y SQUARED
INTEGER	RECIPROCAL	EUCLID	MEDIAN
RISE OVER RUN	COMPLEMENT	LESS THAN	MAGOOSH
PRIME	PARALLEL	INTEREST	BE FLEXIBLE
QUADRATIC	FOIL	GCF	LOW-HANGING FRUIT
EXPONENT	BINOMIAL	DIVISIBLE	PRACTICE
SQUARE ROOT	ISOSCELES	PERMUTATION	GROWTH

Quantitative Concept #8: Data Interpretation

Data interpretation questions have you look at charts, graphs, and diagrams and analyze the information for patterns. Some questions are simply about reading data, while others will ask you to make predictions based on specific graphic trends. Let's take a look at what you'll need to know for the GRE!

Data Interpretation Concepts: The Lowdown

Bars and columns

One common way data will be displayed on the GRE is in bar charts. ETS calls a chart a "bar chart" whether the bars are horizontal or vertical. It's good to know that many sources call charts with horizontal bars "bar charts" and charts with vertical bars "column charts." Regardless of the names we use, there's a subtle difference.

Bar charts

Typically, in a bar chart, when the bars are horizontal, each bar represents a completely different item from some overarching category. For example:

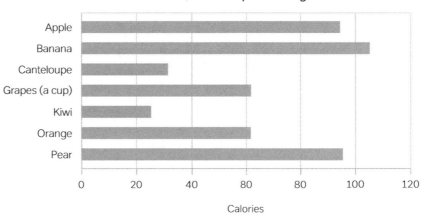

Various Fruits, Calories per Serving

Here, the bars are different fruits. Why these fruits were selected and not others isn't obvious. The order here is simply alphabetical because there is no predetermined way to put fruits into order, whatever that would mean. If there is no inherent order to the categories, and the representatives chosen don't exhaust the category, then the data typically would be displayed in horizontal bars or what many sources would call a *bar chart*.

Column charts

If the set has a logical order to it, such as days of the week or months of the year, and/or the representatives shown encompass all in the category, the data typically would be displayed in vertical bars or what many would call a *column chart*. For example:

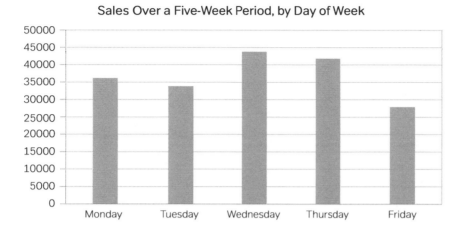

Here, days of the week have a well-defined order, in which they're displayed. Assuming this business only operates during weekdays, this is also a complete set of all the days on which they do business. That's why the vertical columns are used.

Segmented bars and columns

The following is a more detailed version of the "sales by day of week" chart given above:

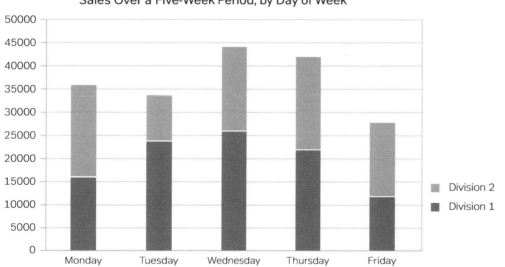

This type of chart gives more nuanced information. Apparently, this company has two divisions, and how each division performs during different days of the week varies considerably. For example, Division 1 clearly has its best days on Wednesdays, while for Division 2, Mondays and Thursdays appear to be neck-and-neck for the best days. Here, the individual pieces are displayed as segments of a column because you might

Edward Tufte (1942–) is widely recognized as the world's expert in the visual display of data. Once, Tufte said: "The only thing worse than a pie chart is several pie charts." Admittedly, the pie chart is an extremely simple diagram that generally conveys far less than most of the other charts and diagrams discussed in this chapter.

be interested in knowing either the revenue of each division separately or the total revenue of the company, which equals the sum of the revenues of the two divisions.

Clustered bars and columns

Sometimes you'll care about the sum of the parts and sometimes you won't. If, instead of being two divisions of the same company, that same data was interpreted as the revenues of two different companies competing in the same market, then the sum of the revenues would be virtually meaningless. In this case, the columns or bars are "clustered," that is to say, displayed side by side. For example:

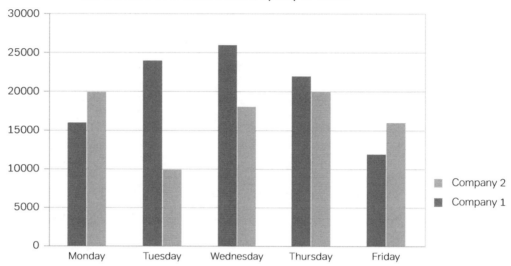

Here, the side-by-side comparison makes it very easy to compare which company outperforms the other on each day of the week.

Scatterplots

One of the most common types of graphs in statistics and in the quantitative sciences is a *scatterplot*. A scatterplot is a way of displaying data in which two different variables are measured for each participant. For example, suppose you ask several people to identify their age and their weight, or both their annual income and the amount of debt they carry, or both their number of kids and number of credit cards. Suppose you measure both the weight and the gas mileage of several cars or the annual revenue and the price, per share, of stock of publically traded companies. In all of those cases, each individual (each person, each car, each company) would be a single dot on the graph, and the graph would have as many dots as individuals surveyed or measured.

An example of a scatterplot

Below is a scatterplot on which the individual dots represent countries.

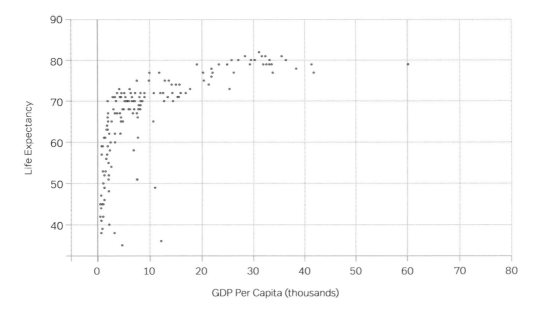

On this graph, the *x*-axis is the gross domestic product (GDP) per capita of the country. The GDP is a measure of the amount of business the country conducts. The size of the GDP depends on both the inherent wealth of the country and the population. When you divide that by the population of the country, you get GDP per capita, which is an excellent measure of the average wealth of the country. The *y*-axis is life expectancy at birth in that country. The sideways L shape tells a story: for countries with a GDP per capita above $20K, life expectancy at birth is between 70 and 80 years, but for the poor countries, those with a GDP per capita less than about $20K, life expectancy at birth varies considerably, and is in many cases considerably less than the 70+ years that's standard for most of the world.

Now, as an example of a scatterplot with two different marks on the graph, here's the same graph again, with some of the points marked differently.

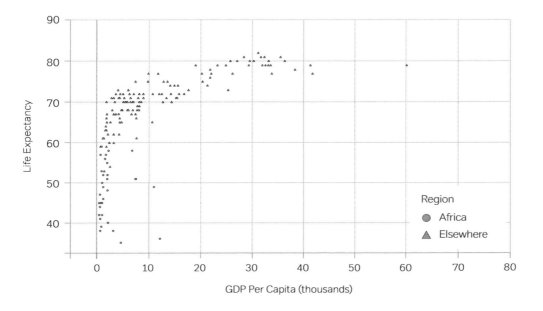

On this graph, the circles are countries on the continent of Africa, and the triangles are countries in the rest of the world. Notice that essentially, the entire continent of Africa is in the vertical arm of the L shape on the left side, while the rest of the world predominantly makes the horizontal arm of the L at the top of the graph. In other words, for most African countries, a person's odds from birth are worse than those of a person born in a non-African country. Suffice it to say, displaying data in a scatterplot can make truly important information visually apparent.

Boxplots

Statisticians like to chunk data in sets. One way to do this is by labeling data using the five-number summary. The five-number summary looks at data like this:

1. Maximum
2. Third quartile, Q_3, the 75th percentile
3. Median, 50th percentile
4. First quartile, Q_1, the 25th percentile
5. Minimum

The beauty of the five-number summary is that it divides the entire data set into quarters: between any two numbers on the five-number summary is exactly 25% of the data.

Because statisticians, like many human beings, are highly visual, they created a visual way to display the five-number summary. This visual form is called a *boxplot*. The five vertical lines represent the five numbers of the five-number summary, and the box in the middle, from Q_1 to Q_3, represents the middle 50% of the data. Between any two adjacent vertical lines are 25% of the data points.

Strikeouts

Here's an example of a boxplot using real baseball data. The data here is the total strikeouts pitched by all National League (NL) pitchers who pitched at least 75 innings in the 2012 season.

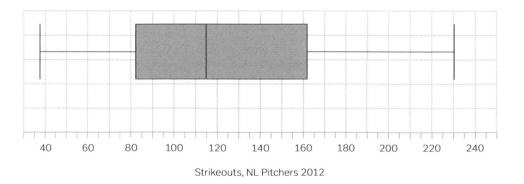

Strikeouts, NL Pitchers 2012

Half of all the NL pitchers here pitched between Q_1 = 83 and Q_3 = 161 strikeouts in the year; these are the pitchers in the big grey box in the center, called the IQR. Meanwhile, only 25% of the pitchers in this data struck out fewer than 83 batters; this bottom 25% is on the lower arm from 38 to 83. And finally, only 25% of the pitchers struck out more than 161 batters in the 2012 season; this top 25% is on the upper arm from 161 to 230. A data interpretation question on the GRE could give you a boxplot and expect you to read all the five-number summary information, including percentiles, from it.

Histogram

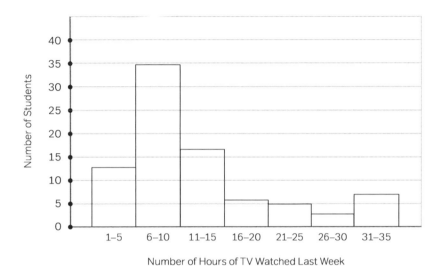

Number of Hours of TV Watched Last Week

Histograms aren't simple bar or column charts. A histogram, like a boxplot, shows the distribution of a single quantitative variable. The makers of this graph asked each high school student, "How many hours of TV did you watch last week?" and each high school student gave a numerical answer. After interviewing 86 students, a list of 86 numbers was generated. The histogram is a way to visually display the distribution of those 86 numbers.

The histogram "chunks" the values into sections that occupy equal ranges of the variable, and it tells how many numbers on the list fall into that particular chunk. For example, the left-most column on this chart has a height of 13. This means that, of the 86 students surveyed, 13 of them gave a numerical response somewhere from 1 to 5 hours. Similarly, each other bar tells us how many responses were in that particular range of hours of TV watched.

The median

The *median* is the middle of the list. In this same histogram problem, there's an even number of entries on the list, so the median would be the average of the two middle terms—the average of the 43rd and 44th numbers on the list. We can tell that the first column accounts for the first 13 people on the list, and that the first two columns account for the first 13 + 35 = 48 people on the list, so by the time we got to the last person on the list in the second column, we would have already passed the 43rd and 44th entries, which means the median would be somewhere in that second column, somewhere between 6 and 10. But we don't know the exact value of the median.

The mean

To calculate the *mean*, you would have to add up the exact values of all 86 entries on the list, and then divide that sum by 86. In a histogram, you don't have access to exact values; you only know the ranges of numbers. Therefore, it's impossible to calculate the mean from a histogram.

Median vs. mean

If it's impossible to calculate the mean, then how can the GRE expect you to compare the mean to the median? Well, here you need to know a slick little bit of statistical reasoning. Consider the following two lists:

> List A = {1, 2, 3, 4, 5}
> median = 3 and mean = 3
>
> List B = {1, 2, 3, 4, 100}
> median = 3 and mean = 21

In changing from List A to List B, we took the last point and slid it out on the scale from $x = 5$ to $x = 100$. We made it an outlier, or a point that's noticeably far from the other points. Notice that the median didn't change at all. The median doesn't care about outliers. Outliers simply don't affect the median. By contrast, the mean changed substantially, because, unlike the median, the mean is sensitive to outliers.

Now, consider a symmetrical distribution of numbers—it could be a perfect bell curve, or it could be any other symmetrical distribution. In any symmetrical distribution, the mean equals the median. Now, consider an asymmetrical distribution. If the outliers are yanked out to one side, then the median will stay put, but the mean will be yanked out in the same direction as the outliers. Outliers pull the mean away from the median. Therefore, if you simply notice on which side the outliers lie, then you know in which direction the mean was pulled away from the median. That makes it very easy to compare the two. The comparison is purely visual, and involves absolutely no calculations of any sort.

The standardized test is a learnable thing. You can become much better at the GRE in a very short time. Just remember to repeat this mantra when that little voice in your head wants to say things like "I'm no good at this."

Normal distribution

A distribution is a graph that shows what values of a variable are more or less common in a population. A higher region of the graph represents more people meeting the variable criteria, and a lower region of the graph, one close to 0, represents fewer people meeting the criteria.

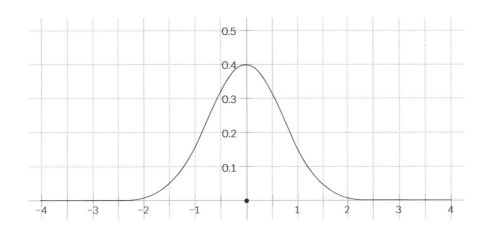

The people who are more than four standard deviations above the mean are the people who are truly exceptional, among the greatest on earth, in one way or another: the professional athletes, the concert pianists and violinists, or the Nobel Laureates of various fields.

By far, the most famous and most useful distribution is the normal distribution, better known as the bell curve. It shows up everywhere, with an almost eerie universality. Suppose you measured one genetically determined bodily measurement such as thumb length or distance between pupils, for every single human being on the planet, and then graphed the distribution. You would wind up with a normal distribution. The same goes for any genetically determined bodily measurement you could make on an animal or a plant: you'd end up with a normal distribution. The normal distribution is the shape of the distribution of any naturally occurring variable of any natural population.

Properties of the normal distribution

All normal distributions on earth, from giraffe height to ant height, share certain central properties.

It's important to appreciate that any normal distribution comes with its own yardstick. For normal distribution, that yardstick is the standard deviation. The very center of the normal distribution is the mean, median, and mode all in one. We use the standard deviation to measure distances from the mean.

In the graph below, the mean (and median and mode) is at $x = 0$, and the units on the x-axis mark off distances in standard deviations. Thus, $x = 1$ is one standard deviation above the mean, and $x = -2$ is two standard deviations below the mean.

From $x = 0$ to $x = 1$, from the mean to one standard deviation above the mean, we find 34% of the population. Because the curve is completely symmetrical, the same is true on the other side: another 34% of the population is between $x = -1$ and $x = 0$. This means that between $x = -1$ and $x = 1$, we find 68% of the population, just more than two-thirds: this accounts for all the people that fall within one standard deviation of the mean. More than two thirds of the population is located at a distance from the mean of one standard deviation or less.

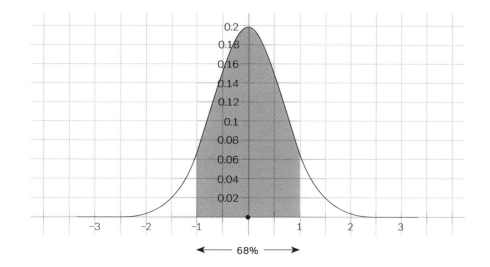

If we go two standard deviations from the mean in either direction, from $x = -2$ to $x = 2$, that always includes 95% of the population. In other words, 95% percent of the population is located at a distance from the mean of two standard deviations or less.

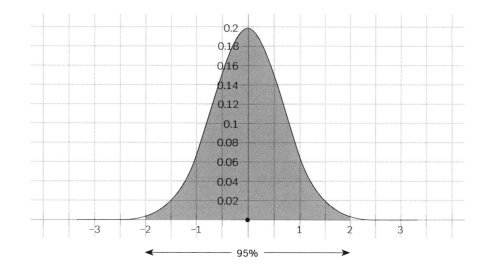

Only 5% of the population is more than two standard deviations from the mean, and that's symmetrically divided between a 2.5% "tail" on the left and a 2.5% "tail" on the right. Folks who are in the upper tail are in the top 2.5% of the population. For example, these would be the folks who score a 168 or more out of the 170 on the GRE math.

If we go out to three standard deviations from the mean in either direction, from $x = -3$ to $x = 3$, that includes 99.7% of the population, with only 0.15% (i.e., 15 people out of 10000) falling in each tail beyond this. The data points that lie more than three standard deviations above the mean are the true outliers.

If you simply remember these two numbers, then you'll have the ability to figure out any GRE math question that addresses the normal distribution:

- **68%** within one standard deviation of the mean (which means 34% on each side)
- **95%** within two standard deviations of the mean

Here's a practice question:

In the country of Dilandia, adult female height follows a normal
distribution, with a mean of 170 cm and a standard deviation of 12 cm.
What percent of the adult females in Dilandia are taller than 182 cm?

(A) 6%
(B) 16%
(C) 25%
(D) 34%
(E) 44%

A height of 182 cm is one standard deviation (12 cm) above the mean (170 cm). The
mean is the median, so 50% of the population is below the mean, shorter than 170 cm.
We learned in the discussion above that between the mean and one standard deviation
above the mean, heights between 170 cm and 182 cm, we'll find 34% of the population.
Adding these, we find that 34 + 50, which = 84% of the heights, will be below 182 cm. If
84% are below 182 cm, then the other 16% must be above 182 cm. Thus, 16% of the adult
women in Dilandia are taller than 182 cm. Answer = **(B)**.

**How do we know whether the 34% region is "less than" or "less than or
equal to"? In other words, how do we know whether to include the height
of exactly 182 cm?** Most of the variables that follow normal distributions are
real-world continuous variables, such as human height. Typically, people report
their height in an integer number of inches or centimeters, but if we were to take
hyperaccurate scientific measurements, every real person would have some decimal
height (e.g., 176.48251 … cm). No one ever would have an exact height of 182 cm, a
height that equaled 182.000000 cm, with an infinite number of decimals of precision.
Such precision is a mathematical fiction that simply doesn't exist in the real world
of measurement. Thus, in most normal distribution problems, we don't worry about
the endpoints of regions: in practical terms, it doesn't matter at all whether we're
discussing heights that are "greater than 182 cm" or "greater than or equal to 182 cm."
Again, as regards real-world measurements, this is a fictional mathematical distinction
that's absolutely meaningless where the rubber meets the road.

Data Interpretation Practice Questions

These questions should help you get an idea of what to expect from the data interpretation questions on the GRE. There are even more practice questions in the GRE practice test at the end of this book.

Question 1

Difficulty: **Easy** · Percent Correct: **86.3%** · Type: **Numeric Entry**

The graph below shows the body mass index (BMI) and basal metabolic rate (BMR) of fifteen males between the ages of 43 and 65.

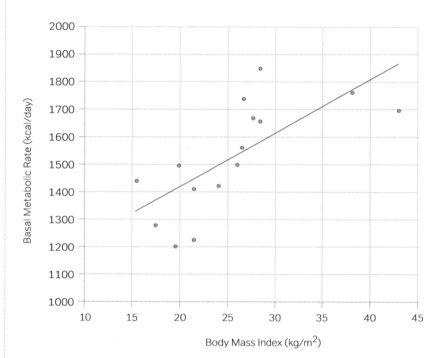

Category	BMI Range (kg/m^2)
Severely underweight	less than 16.0
Underweight	from 10.0 to 18.5
Normal	from 18.5 to 25
Overweight	from 25 to 30
Obese	over 30

The trendline on the graph indicates, for a given BMI, what the expected BMR would be for that individual. In this group, how many individuals have a BMR higher than predicted by this trendline?

The following pie chart shows the breakdown of revenues for a particular grocery store over the first quarter of this year. The bar chart shows the detail of breakdown for frozen foods. Use these graphs to answer the next three questions.

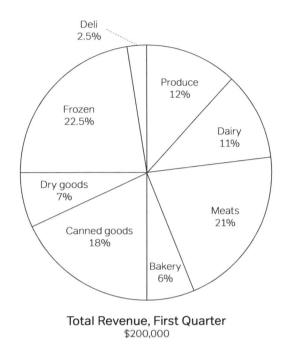

Total Revenue, First Quarter
$200,000

Sales of Frozen Foods, First Quarter This Year

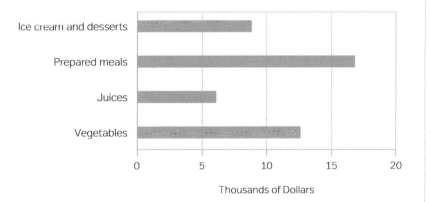

Thousands of Dollars

Question 2

Difficulty: **Easy**   ·   Percent Correct: **88.9%**   ·   Type: **Multiple Choice**

What is the dollar amount of sales of canned goods in the first quarter of this year?

Ⓐ $6,000

Ⓑ $9,000

Ⓒ $18,000

Ⓓ $36,000

Ⓔ $90,000

Question 3

Difficulty: **Easy**   ·   Percent Correct: **59.6%**   ·   Type: **Multiple Choice**

Frozen prepared meals constitute what percentage of the total sales for the first quarter this year?

(A) 2.4%

(B) 8.5%

(C) 20%

(D) 36%

(E) 54%

Question 4

Difficulty: **Hard**   ·   Percent Correct: **57.5%**   ·   Type: **Multiple Choice**

During the first quarter this year, this particular grocery store was finishing its construction of an expanded bakery facility, which, when opened at the beginning the second quarter, will offer dozens of new cakes and pies, a whole new line of pastries, and several flavors of gourmet coffee. Assume that in the second quarter, the bakery sales triple, and all other sales stay the same. The bakery would then account for what percentage of total sales in the second quarter?

(A) 8.7%

(B) 12%

(C) 16.1%

(D) 18%

(E) 25.3%

When you're ready, turn the page to see the answers.

Data Interpretation Answers and Explanations

Question 1

Difficulty: **Easy** · Percent Correct: **86.3%** · Type: **Numeric Entry**

Answer: **7**

The reason human beings use graphs is because we can get so much information "at a glance." The trendline indicates, for a given BMI, what the expected BMR would be for that individual. If the person's dot landed exactly on the line, that person would have exactly what this model predicts for his BMR. By contrast, if his BMR is higher than predicted, then at that BMI position, he would be further up on the BMR scale—his dot would be above the line. Thus, all the people whose BMRs are higher than predicted are represented by dots above the line. All you have to do is count the number of dots above the line. There are seven dots above the line, so the answer is **7**.

With data interpretation graphs, don't be afraid of the easy answer. The whole point of graphs is to make information visual and easy to see!

Question 2

Difficulty: **Easy** · Percent Correct: **88.9%** · Type: **Multiple Choice**

Answer: **D**

What is the dollar amount of sales of canned goods in the first quarter of this year?

(A) $6,000
(B) $9,000
(C) $18,000
D $36,000
(E) $90,000

This is a straightforward read-data-off-the-chart question. The pie chart tells us canned goods sales constitute 18% of $200,000. Don't go to the calculator for such a straightforward percent question!

$$0.018 \times 200,000 = \frac{18}{100} \times 200,000 = 18 \times 2,000 = \mathbf{\$36,000}$$

Question 3

Difficulty: **Easy** · Percent Correct: **59.6%** · Type: **Multiple Choice**

Answer: **B**

Frozen prepared meals constitute what percentage of the total sales for the first quarter this year?

(A) 2.4%
B 8.5%
(C) 20%
(D) 36%
(E) 54%

From the bar chart, prepared meals account for about $17,000 in sales. This $17,000 is what percent of $200,000? Again, please don't jump to the calculator for this.

$$percent = \frac{part}{whole} \times 100\% = \frac{17,000}{200,000} \times 100\% = \frac{17}{200} \times 100\% = \frac{17}{2}\% = \mathbf{8.5\%}$$

Question 4

Difficulty: **Hard** · Percent Correct: **57.5%** · Type: **Multiple Choice**

During the first quarter this year, this particular grocery store was finishing its construction of an expanded bakery facility, which, when opened at the beginning the second quarter, will offer dozens of new cakes and pies, a whole new line of pastries, and several flavors of gourmet coffee. Assume that in the second quarter, the bakery sales triple, and all other sales stay the same. The bakery would then account for what percentage of total sales in the second quarter?

Answer: **C**

(A) 8.7%

(B) 12%

C 16.1%

(D) 18%

(E) 25.3%

This is a tricky question because there's a tempting wrong answer. The bakery accounts for 6% of the total sales in first quarter, so if you triple that, it's 18%, right? Not quite! The new amount would be 18% of the total sales in the first quarter, but we want to know what percent it would be of the total sales in the second quarter. That's a new total because, even though everything else stayed the same, bakery sales increased.

We don't need to consider the actual numbers; we can just work with the percents. Bakery sales triple from 6% to 18%—that's the new "part." Since the bakery goes up 12% from 6% to 18%, and all other sales stay the same, the new total is 112%—that's the new "whole."

$$percent = \frac{part}{whole} \times 100\% = \frac{18}{112} \times 100\% = 16.0714\%$$

You can use the calculator if you like, although you could also approximate that the answer won't be 18% but rather something a little below 18%, because the "whole" has increased a bit.

You can find even more data interpretation questions on gre.magoosh.com!

189

Quantitative Concept #9: Quantitative Comparison Strategies

Recall that there are four types of question formats in the GRE Quantitative section:

1. multiple choice
2. multiple answer
3. numeric entry
4. quantitative comparison

You have probably seen multiple choice on every standardized test in your life since well before even your teenage years, so those aren't new. The numeric entry questions are a great deal like the "just do the math" questions of an ordinary math classroom (i.e., you're presented with the problem and, without prompting, are supposed to calculate the answer). Those aren't new either. Some traditional math classroom problems have more than one answer, which gets into multiple-answer territory.

The question format that's probably newest and most unusual to you is the quantitative comparisons format. Unlike the other three formats, the quantitative comparison format has its own logic and demands a great deal of strategy unique to it. That's precisely why we have a whole section about this format alone.

The Lowdown on GRE Quantitative Comparisons

The basics of this format were presented starting on page 37. It's important to remember that these questions *always* have the same four answer choices beneath the two columns:

(A) The quantity in Column A is greater
(B) The quantity in Column B is greater
(C) The two quantities are equal
(D) The relationship cannot be determined from the information given

You should commit these four to memory, because—again—they're *always* the choices for a quantitative comparison question.

Essentially, the quantitative comparison questions are a kind of inequality question where the job is to determine which mathematical relationship exists between two quantities.

(A) always >
(B) always <
(C) always =
(D) not always anything in particular

It's important to recognize the implicit "always" in choices (A), (B), and (C): those answers are correct only if they express a relationship that's *always* the case, for all the possible values of the variables given. It's also important to appreciate that choice

(D), "The relationship cannot be determined from the information given," means that the information given leaves enough wiggle room that we could pick different possibilities that would produce different relationships. For example, one choice of a value makes column B greater, and a different choice for the same value makes the two columns equal.

Big idea: as soon as it becomes apparent that different possible choices lead to different relationships, it becomes unquestionably clear that (D) absolutely must be the answer.

Here's a sample question that's on the easy side for the GRE:

Point P is a point on the line $y = 3x - 7$.

Column A	Column B
The x-coordinate of point P	The y-coordinate of point P

- (A) The quantity in Column A is greater
- (B) The quantity in Column B is greater
- (C) The two quantities are equal
- (D) The relationship cannot be determined from the information given*

Note: This is the last time we'll list the answer choices for the practice problems in this chapter. On the following problems, you can assume your answer options are exactly the same. Memorize these answer choices, (A) to (D), and you'll be able to get through quantitative comparison questions that much faster on test day.

Point P could be any point on the line. If we pick, say, the y-intercept, (0, –7), then 0 > –7, meaning column A is greater. This is steeply rising line, so we'll sidle to the right a bit, in an attempt to make the y's bigger. Let $x = 10$: this gives us the point (10, 23). Now, 10 < 23, so column B is greater. In this scenario, two choices produce two different relationships, so the answer must be **(D)**.

For algebraic variables, "trying different choices" simply means plugging in different numbers for the variables given. For geometric figures, "trying different choices" means testing all possible shapes and configurations within the parameters given: often this demands subtle visual thinking and a creative geometric imagination. Here is a geometric quantitative comparison that's on the easy side for the GRE:

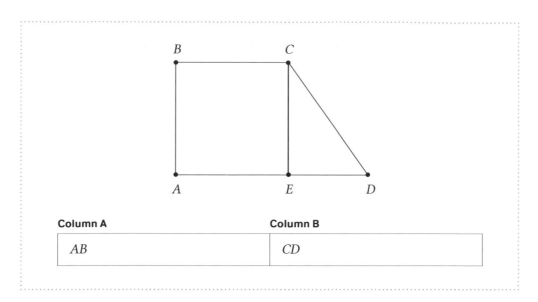

Column A	Column B
AB	*CD*

Before we answer, ask, "What do we *know* is true?" *ABCE* looks like a square; can we assume it's a square? Nope! The angle *CED* looks like a right angle; can we assume that it's a right angle? Nope! Can we assume that any of the sides of quadrilateral *ABCE* are equal? Nope! Can we assume that *CD* is the longest side in triangle *CED*? Nope! The absolutely only thing that we can assume from the diagram is that *A-E-D* is a straight line; in other words, there's no "bend" at point *E*. Straightness is something we can assume from a GRE diagram, but nothing else.

Having said all that, we see in the above configuration, *AB* < *CD*, so this is a case that makes column B greater. Now, let's rearrange, trying to make *CD* small:

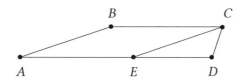

In this arrangement, *AB* > *CD*. We have tried two different geometric arrangements that resulted in two different relationships. Right away, we know that **(D)** must be the answer.

Finding a Relationship

No, we're not pausing our discussion of GRE math to give you romantic advice! Instead, we're talking about the heart of the GRE quantitative comparison problem: finding what kind of mathematical relationship exists between two quantities. This relationship may be an inequality (<, >) or it may be the relationship of equality.

Suppose you have an equation. You probably remember that you can add, subtract, multiply, or divide one side of an equation by just about anything, as long as you remember to do the same operation to the other side. The only restriction is that it's illegal to divide by 0; all other adding, subtracting, multiplying and dividing is perfectly legal.

Suppose you have an inequality. We already discussed inequalities in depth in the algebra section starting on page 76, so we'll just remind you of the highlights here. Suppose our inequality is $11 > -3$, a perfectly true inequality. Adding the same number to both sides or subtracting the same number from both sides is still perfectly legal. If we add 5 to both sides, we get

$$11 + 5 > -3 + 5$$
$$16 > 2$$

This is still true. If we subtract 7 from both sides, we get

$$11 - 7 > -3 - 7$$
$$4 > -10$$

Again, this is still true. Adding or subtracting any number on both sides leaves the inequality unchanged, so we could add or subtract whatever we wanted to each column in a quantitative comparison question and the unknown relationship would remain unchanged.

Recall that multiplication and division are a little trickier. If we multiply or divide our inequality by a positive number, everything is fine. If we still start with $11 > -3$ and multiply by $+3$, we get

$$3 \times 11 > 3 \times (-3)$$
$$33 > -9$$

This is still true. Multiplying or dividing by a positive number leaves the inequality unchanged, so we could multiply or divide each column in a quantitative comparison question by a positive number, and the unknown relationship would remain unchanged.

Obviously, we can't divide by 0. And if we multiply both sides of an inequality by 0, it becomes an equation with 0 on both sides. For example, if we started with the valid inequality $5 > 1$ and multiplied both sides by 0, we would end up with $0 = 0$, which isn't particularly useful. Multiplying both sides of an inequality by 0 is forbidden, and multiplying both sides by a negative is also problematic. As you may remember from the inequality section (page 76), multiplying or dividing by a negative changes the direction of the inequality. **For the quantitative comparison, all we have to know is that multiplying or dividing by anything other than a positive is forbidden, because it would change the unknown relation.**

Thus, the legitimate arithmetic operations that we can perform on both columns in a quantitative comparison question and not change the fundamental relationship between the columns are as follows:

- add any number on the number line to both columns
- subtract any number on the number line from both columns
- multiply both columns by any positive number
- divide both columns by any positive number

For example, consider this quantitative comparison question:

Column A	Column B
$\dfrac{65}{7}$	$\dfrac{28}{3}$

Notice that we could change those improper fractions to mixed numerals that would be close in value.

Column A	Column B
$9\dfrac{2}{7}$	$9\dfrac{1}{3}$

Now, we can subtract 9 from both sides.

Column A	Column B
$\dfrac{2}{7}$	$\dfrac{1}{3}$

Here, we get two much smaller fractions than those at the beginning. At this point, it's very easy to cross-multiply. Are we allowed to cross-multiply? Think about it. Cross-multiplying simply means multiplying both columns by both denominators, 7 and 3 here. Since all the numbers are positive, all multiplication is fine. Therefore, cross-multiplication is fine. After cross-multiplying, we get

Column A	Column B
6	7

Clearly, **(B)** is the answer. By using legitimate arithmetic steps, we were able to boil this down to the simplest of numerical comparisons.

What if variables are involved? Any variable contains a value that's somewhere on the number line, so we can add or subtract a variable because we can add or subtract any number.

With this in mind, consider this algebraic quantitative comparison:

$x > 0$

Column A	Column B
$x - 2$	$2x$

Well, we can add or subtract anything, so let's subtract x from both columns. It doesn't matter whether x is a positive or negative number: subtraction is always legitimate. This leaves us with:

Column A	Column B
−2	x

Now, we have to pay attention to the condition stipulated above the columns. We were told that $x > 0$, so x is some positive number. Remember: **any positive number is always greater than any negative number**. Thus, column B is always bigger, and the answer is **(B)**.

Here's another quantitative comparison along those lines:

$x < 1$

Column A	Column B
$2x + 7$	$5x + 1$

First, subtract $2x$ from both columns, to get all the x's in one place. Once again, adding or subtracting a variable is 100 percent legitimate.

Column A	Column B
7	$3x + 1$

Now, subtract 1 from both columns.

Column A	Column B
6	$3x$

Now, divide both columns by 3. Again, it's absolutely fine to divide both columns by a *positive* number.

Column A	Column B
2	x

Once again, we have to pay attention to the condition stipulated above the columns. Well, x is less than 1, and 1 is less than 2, so x is less than 2. Column A is always bigger, and the answer is **(A)**.

A little bit of algebraic simplification can make some unpleasant-looking algebra reduce to something quite manageable!

Notice that adding or subtracting a variable is fine, but you might wonder about multiplying or dividing by a variable. In general, multiplying or dividing by a variable in a quantitative comparison is a bad idea. When it seems that you might have to do that, chances are that some strategy other than algebraic simplification would be appropriate—for example, it might be appropriate to pick numbers!

Picking Numbers in Quantitative Comparisons

In algebraic quantitative comparisons, one or both of the column values are in variable form. What we discussed in the previous section could be called an algebraic solution—always a possible approach, but that's not the only option. We could also pick numbers.

Let's think about the logic. Suppose a quantitative comparison problem has a variable x. Suppose we plug in $x = 1$, and column B is bigger. Then, we plug in $x = 2$, and column B is still bigger. Then, we plug in $x = 3$, and column B is still bigger. What can we conclude?

Well, unfortunately, a few guesses that point in one direction do *not* guarantee that the same pattern extends all the way up to infinity. We haven't proven anything. Some other choice for *x* down the line might change the relationship. Either the relationship stays the way it is always (answer B) or the relationship changes for some as yet untested values (answer D). In other words, we have eliminated (A) and (C)! If all else fails, at this point, we would be able to guess between (B) and (D), and our odds of getting it correct are much improved if we can eliminate two answers.

By contrast, let's think about this situation: Suppose a quantitative comparison problem has a variable *y*. Suppose we plug in $y = 5$, and column A is bigger. Then, we plug in $y = 6$, and the two columns are equal. *Bam!* As soon as two different values produce two different relationships, we instantly know that no single relationship is true. Thus, **(D)** has to be the answer!

This is the **big idea**: When we pick numbers in a quantitative comparison, the only answer we can "prove" correct is (D). We prove (D) correct if two different values produce two different relationships. If the answer isn't (D), then picking numbers will always give us the same letter answer, but this result only eliminates a couple answers. It doesn't uniquely determine an answer. If we want to verify the answer, we would have to use algebra or logic or some other mathematical thinking. If the answer to the question isn't (D), then picking numbers alone won't finish the job.

Picking numbers *well* is an art. This art depends to a great extent on number sense, already discussed starting on page 56. In some cases, it's important to consider different categories of numbers (positive, negative, zero; integers, fractions, decimals). If numbers of one category give one relationship, then it may be worthwhile to try numbers of another category.

Consider the following quantitative comparison problem:

$y < 1,\ y \neq 0$

Column A	Column B
y	y^2

This quantitative comparison has no words at all, only variables. Furthermore, it isn't clear that any algebraic manipulation of the variables will shed light on the answer. This is an example of a problem in which we have to **pick numbers**.

Here, we can start with a positive fraction, say, $y = \frac{1}{3}$. When we square this, we get $y^2 = \frac{1}{9}$, which is smaller. This first choice indicates (A).

Can we make another choice that changes the relationship? If we can get a different relationship, then we can prove the answer is (D).

That was a positive fraction. Now try a negative integer, say $y = -2$. Then $y^2 = 4$, which is bigger. The second choice indicates (B). So here is a case in which two different values of y produce two different relationships between the columns. As soon as we get two different possible relationships, we know the answer must be **(D)**.

Here's another quantitative comparison:

$10 < p < q$

Column A	Column B
p	$q - 10$

For this problem, you can't pick zero, negative numbers, or fractions between 0 and 1, because both variables are greater than 10. On the left, we have a variable by itself, whereas on the right we have a difference. Let's first look at that difference, because a difference is something we could make either big or small.

If we pick, say, $q = 13$, then the right column has a value of 3. If $p = 11$, then column A is bigger. These choices ($p = 11$, $q = 13$) lead to the answer (A).

Can we make another choice that changes the relationship? If we can get a different relationship, then we can prove the answer is (D).

Well, in our first choices, the difference was relatively small, a single digit number. Suppose we make q much bigger—say, $q = 80$. Then $q - 10 = 70$, which is a much larger difference. That's the value of the right column. If the left column is still $p = 11$, then column B is much larger. This leads to the answer (B).

Once again, two different choices for the variables led to two different relationships. Since more than one relationship is possible, we know that the answer must be **(D)**.

Here's one last quantitative comparison, slightly more challenging:

N is an integer such that *N* > 1.

Column A	Column B
$(N + 1)^2 - 1$	N^2

Let's try the relatively simple choice of $N = 2$. In the left column, we get $3^2 - 1 = 9 - 1 = 8$. In the right column, we get $2^2 = 4$. This choice makes (A) bigger.

Let's try the next value, $N = 3$. In the left column, we get $4^2 - 1 = 16 - 1 = 15$. In the right column, we get $3^2 = 9$. This choice also makes (A) bigger. Hmm.

Can we make another choice that changes the relationship? If we can get a different relationship, then we can prove the answer is (D). Unfortunately, only positive integer choices are possible, and it's not clear that any particular choice of a positive integer would be a "game changer" in terms of changing this relationship. There's an infinite number of choices, and none of them look particularly promising. Our prospects for finding a solution by picking numbers don't look good at this point.

We have gotten (A) as a possible answer twice. Once again, this doesn't prove that (A) is the answer. If we were running short on time, notice that because we have eliminated (B) and (C) as possible answers, we could take a guess. The answer is either (A) or (D). Since two answers have been eliminated, our odds of guessing correctly are much improved.

Suppose, though, we have a little more time to think about this. To get a definitive answer, we would have to use algebra. Remember "The Square of a Sum" formula (pattern #2 on page 70):

$$(N + 1)^2 = N^2 + 2N + 1$$

We can substitute this expression into the left column and simplify the left column:

Column A	Column B
$(N^2 + 2N + 1) - 1$	N^2
$N^2 + 2N$	N^2

Now, since N^2 appears in both columns, we can subtract it from both columns.

Column A	Column B
$2N$	0

Finally, recall the condition specified above the columns: N is an integer such that $N > 1$. If N is greater than 1, then $2N$ will be greater than 2, and thus $2N$ will always be greater than zero. With a little algebra, we see that the answer has to be **(A)**.

Summary

We can use picking numbers on quantitative comparisons to establish definitively that (D) is the answer—when two different values produce two different relationships, then *bam!* we know (D) must be the answer.

If the answer to the question is something other than (D), picking numbers will do no more than suggest a pattern. We would have to use algebra or logic to determine the answer. Picking numbers wouldn't take us all the way in these cases. Consider this problem:

In the following, n is a positive integer.

Column A	Column B
$\dfrac{1}{n} - \dfrac{1}{n+1}$	$\dfrac{1}{100n}$

The easiest positive integer to try is $n = 1$. Then, in the left column, we get $1 - \frac{1}{2} = \frac{1}{2}$, and on the right, we get $\frac{1}{100}$. Well, $\frac{1}{2}$ is clearly bigger than $\frac{1}{100}$, so in this instance, column A is bigger. Right away, we know the answer could only be (A) or (D).

We could plug in a few more numbers {2, 3, 4, ...} but it's helpful to see this probably won't change anything. On the left, we're going to wind up with fractions with relatively small denominators, and the denominator on the right will be in the hundreds, so at least for these choices, it probably will result in the same relationship. We have to try something else. Notice that we can do a little algebraic simplification in the left column.

Column A	Column B
$\dfrac{1}{n} - \dfrac{1}{n+1}$	$\dfrac{1}{100n}$
$\dfrac{1}{n}\left(\dfrac{n+1}{n+1}\right) - \dfrac{1}{n+1}\left(\dfrac{n}{n}\right)$	$\dfrac{1}{100n}$
$\dfrac{n+1}{n(n+1)} - \dfrac{n}{n(n+1)}$	
$\dfrac{1}{n(n+1)}$	

Now that we have used a little algebraic simplification, we'll also use a little number sense. The number 100 is a "big" number. Smaller values of n are not going to make the denominator on the left as big as the denominator on the right. Instead, let's pick a very big number, much bigger than 100—say, $n = 1000$. Then we get the following:

Column A	Column B
$\dfrac{1}{1{,}000(1{,}001)}$	$\dfrac{1}{100(1{,}000)}$

We don't need an exact calculation. The denominator on the right is less than 1,000,000, and the denominator on the left is greater than 1,000,000. The fraction on the right has a smaller denominator, so it has a larger value. Here, we have reversed the relationship. *Bam!* Once again, two different choices for the variables led to two different relationships. Since more than one relationship is possible, we know that the answer must be **(D)**.

Once again, picking numbers well is an art. Just mechanically trying {1, 2, 3, 4, ...} in order is usually not the best approach. Instead, it's helpful to see whether anything can be simplified, as we simplified the left column here. Also, it's helpful to use number sense to see the effect of changing variables' values—whether changes bring the columns closer together or drive them further apart. Picking numbers is most successful when combined with other types of mathematical thinking. That's truly what makes picking numbers an art.

Quantitative Comparison Practice Questions

These questions should help you get an idea of what to expect from the quantitative comparison questions on the GRE. There are even more practice questions in the GRE practice test at the end of this book.

Question 1

Difficulty: **Easy** · Percent Correct: **80.1%** · Type: Quantitative Comparison

In a group of 60 people, the average (arithmetic mean) age of the 40 females is 60, and the average age of the 20 males is 70.

Column A	Column B
Average age of all 60 people	65

- (A) The quantity in Column A is greater
- (B) The quantity in Column B is greater
- (C) The two quantities are equal
- (D) The relationship cannot be determined from the information given

Question 2

Difficulty: **Medium** · Percent Correct: **71.5%** · Type: Quantitative Comparison

x and y are positive.
30 percent of x is y.

Column A	Column B
$\frac{x}{y}$	3

- (A) The quantity in Column A is greater
- (B) The quantity in Column B is greater
- (C) The two quantities are equal
- (D) The relationship cannot be determined from the information given

Question 3

Difficulty: **Medium** · Percent Correct: **68%** · Type: Quantitative Comparison

$2^n + 2^n + 2^n + 2^n = 4^{n+3}$

Column A	Column B
n	4

- (A) The quantity in Column A is greater
- (B) The quantity in Column B is greater
- (C) The two quantities are equal
- (D) The relationship cannot be determined from the information given

Question 4

Difficulty: **Hard** · Percent Correct: **62.3%** · Type: **Quantitative Comparison**

For a certain event, 148 people attended. If all 148 had paid full admission price, the total revenue would be three times the cost of sponsoring the event. (Admission price was the only source of revenue.) As it happens, only 50 paid the full admission price, and the others paid nothing.

Column A	Column B
the total revenue	the cost of sponsoring the event

(A) The quantity in Column A is greater

(B) The quantity in Column B is greater

(C) The two quantities are equal

(D) The relationship cannot be determined from the information given

Question 5

Difficulty: **Hard** · Percent Correct: **57.2%** · Type: **Quantitative Comparison**

For numbers p, q, and r, $(p \times q \times r) < 0$ and $\frac{(p \times q)^2}{r} < 0$

Column A	Column B
$p \times q$	0

(A) The quantity in Column A is greater

(B) The quantity in Column B is greater

(C) The two quantities are equal

(D) The relationship cannot be determined from the information given

Question 6

Difficulty: **Very Hard** · Percent Correct: **49.1%** · Type: **Quantitative Comparison**

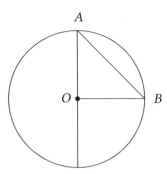

O is the center of the circle.

Column A	Column B
Length of AO	Length of AB

- Ⓐ The quantity in Column A is greater
- Ⓑ The quantity in Column B is greater
- Ⓒ The two quantities are equal
- Ⓓ The relationship cannot be determined from the information given

Quantitative Comparison Answers and Explanations

Question 1

Difficulty: **Easy** · Percent Correct: 80.1% · Type: Quantitative Comparison

Answer: Ⓑ

In a group of 60 people, the average (arithmetic mean) age of the 40 females is 60, and the average age of the 20 males is 70.

Column A	Column B
Average age of all 60 people	65

Ⓐ The quantity in Column A is greater
Ⓑ The quantity in Column B is greater
Ⓒ The two quantities are equal
Ⓓ The relationship cannot be determined from the information given

This is an example of a GRE quantitative comparison question in which we could calculate the answer, but it's much easier just to reason through it without calculation. For quantitative comparison questions, always warm up your imagination and ask yourself, "Could I answer this without doing a full calculation?"

Notice that the two average ages of the groups are 60 and 70, and the value in column B is the average of these two, 65.

Now, pretend instead of this group, we had

30 females, average age = 60
30 males, average age = 70

Well, if the two groups were of equal size, we could just average those two values—the mean age would be 65.

Imagine that 30-30 group is our starting group, and it has an average of 65. Then, we tell ten 70-year-old men to leave the room, and, to take their place, we invite in ten 60-year-old women. If 70-year-olds leave and are replaced by 60-year-olds, what happens to the average age? Of course, if you replace older people with younger people, the average age goes down. At this point, we would have the scenario discussed in the question:

40 females, average age = 60
20 males, average age = 70

And as we just said, the average of this has gone down from its previous value, so this average is less than 65.

The answer is **(B)**.

Question 2

Difficulty: **Medium** · Percent Correct: 71.5% · Type: Quantitative Comparison

x and y are positive.

30 percent of x is y.

Answer: Ⓐ

Column A	Column B
$\dfrac{x}{y}$	3
30 percent of x is y $\dfrac{30}{100}x = y$ $\dfrac{30x}{100} = y$ $30x = 100y$ $x = \dfrac{100y}{30}$ $\dfrac{x}{y} = \dfrac{100}{30} = \dfrac{10}{3} = 3\dfrac{1}{3}$	3

Ⓐ The quantity in Column A is greater

Ⓑ The quantity in Column B is greater

Ⓒ The two quantities are equal

Ⓓ The relationship cannot be determined from the information given

Question 3

Difficulty: **Medium** · Percent Correct: 68% · Type: Quantitative Comparison

$2^n + 2^n + 2^n + 2^n = 4^{n+3}$

Answer: Ⓑ

Column A	Column B
n	4
$2^n + 2^n + 2^n + 2^n = 4^{n+3}$ $4 \times 2^n = 4^{n+3}$ $2^2 \times 2^n = (2^2)^{n+3}$ $2^{n+2} = 2^{2n+6}$ $n + 2 = 2n + 6$ $2 = n + 6$ $-4 = n$	**4**

Ⓐ The quantity in Column A is greater

Ⓑ The quantity in Column B is greater

Ⓒ The two quantities are equal

Ⓓ The relationship cannot be determined from the information given

Question 4

Difficulty: **Hard** · Percent Correct: **62.3%** · Type: **Quantitative Comparison**

For a certain event, 148 people attended. If all 148 had paid full admission price, the total revenue would be three times the cost of sponsoring the event. (Admission price was the only source of revenue.) As it happens, only 50 paid the full admission price, and the others paid nothing.

Column A	Column B
the total revenue	the cost of sponsoring the event

Ⓐ The quantity in Column A is greater

Ⓑ The quantity in Column B is greater

Ⓒ The two quantities are equal

Ⓓ The relationship cannot be determined from the information given

This is a great estimation problem. Let's say that P = the full price of one ticket. If all 148 people had paid full price, the total revenue would have been $148 \times P$, and the revenue would have been three times the cost. Let C = the total cost. Then we have:

$$148 \times P = 3 \times C \ \Rightarrow \ C = \frac{148}{3}P$$

That's the value of column B. Meanwhile, the only revenue they actually took in was from the sale of 50 tickets, $50 \times P$. That's the total revenue, the entry in column A. The question really is "How does $50 \times P$ compare to $\frac{148}{3} \times P$?" Well, you may be tempted to reach for your calculator, but notice that $50 = \frac{150}{3}$, and $\frac{150}{3}$ is clearly greater than $\frac{148}{3}$, so column A must be greater.

Question 5

Difficulty: **Hard** · Percent Correct: **57.2%** · Type: **Quantitative Comparison**

For numbers p, q, and r, $(p \times q \times r) < 0$ and $\frac{(p \times q)^2}{r} < 0$

Column A	Column B
$p \times q$	0

Ⓐ The quantity in Column A is greater

Ⓑ The quantity in Column B is greater

Ⓒ The two quantities are equal

Ⓓ The relationship cannot be determined from the information given

First consider this inequality:

$$\frac{(p \times q)^2}{r} < 0$$

We know that the numerator, $(p \times q)^2$, must be positive because squaring any non-zero number makes it positive. Any values of p and q will always give us a positive value of $(p \times q)^2$.

If the numerator is positive, but the whole fraction $\frac{(p \times q)^2}{r}$ is negative, then we know r is negative. In other words, if r were positive, then the whole fraction would be positive. But the equation tells us that it's really *less* than 0. For that to be true, r must be negative, that is, $r < 0$.

Now, look at the first inequality given, which we're going to rewrite a little:

$(p \times q \times r) < 0$
$(p \times q) \times r < 0$

We used the **associative law** to regroup the factors. Well, we know r is negative, so we know that $(p \times q)$ is positive.

$(p \times q) \times r < 0$
$(p \times q) \times (\text{negative}) < 0$
$(p \times q) \times (\text{negative}) = (\text{negative})$
$(\text{positive}) \times (\text{negative}) = (\text{negative})$
$(p \times q) = (\text{positive})$

If $(p \times q)$ were also negative, the product of $(p \times q)$ and r would be positive.

$(\text{negative}) \times (\text{negative}) = (\text{positive})$

Since $(p \times q \times r) < 0$, we want a negative product. That must mean $(p \times q)$ is positive, that is, $(p \times q) > 0$. Therefore, column A is greater than column B. The answer is **(A)**.

Question 6

Difficulty: **Very Hard** · Percent Correct: **49.1%** · Type: Quantitative Comparison

Answer: **D**

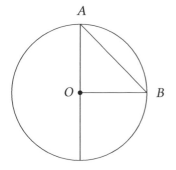

O is the center of the circle.

Column A	Column B
Length of AO	Length of AB

(A) The quantity in Column A is greater

(B) The quantity in Column B is greater

(C) The two quantities are equal

(D) The relationship cannot be determined from the information given

In this problem, exactly what do we know and exactly what don't we know? We know this is circle, and we know that *OA = OB* because they're radii of the same circle. We do *not* know that angle *AOB* is a right angle: in fact, we have no idea what that angle might be. There are three possibilities.

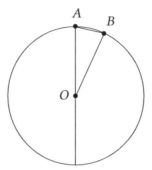

If *AOB* is a relatively small angle, less than 60°, then *AB* will be smaller than *AO*.

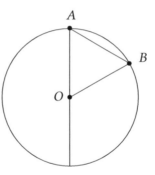

If angle *AOB* = 60°, then triangle *ABO* is equilateral, and *AO = AB*.

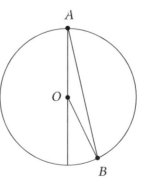

If angle *AOB* is larger, especially more than 90°, then *AB* would be very large, much larger than *AO*.

Because we have no idea about the size of angle *AOB*, we can draw no conclusion about how *AO* compares to *AB*. Thus, the answer is **(D)**.

GRE Quantitative
Reasoning

208

You can find even more quantitative comparison questions on gre.magoosh.com!

Math Fact and Formula Cheat Sheet

Cut out this page and use it to help you solve problems in practice sessions early in your studies. But don't get too attached to it. Remember, the best way to develop your math muscles is by understanding why these rules work rather than memorizing them.

Number properties

The word *number* includes everything on the number line (positive, negative, zero; integer, decimal, fraction).

0 is the only number that's neither positive nor negative.

1 is not a prime number, and 2 is the lowest and the only even prime number.

"Integers" include positive and negative whole numbers: $\{... -3, -2, -1, 0, 1, 2, 3, ...\}$

(even) + (even) = (even)
(even) + (odd) = (odd)
(odd) + (odd) = (even)
(even) × (even) = (even)
(even) × (odd) – (even)
(odd) × (odd) = (odd)

Divisibility rules

2: If N is divisible by 2, then N is even.
3: If N is divisible by 3, then the sum of the digits of N is divisible by 3.
4: The last two digits are divisible by 4.
5: The last digit is 5 or 0.
6: N is divisible by 6 if it's an even number divisible by 3.
9: The sum of digits is divisible by 9.
12: N is divisible by 12 if it's divisible by both 3 and 4.
15: N is divisible by 15 if it's divisible by both 3 and 5.

Algebra

Any positive number is greater than any negative number.

Square of a sum

$(A + B)^2 = A^2 + 2AB + B^2$

Square of a difference

$(A - B)^2 = A^2 - 2AB + B^2$

Difference of two squares

$A^2 - B^2 = (A + B)(A - B)$

Word problems

Distance, rate, time

$d = rt$

Work amount, work rate, time

$a = rt$
Remember: we can't add or subtract times!
We have to add or subtract work rates.

Geometry

Triangles

sum of angles = 180°
largest angle opposite largest side
smallest angle opposite smallest side
sum of any two sides > third side
$A = \frac{1}{2}bh$

Right triangles

$a^2 + b^2 = c^2$
c must be the hypotenuse!

Special right triangles

30-60-90 triangle

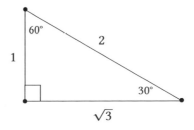

45-45-90 triangle (The Right Isosceles Triangle)

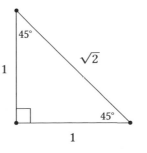

Either of these triangles could be multiplied by any number; the ratios stay the same.

Quadrilaterals

Sum of angles = 360°

For parallelogram, rhombus, and rectangle,

$A = bh$

For square, $A = s^2$

General polygons

Sum of angles = $(n - 2) \times 180°$, where n is the number of sides.

Coordinate Geometry

slope: $m = \frac{rise}{run}$

$y = mx + b$

To find the y-intercept, set $x = 0$.

To find the x-intercept, set $y = 0$.

Every point that satisfies the equation of the line is on the line.

Circles

$\pi \approx 3.14 \approx \frac{22}{7}$

$c = 2\pi r$

$A = \pi r^2$

$\frac{arc\,length}{2\pi r} = \frac{central\,angle}{360°}$

$\frac{area\,of\,sector}{\pi r^2} = \frac{central\,angle}{360°}$

3D shapes

rectangular solid: $V = lwh$, $SA = 2lw + 2wh + 2lh$

cube: $V = s^3$, $SA = 6s^2$

cylinder: $V = \pi r^2 h$

sphere: $V = \frac{4}{3}\pi r^3$

Counting

combinations: $nCr = \frac{n!}{r!(n - r)!}$

Probability

$P(A \text{ or } B) = P(A) + P(B) - P(A \text{ and } B)$

$P(\text{not } A) = 1 - P(A)$

For an even more comprehensive set of mathematical rules, check out our GRE Math Formula e-Book, online at:

magoosh.com/gre/2012/gre-math-formula-ebook

Chapter 4

GRE Verbal Reasoning

Brought to you by Chris from Magoosh

Think of the GRE Verbal as a vocabulary quiz on steroids. Not only will you have to face words like *scurrilous*, *incorrigible*, and *portentous*, but you'll also see these words used in sentences so dense and confusing that they seem to have jumped out of a philosophy dissertation (which, just to warn you, is a very likely source for a reading passage).

The first question type you'll see in the GRE Verbal is a "text completion," which you might know better as a "fill-in-the-blank." You're probably thinking, "Hey, I've seen those before. No sweat." But not so fast! The GRE writers have really outdone themselves. You'll see not only single-blank sentences, in which you have to choose one word that best fits the blank, but also texts with as many as three blanks, which can all be packed into one sentence or, more diabolically still, spread out over an entire paragraph.

Another question type is the "sentence equivalence question," a unique variety of text completion. The good news is that these questions each have only one sentence and one blank. The bad news is you have to choose *two* out of six answer choices. Sorry, there's no partial credit (nor for two- and three-blank text completions, for that matter).

Finally, half of the test will be questions about specific reading passages. The reading passages range from about 100 to 450 words and are drawn from a variety of fields—science, literary critique, social sciences, etc. The GRE includes passages that range from relatively challenging to forbiddingly dense.

Meet the GRE Verbal Section

Though it may not sound like it, *pulchritude* actually means "beauty"; somebody who is beautiful can be described as *pulchritudinous*— though you might not want to say that to their face.

GRE Verbal sections each consist of twenty questions, and for each, you'll have thirty minutes. This gives you 1:30 to answer each question.

So how do you allocate this time between the different questions?

We've done a little calculating and come up with this list of approximate times. Here are the question types on the GRE in order of *least* time-consuming to *most* time-consuming:

- Single-blank text completion (20–45 seconds/question)
- Sentence equivalence (20–60 seconds/question)
- Double-blank text completion (30–75 seconds/question)
- Reading comprehension: paragraph argument question (45 seconds–1:45 min./question)
- Triple-blank text completion (45 seconds–two minutes/question)
- Reading comprehension: multiple-question passage (one to three minutes/question)

Pacing

The ranking above is a rough estimate, meaning that a difficult sentence equivalence question may cost you more time than a straightforward triple-blanker. But it's a good place to start when trying to figure out how to spend your time while practicing GRE Verbal.

Consider these suggestions: Spend no more than a minute on sentence equivalence and single-blank text completions. Spend an average of 1:20–1:30 on double-blank and triple-blank completions. The extra time you saved in single-blank and sentence equivalence should be used on reading comprehension.

Go for the Low-Hanging Fruit

Some questions on the GRE Verbal are easy and others are fiendishly diabolical. The shocking thing is each question, from the one that you get in a blink of an eye to one that has you scratching your head till long after the exam is over, is worth the same.

That's right: similar to the GRE Quantitative, each question within a GRE Verbal section has the same weight.

So don't spend three minutes agonizing over a triple-blank text completion with the words *hagiographic* and *pulchritude* as answer choices. If it's a long paragraph with really difficult words, *skip it!*

In other words, if the question is clearly difficult and time-consuming, move on. Instead, go for the low-hanging fruit—the questions that are easier and take less time. The GRE allows you to scroll from question to question, so take advantage of that feature!

You Can Skip Questions

Don't freak out if you're unable to attempt every question. But there's no penalty for guessing, so be sure to complete each question, even with a random guess. There is, however, a penalty for rushing through a relatively easy question to try to answer every question—you get the easy question wrong. You don't get bonus points for completing the test, so make sure to be accurate where you can.

Verbal Question Types

The questions on the GRE Verbal are split up in a specific format. In order to maximize your score, it's important to know how to navigate through the different question types.

Text Completion Breakdown

Expect the following in each GRE Verbal section:

- One to two single-blank text completions
- Two to three double-blank text completions
- One to two triple-blank text completions

Remember, you get the same number of points for the really difficult triple-blank text completions as you do the really easy single-blank questions. That's not to say you won't spend more time on a double-blank text completion than on a triple-blank one. If you feel any one question is eating up too much time, then skip it and come back later. The upside to this isn't just saving time; often, your brain is more likely to "get it" when, with fresh eyes, you look at the question again.

Reading Comprehension Breakdown

The next grouping you'll see in the GRE Verbal is reading comprehension passages. Short passages are less than twenty lines. Passages between twenty and forty lines are medium passages. Long passages are those over forty lines.

Finally, paragraph argument questions each refer to a single short- to medium-length paragraph, called the argument.

Across the two GRE Verbal sections, here is a rough sampling of what to expect:

- One long passage with four questions
- Four to five short passages with one to two questions each
- Two to three medium passages with two to three questions each
- Three to four paragraph argument questions with one question each

Remember, you can skip a very long passage and come back to it if you have time. We recommend starting with questions that aren't so time-consuming. The thing to remember about a long reading passage is that for those sixty-or-so lines you get four questions. On the other hand, each short passage is about fifteen lines long and offers up to two questions. In other words, in some cases you can answer twice as many short-passage questions with the same amount of reading you would do for a long-passage set.

Sentence Equivalence Breakdown

After a few reading-comprehension questions, you get a handful of sentence equivalence questions, before a final reading comprehension set at the end of the section. There will be a total of eight sentence equivalence questions across both GRE Verbal sections. Keep in mind that these typically require the least amount of time. So as long as your vocab is strong, this is definitely an area that could lead to quick points.

How to Study for the GRE Verbal

Preparing for the GRE Verbal can be daunting. Maybe it's because you feel like you have to learn thousands of new words, or that you have to figure out how to speed-read long passages well enough to then answer multiple questions about them.

But never fear: at Magoosh, we like things to be fun. So we've come up with a few suggestions on how to study for the GRE Verbal without losing your mind, and you may even enjoy the process. If you follow the four guidelines below, you will, in a sense, gain a new mind—one full of academic words and obscure information about the life of phytoplankton.

Read, read, read (and did we mention, read?)

In prepping for the GRE, you're not simply learning a few rules. You essentially have to prove your ability to understand words in an academic context. The best way to do this is to read high-quality, content-rich text. Read articles in publications such as the *New York Times*, the *New Yorker*, or the *Economist.*

Learn words, not definitions

A common preconception—though not necessarily a misconception—is that you only need to study a set list of high-frequency words, and then you're ready to ace the test. Sadly, this isn't 100 percent true. First off, there's no one magic list. Secondly, learning from a list is very unproductive. Finally, and maybe most importantly, you don't know a word just because you can cough up some word-for-word definition, as in the following case:

> ***Belie:*** *fail to give a true notion or impression of (something); disguise or contradict.*
>
> —New Oxford Dictionary

The real question is this: can you use the word in a sentence, and can you identify when the word is being used correctly? For instance, if we said, "The children belied themselves as ninjas during Halloween," you could very well look at the part of the definition that says "disguise" and think, *Hey, that's right.*

The only way to understand a complex word like belie is to understand how the word functions in context. Reading from newspapers and magazines is a perfect way to do so. You should also check out the free Magoosh Vocabulary eBook!

For more on "belie," refer to the appendix.

Targeted practice

Don't just prep at random. Use the study plan at the beginning of this book. Staying on a solid plan can guide you through strategies that can help you boost your GRE verbal score.

The *Atlantic* is also a great magazine for sophisticated topics and GRE-level vocabulary. Unlike the other three mentioned here, the online version of the *Atlantic* allows you to read unlimited articles for free.

Find a GRE Verbal study buddy

"No man is an island" is an expression that can be applied to the GRE test-taker. Don't hide yourself behind a mountain of GRE prep books. Instead, find a study partner. You can quiz each other on words. If you don't know anybody prepping for the GRE, then ask a family member to quiz you with flashcards.

Still Struggling with the GRE Verbal?

This is a common problem for people who've taken the GRE before and want to do so again to up their verbal scores. After all, seeing difficult words, twisted syntax, and dense passages on puzzling topics can make even avid readers tense up. If you typically don't care much for reading or have been out of college for a while, the GRE can seem an incomprehensible language made of academic hieroglyphics. If this describes you, then the worst thing you can do is throw the book down in despair and feel like there's nothing you can do to get a better score.

You can—and you will—get better, but you'll have to invest a lot of time, and you'll need a lot of patience. Just as learning a foreign language can be very difficult and frustrating, so too can be preparing for the GRE. And if English isn't your first language, then you already have learned a foreign language, so you definitely have the requisite grit to tackle GRE Verbal.

So what are some specific things you can do to improve?

Read, read, and read

Are you sick of us saying this yet? Because we'll keep saying it. Over and over. It's *that* important. If you don't read much, your brain isn't going to like you after you force it to try to read a 450-word passage on test day. Only by reading relatively challenging, thought-provoking stuff will you have an easier time deciphering what the sentences and passages in the GRE Verbal are trying to say.

Fall in love with words

Okay, okay, we know … this might sound a little overblown. But honestly, you'll have a far more enjoyable time studying for the GRE if you learn to appreciate words. Maybe the tactile sensation the word *lugubrious* playing out on your lips, the comical imagery conjured up by *troglodyte*, the ethereal quality of *diaphanous*, or the sheer whimsicality of *curmudgeon* will make you a vocabophile. If you need more nudging on your path to falling in love with words, don't forget the Magoosh vocab series on YouTube, "Vocab Wednesdays."

Focus

To say you're having trouble with the GRE Verbal is vague. Identifying specific areas where you're struggling can help boost your score. Is it vocabulary, reading comprehension passages, or specifically just the reading comprehension questions? Whatever the case, target that area when studying.

Remember, a weakness is a chance for you to focus your energy and build a new strength!

A *troglodyte* can refer to a member of a species that were purported to dwell in caves or anyone who is definitely old-fashioned ("I'm going to stick to my rotary phone! Now get out of my cave!")

Vocabulary on the GRE

An excellent grasp of vocabulary is one way to master the GRE Verbal—and, lucky for you—studying new vocabulary doesn't have to be boring. We've put together some amazing resources for you, including study tips and word lists. You can also use our free GRE Vocabulary Flashcards on the web or your mobile device!

Come Up with Clever (and Wacky) Associations

Another way of saying this: use mnemonics—creative ways of remembering words.

Let's demonstrate with the words *gregarious* and *amiable. Gregarious* means "sociable." Let's say you have a friend named Greg, and, indeed, he's outgoing. Now you have a way of remembering this word. As luck would have it, you also have a friend named Amy who, believe it or not, is friendly. So now, when you see *amiable* you think, "Amy-able" and for *gregarious* you think, "Greg-arious."

If you don't know people named Greg and Amy, don't worry. The beauty of mnemonics is they only need to make sense to you. So make up some other way to remember those words! The wackier and sillier a mnemonic, the more likely you are to remember it. Additionally, the mnemonics that make the most sense to you—and the ones you're most likely to remember—are usually the ones that you come up with on your own.

So give it a try with the following words:

Esoteric: known only to those with specialized knowledge
Dilatory: slow; delaying
Polemic: a written or verbal attack against someone

Did you know that if you rearrange the letters in *dilatory*, you get two other GRE words: *adroitly* (done skillfully) and *idolatry* (extreme admiration)?

Use It or Lose It

Let's say you don't know the definitions of any of the words above, so you look them up in a dictionary. Being the good word detective you are, you write down the definitions as well as example sentences on a flashcard.

However, tomorrow, your friend asks you what you learned using Magoosh. You tell them that you learned how to use mnemonics for three words. You remember the words, but you can't remember the definitions. Now, let's say that you decided after reading this book to pick up a copy of the *New Yorker*. While reading the article you think to yourself, "Hey, this is some pretty … oh, oh … what's that word … esoteric stuff."

Now, what's happened? Well, you've recalled a word and used it in a relevant context. Using words will help push them deeper into your memory. That way, when it comes time for the test, you'll spend very little brainpower processing the word.

So whether you're walking down the street, or even watching a television show, see if you can apply the words you've been studying. Otherwise, you'll have a much tougher time learning words if you think that GRE prep ends as soon as you put down your vocabulary books. Use new vocabulary words whenever you can. Your verbal score will thank you.

Don't Bite Off More Than You Can Chew

Learning hundreds of words while only having a shaky grasp of them isn't effective. This is called *cramming*, and it isn't something we recommend doing to get the best verbal score you can!

Instead, learn words at a rate slow enough that they aren't falling out of your head. For some, this rate is five words a day. For others, it's twenty-five. Try starting with just a few words per day, and then increase that number once you have a solid understanding of those earlier words.

Read to Be Surprised

Imagine that you pick up a copy of the *Economist* (we'll give the *New Yorker* a rest for now) and you see the word *dilatory* in an article. It looks familiar, right? Well, your brain should have a sudden jolt of recognition because you just saw the word in the mnemonics exercise above. When you meet a word you learned about as part of your word list but weren't necessarily expecting to see, your brain is surprised by the recognition and is more likely to retain it.

As you continue to learn words, and as you continue to read, you'll have more of these *aha!* moments. Sometimes, you won't remember the word immediately, but you can always look it up to reinforce the definition. And the fact that you've seen that word in context will give you a deeper understanding of how that word is used—an important piece of studying for the GRE.

Vocabulary Takeaways

- Learn words and use them often
- Find creative and wacky ways to remember words
- Read, read, and read some more

Keep these key points in mind as you go through the lists below. Enjoy!

How to Use Vocabulary Lists

In the appendix of this book, we've included over one hundred and fifty GRE-friendly vocabulary words. We also grouped these words into specific categories, making it easier for you to see connections between them. Here are a couple of tips for using these lists:

1. Make the studying meaningful. Use those words in context. We give you a head start with this by also providing example sentences. Learning words from a laundry list of vocabulary by covering up the answer and "testing yourself" turns off your brain. So don't do that.

2. To move words from short-term memory to long-term memory, bite off a little at a time, and do your learning away from the list—that is, think back on the words and definitions. Then, if you forget them, consult the list.

Flashcards

Can't get enough of the Magoosh vocabulary? Well, we can't blame you. That's why we're excited to let you know that you can keeping going with and even extend your vocabulary practice with a bunch of free tools. Magoosh offers a free flashcard app on web and mobile, as well as a Vocabulary Builder app, and a Chrome extension called Magoosh Vocabulary.

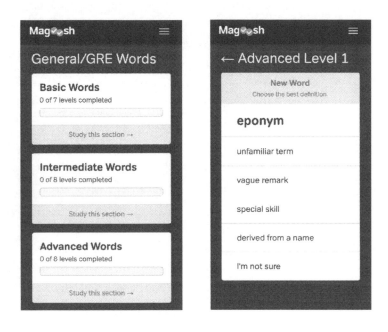

Verbal Question Types: Text Completion

On the surface, text completions sound pretty easy. All you have to do is fill in the blank with the vocabulary word that, given the clues in the sentence, fits best, right?

Not quite.

A text completion can contain anywhere from one to four sentences. The longest text completions can each run an entire paragraph.

A text completion can have between one and three blanks. Every single-blank text completion will be one sentence and will contain five answer choices. The double- and triple-blank text completions, on the other hand, can run anywhere from one to four sentences. Most importantly, each blank in a double- and triple-blank text completion will always have three answer choices.

With a double- or triple-blank text completion, your chances of guessing correctly are quite low. For a triple-blank text completion, you have to get all three correct in order to get the question correct (that's a 1 in 27 chance in guessing).

Below are five important strategies you should follow if you want to do well on text completions.

1. **Don't dive in.** Read the entire stem first. The first blank is often vague and doesn't make sense unless you have read the entire text.

2. **Break down the paragraph.** Text completions are sometimes a full paragraph long, so it's easy to get lost in what they're actually trying to say. A great strategy is trying to understand the "big picture." Breaking down the paragraph in your own words by paraphrasing the information will help you get a grasp on what the sentences are talking about.

3. **Use your own words.** Put your own word(s) in the blank or blanks. Make sure you can justify your answers based not just on the "big picture" but also on some of the specific words or phrases in the sentence itself. Rely on keywords.

4. **Attempt the second (or third) blank first.** Because the first blank is often difficult to deal with, try finding a word for the second or third blank first. Then work your way backwards to the first blank. The caveat: This technique only applies if you can come up with a word for the second or third blank. If you can't, then work with the first blank.

5. **Use the entire text completion as context.** When you've finally chosen your two/ three answers, plug them back into the blanks. Does the completed sentence make sense with how you paraphrased it earlier?

Academic Structures to Know for Text Completions

In both text completion sections, there are certain phrases that may show up that can give the sentence a spin. If you aren't familiar with these phrases, your head is *also* likely to spin.

Take a look at the following two sentences.

> *He was _____, always giving to those in need.*

> *He was anything but _____, always giving to those in need.*

What exactly does "anything but" mean? Well, it's an expression that implies that he's many things, A, B, C, and D … but he's definitely *not* E. In this case, E would be the opposite of the second part of the sentence. A simple way to think about it is to replace *anything but* with *not*. As in, "he was (not) _____, always giving to those in need." The word *stingy* fits in very nicely. Notice how the words in the two blanks of the example sentences are opposite in meaning. *Generous* would make a good entry for the first sentence.

The point here is to show you the meaning of *anything but* and how these idiomatic phrases can be highly misleading if you're not paying close attention. Below are some of the most common phrases you can expect to see on the GRE. Keep an eye out for them when answering text completions, and be sure you feel comfortable with how they're used in sentences.

Nothing but

In most cases, the phrase nothing but means "only (something)."

> *When we went to her house, she was <u>nothing but</u> kind, showering us with gifts.*

> *In his book critiques, Jones was <u>nothing but</u> fair, always judging an author on the merits of his or her latest novel, regardless of previous flops.*

Anything but

In most cases, the phrase *anything but* means "not" (see explanation in the intro).

All but

The phrase *all but* is identical to "almost." It can also mean "everything except the ones mentioned." Contrast the two sentences below to see the differences in how the phrase is used.

> <u>*All but*</u> *the most famous actors of our day will likely not be remembered fifty years from now.*

> *At the end of the marathon, Charles was <u>all but</u> dead; he stumbled across the finish line, mentioning something about his pet iguana.*

At once X and Y

The phrase *at once X and Y* is a tricky structure! First off, X and Y are words or phrases that are opposite in meaning. Second, that's an "and" you see, and not an "or." So this phrase is used to suggest an element of surprise because a person/thing has these opposing qualities.

<u>At once</u> melodious <u>and</u> dissonant, Perkins's symphony is full of beautiful melodies that are suddenly interrupted by a burst of clashing gongs and screeching sopranos.

melodious = X; dissonant = Y

He was <u>at once</u> hysterically funny, making people roll on the floor in laughter, <u>and</u> overly serious as soon as the conversation turned to politics.

hysterically funny = X; overly serious = Y

<u>At once</u> forward-thinking <u>and</u> traditionalist, the mayor's new plan will usher in unprecedented changes while using approaches that have shown enduring efficacy in the civic sphere.

forward-thinking = X; traditionalist = Y

Nothing more than

The phrase *nothing more than* is used to show that somebody isn't very good at something. The word that follows "than" should be a negative description.

He is <u>nothing more than</u> a second-rate musician, busking at a bus stop; his friends are always happy to escape his warbling falsetto.

Harry is <u>nothing more than</u> a seasoned Hollywood hack: his scripts are as numerous as they are contrived.

All the more so

If you want to add emphasis but need an entire phrase to do so, you can use *all the more so*.

Quentin's sudden termination was shocking—<u>all the more so</u> because he helped build the company as many know it today.

For all

The phrase *for all* is another way of saying "despite."

<u>For all</u> his hard work, Michael was passed over for a promotion.

<u>For all</u> their talk on purging the environment of toxins, the two brothers can't do without their hourly smoke break.

If anything

The phrase *if anything* means "if at all." It's meant to suggest that somebody is disagreeing with something and wants to prove that the other case is actually true.

Bob: *It seems like this city is getting more dangerous every day.*

Steve: *Actually, it doesn't seem that much worse from when I first moved here. <u>If anything</u>, the crime rate has actually dropped since the city's population has almost doubled in the last ten years.*

As such

The phrase *as such* can be confusing because it is often misinterpreted as "therefore." However, *as such* must refer to something that came before it.

> **Correct:** *The CEO walked around the office as though he was King Kong, walking over anyone who came in his way. <u>As such</u>, anyone who wasn't upper management tried to avoid him.*

> **Incorrect:** *We missed our train to Brussels. As such, we will have to take another one.*

Not so much A as B

The phrase *not so much A as B* implies that to describe a situation, B is a better word or phrase than A.

> *The scholar was <u>not so much insightful as he was patient</u>: he would peruse texts far longer than any of his peers.*

> *He was <u>not so much jealous as downright resentful</u> of his sister's talents, believing that their parents had put little interest in his education.*

But for

The phrase *but for* is just another way of saying "except for."

> *<u>But for</u> her eloquence, she had little aptitude as an attorney.*

> *His contribution to cinema has been mostly forgotten <u>but for</u> his Oscar-winning role.*

Save (for)

Similarly, the phrase *save (for)* means the same as "except (for)."

> *Watching TV was Mama's favorite activity, <u>save for</u> eating chocolate cream puffs.*

> *Randy did not consider any of the class ruffians friends, <u>save for</u> Donald, who once came to his defense in a playground scuffle.*

Stem from

To *stem from* just means to "come from" or "be caused by."

> *His insecurity <u>stems from</u> his lack of friends in grade school.*

> *The current crises <u>stem from</u> the former administration's inability to rein in spending.*

Text Completion Practice Questions

These examples should help you get an idea of what to expect from text completion questions on the GRE. There are even more practice questions in the GRE practice test in chapter 6.

Single-blank

Question 1

Difficulty: **Medium** · Percent Correct: **56%**

Able to coax a palpable sense of menace from the bucolic backwaters of her native Missouri, Micheaux adroitly shows us, in her latest book, that a surface of idyllic charm can _____ a roiling underbelly of intrigue, corruption, and murder.

- (A) subsume
- (B) belie
- (C) counteract
- (D) preface
- (E) complement

Question 2

Difficulty: **Medium** · Percent Correct: **56%**

For a writer with a reputation for both prolixity and inscrutability, Thompson, in this slim collection of short stories, may finally be intent on making his ideas more _____ to a readership looking for quick edification.

- (A) aesthetic
- (B) prescient
- (C) palatable
- (D) inaccessible
- (E) transcendent

Question 3

Difficulty: **Medium** · Percent Correct: **47%**

That the psychopharmacological journal had already published the findings of the clinician's experiment rendered _____ any prior misgivings she'd had regarding the validity of her control group.

- (A) extant
- (B) moot
- (C) fallacious
- (D) topical
- (E) retroactive

223

Question 4

Difficulty: Hard · Percent Correct: 34%

The author, mocked by many for his simple, almost childlike prose, can at least not be begrudged the distinction of writing with _____ .

(A) geniality

(B) naivety

(C) gusto

(D) anonymity

(E) lucidness

Question 5

Difficulty: Very Hard · Percent Correct: 25%

An element of _____ on the part of the audience is interwoven into the multi-era saga, for two actors portraying the same character at different phases of life are distinguishable enough that the audience is able to discern differences for which the mere passing of years cannot account.

(A) surprise

(B) foreboding

(C) disbelief

(D) confusion

(E) predictability

Question 6

Difficulty: Very Hard · Percent Correct: 27%

The bias for _____ has crept into the current school of physics: superstring theory provides such an all-encompassing—yet tidy—packaging of current streams of thought—quantum physics and Einstein's theory of relativity, among them—that many scientists have been beguiled by the simplicity of the theory into blithely discounting the paucity of data.

(A) thoroughness

(B) inconsistency

(C) elegance

(D) aesthetics

(E) artifice

Question 7

Difficulty: **Easy** · Percent Correct: **70%**

Writing well is not so much a matter of inspiration as it is (i) _____; just as the scientist toils away in an attic, or the athlete trains even in inhospitable conditions, a writer too must be (ii) _____.

(i)	(ii)
Ⓐ forethought	Ⓓ candid
Ⓑ perseverance	Ⓔ yielding
Ⓒ carelessness	Ⓕ tenacious

Question 8

Difficulty: **Medium** · Percent Correct: **56%**

Managers who categorically squelch insights from low-tiered employees run the obvious hazard of (i) _____ creativity; conversely, these very same managers are more likely to (ii) _____ any ideas that flow down from the top brass.

(i)	(ii)
Ⓐ fomenting	Ⓓ unquestioningly embrace
Ⓑ smothering	Ⓔ arbitrarily denounce
Ⓒ sparking	Ⓕ conditionally approve

Question 9

Difficulty: **Medium** · Percent Correct: **50%**

Many imagine philosophers appareled in togas, walking about the Greek agora, (i) _____ questions of great import; yet philosophy (ii) _____ today, only we have traded the agora for the Internet: many online venues exist in which the intellectually curious discuss the very same questions that once reverberated through the open air of Athens' marketplaces.

(i)	(ii)
Ⓐ holding forth on	Ⓓ continues to be imperiled
Ⓑ disproving	Ⓔ is very much alive
Ⓒ dismissing	Ⓕ remains esoteric

Question 10

Difficulty: **Medium** · Percent Correct: **48%**

In censuring the academic committee for apparently being (i) _____ in appointing a chancellor, the university president mistook (ii) _____ for procrastination—the committee had been guilty of nothing more than a scrupulous vetting of all candidates.

(i)	(ii)
Ⓐ biased	Ⓓ prevarication
Ⓑ dilatory	Ⓔ deliberation
Ⓒ overzealous	Ⓕ vacillation

Question 11

Difficulty: **Medium** · Percent Correct: **48%**

Despite protestations to the contrary, Peyermessen had clearly (i) _____ complete sections of text from works that, while (ii) _____, were not unknown to specialists in the field, who accused him of plagiarism.

(i)	(ii)
Ⓐ omitted	Ⓓ dated
Ⓑ lifted	Ⓔ prominent
Ⓒ interpreted	Ⓕ uninformative

Question 12

Difficulty: **Medium** · Percent Correct: **46%**

With numerous exciting public works projects in the offing, residents are understandably (i) _____ ; yet because such prodigious undertakings are inevitably plagued with numerous setbacks, much of the fervor is likely to be (ii) _____ a heavy dose of reality.

(i)	(ii)
Ⓐ vexed	Ⓓ tempered with
Ⓑ concerned	Ⓔ intensified by
Ⓒ agog	Ⓕ precluded by

Question 13

Difficulty: **Hard** · Percent Correct: **44%**

There is a rising consensus amongst immunologists that the observed rise in allergies in the general population can be attributed to (i) _____ exposure to everyday germs. Known as the hygiene hypothesis, this counterintuitive idea could have far-reaching implications; for one, we may now have to be more (ii) _____ those paternal prescriptions to scrub our children's hands at every opportunity.

(i)	(ii)
Ⓐ frequent	Ⓓ wary of
Ⓑ decreased	Ⓔ cognizant of
Ⓒ heightened	Ⓕ indifferent to

Question 14

Difficulty: **Hard** · Percent Correct: **31%**

The theoretical physicist, despite his mathematical training, oftentimes must deal with questions that fall under the realm of the philosophical. Nonetheless, he will often marshal formulae when they serve to (i) _____ a theory, notwithstanding the fact that many such theories are not (ii) _____ empirical analysis, as those theories deal with questions whose answers may ultimately be unknowable.

(i)	(ii)
Ⓐ undermine	Ⓓ unrelated to
Ⓑ conflate	Ⓔ commensurate with
Ⓒ undergird	Ⓕ amenable to

Question 15

Difficulty: **Very Hard** · Percent Correct: **28%**

A new school of thought has it that innate talent can be conveniently (i) _____ a series of readily (ii) _____ factors. Mozart's genius, then, is no divine blessing of the type conferred on a select few, but is simply the result of a patriarchal father who stressed, above else, thousands upon thousands of hours of grueling practice.

(i)	(ii)
Ⓐ reduced to	Ⓓ intrusive
Ⓑ misattributed to	Ⓔ quantifiable
Ⓒ measured by	Ⓕ pervasive

Our immune systems have something like memories: after we have an infection, our body typically remembers that and knows how to fight it, giving us immunity. An allergy is essentially a faulty memory of our immune system. Any allergy is the activation of the powerful machinery of the human immune system to something that, in and of itself, presents little or no biological threat.

Question 16

Difficulty: **Very Hard** · Percent Correct: **19%**

It is (i) _____ that the short story, regardless of its acclaim amongst certain members of the literati, has (ii) _____ amongst the public—all the more so because the novel, in some ways an inherently more demanding form, continues to be popular amongst lay readers who apparently subscribe to the trite credo that bigger is better.

(i)	(ii)
(A) unsurprising	(D) languished
(B) encouraging	(E) burgeoned
(C) telling	(F) imploded

Triple-blank

Question 17

Difficulty: **Medium** · Percent Correct: **60%**

What is currently (i) _____ civil engineers is not so much a predicted increase in annual precipitation as the likelihood that many storms will come in (ii) _____, thereby making flooding in lower lying riparian regions (iii) _____.

(i)	(ii)	(iii)
(A) worrying	(D) more predictable patterns	(G) far more likely
(B) comforting	(E) tighter succession	(H) somewhat infrequent
(C) unimportant to	(F) greater isolation	(I) all but impossible

Question 18

Difficulty: **Medium** · Percent Correct: **51%**

That we can, from a piece of art, (i) _____ the unconscious urges of the artist—urges that remain hidden even from the artist himself—will remain a(n) (ii) _____ issue, as it is one (iii) _____ empirical analysis: we can never definitively know what is submerged deep inside the artist's psyche, let alone reconcile any such revelations with the artist's work.

(i)	(ii)	(iii)
(A) derive	(D) practical	(G) easily subjected to
(B) appreciate	(E) intractable	(H) not readily amenable to
(C) subvert	(F) unambiguous	(I) likely to be resolved by

Question 19

Difficulty: **Hard** · Percent Correct: 45%

The movie is comprised of several vignettes, each presenting a character along with his or her foil: a staid accountant shares an apartment with an (i) _____ musician; a tight-lipped divorcee on a cross-country roadtrip picks up an (ii) _____ hitchhiker; and finally, and perhaps most unconvincingly, an introverted mathematician falls in love with a(n) (iii) _____ arriviste.

(i)	(ii)	(iii)
(A) colorful	(D) garrulous	(G) unpredictable
(B) insatiable	(E) untrustworthy	(H) gregarious
(C) eminent	(F) forlorn	(I) bumbling

Question 20

Difficulty: **Hard** · Percent Correct: 45%

Special effects in movies are (i) _____, in that unlike the story, whose permutations seem to have long ago been (ii) _____, they continue to evolve: if we were magically beamed years into the future (of course that story has been told numerous times before), the special effects would (iii) _____; the story would be awfully familiar.

(i)	(ii)	(iii)
(A) predictable	(D) evaluated	(G) be incomprehensible
(B) exciting	(E) conveyed	(H) hold us in thrall
(C) juvenile	(F) exhausted	(I) remain unchanged

Question 21

Difficulty: **Hard** · Percent Correct: 31%

Jansen's writing strikes many as (i) _____: for one who is capable of enduring even the most recondite topics with a(n) (ii) _____ tone, his prose becomes (iii) _____ in the informal correspondences he had with his contemporaries.

(i)	(ii)	(iii)
(A) pedantic	(D) acerbic	(G) curiously stilted
(B) forbidding	(E) cautious	(H) fully realized
(C) paradoxical	(F) breezy	(I) somewhat unguarded

Question 22

Difficulty: **Very Hard** · Percent Correct: **25%**

Heinrich Feyermahn, in insisting that Galileo did not fully uphold the tenets of scientific rationalism, does not (i) _____ the Italian astronomer, but rather the very edifice of Western thought. For if Galileo is the purported exemplar of rational thinking, and yet is (ii) _____, then the history of science cannot be understood as an endless succession of scientists carrying out their work free of all-too-human biases. Thus, Feyermahn admonishes, in faithfully chronicling the sweep of science in the last three hundred years, historiographers would be (iii) _____ not to include the human foibles that were part of even the most ostensibly Apollonian endeavors.

(i)	(ii)	(iii)
Ⓐ exclusively implicate	Ⓓ found wanting	Ⓖ prudent
Ⓑ partially repudiate	Ⓔ considered enlightened	Ⓗ remiss
Ⓒ fully espouse	Ⓕ dismissed as inconsequential	Ⓘ contrarian

Question 23

Difficulty: **Very Hard** · Percent Correct: **25%**

What tradition has long known, science must labor through its usual rigorous protocols to arrive at the very same assessment. Concerning learning in infants, recent findings (i) _____ this trend: the timeworn yarn that babies are (ii) _____—and oftentimes disregarding—stimuli from their surroundings has been turned on its head; although (iii) _____ exhibiting a mastery of their respective worlds, infants are constantly conducting experiments—very much like scientists themselves—testing their limits vis-à-vis an environment at once enchanting and frustrating.

(i)	(ii)	(iii)
Ⓐ buck	Ⓓ passively receiving	Ⓖ far from
Ⓑ uphold	Ⓔ subtly parsing	Ⓗ known for
Ⓒ underscore	Ⓕ actively misinterpreting	Ⓘ potentially

Question 24

Difficulty: **Very Hard** · Percent Correct: 24%

Perhaps then the greatest failing of this deluge of positive psychology books is not that they (i) _____ the complexity typical of psychology in general—and in this case replace it with a breezy glibness—but that they dispense advice that is so (ii) _____ and littered with platitudes as to be bereft of the very succor the public requires during our (iii) _____ times.

(i)	(ii)	(iii)
Ⓐ invoke	Ⓓ pat	Ⓖ heady
Ⓑ address	Ⓔ evocative	Ⓗ trying
Ⓒ eschew	Ⓕ convoluted	Ⓘ halcyon

Question 25

Difficulty: **Very Hard** · Percent Correct: 22%

The British-led force's landing at Gallipoli made for such a(n) (i) _____ foray into the Ottoman theater of World War I that Max von Oppenheim, a German political adventurer in league with the Ottomans, believed that the attack must have been a (ii) _____ and that Britain had saved her better infantry for an imminent landing upon an area that was (iii) _____.

(i)	(ii)	(iii)
Ⓐ strategic	Ⓓ resounding success	Ⓖ not so heavily exposed
Ⓑ clandestine	Ⓔ mere feint	Ⓗ similarly situated
Ⓒ unpropitious	Ⓕ major provocation	Ⓘ unevenly fortified

Question 26

Difficulty: **Very Hard** · Percent Correct: 16%

Perhaps there is nothing more to the album than its case that experimentalism into uncharted sonic landscapes did not (i) _____ with Stockhausen. Or perhaps its forays—many of which could rightly be dubbed sophomoric—into the avant-garde also lead to the (ii) _____ that to create an unprecedented sound one has to (iii) _____ a discernible melody.

(i)	(ii)	(iii)
Ⓐ come full circle	Ⓓ unsettling conclusion	Ⓖ choose to create
Ⓑ culminate	Ⓔ unwarranted hypothesis	Ⓗ forgo producing
Ⓒ die	Ⓕ uncharacteristic rebuttal	Ⓘ subtly embed

Text Completion Answers and Explanations

Question 1

Difficulty: **Medium** · Percent Correct: **56%**

Answer: **B**

The clues, "able to coax … menace" and "bucolic [rural and pleasant] backwater" show us that the setting of the book might appear pleasant, but just below that surface there's a lot of stuff that isn't very nice. Therefore the surface's "idyllic charm" can cover up/hide/mask these unpleasant things.

(B) *Belie* means "to disguise, to give a false impression of." In this case, the idyllic charm gives a false impression, covering what lies underneath.

(A) *Subsume* means "to include or absorb into." For instance, the paragraph argument question on the GRE used to exist in its own section, but has since been subsumed into the GRE Verbal. This word is a trap for those who try to make the connection between "underbelly" and "subsume."

(C) is incorrect. To *counteract* means "to work against something to neutralize it" (e.g., "the antidote counteracted the poison"). The idyllic charm, however, doesn't neutralize the menace.

(D) is a good trap if you convince yourself that there's a temporal contrast between the surface charm and the menacing underbelly. However, though *preface* means "to introduce something," there are no clues indicating that the charm introduces the menace.

(E) is incorrect. If A complements B, that means A improves upon B, bringing B closer to perfection. If my blue dress shirt complements my black slacks, that means both are improved by being next to each other. There's no such positive connotation in the sentence—the notion that "idyllic charm" matches nicely with a little bit of corruption and murder.

Question 2

Difficulty: **Medium** · Percent Correct: **56%**

Answer: **C**

"Prolixity" and "inscrutability" convey that this person's writing is really, really difficult to understand (inscrutable) and is really wordy (prolix). The "finally intent" indicates that Thompson is now making his works easier to read. **(C)** means "agreeable and satisfactory for." That means he wants to make his writing easier for those who want quick guidance.

Answer (A) is incorrect because *aesthetic*, which means "relating to beauty," doesn't quite capture the idea that the books have become more accessible to readers. Just because something is beautiful doesn't mean it's easier to understand.

Answer (B) is a word that describes a person who is able to know about something before it happens.

(D) is the opposite of the blank.

(E) implies something that goes beyond the normal. The focus of the sentence is the fact that Thompson has made his idea easier to digest. *Transcendent* leans in the other direction.

Question 3

Difficulty: **Medium** · Percent Correct: **47%**

The journal had already published her work, so any fears that she'd had over the article not getting published due to questionable validity are no longer applicable. When something is moot, it's no longer an issue.

Answer: **B**

(A) *extant* means "still in existence."

(B) *moot* fits the context.

(C) *fallacious* means "erroneous." A misgiving is a feeling, and feelings can't be incorrect. Information can be incorrect, as can ideas, but feelings can't. So *fallacious* doesn't quite fit in that sense. Beyond that, fallacious is too strong in its meaning. Since the study was already published, we know that her concerns about the validity don't matter any more. We don't know, though, that they're based on incorrect information.

(D) *topical* means "relevant to current events."

(E) *retroactive* means, in effect, "starting from a point in the past."

Doesn't *moot* just mean "arguable or debatable"? There's another, related definition of "moot" that's a little less common. But that's what they like to test on the GRE—the secondary definitions.

> **moot:** "having no practical significance"

In this case, you could paraphrase the sentence to say that her concerns aren't important anymore since the journal already published the work—even if there was a problem with the control group, it's too late to change it.

Question 4

Difficulty: **Hard** · Percent Correct: **34%**

The clue is "simple, almost childlike." The author writes in a very straightforward manner, and, in a way, is mocked by the writer of the sentence. But you're looking for a positive word, one that relates to straightforward/simple/easy to understand. This leads you to **(E)**.

Answer: **E**

Why doesn't *naivety* work? This is a shift sentence. "Can at least not be begrudged" tells us that, although he's mocked for his childlike writing, he at least writes with _____ (a positive quality). So you're looking for a positive quality of the author's writing that contrasts with his childlike prose (for which he is mocked).

Naivety doesn't quite fit the context of the sentence here because it carries a negative connotation, especially when describing adults. The word *naivety* means "simpleness" in a bad way. Calling someone "naive" means that you're calling them something close to "immature."

The author's writing is childlike, but at least it's positive in its _____. Naivety is a negative word, so it won't work, even though it matches with *childlike*. In contrast, *lucidness* matches "simple" and is a positive word (it means "very clear" related to writing). Having clear writing is a good thing, because that means people can understand what you write. *Gusto* and *geniality* are positive, but they don't fit with the clue that the writing is simple.

Can you explain the use of "begrudge" in this sentence? Begrudge has two different meanings, making it a tricky word:

> *To envy the possession or enjoyment of*
> *To give or expend with reluctance*

The second definition is close to "deny," but it doesn't actually mean "deny." It means "give very reluctantly."

By saying that readers can't begrudge the writer of something, the sentence is saying that readers must willingly grant that something is true about the writing.

Question 5

Difficulty: **Very Hard** · Percent Correct: **25%**

Answer: **C**

The key to unraveling this tough question is to break up the sentence into digestible parts, simplifying along the way:

> *"An element of _____ on the part of the audience … saga"* = The word in the blank is an inherent quality of the multi-era saga:
>
> > *"Two actors … difference"* = the audience can tell how two actors playing the same character differ physically
> >
> > *"passing years … account"* = these differences are greater than those that naturally happen when a person ages

Therefore, an inherent part of watching the multi-era saga is an element of **(C)** *disbelief*, since the audience knows that the same character is actually played by two different people.

(A) is incorrect, as there's no context suggesting that the audiences are surprised by the fact that two actors are playing the same character.

(B) *foreboding* means "a sense that something bad will happen." This negative word isn't supported by the context.

(D) is incorrect, as the audience isn't confused since they're able to tell the difference between two actors playing the same character onscreen.

(E) *predictability* might describe the situation in general, i.e., the audience will be able to predictably tell the difference between two actors portraying the same character. However, "predictability" doesn't make sense as the specific word that fits in the blank, since it's implying that the audience itself is predictable.

Question 6

Difficulty: **Very Hard** · Percent Correct: **27%**

This is a very tough and convoluted question. One of the first words to jump out is "all-encompassing." That alone biases us toward us (A). However, the rest of the sentence isn't just about thoroughness. The "yet tidy" is an important idea that runs throughout the sentence: the idea of "simplicity of theory." So the bias is toward something that seems simple, yet all-encompassing. The word *elegance* (**C**) doesn't just connote fine evening attire. A very different definition relates to the scientific method. When a theory is able to account for some phenomenon in a simple yet compelling manner, it's said to be "elegant." One example of elegance in theories is evolution. Whether or not it's consistent with a particular person's beliefs, evolution provides a simple way of explaining how two things as different as a whale and a horse can have arisen from some very different ancestor: the process of natural selection.

Choice (B) doesn't work because nowhere in the sentence is there a clear indication of an inconsistency. True, the theory is simple and all-encompassing, and it also has very little data. Yet a consistent explanation can be simple and all-encompassing and not be based on much data.

The word in choice (D) means "relating to the nature of beauty." There's no mention of the beauty of the theory but rather its simplicity.

(E) *artifice* means "trickery." There's no context to support this interpretation.

Answer: **C**

Question 7

Difficulty: **Easy** · Percent Correct: **70%**

The first clue in this sentence is "not ... a matter of inspiration." We need words like (A) or (B). To know which one, we have to read the part of the sentence that comes after the semicolon. "Toil away" and "train ... inhospitable conditions" is consistent with **(B)**, which means "to not give up, despite adversity."

The second blank is consistent with the first blank. The basic structure is as follows:

Writing is not quality A, it's quality B. Examples of quality B. A writer is similar to these examples, showing (once again) writer has quality B.

(F), which means "not giving up," is similar to (B). (D), which means honest and direct, doesn't match the context. (E), which means "giving in," is the opposite of the answer.

Double-blank

Answers: **B** **F**

Question 8

Difficulty: **Medium** · Percent Correct: **56%**

Assuming you don't know what "squelch" means, a good way to attack the first blank is noticing that "run the obvious hazard" indicates that the first blank is negative. (C), therefore, is clearly out. (A) is a slightly negative word, but mostly because "foment" typically precedes a word that's negative, such as "unrest" or "agitation." You really wouldn't "foment" creativity, which is a positive trait. That leaves us with **(B)**, which is a synonym with "squelch," meaning "to suppress."

For the second blank, notice the word "conversely" indicates that what follows is the

Answers: **B** **D**

opposite of the first part in the sentence. Here, these same managers do the opposite of smother—**(D)** *unquestioningly embrace*—whatever those who are higher up in the hierarchy say. (F) is wrong because (F), while positive, is too soft; "conditional" implies something that isn't 100 percent but rather weakened slightly; in this case the "approval" isn't very strong.

Question 9

Difficulty: **Medium** · Percent Correct: **50%**

Answer: **A** **E**

The best way to attack this question is read up to the second blank, since there isn't enough context before the semicolon to be able to solve the first blank. Up until this point, any of the three words would work. Even then, you'll have to read to the part that discusses how philosophy's place today is similar to its role in ancient Greece ("only we have traded the agora for the Internet"; "the very same questions …"). Therefore, the second blank is **(E)**.

The first blank, then, becomes slightly clearer. People imagine philosophy as something that applies to the ancient times. (B) and (C) imply that philosophy is ignoring these questions. (Also, (B) *disproving* is fishy: do you "disprove questions"?) But notice the end of the sentence "once reverberated through … marketplace." Clearly the image of philosophers in ancient Greece ("appareled in togas") was likely to **(A)** *hold forth on*, or discuss at length, the questions of philosophy.

Question 10

Difficulty: **Medium** · Percent Correct: **48%**

Answers: **B** **E**

"Censuring" indicates that the university president is upset with the committee because he believes it procrastinated. Therefore, the first blank is a synonym for procrastinating. **(B)** *dilatory*, which means "slow to take action," works well. For the second, you want a more positive word than *dilatory*, one that's also a match with "scrupulous vetting" (a careful checking). **(E)** *deliberation* works well.

Question 11

Difficulty: **Medium** · Percent Correct: **48%**

Answers: **B** **D**

"Accused him of plagiarism" supports **(B)** *lifted*, for the first blank. (C) *interpreted* isn't the same as plagiarism, which is actually the taking (or lifting) of text and trying to pass it off as one's own. "Were not unknown to …" matches up best with **(D)** *dated*. You can simplify the part of the sentence around the second blank to this:

Even though the texts were _____, they were not unknown to specialists in the field.

So the specialists still know about the texts. The best way to find this answer is to plug in the answer choices and see which one works best:

Even though the texts were prominent, they were not unknown to specialists in the field.

This doesn't work because if the texts were prominent, certainly the specialists would know about them. But the sentence states "even though," so this choice doesn't fit.

Even though the texts were uninformative, they were not unknown to specialists in the field.

At first, this looks like a slightly tempting answer choice. However, if you look elsewhere in the sentence, you'll see that Peyermessen was plagiarizing these texts—why would he plagiarize texts that are uninformative? Well, he most likely wouldn't, and so this isn't the best answer choice.

This leaves you with *dated*. Even though the texts were dated, they weren't unknown to specialists in the field. So even though the texts were old, specialists still knew about them.

Question 12
Difficulty: **Medium** · Percent Correct: **46%**

The second blank is easier to deal with than the first. "Inevitably plagued … setbacks" indicates that much of the fervor (excitement) is going to be lessened. To temper something is to moderate it or put a "damper on it." Therefore **(D)**.

The first blank is trickier because of the word "offing." This word doesn't actually mean you're getting rid of something (like the slang verb "off"—as in to do away with someone). In the sentence, "in the offing" means "currently in production." Therefore, people are going to be excited and eager, or **(C)** *agog*. The first blank connects well with the clue "fervor," which comes toward the end of the sentence. Notice how the "yet" signals a shift in the sentence. The first part of the sentence describes how people are going to be happy. The second sentence discusses why that enthusiasm should be tempered or lessened.

Answers: **C** **D**

Question 13
Difficulty: **Hard** · Percent Correct: **44%**

The "counterintuitive idea" indicates that the first blank is the opposite of what you would expect—a rise in allergies has resulted from a **(B)** *decreased* exposure to germs (you would think that an increase, not a decrease, in germs leads to something bad). Therefore, when it comes to getting rid of germs ("scrub our children's hands"), you have to be more on guard or **(D)** *wary of.* To say that you're more aware of something doesn't imply that you're more or less likely to do it. Therefore, (E) is wrong.

Answers: **B** **D**

Question 14
Difficulty: **Hard** · Percent Correct: **31%**

The "nonetheless" indicates that the physicist is still a mathematician and will "marshal formulae …" to support or **(C)** *undergird* a theory. "Questions … unknowable" indicates that theories aren't subject or **(F)** *amenable* to empirical analysis.

Answers: **C** **F**

Why can't *commensurate* with go in the second blank? "Commensurate" means "corresponding in size or degree; in proportion." And at first it may seem like it works in the sentence, but if you look a little closer, you'll find that the two things being compared aren't proportional or equal.

The author is talking about the philosophical part of a physicist's job—the theoretical nature. You know too that empirical analysis won't help to answer some of these questions. The sentence even says that they aren't knowable. Ask yourself, "Does it make sense to say that theories aren't proportional to empirical analysis? Are these ideas equal to scientific testing?" The answer is "no." It doesn't quite make sense because the two things are qualitatively different—one is an idea and the other involves testing an idea. Maybe this will be clear with an example of "commensurate" in a couple sentences:

> *The punishment should be commensurate with the crime.*

> *His reward was commensurate with the responsibility he had.*

It does make sense to use *amenable* because the sentence talks about taking a theory that can't be changed in order to be tested. You can imagine changing a theory to make it testable. Or in this case, you can imagine a theory that cannot be modified in order to be tested.

Question 15

Difficulty: **Very Hard**   ·   Percent Correct: **28%**

Answers: **A** **E**

This sentence is difficult mainly because of the first blank. (C) *measured* by is a tempting answer; however, it lacks a couple of important things.

The phrase "innate talent" is very important here. According to the second part of the sentence, the new school of thought tells you that talent like Mozart's is, in fact, not "innate," but instead learned.

The "innate talent" described in the beginning, then, must somehow mean something else: those "_____ factors." If you use "measured by," it doesn't give you the needed shift away from "innate." There would be no reinterpretation and the talent could still be correctly considered innate, which doesn't match up with the example of Mozart.

The word "conveniently" is important to notice for the tone of the passage. That word can impart two possible connotations—that something is actually useful, or that it's *overly* simplified. This second sense is a bit sarcastic. There's little or no indication that this school of thought is actually helpful, so with the word "simply" showing up later, you can assume the author thinks this school of thought is oversimplified. This slightly negative tone also supports **(A)** *reduced* to for the first blank.

Why couldn't *misattributed to* be used? This sentence is describing "a new school of thought." The author isn't making an argument about where Mozart's talent came from. Instead, he's explaining how this new school of thought views Mozart.

Now, note the structure of this sentence. The first part, with the two blanks, makes a general statement:

"A new school of thought has it that innate talent can be conveniently _____ a series of readily _____ factors ..."

You don't know what that statement is because words are missing. The next part of the sentence explains it with a specific example:

"Mozart's genius, then, is no divine blessing ... but is simply the result of ... grueling practice."

So the "new school" believes that "Mozart's genius is no divine blessing." This school wants instead to explain Mozart's abilities through his father and his training.

Now, consider the word "misattribute." Is the school trying to misattribute his talent? That is, are they *trying* to make an error? Of course not. No one would *try* to misattribute his talent to other factors. The opposite is true—they want to *attribute* his talent to practice.

In fact, the "new school" wants to go so far as to say that Mozart's talent was *nothing but* the result of practice. *Reduced to* gives you this idea of explaining something by reducing it down.

Why couldn't *intrusive* be used? (D) *Intrusive* is a tempting answer because the second part of the sentence does refer to some intrusive behavior by Mozart's father. However, the second part of the sentence gives you evidence for **(E)** *quantifiable* by saying that "Mozart's genius, then, is no divine blessing." This represents the old way of thinking: that talent magically or divinely appeared in a person. Instead, the new school of thinking believes that his talent "is simply the result of a patriarchal father who stressed, above else, thousands upon thousands of hours of grueling practice." In other words, the new school of thought believes that there are "known," or "quantifiable," reasons that Mozart's talent came to be—not *intrusive* reasons that Mozart's talent came to be.

Question 16
Difficulty: **Very Hard** · Percent Correct: **19%**

Answers: **C D**

The word "surprising" would fit nicely in the first blank. For example, *The short story surprisingly hasn't been adopted by the public because the novel is "more demanding ..."* However, "surprising" isn't an answer choice. (A) *unsurprising* is the opposite.

(B) *encouraging* doesn't fit the overall tone of the sentence, especially with the second half starting with "all the more so." Why would it be encouraging that the public follows a "trite credo"?

(C) *telling*, which means "striking or revealing," matches up better with the second sentence: "It is all the more striking that the short story hasn't been popular, because the novel, which requires more of the reader, has been popular."

What does "all the more so" mean? The phrase "all the more so" means "especially so," and is used to emphasize a statement by adding more information. This is an escalation of the idea found in the first part of the sentence and especially in the first blank. The writer is making a more insistent point in the second part of the sentence about what was said in the first part. That's why it's so important to pay attention to the second sentence for clues: all the clues are in this sentence.

Why doesn't *unsurprising* work for the first blank? Look first at the sentence **without** the last clause:

> *It is _____ that the short story, regardless of its acclaim amongst certain members of the literati, has _____ amongst the public—all the more so because the novel, in some ways an inherently more demanding form, continues to be popular amongst lay readers.*

If you had just this sentence, it might be clearer. This gives the reason why the short story *should* be popular, so its unpopularity is surprising. If you just stop here, it might be clearer that the first blank would be "surprising" or something similar.

But the final clause does cause some confusion:

> *. . . who apparently subscribe to the trite credo that bigger is better.*

This is an explanation of **why** this surprising situation is true. Note the negativity ("apparently," "trite credo") here. The author is being negative about the idea that "bigger is better" because he feels that it's *not true*. So it's surprising that people actually follow this "credo," especially when novels are actually more difficult!

It helps to keep in mind what the *author's* beliefs are so as not to be tricked by other people's opinions like this. The author finds it surprising, even if the *people* who think "bigger is better" would not.

If short stories are becoming less popular, doesn't that contradict what the second sentence tells us? The first half is discussing short stories, while the second half is discussing novels. Short stories and novels are two different things! So there's no contradiction if the writer says that the short story has "languished amongst the public."

Question 17

Difficulty: **Medium** · Percent Correct: **60%**

The phrase "not so much thing A as thing B" means that thing B is more important or more accurate of a description than A. It doesn't mean that thing A isn't also a contributing factor. For instance:

> *Bob was not so much tired as he was hungry.*

Bob may be tired, but not to the same extent as he is hungry. In the text completion, civil engineers aren't expecting only rain but also something that's even more—something that will contribute more to flooding. Given the "not so much thing A as thing B" structure, it wouldn't make sense to say that thing B—the second blank—must be something that contributes less to the flooding than the predicted increase in precipitation. Therefore, **(E)** *tighter succession*, which indicates more storms in less time, works best.

For the third blank, we need a word that indicates that the possibility of flooding will increase, which leads to **(G)** *far more likely*. Finally, the first blank will require a word to show how civil engineers would react to the increased prospect of flooding. **(A)** *worrying* works best.

Question 18

Difficulty: **Medium** · Percent Correct: **51%**

Answers: **A** **E** **H**

The very last part of the sentence says that you can't figure out an artist's "unconscious urges" by analyzing his or her artwork. Therefore, **(A)** works best. When you *derive* something, you figure it out. (B) *appreciate* doesn't really capture the sense of "figuring out/discovering," which ties back to the clue "never definitively know."

At this point, you can figure out that deriving unconscious urges is a thorny problem. **(E)** *intractable*, which means "difficult to deal with," matches this meaning nicely.

Finally, "empirical analysis" deals with testing observable, measurable phenomena. Therefore, this issue is **(H)** *not really amenable* to empirical analysis.

Question 19

Difficulty: **Hard** · Percent Correct: **45%**

Answers: **A** **D** **H**

This text completion requires sifting through the unimportant words to find the one word that each blank is being contrasted with. The reason we know that the blanks involve contrasts is the word "foil." In a literary or narrative context, a foil is a character who contrasts greatly with another character. The structure for each phrase set off by semicolons is [adjective + person 1] and then [opposite adjective + person 2]. In each case, the blank is the opposite adjective. As long as you can quickly find the adjective that describes the first person and think of its opposite, you have cracked the structure. The vocabulary, however, is still tricky.

The first blank contrasts with "staid accountant." Somebody who is "staid" is very serious, unlikely to take risks and, overall, dull. **(A)** *colorful*, in terms of character, describes someone with a very exciting and lively personality.

For the second blank, we need the opposite of "tight-lipped," or "uncommunicative." **(D)** *garrulous* is the exact opposite.

For the third blank, we need the opposite of "introverted," which is **(H)** *gregarious*.

Question 20

Difficulty: Hard · Percent Correct: 45%

"Unlike" shows that there's a contrast between special effects and story. Special effects continue to evolve. They are **(B)** *exciting.* The different types of stories, on the other hand, have been **(F)** *exhausted.* The third blank continues this idea: in the future, special effects will still be exciting. They'll still **(H)** *hold us in thrall.*

Doesn't *juvenile* mean "still developing?" Not in this context. If you used the word *juvenile* in the first blank, it would mean that the special effects only appeal to children. It's very often a negative word, and you need something positive for that first blank. Only occasionally is *juvenile* a neutral word, and that's usually in a more technical (medical or legal) sense.

What does the phrase "hold us in thrall" mean? *Hold in thrall* can be used either to mean "excite" or, in its older and more literal sense, "enslave" (or something less powerful than "enslave," such as "confine" or "detain"). It might be more useful to consider that something that holds someone in thrall is "captivating," stemming from a more literal meaning that's close to "hold captive."

Question 21

Difficulty: Hard · Percent Correct: 31%

The best way to attack this sentence is to deal with the second and third blanks first. First off, there's the "even … recondite topics," which indicates that the second blank is **(F)**. That is, the author can make even the most obscure topics seem interesting and light. The word "becomes" signals a shift between the second and third blanks. Therefore, **(G)** *curiously stilted,* which means "awkward and unnatural," works best.

Notice that once you've solved the second and third blank, you get a sentence that says that Jansen can write about the most obscure topic in a relaxed, informal way, but when he has to write informally, he's anything but relaxed. This is an example of a paradox, i.e., something that's true but somehow contradictory. Therefore, **(C)** *paradoxical* fits in the first blank.

Question 22

Difficulty: Very Hard · Percent Correct: 25%

Feyermahn accuses Galileo of being only partially rational. His argument is that all of scientific thought is built on human endeavor, which is prone to biases and therefore not entirely objective. For the first blank, you want words showing that Feyermahn isn't criticizing only Galileo. **(A)** *Exclusively implicate* works best.

The second sentence implies that Galileo isn't perfectly rational, and thus **(D)** *found wanting,* which means "lacking," works best. (F) *Dismissed as inconsequential* is too extreme. The sentence is only implying that Galileo came up short. The third sentence moves to modern chroniclers of science, whom Feyermahn urges to be aware of the human weaknesses of scientists. Those writers of science who choose not to would be **(H)** *remiss,* or negligent. (I) *Contrarian* implies a deliberate stubbornness that isn't supported by the context.

Why is _partially repudiate_ incorrect? _Repudiate_ means, roughly, "to go against or to deny the truth or validity of something." So _repudiate_ does kind of fit, but the word that throws everything off is the word _partially._

Feyermahn's criticism of Galileo's scientific rationalism brings into question the entire foundation and history of Western scientific thought:

> "does not _____ the Italian astronomer, but rather **the very edifice of Western thought**."

That's a pretty big thing!

To say that Feyermahn _partially repudiated_ Galileo would be to say that he only questioned or denied part of Galileo, and by extension, only part of "the very edifice of Western thought." But you know from the rest of the passage that he called into question both Galileo's entire body of scientific work and the entire historical view of western science. So "partially repudiated" just doesn't fit the blank.

Question 23

Difficulty: **Very Hard** · Percent Correct: **25%**

Answers: Ⓐ Ⓓ Ⓖ

The "timeworn yarn" implies that tradition, in this instance, is incorrect. Therefore, the first blank is **(A)** _buck_, which means "to go against." For the second blank, we find the clue deeper in the sentence ("constantly conducting experiments"). Therefore, the idea that babies are **(D)** _passively receiving_ has been turned on its head, or shown not to be true.

For the final blank, we have a simple shift. The "although" implies that while they are novice scientists, so to speak, they're **(G)** _far from_ "exhibiting mastery."

What does "what tradition has long known, science must labor through its usual rigorous protocols ..." mean? And how does _buck_ fit in the first blank? "What tradition has long known, science must labor through its usual rigorous protocols to arrive at, albeit the very same assessment."

In other words, people already know things, but science has to work very hard to prove them true.

> "Concerning learning in infants, recent findings (i) _____ this trend ..."

Now you're looking at a specific case. People know things about infants, and science works very hard to evaluate what people know. You don't know whether the scientist's results support the "trend" in this sentence or undermine it. You have to read on to find out.

> "The timeworn yarn that babies are (ii) _____—and oftentimes disregarding— stimuli from their surroundings has been turned on its head ..."

Now, you know the "timeworn yarn" has been "turned on its head." This is your clue for the first blank, and a clear shift from the very first sentence. In this case, science isn't proving common knowledge. It's actually going against common knowledge. Thus, recent findings *buck* the trend.

Why is the answer to the third blank *far from*?

> *"although (iii) _____ exhibiting a mastery of their respective worlds, infants are constantly conducting experiments—very much like scientists themselves—testing their limits vis-a-vis an environment at once enchanting and frustrating."*

Here, infants are compared to scientists—both test their limits. This makes sense given our answers to the first and second blanks: recent findings "buck" the trend that infants "passively receive" stimuli.

However, the part "although (iii) _____ exhibiting a mastery of their respective worlds" sets a limit on infants and scientists. Both infants and scientists test their limits and explore their environments, but neither are masters of their respective worlds.

The author is acknowledging that there's a limit before introducing the main idea. Let's look at an example:

> *"Although far from having the talent to be a professional, Bob is a good chess player."*

Before the writer says, "Bob is a good chess player," she introduces a limit on that statement.

That's what happening in this sentence. The "although" tells the reader to want a contrast of some kind with "constantly conducting experiments and testing limits." Infants do this, but that doesn't mean they exhibit mastery of their world. The author wants to acknowledge the limit of his statement. "Potentially exhibiting mastery" nor "known for exhibiting mastery" would contrast properly with "constantly conducting experiments and testing limits."

Question 24
Difficulty: **Very Hard** · Percent Correct: **24%**

Answers: **C D H**

"Replace it with a breezy glibness" indicates that psychology books avoid, or **(C)** *eschew*, complexity. The second part of the sentence is tricky. The word "succor," which means "support in times of hardship," is a good way to figure out the remaining two blanks. Tough times require succor, so **(H)**, for the third blank, works perfectly. (G) *heady* means "exhilarating," which doesn't fit the context.

For the second blank, you need a word similar to "platitudes," which are trite, useless sayings (not helpful during trying times). **(D)** *pat* means that the advice is unconvincing and lacking in depth. (F) is a pretty good distractor because it sort of matches up with "littered with." But more context would be needed. The key here isn't that it is littered or filled with just anything; it's the fact that it is filled with platitudes that makes the advice in many books so unhelpful.

Question 25

Difficulty: **Very Hard** · Percent Correct: 22%

This is a very tough question, since a few of the answer choices seem to work. For instance, the landing could have been (A) *strategic* and a (D) *resounding* success, except that there are a couple of subtle phrases that argue against this interpretation. For one, it doesn't make sense to describe a person's reaction to a highly strategic battle as something that "must have been" a success. If something were so strategic, then likely he would have believed that it was a success. This is of course very subtle.

A clearer clue is the idea that Britain had "saved her better infantry for an imminent landing" somewhere else, meaning that the first landing was so unsuccessful that it appeared that Britain hadn't sent "her better infantry to fight." With this interpretation, **(E)** *mere feint*, or a pretend movement meant to deceive, fits. And **(C)** *unpropitious*, or not favorable or indicating a high level of success, falls into place.

Finally, for the third blank, you need to remember that the first attack was a complete disaster, so much so that Oppenheim thought it was a trick. Therefore, Oppenheim would be expecting the troops to make a landing in an area that made more strategic sense. **(G)** *not so heavily exposed* works best.

Why doesn't *unevenly fortified* work for the third blank? There are two basic reasons the British force's landing at Gallipoli could have been a failure: the place they landed was not safe, or the area they then moved to attack was too well defended. This makes "unevenly fortified" tempting, because it's true that an unevenly fortified defense would be easier to attack than a strongly fortified one. But this blank is **not** about what the British attacked; it's about them *"landing upon **an area**"* where they exited their ships. That landing area is better when safe—in other words, "not so heavily exposed."

Question 26

Difficulty: **Very Hard** · Percent Correct: 16%

The first part, "Perhaps there is nothing more to the album than its case that ..." could be rephrased as "Perhaps this album contains only the argument that experimentalism ..." The author presents the idea that the album doesn't have much artistic depth.

If you choose either (A) *come full circle* or (B) *culminate* for the first blank, it implies that the author is saying this album achieves more than Stockhausen did. Therefore, **(C)** *die* is the best choice: perhaps the album argues that musical experimentalism isn't over, isn't dead.

It's best to deal with the third blank next, which could be rephrased as: "That to create ... one has to _____ a clear, recognizable tune." From the first sentence, you know that the album is a poor attempt at "creating new things with sounds" and is "sophomoric," or overconfident and immature. So this band listened to avant-garde music, like that of Stockhausen, but didn't really understand it. Then they made their own album, thinking they understood avant-garde music, but it came out "sophomoric." It might be erratic and unpleasant. You can infer that the third blank

Answers: C E G

Answers: C D H

has something to do with "giving up" a clear, recognizable tune, leading to **(H)** *forgo producing*. This makes sense considering the author doesn't like the album.

You can see that the last part says something like "in order to create a totally new, never-before heard sound, one has to give up a clear, recognizable tune." Your choices are that this concept is an (D) *unsettling conclusion*, (E) *unwarranted hypothesis*, or (F) *uncharacteristic rebuttal*.

A rebuttal is a counterargument, but the author isn't saying that the album is a counterargument to anything, nor that it is uncharacteristic. It may be a hypothesis, but based on the characteristics of the album, it doesn't seem "unwarranted." A conclusion is a final statement. If in fact you believe that the album has value as avant-garde music, you'll be led to the **(D)** *unsettling conclusion* that you must get rid of melody in order to create "an unprecedented sound." This is a good fit.

Verbal Question Types: Sentence Equivalence

Sentence equivalence questions have somewhat confusing instructions: *Select the two answer choices that, when used to complete the sentence, fit the meaning of the sentence as a whole and produce completed sentences that are alike in meaning.*

Even if a sentence equivalence question itself looks straightforward, you may be unsure how to proceed. Imagine, for example, a sentence for which three answer choices work. Two of them are synonyms, and one of them isn't. You feel, however, that one of the synonyms only partially works in the sentence, and that the one tempting word that doesn't have a synonym in the answer choices works even better. This could keep your mind spinning. What, then, is the answer?

Let's take a look at a sample question that could put you in such a jam.

The proliferation of anti-smoking images has clearly had a(n) _____ effect: both the number of total smokers and the rate of lung cancer has fallen in recent years.

- [A] salutary
- [B] lasting
- [C] dramatic
- [D] ephemeral
- [E] unremarkable
- [F] beneficial

There are a few answer choices that could work here: [A] *salutary*, [B] *lasting*, [C] *dramatic*, and [F] *beneficial*. However, *lasting* is a bit suspect, because there's nothing in the sentence that implies the changes in behavior are permanent.

So now you're down to three answers. Let's say you really like answer choice [C] *dramatic*. In fact, this is possibly the very word you came up with for the blank. However, because answer choices [A] and [F] are synonyms that work for the blank, there's no way [C] can be the answer. This is an important tip to keep in mind: **If two synonyms work for the blank, then another word cannot be the answer.**

Of course, in the world of the GRE and sentence equivalence questions in particular, it isn't always that straightforward. What if you didn't know the definition of [A] *salutary*? Would it then make sense to choose [C]? No. The vast majority of sentence equivalence answers are synonyms. Even in those sentence equivalence questions in which the two correct answers aren't strict synonyms, synonymous sentences result when you plug the words in. [C] *dramatic* and [F] *beneficial*, however, are very different words and create very different sentences. Therefore, your best bet is to first choose [A] *salutary* even though you don't know what it means. The assumption here is that [A] *salutary* is one of the two synonyms. Then you want to choose either *dramatic* or *beneficial*. One of them will most likely be the answer.

You may hesitate, thinking that the odds are 50/50. However, if you pick [C] and [F], while avoiding the word you don't know, your chances of answering the question correctly are nil, because such different words clearly create different sentences.

Here are some good strategies for dealing with sentence equivalence questions:

- Always look for synonyms.
- If you can't find any synonyms in the answer choices (given you know the definition of every word), then the correct answers will be words that aren't technically synonyms.
- If you don't know a few of the words, don't just pick two words because they're synonymous; sometimes two pairs of synonyms exist within the six answer choices.
- If no pair of words that you know creates synonymous sentences, choose a word you don't know and match it with one of the answer choices that works.

If the tips above sound like taking some big gambles, that's because approaching sentence equivalence in terms of guessing is so complex compared to the typical one in five-choice questions. Basically, you'll want to do anything to increase the odds of guessing correctly. And, to do so, the steps above will be a helpful approach.

MANTRA

Everyone else is also struggling on this really dense reading passage.

The little negative voice loves to use the really tough questions as proof that you're not doing well. But, truth be told, almost everyone finds the tough questions tough. Often those who were able to arrive at the correct answer were the ones who were able to turn off the negative voice in their heads.

Sentence Equivalence Practice Questions

These examples should help you get an idea of what to expect from sentence equivalence questions on the GRE. There are even more practice questions in the GRE practice test in chapter 6.

Question 1

Difficulty: Easy · Percent Correct: 80%

After the botched elections, the country descended into _____, with many of the stronger taking advantage of the weaker amidst the lawlessness.

A turmoil

B antipathy

C exclusivity

D corruption

E indifference

F chaos

Question 2

Difficulty: Easy · Percent Correct: 78%

Augustine's sylvan sketches evoke a _____ in the viewer that echoes the very repose during which the artist himself rendered these woodland scenes.

A weariness

B contemplativeness

C tranquility

D mistrust

E serenity

F skepticism

Question 3

Difficulty: Easy · Percent Correct: 64%

A tantalizing paradox in the field of number theory—especially for the neophyte— is that even one with little training can pose a legitimate question that can _____ a seasoned expert.

A impress

B baffle

C undermine

D confound

E convince

F discourage

The Russian writer **Alexandr Solzhenitsyn** (1918–2008) survived living in a Gulag (forced prison camp) and was eventually expelled from the Soviet Union, despite the fact that he had won the Nobel Prize in Literature. After the Soviet Union collapsed in the early 1990s, he returned to his native Russia, where Putin eventually presented him with an award for his humanitarian achievements.

Question 4

Difficulty: **Easy**   ·   Percent Correct: **60%**

That Alexander Solzhenitsyn languished for many years in a Siberian prison camp can perhaps account for the _____ tone of many of his novels.

- [A] bleak
- [B] sentimental
- [C] cogent
- [D] sanguine
- [E] persistent
- [F] grim

Question 5

Difficulty: **Medium**   ·   Percent Correct: **57%**

Pearson's prose has become increasingly _____; even those who once extolled his intricate metaphors now believe that the excessive use of such language only serves to undermine any semblance of narrative.

- [A] unguarded
- [B] ornate
- [C] embellished
- [D] vague
- [E] lucid
- [F] truculent

Question 6

Difficulty: **Medium**   ·   Percent Correct: **49%**

Corrupted by handshakes and sly winks, the government was run by a leader who cared only for his _____ and nothing for his languishing people.

- [A] contemporaries
- [B] adversaries
- [C] cronies
- [D] relations
- [E] chums
- [F] legacy

Question 7

Difficulty: **Hard**   ·   Percent Correct: **38%**

To most, the word *architecture* connotes a grandeur typically associated with the Old World—flying buttresses, Doric columns, baroque flourishes, byzantine arabesques—and thus many of the more _____ structures, especially those not obviously inspired by neoclassicism, are often thought to be cobbled together haphazardly instead of following some prescribed architectural idiom.

A modest
B secular
C unassuming
D dilapidated
E ramshackle
F sedate

Question 8

Difficulty: **Hard** · Percent Correct: **32%**

Academics, when locking rhetorical horns, can toss off the most pointed barbs by deploying nothing more than an understated phrase, so it should come as no surprise that they are also prone to seeing _____ where none exist.

A slights
B conspiracies
C misinterpretations
D rivalries
E misperceptions
F snubs

Question 9

Difficulty: **Very Hard** · Percent Correct: **28%**

The travel writer must invite _____; few travelogues, if any, have ever been inspired by a languorous afternoon poolside.

A travail
B tribulations
C excitement
D scandal
E tranquility
F serenity

Question 10

Difficulty: **Very Hard** · Percent Correct: **19%**

The city council was notorious for voting down any measure that would restrict its ability to wield power, so that it _____ a bill aimed to narrow the ambit of its jurisdiction was surprising only to the small few who had come to believe that the council would pull an about-face.

A championed
B took exception to
C discarded
D was in favor of
E tabled
F objected to

Sentence Equivalence Answers and Explanations

Question 1
Difficulty: **Easy** · Percent Correct: **80%**

Answers: **A F**

The keywords here are "botched elections," "descended," and "amidst the lawlessness." "Botched elections" and "descended" show the word in the blank is negative. "Lawlessness" has to be similar to the word in the blank.

[A] *turmoil* means "chaos." If a country is in turmoil, there is great confusion.

[B] *antipathy* means "aversion or strong dislike."

[C] *exclusivity* denotes the exclusion of other things, which doesn't match the context of this sentence.

[D] *corruption*, while negative, doesn't match with lawlessness. Nor does corruption have a similar word among the answer choices.

[E] *indifference* means "not caring."

[F] *chaos* is similar to "turmoil" and both imply a sense of lawlessness.

Question 2
Difficulty: **Easy** · Percent Correct: **78%**

Answers: **C E**

"Repose" is a sense of calm. The sentence shows that there's a similarity between the state in which the artist painted the scenes (a sense of calmness) and the viewer's response.

[A] *weariness* is "tiredness."

[B] *contemplativeness* means "thoughtfulness." This word doesn't contrast as well with *repose* as do [C] and [E].

[C] *tranquility* is "peace."

[D] *mistrust* isn't supported by the context.

[E] *serenity* means "peace."

[F] *skepticism* is "mistrust."

Question 3
Difficulty: **Easy** · Percent Correct: 64%

Answers: **B D**

This is one of those sentence equivalence questions where many different words could fit in the blank. In such cases with an unclear blank, it's a good idea to go to the words and look for synonym pairs.

The only real trick here is [A] and [E]. But the two words don't overlap as well as we need—you can convince a friend to go to the movie, but you would hardly say he's impressed.

Only **[B]** and **[D]** are similar words, making them the answers.

Question 4

Difficulty: **Easy** · Percent Correct: **60%**

"Languished" means "to suffer from being in an unpleasant place." Therefore, we can assume that his tone is going to be negative. "Prison camp" reinforces this.

[A] *bleak* means "not hopeful."

[B] *sentimental* means "overly emotional" and suggests a longing or nostalgia for something.

[C] *cogent* relates to an argument that's persuasive.

[D] *sanguine* means "cheerful, optimistic."

[E] *persistent* is "constant, not changing." The word lacks the connotation of hopelessness/despair that we need here.

[F] *grim* means "lacking any hope or cheer."

Answers: **A F**

Question 5

Difficulty: **Medium** · Percent Correct: **57%**

The clues are "once extolled … intricate metaphors … excessive use."

Pearson was once praised for his metaphors, but now he overuses them. Therefore, his language has become vague, difficult to understand, and *embellished*. Obviously many of these words can fit. When this is the case, always remember: two answers have to be similar words. The two synonyms, **[B]** and **[C]**, work because they both mean "to become more decorated and detailed." As Pearson uses more intricate metaphors, his prose becomes more *ornate*.

Answers: **B C**

Question 6

Difficulty: **Medium** · Percent Correct: **49%**

The clues are "Corrupted … cared only … nothing for his languishing people."

The government is corrupt and the leader is allowing his people to suffer. He cares only for his colleagues/friends/henchman. [B] *adversaries* doesn't make sense since the sentence doesn't suggest that the leader would care for his enemies. [F] *legacy* also doesn't work because the sentence never suggests that the leader would care about his lasting reputation or lineage. [A] *contemporaries* and [D] *relations* are too vague. The pair that works best with the context of the sentence is **[C]** *cronies* and **[E]** *chums*, since they both imply the closeness that "handshakes and sly winks" hint at.

Answers: **C E**

Question 7

Difficulty: **Hard** · Percent Correct: **38%**

The trap here is to narrow-sightedly contrast *grandeur* with the blank. If you do so, you'll end up with [D] and [E]. The contrast, however, isn't between *grandeur* and dilapidation, but rather, between what constitutes "architecture" and what does not. Therefore, **[A]** and **[C]** fit this context much better. The contrast is between everyday buildings and the grand structures of the Old World.

Answers: **A C**

Question 8

Difficulty: Hard · Percent Correct: 32%

This is a very tough question because of the way that the answer choices are arranged. An uncommon definition of "slight" is used and two words that could arguably both work on their own (*conspiracies*, *rivalries*) create meanings that are a little too different for comfort. Finally, to make things even more difficult, two matching words, [C] and [E], describe the context of the sentence but not the specific word that goes in the blank.

First off, in academic writing, a great insult can come from an understated phrase. In other words, it only takes a few, low-key words for an academic to insult someone. Therefore, it shouldn't be surprising that academics are likely to see insults where none exist. **[A]** and **[F]** are similar to the word "insult" and are the two answers to this question.

[B] could work, but it doesn't have a matching word. Be careful with "conspiracy." By a stretch, "conspiracy" could work in the original sentence, but a "conspiracy" and a "rivalry" are two different things.

[C] and [E] are similar words but don't fit the blank—though they do fit the general context. *Misperceptions* and *misinterpretations* result because academics are prone to seeing insults/slights/snubs where none exist. It wouldn't make sense to say that misperceptions result because academics are prone to seeing misinterpretations where none exist. The misperception is that they're seeing insults where none exist.

What does this sentence even mean? To understand this sentence you'll need to know the definitions of words like "rhetorical," "deploying," and "barbs."

- "Academics, when locking **rhetorical** horns, can toss off" = Academics, when debating [a rhetorical fight], throw
- "the most pointed **barbs**" = insults
- "by **deploying** nothing more than an understated phrase" = by using an understated phrase
- "so it should come as no surprise that they are also prone to seeing slights **where none exist**" = so it's not surprising that they tend to see insults where there actually are none

Putting the simple version together, then, you have the following:

Academics, when debating, can throw insults by using an understated phrase, so it's not surprising that they tend to see insults where there are none.

Essentially, this sentence states that when academics argue with one another, they don't yell insults. Instead, they respond with subtle statements. The statements are so subtle that it's hard to tell that they're even arguing back. Because professors argue this way, they sometimes mistake any subtle statement as an insult even when there isn't an insult there.

Question 9

Difficulty: **Very Hard**   ·   Percent Correct: 28%

The second part of the sentence states that travelogues don't result from relaxing travel. Therefore, the first blank indicates a word that's the opposite of relaxing. **[A]** and **[B]** both imply difficulty and challenge.

[E], [F], while synonyms, are the opposite of the blank.

[C] could work in isolation but creates a different sentence than the one that results from [A] and [B].

[D] could possibly work in isolation, but again it creates a very different sentence than the rest of the answer choices.

Answers: **A** **B**

Question 10

Difficulty: **Very Hard**   ·   Percent Correct: 19%

This sentence is tricky. It seems as though the city council's action was surprising. But notice the word "only" after the word "surprising." Only those who expected the council to deviate from their normal behavior were surprised. Most people didn't expect that, so the blank should align with the council's normal behavior.

Their typical habit is "voting down any …" Therefore, **[B]** and **[F]**.

[C] is tempting, but there's no synonym in the answer choices, since "discard" is far more permanent than "table."

[E] means "to put aside for later." It doesn't mean "to consider."

Answers: **B** **F**

Verbal Question Types: Reading Comprehension

In order not to give any test takers an advantage, the GRE tries to pick topics that as few people as possible know about. Some ETS doozies have included women bicyclists in nineteenth-century America, predation on anesthetized tadpoles, and radioisotope dating in icebergs.

Out of all the sections on the GRE, it might very well be reading comprehension that students pay the least attention to. They likely figure, "I know how to read. I'll just do a couple of practice passages—if that—to get the hang of it."

Yet reading comprehension is, for many, the most difficult section to improve on. For one, reading comprehension isn't just about reading; it's about understanding how the test writers phrase questions and create trap answers. These questions will test your ability to work without utter certainty (the way you would in math) and instead weigh two answers that are almost identical, one being slightly better than the other. Discerning these nuances—in a stressful environment, no less—is one of the keys to doing well on the reading passages.

Doing well is also about pacing. You might be able to apply the strategies you learn here, but if you do so in a way that wastes time, you're hurting yourself. Practicing speed without compromising accuracy is no easy feat, and it takes plenty of grit—you may want to give up long before you start seeing substantial progress. You'll also have to be patient, especially if you're not an avid reader, as your brain adapts to the kind of elevated language seen on the test. But practicing diligently will reward you on test day. You'll develop a sense of pacing that shouldn't interfere with your performance on the rest of the GRE Verbal.

Finally, practicing reading comprehension questions is important for your performance on the entire test. Even if you're a strong reader and are faced with what you think are relatively easy questions, you might still be worn down by the time you reach the end of the verbal section. That's why honing your ability to focus for several hours is so important: the amount of concentration required on the reading passages can be a significant drain on your stamina.

In the pages that follow, you'll learn the different passage types, the different question types, and strategies to both understand the passages and not fall for those ever-so-subtle traps the test writers are fond of laying.

Reading Comprehension Passage Types

1. **Short passages:** ten to twenty lines, usually two questions
2. **Paragraph arguments:** eight to twelve lines, always one question
3. **Medium passages:** twenty to forty lines, typically three questions
4. **Long passages:** fifty-plus lines, four questions

The GRE Verbal reading comprehension questions can be divided into two large categories: the paragraph argument questions with shorter prompts, and the longer passages with multiple questions. The strategies that follow are relevant short, medium, and long passages. Since paragraph argument questions involve specific kinds of challenges that are different from general reading comprehension, we treat these questions separately in the later sections of this chapter.

Reading Comprehension Question Types

1. **Standard five-answer questions:** This applies to all reading comprehension questions in the GRE Verbal, except for the question type mentioned directly below.

2. **Multiple-answer questions:** For the multiple-answer question, the instructions are as follows: *"Consider each of the choices separately and select all that apply"*

   You'll know that you're dealing with a multiple-answer question type when you see a question that has exactly three answer choices—A, B, and C—all of which have squares rather than circles around them. The correct answer(s) can be just one answer choice, a combination of two answers, or all three answers.

   There will be one to three multiple-answer questions per GRE Verbal section.

Meet the GRE Reading Passage

What exactly is a GRE reading passage? And what makes it so special (and difficult!)? To answer this, we're going to give you two short passages that cover an identical topic.

> *Detecting art forgeries has become less difficult, thanks to innovations in technology. Computer algorithms are now able to determine the number of brushstrokes common to each artist. A forger, guided only by the naked eye, would have difficulty determining how many brushstrokes an artist used on a particular canvas because these intricate details require many brushstrokes. Forgeries, once thought to be genuine, are now thanks to computer analysis—turning up in auction houses throughout the world.*

> *The use of technology to detect art forgeries has become increasingly common now that computer algorithms are able to capture details so subtle that they elude the human eye altogether.* **Nonetheless**, *the forgers are gaining an understanding of the way that the algorithms function and as a result are creating forgeries capable of foiling the algorithms.* **While** *such attempts at reverse engineering a painting are not always successful—often a forger will focus on an aspect of the painting that is only part of or not at all included in the algorithm—sometimes the computer technology is beguiled by the hand of an adept forger into identifying a forgery as a genuine work of art.* **Yet** *computer algorithms should not be discounted altogether, because they are still capable of exposing fake works and, when used in conjunction with an art expert's testimony, provide the most accurate means we have of determining the authenticity of a work of art.*

The first paragraph is highly readable and engaging—the type of article you'd expect to read in a popular magazine. The second paragraph, on the other hand, might lead readers of a popular magazine to unsubscribe. The sentence structure is more advanced, the style more sophisticated. The third sentence in particular is convoluted; students will likely reread it several times (which we don't recommend doing—but more on that later). Phrases such as "beguiled by ... art" are elevated in style, making the sentence even more difficult to parse.

While it's easy to get lost in the thicket of words, the GRE passage writers are very deliberate about including "signpost" words—words that indicate the relationship between sentences and clauses within those sentences. Understanding how these important words function will help you navigate the twists and the turns of the passage.

In the second passage, we have boldfaced these signpost words. Generally speaking, they fall into three categories: Same, Opposite, Cause and Effect.

1. **Same:** the statement in one clause/sentence is similar to the idea that preceded it

   Examples: *additionally, also, moreover, likewise, too, furthermore*

   Example sentence: Researchers have found evidence that the indigenous sloth population is decreasing. **Additionally**, evidence shows that the native toucan population is languishing.

2. **Opposite:** the statement in one clause/sentence is opposite to another written idea

   Examples: *yet, though, however, but, nonetheless, nevertheless, at the same time, notwithstanding, still, that said*

   Example sentence: **Though** evidence shows that the indigenous sloth population has decreased in recent months, much of this can be attributed to seasonal variations in the animal's numbers.

3. **Cause and Effect:** the idea expressed in one clause is the result of an idea discussed in an adjacent clause

   Examples: *since, so, because, consequently, as a result, due to, given*

   Example sentence: **Given** the recent destruction of the rainforest, the sloth population is deprived of its natural habitat and is rapidly decreasing in number.

Picking up on these signpost words, especially those that indicate "opposite," will help you see a pattern common to many GRE passages. In our earlier excerpt, the author conveys a thought (forgers can't always fool the algorithms) only to limit the statement in the following sentence (but they're often able to do so).

This is called qualifying a statement. It's what often makes GRE passages tricky to understand, since the author isn't taking a "yes-or-no" position on an issue. Instead, he or she is arriving at a reasoned position that leans toward "yes" or "no." In this case, the author believes that it's not easy to trick a computer, but (first qualification) an adept forger can do so. Finally, the author adds that computers are still an important part of identifying forgeries.

Anticipating the signposts and the qualifications will help you better package the information as you read—and better navigate the twists and turns of the passage. We will build on this idea in the following section.

Attacking the Passage

It might seem obvious that the first thing to do is read the passage. But what exactly does it mean to "read" the passage? For instance, you could skim fifty lines, getting a general sense of what the passage is about, but not really being able to articulate any of the supporting details or counterarguments. Likewise, you could carefully read each paragraph, taking assiduous notes.

The two strategies are on opposite sides of the spectrum, and neither is recommended for the GRE. Instead, your reading pace should be somewhere in the middle. What's just as important, though, is *how* you read the passage. You'll want to use an important technique: active reading.

Five Essential Tips for Active Reading

1. **Get excited!** Perhaps art forgeries interest you. But for many readers, they're unfamiliar footing, because few of us have ever really given the topic much thought. The GRE intentionally picks such topics because they don't want to give students with specialized knowledge an advantage. To ensure this, they select topics that can be highly esoteric (the advent of bicycle riding in nineteenth-century America is one such topic from *The Official Guide to the GRE revised General Test*, Second Edition).

   Coupled with the dense prose, these obscure topics induce boredom in many test takers. Even if they can't stop their minds from wandering, readers nonetheless start stringing words together, losing a sense of the main ideas in each paragraph. They hope that by brute force they'll get to the end of the passage and will have a sudden moment of enlightenment. Not very likely! By not engaging the "active-reading brain" from the beginning, readers tend to make "word salad" out of the passage.

   To combat this tendency, convince yourself that the topic matter is super interesting, that it rivals front-page news (the proliferation of mollusks in the South Pacific? Whoa, tell me more!). This mindset will help turn your "active-reading brain" on so that you can take advantage of the other tips.

2. **Understand the big ideas in each paragraph.** Each paragraph is packed with lots of information: big ideas, supporting details, qualifications, and even multiple viewpoints. As much as possible, try to mentally summarize the main idea of the paragraph—or take "mental snapshots." Yes, this means pausing for a quick few seconds as you absorb and assimilate the information. But by gaining this deeper understanding, you'll save time when you come to the questions because you'll have a stronger grasp on the passage.

   Your goal isn't to mentally summarize everything, but rather to get a sense of the function of each paragraph. This "paragraph sense" will allow you to know where to look for the evidence to answer the question. It will also give you a sense of how the paragraphs connect, which can be important.

3. **Don't get bogged down by the tough parts.** As mentioned in the previous tip, you don't want to spend too much time trying to understand a paragraph. Often, there's a sentence, usually toward the end of a paragraph, that's difficult to understand. Although it's easy to get a feeling of dread that you'll miss something huge if you don't entirely understand the sentence, that's typically not the case. If you can sum the sentence up at the level of specificity, say, of "the author is disagreeing with some aspect of theory," that will be enough.

   The point is you might not even have to deal with this thorny patch of text. But if you do, then going back to the passage—which is one of the key elements of attacking questions (more on that in a later section)—will allow you to see the text with "fresh eyes" and without the cognitive load of having to read the entire passage.

4. **Note any counterarguments or additional points of view.** The passages—especially the long ones—will usually describe a complex issue. The author will either take a specific stance or describe a specific stance within the debate. Then, another viewpoint will be offered, a counterargument to the point the author brought up. It's not as straightforward as the author saying, "I think that forgers cannot outsmart computer technology," and the counterargument saying, "I think they can." Rather, it will be far more nuanced, something along the lines of "even if forgers are unable to replicate an artist's brushstroke, they only need to be able to do so with enough accuracy to foil a computer." The counterargument might be "even a deviation in brushstroke that is too minor for the human eye to detect is sufficient for a computer to detect." Again, the difference is over something very detailed in the argument—a difference in brushstrokes, if you will.

   A question or two on these small areas of contention often pops up. By being alert to these counterarguments the first time you read through, you give yourself a much better shot of answering the questions correctly.

5. **Watch for signposts.** Signposts, as we discussed earlier in this chapter, both hold the passage together and tell you where the passage is going. Knowing the signposts and how they function is a big part of active reading. If you forget the specific definition of a signpost ("notwithstanding" is commonly misconstrued, for one) or gloss over it altogether, you'll likely misunderstand what the author is saying.

Active Reading in Action

Now that we've discussed how to actively read, it's time to apply what we've learned. The following passage is both difficult and not that interesting (at least for most). So you might want to review the first tip, the one about getting excited!

You should also do the following: after each paragraph, jot down a paraphrase of what you just read. Ultimately, you'll want to take a "mental snapshot" of the passage, but for now, write out your paragraph paraphrases *and* a one-sentence summary of the entire passage once you finish reading. For the last paragraph, which is very long, try to paraphrase two main points.

For the summary, don't be too specific (that's not the point), but also don't be too general and just write down the topic (it's about how the human brain learns). To give you a sense of what you should come up with, we've included example paragraph paraphrases and an example passage summary after the passage.

The view that the brain is unable to regenerate and grow was long ago overturned and replaced with the view that the brain is plastic, meaning that it can and does heal itself in response to injury. However, recent studies performed on the brains of deceased individuals indicate that scientists have in fact underestimated the plasticity of the human brain.

The studies found that oligodendrocytes, the cells that form myelin sheaths, which allow the brain's one hundred billion neurons to communicate with one another, do not perish the way they do in the brains of rat and mice—which until now had formed the basis of understanding of the human brain. Rather, oligodendrocytes in human brains lose only one per three hundred cells per year, a state contrasting greatly with that found in the brains of mice and rats, in which the oligodendrocytes are replaced every time the animal needs to produce more myelin. The implication is that the human brain is more prepared for trauma because it can quickly replenish myelin, unlike the brains of rats and mice, which must create entirely new oligodendrocytes to do so.

To substantiate such a claim, researchers must demonstrate more convincingly the relationship between the ability of existing oligodendrocytes to replace old oligodendrocytes and the speed of myelin regeneration. Moreover, scientists need to show that myelin regeneration is not the only significant factor to contribute to plasticity. For instance, the brain tends to employ both hemispheres to a far greater degree than before following trauma, especially if that trauma involves a task typically limited to one side of the brain. For example, those with strokes to the left hemisphere, which is responsible for speech, will enlist parts of their right hemisphere when forming sentences. Determining to what degree, compared to the brain of a mouse, the human brain engages both hemispheres will provide researchers with a deeper understanding of what role oligodendrocytes play in plasticity. Nonetheless, such a relationship might be difficult to ascertain since the oligodendrocytes themselves might play a role in how efficiently the brain uses both hemispheres to perform a task traditionally limited to one hemisphere. What is clear from the research is that to understand plasticity, researchers must study the human brain whenever possible.

Example Paragraph Phrases and Passage Summary

Note: We've included abbreviations of the more difficult terms, which is something you should, too. For instance, even if you're taking mental snapshots, you shouldn't repeat "oligodendrocytes" syllable for syllable since it adds unnecessary strain to your brain. Instead, just abbreviate as something simple like "oligos."

1st paragraph: Plasticity has been the dominant view for a while but human brains may be even more plastic than previously thought.

2nd paragraph: Oligos form myelin, which helps brain function. Rats need to replace oligos, unlike humans; human brains are therefore more plastic.

3rd paragraph: Oligos might play a part in how both hemispheres are used, so it's hard to determine how plastic the human brain is.

Passage summary: The primary purpose of this passage is to talk about myelin regeneration and how it's different in humans from that of mice and rats.

Final note: Like learning any new skill, learning active reading might at first seem awkward and time consuming. But by practicing and getting the hang of juggling lots of information in your head, you'll become faster. The real upside is the confidence you'll have answering questions, which can suck up a lots of time if you find yourself vacillating between a few answer choices.

Attacking Questions

Answering questions isn't just a matter of reading the question and looking for the answer. In fact, that could result in missing a question that you might have gotten right had you followed the method below, which we call RIPHAM.

Read question

Yea, this one is pretty obvious. But what is important is that you read the entire question, word for word. In a timed situation, it's easy to miss an important word or two that can lead you to misinterpret the question. And skimming the question—taking in only a few words—can lead you to reconstruct a different meaning than the one intended.

Ignore answers

This is much easier said than done because the answer choices are right in front of you, like a finish line at the end of the race. Yet you should think of them not as offering salvation, but as luring you with a false promise of success. The reason is that when we go directly to the answers, our brains are in "confirmation mode." That is, we get attached to the part of the answer choice that sounds right. The test writers know this, so they create answer choices that are mostly correct, save for a word or two that makes the answer choice slightly off (we'll talk about this later in the section on answer choice traps).

Paraphrase question

This step, while not always necessary, makes the next step a lot easier. What often happens is that when you read the question and head to the passage to look for supporting text, you suddenly forget what the question was asking. To prevent this from happening, take a short second to simplify what the question is asking. That way you'll be able to "store" this information as you hunt for the supporting evidence.

Hunt in the passage

The answer to every reading comprehension question is always in the text. This part of the passage is called the supporting text. This might seem like an obvious point, but it's one that many seem to forget as they struggle with two answer choices: one that's right and one that's almost right. It's easy to convince yourself of either one if you stare at them long enough. But by going back to the passage, you can rely on the supporting text to help you make an informed decision.

Luckily, many questions give you a specific line reference so you know where to hunt for the information to support your answer to the question. When you see that line reference, read one sentence above the cited line (for context) and, if necessary, one sentence below. The answer is almost always contained in those lines. And for those thorny patches we talked about earlier, you're more likely to understand the text the second time around. But don't skim too quickly. Make sure you're taking in the information.

Other questions don't tell you where in the passage to look. But these questions do give you keywords that are clustered in a certain part of the passage. So if you actively read correctly, you'll have a sense of where words occurred—a "geography of the page"—and you'll know where to hunt for the supporting text. For instance, if the question is asking about "myelin replacement in rats," you might remember that this phrase appeared in the second paragraph. If not, you skim the entire passage looking for the phrase. Make sure to have at least a few words in this phrase. You don't want to search just for "rat" or "myelin."

Finally, you can tackle questions that ask about the main idea or the function of the paragraph both by returning to the passage and by relying on your mental snapshots. If the question asks about the function of a specific paragraph, you might want to quickly reread that paragraph. If you've actively read the first time around, you can skim the paragraph more easily. And for main idea questions, you can rely on your first read-through. If that's not enough, don't read the entire passage but reread the first paragraph and the topic sentences of the subsequent paragraphs. This will give you an idea of the author's main idea vs. ideas that are too narrow.

Anticipate answer

This step is about how you engage with the supporting text. Once you've found this information, make sure you're able to understand how it answers the question. Then, rephrase the text in your own words so you can simplify the ideas (which will be important for the next step). Essentially, you're providing the answer to the question; you're doing the thinking rather than letting the answer choices do the thinking for you.

Remember, to rephrase is not the same as to reinterpret, so make sure you stick to the text as much as possible.

Match

Finally, match your answer—which should be based on a simplification of the text—to an answer choice. In the case that you're left with two answers, as often happens on tough questions, don't be afraid to go back to the text yet again. To help differentiate between those two answer choices, you'll also need to know the way test writers create traps, the way they create that almost-right answer, and just what exactly makes it incorrect.

Answer traps

The key to understanding answer traps is to constantly be asking yourself the following: "What makes a wrong answer choice wrong?" Most wrong answer choices will fall into one of the following categories:

1. **Uses words in passage but twists the author's meaning.** One thing our brain loves is familiarity. We latch on to words and phrases we remember seeing in the passage, convincing ourselves that the answer is correct. Meanwhile, we forget to put all those words together to see that they result in a statement that's incorrect. In other words, the test writers will twist what the author is saying while using familiar words.

2. **True, but in a different part of the passage.** Sometimes an answer choice is actually correct, in the sense that it is supported by the passage. The problem that it doesn't answer the question at hand. Therefore, always read the question carefully so you know what it's asking.

3. **True in the real world, but not found in the passage.** Sometimes, an answer choice will sound true, as far as common sense goes. But it won't actually be covered in the passage. If it's not supported by the passage, it's incorrect.

4. **Everything is right except one thing.** We call this the "rotten fruit" error. Think of how you shop for fruit. When you pick up an apple, you don't look at the one shiny spot and say, "Hey, I'll buy this apple." Instead, you turn it over meticulously, looking for that one rotten spot. Likewise, on the reading comprehension answer choices, you shouldn't just look at the part that's right. Instead, you should "turn over" the entire answer choice, making sure that each word/phrase is valid.

Putting It All Together

Now that you've actively read the passage on neuronal regeneration and the different kind of traps the test creates, let's try a few practice questions. As you answer these questions, remember to apply the RIPHAM method and to see which one of the above four categories the wrong answer choices fall into. (On actual practice questions, you might only want to do that when you're down to two possible answers).

Question 1

The passage mentions that both hemispheres of the brain respond to injury in order to

(A) discuss how myelin regeneration may serve a greater function than previously thought

(B) show that brain plasticity is not limited to one factor

(C) suggest that oligodendrocytes might have a role in how the two hemispheres work

(D) highlight one way in which stroke patients recover

(E) question the connection between oligodendrocytes and the speed in which myelin is replaced

Explanation

Reread this supporting text:

> *Moreover, scientists need to show that myelin regeneration is not the only significant factor to contribute to plasticity. For instance, the brain tends to employ both hemispheres to a far greater degree than before following trauma, especially if that trauma involves a task typically limited to one side of the brain. For example, those with strokes to the left hemisphere, which is responsible for speech, will enlist parts of their right hemisphere when forming sentences.*

From this text, You'll see that (B) is the correct answer. (A) takes elements from the passage and twists them into the wrong idea. Both (C) and (E) refer to the wrong part of the passage. And nothing about (D) is correct.

Question 2

According to the passage, one reason that knowing how much the human brain relies on both hemispheres does not provide an adequate basis for determining the role of oligodendrocytes in brain plasticity is that

(A) brain trauma is rarely limited to one side of the brain

(B) myelin regeneration might not be the only measure of brain plasticity

(C) the human brain is too complex for scientists to understand

(D) the oligodendrocytes might be involved in how the brain uses both hemispheres

(E) it's only recently that scientists have begun to use human brains to understand how new cells grow

Explanation

You might notice that this question stem is very complex. In this case, you'll want to use the "P" from RIPHAM, which stands for "paraphrase."

> **Simplified:** Knowing how much the human brain relies on both hemispheres doesn't tell us how oligos are related to plasticity because …

Reread this supporting text:

> *Determining to what degree, compared to the brain of a mouse, the human brain engages both hemispheres will provide researchers with a deeper understanding of what role oligodendrocytes play in plasticity. Nonetheless, such a relationship might be difficult to ascertain since the oligodendrocytes themselves might play a role in how efficiently the brain uses both hemispheres to perform a task traditionally limited to one hemisphere. What is clear from the research is that to understand plasticity researchers must study the human brain whenever possible.*

You'll see that **(D)** is the correct answer. (A) is wrong and not supported at all by the text. (B) doesn't answer the question. (C) is debatable and not supported by the text. (E) contains information not mentioned in the passage.

Miscellaneous Reading Tips

1. **Practice, as much as possible, using official material.** Content-wise, nothing beats practicing with actual GRE questions from ETS. The style and tone of the passages, the way questions and answer choices are worded, and the subtlety between the correct answer and the incorrect answers can only be found in actual questions.

2. **Know why the wrong answers are wrong.** The wrong answers are the soul of the reading comprehension questions. Oftentimes, you may know the general answer to a question. General knowledge isn't what the GRE is testing, though. It's testing whether you can tell the difference between an answer choice that's almost right and one that's right. Only by having a strong sense of why the correct answer is correct and the incorrect answer incorrect will you truly have mastered a question.

3. **Reread passages.** Are you worried by the thought of practicing over and over with the same reading passages? It's understandable, but unless you have an amazing, photographic memory, you'll probably have forgotten most, if not all, of a passage you read six weeks ago.

   It's also not about getting questions right. It's about knowing why the correct answer is correct and the wrong answer wrong. The chances that you'll remember the exact distinctions between answer choices are fairly small. Think of it this way: each time you go through the same passage and answer choices is a fresh opportunity to exercise your analytical muscles.

4. **Be aware of your mistakes.** Often, there's a pattern to your mistakes. It could be that you infer too much on inference questions or that you often miss the single word in the passage that makes all the difference. It could be misinterpreting answer choices. Anticipating your personal common mistakes can help you improve.

Paragraph Argument

Among the GRE reading comprehension passages will be a few that Magoosh calls "paragraph argument questions." About three of these will appear as reading comprehension passages on any GRE Verbal section. The GRE lumps these in with other reading comprehension questions, but they're quite different in a few ways.

The paragraph argument questions have short prompts (25–100 words) that present an argument, and they always have only one question that asks you to analyze that argument.

To dive in deeper, let's discuss what makes up an "argument" in paragraph argument questions.

At a very basic level of analysis, every argument has two parts: (a) the premise and (b) the conclusion. The premise is a factual statement. For GRE-taking purposes, you should assume that the factually presented premises in paragraph argument questions are true. The conclusion is the viewpoint that the author of the argument wants you to believe. The words "therefore," "consequently," and "thus" are common signposts for conclusions. Unlike the premise, the conclusion is often a prediction.

Consider this simple argument:

Amrita is about to take a trip to Ireland. Mike is going to be so jealous of her.

Obviously, any argument about individual people and their feelings wouldn't be academic enough for the GRE, but we can use this argument for practice. The premise is the first sentence. That's a factual statement. For the purposes of analyzing this argument, we'll assume that this is the truth.

The second sentence—the prediction—is the conclusion of the argument.

While your job on the GRE is to believe that the premises are true, you're under no obligation to believe any argument. In fact, when you recognize a paragraph argument question on the GRE, you should immediately put your "critical-thinking hat" on. It's a good idea to activate "suspicious mode" and think, "Hmmm, do I *know* that this is true?"

Do we know that this argument about Amrita and Mike is true? Do we know that the conclusion is true? Not necessarily. In order for it to be true, there would have to be an unstated link between the premise and conclusion. Such a link is called the "assumption" of the argument, and it holds the argument together like a linchpin. Here, an assumption might be "*Mike is always jealous of other people's trips*" or "*Mike loves Ireland and is jealous when anyone else travels there.*" If either one of those were true, the above argument would be considerably more plausible. Conversely, if we knew for a fact that either one of those were definitely not true, then this would call the entire argument into question.

If you have experience with the GMAT or are planning on also studying for the GMAT, it's good to know that the "paragraph argument" is virtually identical to the "critical reasoning" questions on the GMAT.

The assumption is critical to most paragraph argument questions. Identifying it will allow you to answer the question.

But before we learn to do so, let's take a look at a GRE-like paragraph argument question.

In effort to combat three consecutive years of boll weevil infestations, cotton farmers have started using Eradicon, a chemical just released to market, capable of emitting an odor that effectively repels the boll weevil. The agricultural board expects that cotton production on those farms using Eradicon will return to levels similar to those from three years ago.

Which of the following, if true, does the most to weaken the agricultural board's expectations?

So that's what a paragraph argument question will look like on the GRE. Now, let's dive in!

Because of the word "weaken," we know this is a question that requires you to weaken the argument. "Undermine," "argue against," "call into question," and "diminish" are some such words.

One strategy is to read the question first. That way, when you go to read the paragraph, you'll know what you'll need to do.

Finally, each paragraph argument will be followed by five answer choices, exactly one of which is correct. They're never multiple-answer questions.

  Ⓐ Eradicon has been proven to repel boll weevils in a laboratory setting.

  Ⓑ Those cotton farmers who chose not to use Eradicon tended to witness a greater drop in cotton production during the last three years than those who started to use Eradicon.

  Ⓒ Most boll weevil infestations happen in the early spring, when cotton plants are highly vulnerable.

  Ⓓ When used for more than a week, Eradicon begins to leach the ground of nitrates, without which cotton plants cannot adequately grow.

  Ⓔ Farmers need to spray Eradicon on their fields once every few days for it to be effective.

Attacking the paragraph argument

The first step is to identify the premises. With most paragraph argument questions, these come at the beginning. The premises, again, are facts upon which the conclusion rests. In this case, the following are premises:

1. There have been three consecutive years of infestation
2. Farmers have started using Eradicon
3. Eradicon emits an odor that repels the boll weevil

These premises must be accepted as fact and should not be challenged.

Next, we need to identify the conclusion. Words such as "therefore" and "thus" often indicate the conclusion. In this case, it's the agricultural board's expectation that serves as the conclusion:

> **Conclusion:** *Cotton production on those farms using Eradicon will return to levels similar to those from three years ago.*

The assumption

The next step, and perhaps the most difficult, is to anticipate the answer by identifying the assumptions. The reason this is challenging is that the assumptions are unstated. Yet, if the assumption is untrue, as we learned in the Amrita and Mike example, the argument falls apart.

For this question, an assumption is that boll weevils do *not* develop an immunity to Eradicon. If they do, the conclusion is invalid. In a "weakening" type of paragraph argument question, the correct answer could point out an assumption and then attack it, e.g., most boll weevils develop an immunity to Eradicon after a few months. In a "strengthening" type of paragraph argument question, the correct answer will address an assumption, e.g., boll weevils aren't able to develop an immunity to Eradicon.

By thinking of assumptions and what the correct answer must look like, you avoid rushing into the answer choices and falling into any one of several traps, which we will discuss later.

Another assumption is that cotton crops aren't vulnerable to some other pest. In other words, the argument assumes that A causes B, where A is the boll weevil infestation and B is the reduction in crops.

This A causes B, or A $\Rightarrow$ B, is a common kind of assumption.

A related assumption is that *only* A causes B. It's possible that while boll weevils certainly don't help cotton production, there could be another cause that has led to the cotton decrease, so eliminating the boll weevils won't help cotton production return to its level of three years ago. We can denote this as follows, where C is any other factor that's hurting cotton growth:

$$C \Rightarrow B$$

There are other assumptions about the effect Eradicon will have. Granted, it might effectively repel boll weevils (as the premises states), but it might, by some other means, hurt cotton production.

In thinking about the assumptions, you can anticipate the correct answer. It might not exactly match the assumptions you generated, but you'll be better able to spot the correct answer since you've already done the critical thinking. Sometimes, usually with the easier paragraph argument questions, the thirty seconds you spent thinking of assumptions will lead you right away to the answer.

While it might seem like all this thinking through of the question is just a waste of time, the big time drain comes from not sufficiently thinking of the assumption and then going straight to the answers. You'll find yourself typically going back and forth between two of three answer choices, choosing one that you're not confident about, and often getting it wrong.

Back to the question

Now, take a stab at the paragraph argument question using the technique we just discussed. You might be able to generate an assumption we didn't mention. And if you have trouble describing an exact assumption, that's fine. Just thinking about the gaps in the argument will help. With practice you'll get better at explaining the gaps that exist.

Below, we'll describe why the wrong answers are wrong and why the correct one is correct.

(A) *Eradicon has been proven to repel boll weevils in a laboratory setting.* We already know from one of the premises that the odor from Eradicon repels boll weevils. The information in the answer choice is irrelevant to how the use of Eradicon will ultimately affect cotton production.

(B) *Those cotton farmers who chose not to use Eradicon tended to witness a greater drop in cotton production during the last three years than those who started to use Eradicon.* This answer choice indicates that Eradicon is likely effective, since those farmers who used it witnessed a greater increase in cotton production than did other farmers. True, there could be some other variable that led to this increase. Regardless, this information does nothing to challenge the conclusion.

(C) *Most boll weevil infestations happen in the early spring, when cotton plants are highly vulnerable.* The prompt doesn't mention anything about the seasons and how that would affect cotton growth.

(D) *When used for more than a week, Eradicon begins to leach the ground of nitrates, without which cotton plants cannot adequately grow.* **Correct answer:** This answer choice shows that Eradicon, while effective against boll weevils, is actually destructive to the cotton plant itself. Sure, the boll weevils may have scurried off to different pastures, but now the cotton plant is unable to grow. Therefore, cotton production is unlikely to return to previous levels, and this answer choice effectively weakens the conclusion.

(E) *Farmers need to spray Eradicon on their fields once every few days for it to be effective.* See below in "traps."

Traps

You might have noticed that one answer choice did the opposite of what the question asked—it strengthened the argument. What often happens is that a few answer choices are irrelevant, such as (A) and (C) in this question. Another answer choice is the opposite, meaning that if the question is asking you to strengthen the argument, the trap answer weakens the argument, and vice versa.

Usually, you'll be left with two answer choices, one of which is correct. The other answer choice is tempting because it seems to weaken the conclusion, in the case of a "weaken question" and strengthen the conclusion in the case of a "strengthen question."

One way to realize that you're dealing with one of these kinds of answer choices is that you'll often have to make a certain assumption for it to be the correct answer. Returning to (E), note that if we assume that farmers don't spray Eradicon every few days, then it's not going to be effective and the conclusion will fall apart. However, we have to make this other assumption. It's just as likely that the farmers will spray Eradicon every few days, especially considering what's at stake.

To sum up the technique we used above,

1. Read paragraph argument question first to determine if it's a weaken, strengthen, or other variety
2. Read the prompt, looking for the conclusion
3. Identify assumptions (two or three is sufficient)
4. Find an answer choice that matches up
5. Keep your eye out for traps

Paradox questions

Another type of paragraph argument question you can expect to see in the reading comprehension portion of the GRE Verbal involves a paradox. What makes this kind of paragraph argument question different from those questions described above is that there's no *conclusion*. Instead, you're given two premises that seem to contradict one another. However, like those other paragraph argument questions, you can only pick one answer that best resolves this discrepancy. Let's take a very simple example, one that you wouldn't see on the test:

> Jim ran three miles more each day in July than he did in June. Jim weighed himself at the end of July and was five pounds heavier than he was at the end of June.

The discrepancy here is that we wouldn't expect somebody who increases the amount he or she exercises to gain weight. The correct answer would help us show how these two facts, while seemingly contradictory, are actually true. Here is one possible answer:

Jim drank protein powder three times a day, increasing his average caloric intake from 3,000 to 4,500 calories.

The correct answer should give you a eureka moment. In this case, it's the increased caloric intake in the month of July that led Jim to put on pounds, despite the extra running.

In terms of approaching the question, you should spend about twenty to thirty seconds seeing if you can anticipate what the answer must look like. That is, think of a possibility that might resolve the paradox. This process isn't intended to match up with the answer even half the time. But by thinking about the discrepancy at a deeper level, you're less likely to fall for one of the wrong answers or distractors.

See if you can come up with good reasons to eliminate the following distractors:

1. Jim was more likely to run up hills in June than he was in July.
2. Jim biked more in June than he did in July.
3. Jim was on a crash diet in May and consumed very few calories.
4. Jim began gaining weight steadily through the month of July.

Explanations

1. Does running up hills really make you burn much more calories? Perhaps. But this answer choice is far too vague. "More likely" could mean a couple of light hills a week, or it could mean 15,000 feet weekly elevation gain. Whenever you feel like "it depends," because you don't have enough information, you should be careful picking that answer choice.
2. This is very similar to the first answer. It's vague. We need to know how much more Jim biked.
3. This is about the month of May, not the months of June and July. Therefore, it's irrelevant in resolving the paradox.
4. This is consistent with the premises. For that reason, you might be tempted to choose this as the correct answer. But remember: you're trying to resolve the paradox, not reinforce it.

MANTRA

If I get this question wrong, it's only one question out of many.

Even if you're going for a perfect score, you can miss a question. You don't have to answer each question correctly to prove that you know what the GRE is testing. The reality is that these tests are filled with difficult questions. Don't let these questions bully you and take you out of your rhythm. Instead, use the skip function and maintain your poise on the next, much easier questions.

Now let's turn to an actual GRE-style paragraph argument question that involves a paradox:

> In the last three years, the number of pink bottlenose dolphins in Eremonte Coastal Reserve has dramatically increased, as the number of turtles the dolphins feed on has increased significantly. While marine biologists have confirmed the increase in dolphins, tourists coming to the park, hoping to see the dolphin, have been disappointed, and tour guides themselves say that the sightings of the dolphins are no more common than they were in previous years.
>
> Which one of the following most helps to explain the apparent contradiction above?
>
> (A) Tour operators, in the hopes of driving more business, feature the dolphin prominently in their promotional brochures.
> (B) Only one tour has an official who reported sighting a pink bottlenose dolphin.
> (C) The turtles on which the dolphins feed tend to congregate in deeper waters of the park, where the guided tours do not travel.
> (D) There has been an increase in the number of nurse shark sightings, yet there has not been an overall increase in the number of nurse sharks in the reserve.
> (E) Sightings of the dolphin tend to be increasingly rare the farther from the coast boats travel.

Explanation

Answer (A) reinforces the idea that the park is trying to bring in more tourists to see the dolphins. It doesn't explain why this influx of tourists is no more likely to see the dolphin than in previous years, when the dolphins were not as numerous in the park. (B) reinforces the notion that there aren't many dolphins. In other words, it provides more evidence for the premises but does nothing to resolve the discrepancy. **(C)** is the correct answer. Remember that the dolphin feeds on the turtles that gather in deep water where the boats cannot reach. Notice as well that there has been a significant increase in the turtles. Therefore, the dolphins are far more likely to be feeding on turtles in the areas of the park where the guided tours cannot reach. This resolves the paradox that there have been fewer dolphin sightings despite the increase of dolphins in the park. (D) is wrong because it reverses the paradox: fewer animals but more sightings. (E) doesn't work because the answer focuses on dolphin sightings outside of the park. Whether or not such sightings have increased or decreased doesn't help us resolve the issue of in-the-park sightings.

Encephalization quotient (EQ) is a complex ratio indicating how big the brain of an animal is, given its body mass. Humans have the highest EQ on the planet, 7.44, but dolphins are second at 5.31. All other animals have EQs less than three: the next highest are chimpanzees and ravens, tied at 2.49.

The names that appear in paragraph argument questions on the GRE are often fictitious. We've kept that theme alive, conjuring up such fictitious locals as Eremonte Coastal Reserve—which we hear is nice this time of year.

The American
economist **Thorstein
Veblen** (1857–1929)
was a witty critic
of capitalism.
For example, he
coined the term
"conspicuous
consumption."
Throughout the
20th century, social
thinkers have
appreciated that
Veblen provided a
non-Marxist critique
of capitalism.

Boldface

You can spot the boldface-style paragraph argument questions from a mile away because they have bold text as part of the prompt! Most of the questions of this type actually have two different sections in bold. The key to the boldface questions is to pay attention to the role of each sentence. This is always good practice for dissecting any argument. If you can label the role of each sentence in any argument, you understand that argument well.

Here's an example boldface question:

In economics, a "Veblen good" is an item that people buy in greater quantity when the price goes up. **According to the law of supply and demand, when the price of an ordinary item goes up, demand drops, i.e., people buy fewer of them.** A Veblen good is a luxury item to which status is attached, such as a designer outfit or luxury car. As the price of such an item increases, its prestige increases, which makes the item that much more desirable. **Therefore, as the price increases, the demand also increases, and more of these items are sold.**

In the argument, the two portions in boldface play which of the following roles?

(A) The first is a piece of evidence supporting the main conclusion; the second is the main conclusion.

(B) The first is a view that the author opposes; the second is the main conclusion.

(C) The first is a prediction; the second gives evidence for this prediction.

(D) The first is a general rule, the violation of which seems to indicate a paradox; the second is the resolution of that apparent paradox.

(E) The first is an ironic description of what could happen in the marketplace; the second is a more realistic description of what actually happens.

As you can see, these are tricky! The four incorrect answer choices are designed to be tempting and confusing distractors. As we saw with the other paragraph argument questions, it's often helpful to have your own clear idea about the argument and your own clear sense of an answer to the prompt question before you get confused by the answer choices.

Let's start with the prompt argument. In this argument, the first bold statement is the law of supply and demand, which, as you may remember from Economics 101, is a big deal. It's a general rule that products on the market are supposed to obey. Apparently these Veblen goods don't obey this general rule, which is a bit of a paradox. The final sentence, the second bold statement, makes clear why these Veblen goods don't obey the general rule. So the first bold statement is a general rule and the second is an explanation of why something doesn't obey this general rule.

Explanation

(A) is incorrect because the first bold statement isn't evidence in the sense of a clear factual statement, and it certainly doesn't support the second statement. For (B), we have no idea whether the author opposes the law of supply and demand, but it would be quite odd for any economist to oppose something this widely accepted. The second statement isn't really a conclusion. Therefore, (B) is incorrect. The law of supply and demand isn't simply a prediction, and the second bold statement is certainly not consistent with it. So (C) is incorrect. **(D)** is the correct answer because of what we mentioned in the last paragraph on page 274. Lastly, (E) isn't right because there's nothing ironic or hypothetical about the law of supply and demand, and the second bold statement, while realistic, isn't a generally applicable rule.

Parting thought

We've covered the majority of the passage questions you'll see on the reading comprehension portion of the GRE Verbal. Try to complete as many of these questions as possible. If this is your first time wrestling with passages, this may seem like a slow and laborious process, but that's simply because it's new to you. Take heart. As you practice these, you soon will be unraveling these texts with efficiency!

○ ● ○ ————
● ○ ○ ————
○ ● ○ ————
○ ○ ● ————
● ○ ○ ————

Paragraph argument

Reading Comprehension Practice Questions

These examples should help you get an idea of what to expect from reading comprehension questions on the GRE. There are even more practice questions in the GRE practice test in chapter 6.

Question 1

Difficulty: **Easy** · Percent Correct: **83%**

Political Analyst: "Although citizens of this state normally oppose any new taxes, they are overwhelmingly in favor of taxes that support the medical initiative. Candidate Johnson vowed to cut these taxes, and he was trounced in the primary elections. **Furthermore, in a poll that asked citizens, 'Would you pay higher taxes if it meant having the benefit of the new medical initiative?' an astonishing 82% replied, 'Yes.'** This is a pattern of support for taxes we have not seen before in this state."

In the political analyst's argument, the portion in boldface plays which of the following roles?

(A) It is an explanation that the argument concludes is correct.
(B) It is a finding that calls the main conclusion into question.
(C) It introduces a judgment that the argument opposes.
(D) It provides evidence in support of the main conclusion of the argument.
(E) It is the main conclusion of the argument.

Question 2

Difficulty: **Easy** · Percent Correct: **71%**

A table made entirely from the trunk of a tree said to have lived 1,000 years was recently claimed to be made from that of a much younger tree. In order to rebut this charge, the craftsman summoned a team of dendrochronologists to prove that the tree lived to be at least 1,000 years old. Dendrochronology, or the technique of using tree rings to date wood, is based on the fact that for each passing year a tree develops exactly one ring, as seen in a horizontal cross-section of the trunk. Given that dendrochronology is accurate for trees that lived less than 2,000 total years, the dendrochronologists will be able to determine whether the work comes from a tree that lived to be at least 1,000 years old.

Which of the following is an assumption that the argument makes?

(A) The craftsman has not used the trunk of the same tree in other works of art he has produced.
(B) The tree was not less than 1,000 years old when it was cut down.
(C) The craftsman worked on the wood consistently, without taking breaks of more than one year.
(D) The wood used in the table is large enough to contain a span of 1,000 tree rings.
(E) Dendrochronology has shown to be inaccurate for the oldest trees in the world, since parts of the trunks are so worn down that traces of tree rings are difficult to discern.

Question 3

Difficulty: **Easy** · Percent Correct: **66%**

The price of the SuperPixel high definition television, by Lux Electronics, has typically been out of the range of most consumers, a few of whom nonetheless save up for the television. This past July, the SuperPixel reduced its price by 40%, and sales during that month nearly tripled. TechWare, a popular electronics magazine, claims that the SuperPixel television should continue to see sales grow at this rate till the end of August.

Which of the following suggests that TechWare's forecast is misguided?

(A) Most of the customers who had been saving up for the SuperPixel bought the television in July.

(B) Sales of the MegaPixel high definition television, an even more expensive model than the SuperPixel, saw declining sales in the month of July.

(C) Electronics sales tend to peak in August and December.

(D) The SuperPixel tends to be an unreliable television and Lux Electronics makes a considerable profit from repairs.

(E) The SuperPixel is the only model for which Lux Electronics plans a price reduction.

Question 4

Difficulty: **Medium** · Percent Correct: **57%**

Epidemiologist: Malaria passes into the human population when a mosquito carrying the malaria protozoa bites a human who has no immunity. The malaria parasite can remain in the blood of an infected person for up to forty days. The disease cannot be passed from person to person, unless a non-infected person is exposed to the blood of an infected person. Theoretically, malaria could be eradicated in any given area if all the mosquitoes carrying malaria in that area are exterminated. If such a course of action is carried out at a worldwide level, then the global eradication of malaria is possible.

Which of the following, if true, suggests that the epidemiologist's plan for eliminating malaria is not viable?

(A) A person who is infected with malaria can infect a mosquito that is not carrying malaria, if that mosquito bites such a person.

(B) Some strains of malaria have protozoa that have been documented to last more than forty days inside the blood of a human.

(C) Malaria is still endemic in many parts of the world, and many health workers believe that the global eradication of malaria is not possible.

(D) Some people in areas where malaria is rife have developed an immunity to mosquitos, yet they also show a higher incidence of genetic disorders such as sickle cell anemia.

(F) Mosquitos in many developing parts of the world are responsible for passing on a variety of viruses to human hosts.

Question 5

Difficulty: **Very Hard** · Percent Correct: **24%**

Art Historian: Recently, computer analysis has revealed that a few of a famous Flemish artist's works are forgeries, and are actually the work of noted forger Elmyr de Hory. While such a development may emit violent reverberations through the art world, even those museums that have a wealth of the Flemish artist's work in their collections should not be overly concerned. Hundreds of this Flemish artist's works were tested to determine whether they were forgeries, yet only a slim few turned out to be actual forgeries. Thus, the master's reputation as one of the greatest artists humanity has ever produced will surely remain undiminished.

Which of the following, if true, casts the most doubt on the art historian's conclusion?

(A) The computer analysis involved is more likely to mistake an actual work as a forgery than to mistake a forgery as an actual work.

(B) Many of the Flemish artist's well-known portraits are in the collection of private owners and were therefore not subjected to computer analysis.

(C) Some of the works upon which the Flemish artist's standing rests were identified by the computer analysis to be the work of de Hory.

(D) Some museums, worrying that their most prized painting from the Flemish artist would be deemed forgeries, and thus lose value, only offered up the artist's lesser known works for computer analysis.

(E) Though few in the art world dispute the outcome of the computer analysis of the Flemish artist's work, many contend that the identified forgeries are not the work of Elmyr de Hory but some other highly skilled forger.

Question 6

Difficulty: **Easy** · Percent Correct: **89%**

Company X and Company Y have each been building a rocket ship able to travel to Mars. After five years of design and construction, the rocket ships have been unveiled to the public, which instantly noticed the rocket ships are so similar in design as to be indistinguishable. Therefore, one of the companies must have had information pertaining to the design of the other rocket ship.

Which of the following, if true, would most call in to question the validity of the argument?

(A) The engineers responsible for the design and construction of the rocket ship are subjected to a rigorous vetting process.

(B) Each space ship uses a different color scheme, which matches that of each company's logo.

(C) Several employees currently in the employ of Company X were working for Company Y before the construction of the rocket ship.

(D) Given the current materials, there is only one possible design that satisfies the aerodynamic requirements to reach Mars.

(E) Both companies have been highly profitable and have been heavily funded throughout the five years in which the rocket ships have been constructed.

Question 7

Difficulty: **Hard** · Percent Correct: **39%**

State park officials recently released a report urging hikers in Rockridge Mountain Park to exercise caution during the months of April and May. According to the report, the number of mountain lion sightings in the park reaches its peak in the months of April and May.

All of the following could account for the increased number of mountain lion sightings EXCEPT

(A) During April and May, which feature the best hiking weather of the year, more people visit the park than during any other time of year.

(B) Throughout the year, local newspapers report any mountain lion sightings, and most reports come during the months of April and May.

(C) The red-tailed deer, the mountain lion's primary food source, is most abundant during these months and tends to favor hiking trails.

(D) In spring, the trail conditions are best for mountain bikers, who, because they make less noise than hikers, are more likely to startle mountain lions.

(E) Creek beds high in the mountains tend to dry up in spring, so mountain lions often descend into the lower elevations, where hikers are more common.

Question 8

Difficulty: **Hard** · Percent Correct: **34%**

Consumer Advocate: Happy Smiles Daycare, a popular child-care facility in Rolling Hills, boasts an average child-to-caregiver ratio of 5:1, a number it cites as the lowest in the county. Furthermore, the daycare claims that compared to some other daycare centers in the county, it doesn't include helpers, or those who are involved in cleanup and diaper changing, when computing the ratio. Yet Happy Smiles Daycare's claim that parents with children aged 1–3 will find no other facility with such a low child-to-caregiver ratio isn't accurate.

Which of the following, if true, provides the best justification for the Consumer Advocate's position?

(A) Happy Smiles Daycare has two rooms, one for children 1–2 years old and another for those 2–3 years old, both of which have a child-to-caregiver ratio of 5:1.

(B) Kenton School, which has fewer than 100 students and a legitimate child-to-caregiver ratio of 6:1, provides classes for each year up to age 6, though the classes for those over 3 years old have a child-to-caregiver ratio more than three times that of the other classes.

(C) The number of students enrolled in Happy Smiles Daycare remains relatively fixed throughout the year.

(D) Tiny Tots Daycare, which boasts a 4:1 child-to-caregiver ratio, includes any adults who are in a classroom throughout the day.

(E) Looming budget cuts indicate that Happy Smiles Daycare may not be able to sustain such a low child-to-caregiver ratio in coming years.

Question 9

Difficulty: **Very Hard** · Percent Correct: **27%**

The prevalence of a simian virus has been directly correlated with population density in gorillas. Recent fieldwork in the Republic of Dunaga, based on capturing gorillas and testing the gorillas for the virus, has shown that Morgania Plain gorillas are more than twice as likely to be infected than are the Koluga Mountain gorillas. Nevertheless, the population density of Koluga gorillas is significantly greater than that of Morgania gorillas.

Which of the following could best account for the discrepancy noted above?

(A) During periods of little rainfall, Koluga gorillas often wander down into the plains in search of food.

(B) Dormant strains of the simian virus are often difficult to detect.

(C) Due to the Morgania gorilla's natural habitat and its less reclusive nature, researchers have tested a greater number of Morgania gorillas than Koluga gorillas.

(D) Infected Koluga gorillas behave very aggressively and are more difficult to subdue for testing.

(E) The Koluga and the Morgania both have similar markings on their backs but are classified as different subspecies.

PASSAGE

Chopin the pianist has been greatly overshadowed by Chopin the composer. When Chopin the pianist is mentioned, it is his dreamy gaze and supple wrists (as well as countless female admirers gathered around the piano returning that same dreamy stare). But Chopin was a formidable pianist in his own right; after all, he was able to play, from start to finish, all twenty-four of his *études*, a set of pieces so demanding that even today's great pianists feel taxed after performing them. Two things could account for this oversight: for one, any pianist for whom no extant recordings exist is likely not to weather time well. Secondly, Chopin's coeval and friend, Franz Liszt, was of such legendary prowess that Chopin himself wished he could play his own études the way Liszt did. Nevertheless, Chopin deserves to be remembered not just as a composer of challenging pieces but as a pianist capable of executing, with panache, these very pieces.

Question 10

Difficulty: **Medium** · Percent Correct: **54%**

Which of the following, if true, would cast the most doubt on the author's contention regarding Chopin the pianist?

(A) Chopin rarely, if ever, played the piano works of other composers.
(B) Apart from a cello concerto and a few other works, Chopin composed mainly for the piano.
(C) Chopin seldom performed his études in concerts, preferring to play in front of a small group.
(D) Not all of Chopin's compositions are as difficult to execute as his études.
(E) Chopin himself acknowledged that he was primarily a composer, and would have composed even more difficult pieces had he the ability to play them.

Question 11

Difficulty: **Easy** · Percent Correct: **64%**

In the context in which it appears, "weather" most nearly means

(A) perish
(B) subsist
(C) withstand
(D) transform
(E) sustain

Gustave Flaubert (1821–1880), the author of *Madame Bovary*, said: "There are three things in the world I love most: the sea, [Shakespeare's] *Hamlet*, and Mozart's *Don Giovanni*."

PASSAGE

In *Don Giovanni*, what is perhaps Mozart's best-known opera, there exist two distinct endings, a phenomenon not entirely unknown during the composer's time, but one that invites the obvious question: why did Mozart decide to include alternate endings for *Don Giovanni*, when he did not do the same with his other famous operas, *Die Zauberflöte* and *Le Nozze di Figaro*? Another question, and one not so obvious, is why Mozart himself was uncertain as to which of the two endings to choose, as is evidenced in his correspondence with Lorenzo Da Ponte, the opera's librettist.

A common answer is to treat both these questions as one: Mozart was uncertain as to which ending to provide, so he wrote both endings. Such a reply ignores an important consideration: why did Mozart decide to provide these specific endings? Libard provides a reasonable answer: The traditional ending—in the sense that it is the one that was popular during the composer's day, and continues to be so today— is clearly more palatable for audiences. The hero, Don Giovanni, is chided for his libertine ways and then the cast appears in tutti, bellowing a merry chorus as the curtain falls. The audience is left having a light dose of entertainment, which, after all, was the aim of many of the operas of Mozart's time. Fine, but then what of the tragic ending? Libard—trading the sensible for the pat—offers little more than that such an ending reflects the political climate of the day.

This alternate ending—Don Giovanni is suddenly cast down to Hell, and instead of being redeemed, the hero emerges from the underworld chastened, and the curtain falls—was interpreted by the critics of the day as heavy-handed didacticism. While such a view is not entirely without merit—Mozart ultimately aimed to impart some lesson for his incorrigible Lothario—it still leaves the question unanswered as to why there are two endings, and what exactly Mozart aimed to communicate that could not be housed in a traditional ending.

One answer offered recently by musicologist Gustavo Lucien is that Mozart balked at including a traditional ending, feeling that it was incongruous with the serious tone of most of the opera. In fact, *Don Giovanni* falls more under the rubric of *opera serie* than *opera buffa*, the latter typically featuring light endings in which the entire cast sings in an upbeat, major key. Da Ponte, however, insisted that forthwith casting Don Giovanni to Hell, and offering him scant opportunity for redemption, would likely leave the audience feeling ambivalent. Such an ending would also suggest that the librettist had been unable to think of a tidy resolution. Da Ponte, then, was not so much against a tragic ending as an abrupt tragic ending. Perhaps even Mozart was unsure of what to do with Don Giovanni once he was in Hell, and may have even been working out a different ending, using the light ending as a stopgap till he achieved such an aim. In that case, the fate of Don Giovanni can best be explained by the fact that Mozart—through debts, ill-health, and the composer's obligation to compose works for his patrons—was unable to return to a work he had tabled.

Question 12

Difficulty: **Medium** · Percent Correct: **46%**

In the context in which it is used "tabled" most nearly means

(A) considered

(B) discarded

(C) toiled over

(D) unintentionally forgotten

(E) put aside indefinitely

Question 13

Difficulty: **Very Hard** · Percent Correct: **19%**

The author of the passage would take exception to all of the following statements regarding Libard's response to the existence of dual endings to *Don Giovanni* EXCEPT

(A) Libard's explanations of *Don Giovanni*'s multiple endings are not uniform in their usefulness.

(B) Libard offers little insight into both of the questions posed in the first paragraph.

(C) Libard's understanding of eighteenth-century audiences is flawed.

(D) Libard's interpretation of the tragic ending to *Don Giovanni* has more in common with that of Lucien than with that of Lorenzo Da Ponte.

(E) Libard's views, while not entirely accurate, are consistently probing.

Question 14

Difficulty: **Hard** · Percent Correct: **45%**

Consider each of the choices separately and select <u>all</u> that apply.
According to the passage, Mozart's use of a tragic ending allowed him to accomplish which of the following?

[A] He was able to teach a moral regarding wanton behavior.

[B] He was able to be consistent with the conventions of the opera prevalent during his time.

[C] He was able to provide a resolution that would allow audiences to feel satisfied.

PASSAGE

The efficacy of standard clinical trials in medicine has recently become the subject of contentious debate between those practitioners who maintain that such trials, despite admitted shortcomings, still represent the best means we have for learning about the effects of pharmaceutical drugs on the human body, and those who maintain that the current system of collecting knowledge of such effects is but one possibility and most likely not the most efficacious one. Gimley and Lebsmith, in their recent work, fall into the latter camp and indeed go further by challenging the idea that the standard medical trials can yield meaningful information on pharmacogenetics, or how a drug interacts with the human body.

Gimley and Lebsmith's foremost criticism is that the effect of a drug differs depending on a person's physiology. To be sure, there are cohorts, or groups, that react to a drug in a specific manner, but clinical trials are unequipped to identify such groupings. The main reason is that clinical trials are allied to the notion that the larger the number of subjects in a study, the greater the validity of a drug, should it show any promise.

Therefore, even if a drug can exercise a marked effect on a subset of subjects within a trial, this information will be lost in the statistical noise. Another criticism of Gimley and Lebsmith concerns the very idea of validity. Pharmaceutical companies will run hundreds of trials on hundreds of different medications. Given the sheer number of trials, a few are likely to yield positive results, even if there is no demonstrable effect. Gimley and Lebsmith cite the fact that most pharmaceuticals that have exerted a positive effect in the first round of testing are likely to fail in the second round of testing.

Gimley and Lebsmith argue that a more effective approach is to identify groups who exhibit similar genetic subtypes. This very approach is currently in use in groups possessing a particular molecular subtype of breast cancer. Furthermore, these groups are not only trying one specific drug, but also a combination of such drugs, subbing them in and out to measure the effects on a subject, a procedure Gimley and Lebsmith endorse. Nonetheless, such an approach is often both time-consuming and costly. However, given the constraints of current medical trials, trials that target subtypes— even if they do not yield any significant advances—will encourage a culture of experimentation on how clinical trials are conducted in the first place.

Question 15

Difficulty: **Very Hard** · Percent Correct: **28%**

What is the primary purpose of this passage?

- (A) To evaluate and survey diverse opinions on the current state of a field
- (B) To point out an oversight in the work of two scholars
- (C) To discuss a field of inquiry and several ways in which that field can be improved
- (D) To describe a current debate and the analysis of specific researchers
- (E) To assess the effect the work of two scholars has had in their field

Question 16

Difficulty: **Hard** · Percent Correct: **39%**

Which of the hypothetical trials best parallels a shortcoming in clinical trials as described by Gimley and Lebsmith?

(A) A subset of patients displays a slightly negative reaction to a drug, but that outcome is masked by the majority of subjects' responses, which are neither positive nor negative.

(B) A drug exercises a strong negative effect on a subgroup but this effect is masked by the majority of subjects' responses, which are neither positive nor negative.

(C) The majority of patients in a trial exhibit a negative effect to a drug, yet the fact that a few subjects exhibited a positive effect diminishes the intensity of the negative effect.

(D) A trial targeting a particular genetic subtype struggles to recruit enough subjects to establish that an observed effect of a drug would be valid across a larger population.

(E) Several subjects in a trial exhibited positive effects from a drug used during an initial phase of an experiment, but once another drug was substituted for the drug used in the initial phase, those patients failed to exhibit any positive effects.

Question 17

Difficulty: **Medium** · Percent Correct: **58%**

It can be most reasonably inferred that those on the side of the debate endorsing standard medical trials are likely to believe which of the following?

(A) Those favoring standard clinical trials believe that such trials represent the only means scientists have of studying pharmacogenetics.

(B) The experimental methods espoused by Gimley and Lebsmith may ultimately come to displace those currently in use.

(C) The most effective method of gathering information concerning pharmacogenetics will not be without flaws.

(D) Clinical trials that focus on a specific genetic subtype will be better able to isolate the effects of a specific drug.

(E) Many drugs exhibiting a positive effect on subjects in the first round of testing will fail to exhibit the same positive effect in subsequent tests.

PASSAGE

Outsourcing, or the allocation of specific aspects of a corporation to a business entity specializing in those areas, has become such an integral part of a company's organizational structure that few question outsourcing's long-term viability.

Two recent studies on this topic are no exception; both focus on ways in which outsourcing can be improved. Each, for the most part, discusses different aspects of outsourcing. Yet there is one area in which the recommendations of both theories overlap somewhat. Peavy chiefly discusses ways in which companies can mitigate the potential negative effects of confidential information reaching competitors. Presently, when a corporation outsources even a small operational function, it must share information pertaining to this function. In other words, the more of its operation a company entrusts to another business entity, the more confidential information that company will have to release. According to Peavy, one way to minimize the negative consequences should any of that information fall into a competitor's hands is to impose stronger penalties on any business entity entrusted with such information, should it divulge that information. However, Peavy is concerned mostly with exploring the effect of increasing the severity of penalties for any one instance of leaked information, and he devotes only one chapter to an existing structural check on such "information leaks": as a company specializing in outsourcing assumes more clients, its legal liability will increase with each company that becomes a client, an effect, he notes, that becomes more conspicuous the more a company diversifies.

Morgan, on the other hand, looks at those business entities that performed the outsourced work. As such entities grow, their ability to provide specialized services to a specific client diminishes. Since, like most business entities, they are driven to grow profits, often doing so by diversifying, the needs of a specific client are often subordinate to this larger goal. Morgan's aim is to educate corporations engaged in outsourcing so that they choose a firm that focuses on providing one service. This view, however, is somewhat shortsighted, since the long-term trajectory of a company is not always clear and a firm may end up diversifying.

In this regard, there is a curious overlap between the two studies: in some ways both see problems with diversification, Peavy focusing on the liability and Morgan on the diminishment in quality of the services rendered. Yet it is important to note that Peavy focuses on how diversification negatively affects a company providing services to companies outsourcing, whereas Morgan focuses on how the latter is negatively impacted.

Question 18

Difficulty: **Medium** · Percent Correct: **58%**

The author of the passage considers Morgan's plan to educate corporations "shortsighted" since it

- Ⓐ seeks to educate only corporations and not business entities to which corporations outsource work
- Ⓑ assumes that companies that plan to diversify may not end up doing so
- Ⓒ provides advice that might not be relevant in the near future

(D) fails to distinguish between corporations and companies to which corporations outsource work

(E) confuses specialized services with services pertaining to the entire operation

Question 19

Difficulty: **Medium** · Percent Correct: **59%**

The primary purpose of the passage is to

(A) describe the way in which two theories conflict

(B) propose two different solutions to the same problem

(C) discuss how two studies arrive at contradictory conclusions

(D) explore two reactions to a phenomenon and draw a parallel

(E) support one theory and discredit a second

Question 20

Difficulty: **Medium** · Percent Correct: **51%**

It can be inferred from the passage that which of the following would be most immune to the "structural check"?

(A) A company doing outsourcing work that does not diversify in terms of the services it provides

(B) A company involved in outsourcing that has been entrusted with confidential information from a large number of companies across varying industries

(C) A business entity that provides one narrow function for a number of corporations

(D) A company that does not have a clear vision of its long-term trajectory

(E) A business whose sole existence is based on providing ancillary services to exactly one corporation

Question 21

Difficulty: **Hard** · Percent Correct: **33%**

According to the passage, which of the following is common to both Peavy's and Morgan's studies?

(A) Both welcome diversification in business entities providing services for corporations.

(B) Both discuss the effect that outsourcing has on the long-term viability of a corporation.

(C) Both explore the way in which diversification and growth within a corporation can affect outsourcing.

(D) Neither focus on the impact of diversification on business entities providing services for companies outsourcing.

(E) Neither questions whether outsourcing itself is a beneficial practice for corporations.

Most dinosaurs, including all the large lizards, died in the Cretaceous-Tertiary extinction 65 million years ago. Nevertheless, there are still dinosaurs loose in the world today: all modern birds, biologically, are members of the clade *Dinosauria*—technically, the ordinary birds we know and love are dinosaurs!

PASSAGE

For much of the twentieth century, paleontologists theorized that dinosaurs, like reptiles, were ectothermic, their body temperature regulated externally. These scientists, however, based their conclusions on faulty reasoning, claiming that scaly skin was common to all ectotherms (amphibians, which are ectothermic, do not have scaly skin) and that the dinosaur's size could account for ectothermy (some adult dinosaurs weighed as little as ten pounds). Supplanting this theory is an entirely new line of thought: dinosaurs were actually mesothermic, neither warm- nor cold-blooded. By taking this middle ground, some paleontologists maintain that dinosaurs were faster than similar-sized reptiles yet did not require as much food as similar-sized mammals. To substantiate this theory, paleontologists intend to study how birds, dinosaurs' closest extant relatives, might have at one time been mesothermic.

Question 22

Difficulty: **Medium** · Percent Correct: **51%**

For the following question, consider each of the choices separately and select <u>all</u> that apply.

Which of the following does the passage imply regarding birds?

- [A] They hold value in their evolutionary proximity to dinosaurs.
- [B] They require more food than a similarly-sized mammal.
- [C] Over time they might have undergone a change in how they regulate body temperature.

Question 23

Difficulty: **Medium** · Percent Correct: **55%**

The two parts in parentheses serve to do which of the following?

- (A) Summarize two claims that the author of the passage ultimately repudiates
- (B) Highlight commonalities between amphibians and dinosaurs
- (C) Provide rebuttals to commonly held views regarding physical aspects of dinosaurs
- (D) Describe a recent theory that the author of the passage supports
- (E) Furnish information regarding contradictory notions of dinosaur behavior

Question 24

Difficulty: **Very Hard** · Percent Correct: **18%**

For the following question, consider each of the choices separately and select <u>all</u> that apply.

Based on the information in the passage, it can be inferred that which of the following is a possible benefit conferred by mesothermy?

- [A] Controlling for size, it allows for greater speed than does ectothermy.
- [B] Controlling for size, it leads to less dependence on food than does ectothermy.
- [C] It allowed prehistoric birds to fly.

PASSAGE

Most scholarship regarding the sudden disappearance of the Olmec civilization 2,500 years ago has focused on the change in meteorological conditions favorable to subsistence crops. Much of this research, though, has overlooked the role that changing geography, most notably the course of rivers, played. The Coatzacoalcos River, the main river passing through La Venta, could have had notable tributaries diverted as a result of climate change, leading not only to severe flooding in certain areas, but also to a lack of sufficient water for subsistence crops planted near the erstwhile alluvial plain. Such a view, however, fails to account for the resilience of a people capable of transferring crops and moving settlements as need be. What was more likely responsible for the downfall of the Olmec civilization was internal dissent brought on by ecological change, since a leadership unable to control events was likely to be perceived as weak. Without the central governance needed to adapt crop subsistence patterns, the Olmec likely became a collection of feuding clans and within a few generations all but disappeared.

Question 25

Difficulty: **Medium** · Percent Correct: **47%**

Which of the following, if true, would best undermine the theory the author of the passage provides for the sudden disappearance of the Olmec?

(A) Much of the flooding that resulted came not from any diverted tributaries but by rainfall that intensified over the course of a decade.

(B) Not all the major subsistence crops were planted along the Coatzacoalcos River.

(C) Internal dissent was long offered as a theory for the disappearance of the Mayans, but in recent years there is near unanimous agreement that the disappearance was mostly caused by a meteorological phenomenon.

(D) The Olmec split into two groups that warred persistently for several decades before both succumbed to meteorological changes that made settlement of the area virtually impossible.

(E) The Olmec leadership successfully relocated settlements near one of the new tributaries of Coatzacoalcos, yet years of constant flooding precluded the growth of subsistence crops.

Question 26

Difficulty: **Medium** · Percent Correct: **54%**

Which of the following best describes the primary function of the third sentence ("The Coatzacoalcos … plain")?

(A) To call into question information mentioned in the sentence that immediately precedes it

(B) To introduce the role meteorological conditions played in the change in crop subsistence patterns

(C) To highlight evidence offered up by most scholarship on the disappearance of the Olmec

(D) To provide a specific example supporting a hypothesis that differs from that mentioned in the first sentence

(E) To indicate how major geographical changes affected the Olmec's ability to govern effectively

Question 27

Difficulty: **Medium** · Percent Correct: **49%**

For the following question, consider each of the choices separately and select <u>all</u> that apply.

Which of the following is an assumption the author of the passage makes?

A The crops displaced by the flooding of the Coatzacoalcos River would not be viable if replanted in areas unaffected by flooding.

B Adapting crop subsistence involves some level of central governance.

C Feuding clans are not capable of sustaining a viable population in the wake of ecological catastrophe.

PASSAGE

Once American men returned from the World War II battlefields, they quickly displaced the women who had temporarily filled jobs otherwise reserved for men. With many women reverting to their domestic role, the dramatic increase in birth rate is perhaps not too surprising. Yet such factors alone cannot explain the increase in the number of births from 1946–1951. Murray suggests that both women's and men's perspectives changed, mostly because of America's success in the war, leading to rapid population growth. However, this position ignores the many middle- and lower-middle-class women who continued working in factories and who contributed to the dramatic surge in population. Regarding this subset, the more plausible view is that couples were more likely to conceive based on the fact that they considered themselves parts of dual-income households—if necessary, the woman of the home could work.

Question 28

Difficulty: **Easy** · Percent Correct: **64%**

According to the author, middle- and lower-middle-class women were more likely to conceive based on which of the following?

(A) Positive attitude
(B) Sense of patriotism
(C) Ability to return to former jobs
(D) Financial outlook
(E) Overall level of health

Question 29

Difficulty: **Medium** · Percent Correct: **58%**

As used in the final sentence, "plausible" most nearly means

(A) accepted
(B) common
(C) credible
(D) praiseworthy
(E) controversial

Question 30

Difficulty: **Medium** · Percent Correct: **54%**

The passage implies that the main shortcoming in Murray's view is that it

(A) ignores the role women play in dual-income households
(B) fails to account for a particular segment of society
(C) relies too much on people's perception of their wealth
(D) overemphasizes women who continued working in factories
(E) only considers women's perspectives

Reading Comprehension Answers and Explanations

Question 1

Difficulty: **Easy**   ·   Percent Correct: **83%**

Answer: **D**

The boldfaced part is evidence that's used to support the argument, which says citizens are in favor of tax increases supporting medical initiatives. This matches up best with **(D)**.

(A) is wrong because the boldfaced part isn't an explanation.

(C) is wrong because nothing is being called into question in the paragraph.

(E) is wrong because the first sentence was the main conclusion.

Question 2

Difficulty: **Easy**   ·   Percent Correct: **71%**

Answer: **D**

Premise: The number of rings on a tree determines the age of the tree.

Conclusion: Using this fact, tree experts will be able to determine the age of the table.

Assumption: The table has to come from a cut of wood that actually has 1,000 rings. If the table comes from only a slice of wood, then it won't contain all 1,000 rings. Remember, according to the prompt, the rings are contained in a horizontal cross section of the trunk. So if the width of the trunk is greater than the length of the table, then you cannot say for sure whether the wood used in table comes from a tree that's at least 1,000 years old. This logic matches best with answer **(D)**.

(A) is completely irrelevant since it relates to other works of the craftsman. The only work that's in question is the table.

(B) is really misleading. The conclusion is that the tree experts can determine (yes/no) whether the tree is at least 1,000 years. If you negate the assumption in (B), that the tree *was* less than 1,000 years old, then the tree experts will be able to definitively determine the tree's age. That's consistent with the conclusion. Negating an assumption should result in the argument falling apart. That happens with (D), since if the table isn't large enough to contain all the tree rings, then the experts won't be able to determine whether the tree was at least 1,000 years old.

(C) doesn't relate to the age of the tree.

(E) is consistent with the prompt: dendrochronology is accurate only for trees less than 2,000 years old.

Question 3

Difficulty: **Easy**   ·   Percent Correct: **66%**

Answer: **A**

The SuperPixel television is very expensive, so it's not surprising that, with the drastic price reduction, many people bought it (the television is popular and many save up to buy it). However, the argument assumes that the surge in sales that occurred in July, when the price reduction happened, will continue into August.

(A) provides a reason to doubt the claim: many who had been saving to buy the

TV bought one in July. Therefore, the price reduction led many consumers (those who represented a pent-up demand) to buy the TV. In August, there will no longer be a pent-up demand, so sales shouldn't be expected to be as high as in July. (A) is therefore the answer.

(B) doesn't relate to SuperPixel and is thus irrelevant.

(C) would suggest that August would be a great sales month, as the paragraph predicts.

(D) relates to SuperPixel sets that have already been bought and are in need of repair. This answer is therefore irrelevant.

(E) suggests that there will be no competition from other Lux models. (E) doesn't provide a reason why sales would not decrease in August.

Question 4
Difficulty: **Medium** · Percent Correct: **57%**

Answer: **A**

The paragraph is essentially saying that if we kill every malarial mosquito, then once the last such mosquito is killed, we have effectively eradicated malaria.

(A) exposes the flaw in this plan. Since people can carry malaria for up to forty days, all they have to do is infect a non-malarial mosquito, and the whole process starts over again.

The focus of this prompt is how eradicating all the mosquitos still will not result in the eradication of the disease. Unlike (A), which shows the mechanism whereby a non-infected mosquito can be infected by a human, (B) doesn't show how malaria would get back into the mosquito population once it had been eradicated. Sure, a malaria strain could last one hundred days inside a human. But unless the malaria protozoa enter back into the mosquito population after being eradicated, it doesn't matter how long the protozoa lasts in the blood of a human—it cannot be passed from human to human.

(C) is wrong. What health workers believe doesn't directly affect the argument. It may suggest that the plan has doubters, but nothing more.

(D) brings in two irrelevant topics: immunity and sickle cell anemia.

(E) just describes mosquito behavior in general and isn't specific to the paragraph.

Question 5
Difficulty: **Very Hard** · Percent Correct: **24%**

Answer: **C**

The argument: only a few of a famous artist's works, according to a computer program, are forgeries; therefore, the artist's reputation will be unaffected. The correct answer will indicate that the artist's reputation will actually be compromised by the computer results.

(A) points to the fact that the results of the computer tests may not be accurate. In other words, if it's likely that some of the Flemish artist's paintings identified as forgeries aren't actually forgeries, then the conclusion is supported.

Assume that (B) is correct: many of the artist's well-known works are in a private collection. Does that mean the artist's reputation will be hurt? Without knowing whether the works in private collections are or are not forgeries, you don't know what impact they'll have on his reputation. Had (B) said that the artist's well-known works in private collections were also identified as forgeries, then it would have been the correct answer.

If **(C)** is true, then the artist is in trouble, since the reason he's considered a great artist in the first place is because he painted these works. To give a real-life example, let's say you find out the best-known works of da Vinci (yes, that means you, Mona Lisa) were actually painted by a forger. Your perception of da Vinci as a great painter would surely change.

If you assume (D) is true, does that weaken the argument? Well, you know that some of the artist's lesser-known works are forgeries. That itself doesn't hurt his reputation, since these paintings aren't important. You could argue, "What if the better-known works the museums didn't offer up are forgeries?" Well, then that would make (D) the answer. But you can't assume that's the case, because it could very well be that none of the better-known works are forgeries.

(E) is incorrect. It's the original artist's reputation at stake; if his paintings are forgeries, it doesn't matter who the forger was.

> **Important strategy:** Try assuming the wrong answer to be true and working backwards. In other words, "poke holes" in the answer choice by assuming that it is true. Often, you try to find ways in which an answer could be true, and that practice can cause trouble on some of the more difficult questions. Notice that, in (D), it's tempting to add on a further assumption: "If I assume that the better-known paintings in the museum are also forgeries, then (D) works." Bringing in extra assumptions is what can happen when you're trying to prove that an answer is right, instead of trying to "poke holes in it."

Doesn't answer choice (C) simply restate the first sentence of the passage?
Let's look at the difference:

1. Recently, computer analysis has revealed that a few of a famous Flemish artist's works are forgeries and are actually the work of noted forger Elmyr de Hory.
2. Some of the works **upon which the Flemish artist's standing rests** were identified by the computer analysis to be the work of de Hory.

So, initially, just "some of the famous works" turned out to be forgeries. But in fact, some of the works *that made the Flemish artist so important* turned out to be forgeries.

This is a key distinction. The fact that the artist's standing depended upon these works, which are in fact not his, casts serious doubt on the claim that "the master's reputation as one of the greatest artists humanity has ever produced will surely remain undiminished."

What makes answer choice (C) the best answer compared to choices (B) and (D)? Answer choice (C) casts the most doubt on the conclusion, out of all the answer choices, and here's why:

This answer choice is saying that the most important works were actually forgeries. This definitely would destroy the conclusion that "the master's reputation ... will surely remain undiminished" or "museums ... should not be overly concerned."

Answer choice (C) is much more certain because it clearly says that the works are forgeries. Answer choice (D) only suggests the possibility that some works went untested and could possibly be forgeries. And answer choice (B) discusses where forgeries may be, but not their impact: the fact that private owners may have some potential forgeries doesn't really break down the conclusion.

Since you're looking for the **best** possible answer, you select answer choice **(C)**.

Question 6

Difficulty: **Easy** · Percent Correct: **89%**

Premise #1: Company X and Company Y both build rocket ships that can get to Mars.

Premise #2: Company X's and Company Y's rockets have the exact same design.

Conclusion: One of the companies copied the other.

(A) isn't strong enough to be confident that some kind of spying wasn't going on. Anyhow, even if the engineers don't say anything, there are presumably non-engineers aware of the rocket who could share information to the other company.

(B) is wrong since the focus in the passage is on how the design of the two rockets is identical. The color is irrelevant.

(C) strengthens the conclusion, since it gives you a compelling reason how information regarding design could leak.

(D) is saying that there's only one way to build a rocket capable of getting to Mars. Therefore, the designs will certainly converge so that they're practically indistinguishable.

(E) doesn't account for how the two rockets look so similar. It only tells you that both have lots of funding.

Answer: **D**

Question 7

Difficulty: **Hard** · Percent Correct: **39%**

This is an EXCEPT question. Four of the answers will clearly account for the increased number of mountain lion sightings in the Rockridge Mountain Park, and these four valid explanations won't be correct. One of the answers will either be irrelevant or even suggest that there should have been fewer sightings, and this one oddball will be the correct answer.

The correct response is choice **(B)**. The argument isn't about how many sightings are reported in the paper, but simply how many take place. The fact that a newspaper always reports these sightings doesn't cause the mountain lion to be seen. This is totally irrelevant, so it's the best answer to the EXCEPT question.

If more people are in the park, that's more eyes, which increases the likelihood of seeing a mountain lion. Choice (A) is a valid explanation, so it's not a correct answer.

If the red-tailed deer is on the hiking trails in these months, then the mountain lion will follow, and hikers will see more of the lion. Choice (C) is a valid explanation, so it's not a correct answer.

Bikers are more common in the spring, and more likely to startle lions, so the number of sightings by bike riders would increase in the spring. Choice (D) is a valid explanation, so it's not a correct answer.

Answer: **B**

Spring is the time when mountain lions come down to where the hikers are, increasing the likelihood that hikers will see them. Choice (E) is a valid explanation, so it's not a correct answer.

For choice (D), it said that the "bikers make LESS noise than hikers." Why are "the bikers more likely to startle mountain lions?" It should be less likely for bikers. The choice itself doesn't make any sense.

It's normal to associate startling something or someone with making more noise, so that does seem to make more sense at first glance. But think of the situation: if you're on a trail and there's a mountain lion nearby, in which situation are you more likely to see it?

If you're hiking and making a lot of noise, the mountain lion could hear you sooner and leave before you catch sight of it. If you're biking quickly and making less noise, the mountain lion is less likely to hear you and run off before you can see it. Even though you're making less noise, you're more likely to startle or surprise the mountain lion when you come across it! So you're more likely to see mountain lions because you would come across them quietly before they have the chance to run away. If you look back to the question stem, answer choice (D) could account for the increased mountain sightings, so it's not the correct answer.

Why isn't (A), instead of (B), the answer because more people on the mountain wouldn't cause more lions to appear? Choice (B) is the answer because it only refers to how many reports are published on sightings, not the sightings themselves. The number of reports published doesn't help account for (or cause) a greater number of sightings to occur. This works well since you're looking for an answer that doesn't help account for the increased sightings.

Choice (A) helps account for the increased sightings because a greater number of people in the park could cause more sightings. The more people there are in the park, the more likely it is that someone will see a mountain lion.

Question 8

Difficulty: **Hard** · Percent Correct: **34%**

Answer: **B**

The consumer advocate has evidence that Happy Smiles Daycare doesn't have the lowest child-to-caregiver ratio in the county. The answer that provides the best evidence is **(B)**. Kenton School has a 6:1 child-to-caregiver ratio, but that ratio accounts for those students who are older than 3 as well.

Happy Smiles, on the other hand, only bases its ratio on children aged 1–3. Since Kenton School has a ratio for 3–6-year-olds that's more than three times that of the 1–3-year-old range, we can conclude that the ratio in the 1–3-year-old age range is lower than 6:1. In other words, the student-caregiver ratio in older classes must be higher than 6:1, and the ratio in younger classes must be lower than 6:1, with the two making a total ratio of exactly 6:1. And because the ratio in the older classes must be much higher than the ratio in the younger classes, the ratio in the younger class will be very low—even lower than 5:1.

(A) just confirms what the paragraph says.

If anything, (C) strengthens Happy Smiles Daycare's claim. The school isn't basing its numbers on a period when it has a much lower child-to-caregiver ratio than usual.

(D) doesn't weaken the claim in the paragraph, because the paragraph specifically says that Happy Smiles Daycare doesn't include helpers in its child-to-caregiver ratio.

(E) is irrelevant to the argument, which is based on the present.

What does the last sentence of the paragraph mean? Here's the sentence: "Yet Happy Smiles Daycare's claim that parents with children aged 1–3 will find no other facility with such a low child-to-caregiver ratio is not accurate."

Let's break this down so the double negative is a little less confusing.

You may start with identifying what Happy Smiles Daycare's claim is.

Their claim is that parents with children aged 1–3 won't find any other facility with such a low child-to-caregiver ratio.

Now, let's look at the rest of the sentence without the claim itself:

Happy Smiles Daycare's claim is not accurate.

So the sentence is stating that Happy Smiles Daycare's claim is *not* true. The consumer advocate is actually arguing that there's another facility with a child to caregiver ratio of lower than 5:1, for children aged 1–3.

How can we be sure that Kenton School has a child-to-caregiver ratio that's lower than 5:1? For Kenton School, let's assume that there are 100 total students, just to make things easier. Now, you know that it provides childcare for students all the way up to age 6, not just age 3. So let's say that there are 50 children ages 1–3, and 50 ages 4–6.

Now, the total overall child to caregiver ratio is 6:1, which means that there are about 17 caregivers total for the 100 children. However, the classes for the 4–6-year-olds have a ratio more than three times that of the younger children. So maybe there are 13 caregivers for the younger children, but only 4 caregivers for the older children. This would mean that the ratio for the older students is 50:4, or 12.5:1, and the ratio for the younger students is 50:13, or about 4:1. You only care about the ratio for these younger students. This ratio is lower than the Happy Smiles Daycare of 5:1, so this helps to support the argument.

Question 9
Difficulty: **Very Hard** · Percent Correct: **27%**

The greater the population density, the greater the chance a gorilla is infected. Koluga gorillas have a greater population density than Morgania gorillas, and therefore you would expect them to be more likely to have the virus. But based on captured gorillas, the Morgania gorillas are more likely to be infected.

The paradox can best be resolved by **(D)**. If scientists are far more likely to capture non-infected than infected Kogula gorillas, then that accounts for the difference in results.

(A) would be correct if the passage mentioned that researchers only captured the

Answer: **D**

gorillas in the plains, and uninfected Koluga gorillas were more likely to venture out of their natural habitat.

(B) doesn't differentiate between the two gorillas, so it's unlikely to help resolve the discrepancy.

(C) is similar but different. It's not the total number of captured Kogulas that's important. "Twice as likely" is based on rate, not the total number.

(E) is out of scope.

Multiple-question

Question 10

Difficulty: **Medium** · Percent Correct: **54%**

Answer: **E**

Only **(E)** directly casts doubt on Chopin's playing ability, "more difficult pieces … had he the ability to play them."

Even if Chopin never played other composer's works, it isn't necessarily because those works were too difficult. You need to choose something stronger than (A).

The issue is Chopin's piano-playing ability. So whether he could play other instruments is unimportant. (B) is out.

(C) doesn't relate to issue. Even if his études were Chopin's most difficult pieces, that doesn't diminish his piano-playing prowess.

Question 11

Difficulty: **Easy** · Percent Correct: **64%**

Answer: **C**

In context, you learn that players with extant recordings (works still in existence) seem to "weather" time better than those who don't have extant recordings.

(C) means "to hold up/endure," and that option works best.

(B) means "to barely survive," a meaning that doesn't quite fit the context.

(E) has a few meanings. One meaning is something like "suffer through," which makes this a tempting choice. People sustain blows, injuries, or other painful things. It doesn't mean they survive them, just that they get them. In this sentence, you need something that means "suffer through" but "not be defeated by"—and that's "withstand."

Besides that, you can get a sense that "sustain time" doesn't work just by saying it aloud. It doesn't sound right in English. "Withstand time" is much more natural.

Question 12

Difficulty: **Medium** · Percent Correct: **46%**

Answer: **E**

You learn earlier in the paragraph that Mozart had put aside *Don Giovanni*, hoping to come back to it once he had thought of a better ending. Therefore, in this context, "table" means "to put aside for later." **(E)** is the answer.

Question 13

Difficulty: **Very Hard** · Percent Correct: 19%

Answer: **A**

This is a trickily worded question that amounts to a double negative. "Take exception" means "to disagree with." Because this is an EXCEPT question, the answer is something with which the author would either agree or not clearly disagree.

The author would agree with **(A)** because Libard offers two explanations to the questions posed by the author. The author considers one explanation reasonable and the other lacking. Therefore, the author would agree that Libard's explanations aren't "uniform in their usefulness."

(B) is incorrect because Libard offers insight into one of the questions.

(C) is incorrect because, if anything, the passage supports that Libard understood eighteenth-century audiences. In his first explanation—the one the author approves of—Libard shows insight into eighteenth-century audiences.

Libard's views are inconsistent with those of Lucien, therefore (D) is incorrect.

(F) is wrong because Libard's views *aren't* "consistently probing."

Question 14

Difficulty: **Hard** · Percent Correct: 45%

Answer: **A** only

The passage, in the third paragraph, says that "Mozart ultimately aimed to impart …" Therefore, **[A]** is the correct response.

The passage says the tragic ending was not typical. Therefore, [B] is incorrect.

[C] describes the traditional ending not the tragic ending. [C] is incorrect.

Question 15

Difficulty: **Very Hard** · Percent Correct: 28%

Answer: **D**

The passage only focuses on Gimley and Lebsmith. Therefore, the phrase "diverse opinions" makes (A) incorrect.

(B) is wrong. While the passage mentions some objections to a few of Gimley and Lebsmith's recommendations, this happens at the very end and therefore isn't the main idea of the passage.

(C) is a very alluring trap answer. However, it changes the meaning of the passage slightly. The key is the word "inquiry," so you know this corresponds to the work of Gimley and Lebsmith. Given this fact, answer (C) is essentially saying that the passage is concerned with a field of study (how to change the structure of clinical trials); it isn't concerned with improving that field of study, which amounts to improving the study of how to change the structure of clinical trials. The passage is focused on the work of those hoping to improve the way in which clinical trials have been challenged. In doing so, the passage offers a few insights into how clinical trials can be improved.

Finally, the only mention of how anything "can be improved" is mentioned in response to Gimley and Lebsmisth's recommendations. Those recommendations, however, don't constitute a "field of study."

(D) is correct because the purpose of the passage is to talk about the current debate involving clinical trials:

> "The efficacy of standard clinical trials in medicine has recently become the subject
> of contentious debate between those practitioners who maintain that such trials,
> despite admitted shortcomings, still represent the best means we have for learning
> about the effects of pharmaceutical drugs on the human body, and those who
> maintain that the current system of collecting knowledge of such effects is …"

Yes, that's a long, unwieldy sentence. But notice how the two sides of the debate are mentioned. The rest of the passage is mostly concerned with discussing the findings of one of those sides (Gimley and Lebsmith).

(E) is wrong because the focus of the passage isn't to discuss the effect that the scholars have had on their field. Again, the focus is the current debate on clinical trials and the work/insights of two specific researchers who fall on one side of that debate. Sure, the passage implies that the two have made useful offerings, but that observation isn't why the author wrote the passage.

Question 16

Difficulty: **Hard** · Percent Correct: **39%**

Answer: **B**

Gimley and Lebsmith's criticism of the trials are as follows:

> "Therefore, even if a drug can exercise a marked effect on a subset of subjects
> within a trial, this information will be lost in the statistical noise."

(A) is close, but there's a subtle difference from the text quoted above. What we're looking for is a "marked effect" (a strong effect) on a group of subjects. (A), however, talks about a "slightly negative reaction" among a subset.

(B) is very similar to (A). But notice how it says "strong negative effect." Also, the large number of subjects that "are neither positive or negative" matches up much better with "statistical noise." (A), by contrast, says "positive," which would be better described as counterbalanced by a clear effect. Therefore (B) is the best answer.

(C) changes the meaning from a subset exhibiting a strong effect to the rest (the majority) exhibiting a strong effect. Also, it's the subset that slightly weakens the extent of the strong effect and not the other way around.

(D) would be the perfect answer to one of the doubts the passage has about Gimley and Lebsmith's reservations. The question, however, concerns a shortcoming identified by Gimley and Lebsmith in clinical trials.

(E) refers to the new type of clinical trial espoused in the last paragraph.

Question 17

Difficulty: **Medium** · Percent Correct: **58%**

Answer: **C**

Supporting text: "… those practitioners who maintain that such trials, despite admitted shortcomings, still represent the best means we have for learning about the effects of pharmaceutical drugs on the human body."

This side of the debate represents those who support clinical trials. Notice the text says, "represent the best means we have." Also, notice the "despite admitted shortcomings." In other words, it's understood that those who endorse clinical trials admit that the trials aren't perfect but are still the most effective means of learning. This matches up best with **(C)**.

(A) is incorrect because the passage says that those favoring clinical trials do so because such trials represent the *best* means, not the *only* means.

(B) is incorrect because it's something that those who don't agree with Gimley and Lebsmith would be opposed to.

(D) is tempting. We know that the question is asking about those who wouldn't be fans of Gimley and Lebsmith's work because they believe that clinical trials are the best way of learning about a drug's usefulness. However, (D) goes a little bit too far in saying that the trials won't be able to isolate any of the effects. In other words, this is inferring too much—at least based on the passage—as to what those who are pro current-clinical-trials would think about Gimley and Lebsmith's work. Compare this to (C), in which there's clear textual support for the reasoning.

Though (E) is mentioned in the passage, it's done so in relation to why Gimley and Lebsmith criticize current medical trials.

Question 18

Difficulty: **Medium** · Percent Correct: **58%**

Answer: **C**

Supporting text: "Morgan's aim is to educate corporations engaged in outsourcing so that they choose a firm that specializes in providing one service. This view, however, is somewhat shortsighted, since the long-term trajectory of a company isn't always clear and a firm may end up diversifying."

In other words, a company that presently specializes in one service may end up diversifying in the future. This matches best with **(C)**.

While answer (A) accurately describes Morgan's work, it doesn't describe why he considers a view shortsighted.

(B) reverses the meaning. Morgan is focused on companies that **didn't intend** to diversify **but ended** up diversifying **all the same**, not, as this answer states, companies that plan to diversify but then don't end up doing so.

(D) is wrong since no such distinction is mentioned in relation to short-sightedness.

(E) is wrong. While Morgan does focus on specialized services, he's concerned with companies providing outsourced services becoming less specialized as they diversify.

Question 19

Difficulty: **Medium** · Percent Correct: **59%**

Answer: **D**

The passage describes how two theories relate to outsourcing. The focus isn't how these two theories are similar. Instead, the author says that they deal with different aspects of outsourcing. The author does, however, make a connection between these two seemingly disparate studies ("Yet, there is one area in which the recommendations of both theories overlap somewhat."). In the last couple of sentences of the passage, the author describes this overlap. This points best to **(D)**.

(A) is wrong because the author doesn't describe a conflict between the two points of view. He says that they're different but overlap slightly, although the way in which they overlap slightly isn't exactly similar. One focuses on how diversification can affect the outsourcing company, and the other focuses on the company that the work is outsourced to. This observation is not the same as saying the two theories are in conflict.

(B) is wrong because neither Morgan's nor Peavy's insights can be described as a solution.

(C) is the best trap answer. If (C) were the answer, however, the passage would be focused on how the two theories have conclusions that clash. The passage, though, just says that the two theories don't overlap, except for one small area: diversification. In order to adequately describe that one specific area, the author gives a background on the subject. The very last sentences discuss how Morgan and Peavy focus on different aspects of diversification: Morgan says it hurts the outsourcing company and Peavy says that it hurts the company that does outsourced work. These, however, aren't contradictory conclusions.

(E) is also wrong because the author doesn't discredit either theory.

Question 20

Difficulty: **Medium** · Percent Correct: **51%**

Answer: **E**

Supporting text: "Devotes only one chapter to an existing structural check on such 'information leaks': as a company specializing in outsourcing assumes more clients, its legal liability will increase with each company that becomes a client, an effect, he notes, that becomes more conspicuous the more a company diversifies."

Simplified: a company that does outsourced work is at a greater risk of leaking information the more companies it provides services for.

Anticipating the answer: The question asks you for the answer most immune from this outcome. Therefore, the best answer choice would be one that describes some company that does outsourcing but also limits the number of companies it represents. Ideally, this company would be one that has only one client.

(A) is tempting. But remember, it's not the number of different services that's a factor here but the number of clients a company doing outsourced work takes on.

(B) is the opposite of what you're looking for. Remember, the question said "immune."

(C) is wrong because the "number of corporations" indicates that there would be a great structural check.

(D) is wrong since a company's long-term trajectory doesn't relate to the issue of structural checks and liability.

(E) is correct: since a company is providing a service for exactly one company, it would be immune to the structural check.

Question 21

Difficulty: **Hard** · Percent Correct: **33%**

Supporting text: "Outsourcing, or the allocation of specific aspects of a corporation to a business entity specializing in those areas, has become such an integral part of a company's organizational structure that few question outsourcing's long-term viability. Two recent studies on this topic are no exception."

Key takeaway: This question is tricky, since the answer could come from anywhere in the passage. You might expect the supporting text to come at the end. This kind of "trick" is quite common on higher-level questions. So if you find yourself unable to justify an answer based on the text, you may be looking at the wrong part of the passage.

(A) is incorrect since both Peavy and Morgan regard diversification as something that can cause a negative impact.

(B) is wrong because the long-term viability of a corporation isn't discussed in the passage.

(C) is wrong since the diversification in the passage is focused on the business entity that does the outsourced work, not the corporation that outsources work. Notice that throughout the passage "corporation" is only used to refer to the latter.

(D) is wrong because *both* focus on the impact of diversification in business entities that do outsourced work.

(E) is correct since, as it says in the supporting text, "few" researchers "question outsourcing's long-term viability."

Answer: **E**

Question 22

Difficulty: **Medium** · Percent Correct: **51%**

"To substantiate this claim" implies that scientists would like to use birds for a specific purpose—this is their "value." It comes from being "the closest extant relatives," which means they are relatively close to dinosaurs, evolutionarily speaking.

The passage mentions that a dinosaur required less food than would a similar-sized reptile. However, there's no mention about how much food a bird requires. Sure, birds, like dinosaurs, might have been mesothermic, but mesothermy relates to body temperature regulation, not to the amount of food consumed.

The last sentence states that birds "might have at one time been mesothermic." That is, they might have changed from mesotherms to endotherms. From the first sentence, we learn that endothermic describes body regulation. Therefore, birds possibly changed in the way their body temperatures were regulated.

Answers:

Question 23

Difficulty: **Medium** · Percent Correct: **55%**

Notice the structure of the sentence, "based their conclusions on faulty reasoning, **claiming that scaly skin was common to all ectotherms ...**"

The boldfaced part is the specific claim. Look at the subsequent part in parentheses

Answer: **C**

303

and how it relates to the boldfaced part above: "(amphibians, which are ectothermic, do not have scaly skin)."

This is a clear denial of the boldfaced part. The exact same thing happens with the second claim of scientists: "the dinosaur's size could account for ectothermy."

Here is the objection (in parentheses) that states the boldfaced part is untrue: "(some adult dinosaurs weighed as little as ten pounds)."

This points to answer (C).

(A) is wrong because the author, while rejecting the claims that are in boldface above, uses the parentheses to say why the boldfaced parts are incorrect. The author isn't summarizing the claims in the parentheses.

(B) is talked about elsewhere in the passage. The focus of the parentheses is on pointing out the inaccuracy of commonly made claims about the relationship between ectothermy and dinosaurs.

(D) is wrong since the theory the author supports (that of mesothermy) is described later in the passage.

The information in parentheses might contradict the information that comes immediately before it; however, (E) mentions "dinosaur behavior," which isn't discussed in this passage.

Question 24

Difficulty: **Very Hard**   ·   Percent Correct: **18%**

The line "some paleontologists maintain that dinosaurs were faster than similar-sized reptiles" points to [A]. Remember, the new theory is that dinosaurs were mesotherms, and the passage discusses the advantages of this form of body temperature regulation.

[B] would be correct if "ectothermy" was replaced by being a "mammal." The passage clearly mentions food dependency in relation to mammals.

[C] might be tempting if you try to make a connection between birds, mesothermy, and flight—three things mentioned in the passage but not in relation to each other. Nowhere does it say that birds were able to fly because they were mesothermic. In fact, based on what little we know from the passage, it's entirely possible that birds were able to fly before this hypothesized period of mesothermy in their evolutionary history.

Question 25

Difficulty: **Medium**   ·   Percent Correct: **47%**

Answer: **E**

The author's theory is that it wasn't just geological change but internal dissent brought on by climate change. You're looking to disprove that internal dissent was a major factor. What makes this question so difficult is that the right answer can still mention flooding, as long as it casts doubt on the claim that internal dissent was the final blow. Only (E) really gets at the idea that it was meteorological/geographic change, and not internal dissent, that led to the ultimate dissolution of the Olmec. Therefore, if (E) is true, it undermines the author's argument.

Notice that in (E), "The Olmec leadership successfully relocated settlements" shows that internal dissent wasn't an issue.

(A) is by no means a terrible answer. It's an okay answer, but unlike (E) it doesn't really attack the author's theory that internal dissent was part of what led to the downfall of the Olmec. So (A) could coexist with "internal dissent." That is, there could have been rainfall that increased over a decade *and* the Olmec could have had internal dissent issues. Another issue with (A) is that it mentions another theory ("could have had notable tributaries …"), not the author's theory.

Even if not all the major crops were planted along the river, this fact doesn't relate to the author's idea that internal dissent played a major role. For this reason, (B) is wrong.

(C) is tricky. Notice that it mentions the Mayans. What applies to the Mayans doesn't necessarily apply to a different people, i.e., the conditions could have been very different with the Olmec.

(D) is consistent with the author's view and actually paraphrases the author's theory.

Question 26

Difficulty: **Medium** · Percent Correct: **54%**

Answer: **D**

The passage begins by saying that meteorological change made it difficult to grow certain crops, thereby leading to the disappearance of the Olmec. The second sentence says this view isn't complete and mentions the changing course of rivers. The third sentence provides an explanation of the effect that the changing river courses had on the disappearance of the Olmec. This matches up best with **(D)**. In this case, the hypothesis is the one mentioned in the first sentence, i.e. meteorological changes. And the specific example is the Coatzacoalcos River.

(A) is tempting, but the third sentence is consistent with the second sentence. It's the first sentence, specifically the meteorological hypothesis, that both the second and third sentences disagree with.

(B) focuses on meteorological conditions. However, the second and third sentences move away from this explanation and focus on changes in geography, specifically rivers.

(C) is wrong since "most scholarship" refers to the first sentence.

(E) is tempting since it mentions information in the third sentence and the one immediately following it. However, if you look at the fourth sentence, it somewhat discredits the view in the third sentence. Therefore, "the Olmec's ability to effectively govern" is part of a new theory.

Question 27

Difficulty: **Medium** · Percent Correct: **49%**

Answers: **B C**

The passage states that the Olmec should have been able to transfer subsistence crops to other areas after the original planting areas had been flooded. Therefore, the author assumes that crops can simply be replanted. [A] is saying the opposite, that such crops wouldn't be viable if moved elsewhere, and is therefore challenging the author's claim.

The author claims that moving crops shouldn't have been too much of a problem with a centralized government. But because there was internal dissent, there was no central governance, and so the Olmec weren't able to move the subsistence crops. The author is assuming that to move subsistence crops there has to be some level of central governance. Therefore, **[B]** is one correct answer.

The author ends the passage by saying that the Olmec became a "collection of feuding clans and thus all but disappeared." The "thus" implies a cause and effect and points to the author's assumption that a motley of feuding clans isn't capable of sustaining a population. Therefore, **[C]** is another correct answer.

Question 28

Difficulty: **Easy** · Percent Correct: **64%**

Answer: **D**

According to the passage, women in middle- and lower-middle-class families "considered themselves parts of dual-income households," meaning that they would be able to make money for the family "if necessary." Therefore, **(D)** is the best answer.

(A) describes Murray's research, which doesn't specifically mention "middle- and lower-middle-class women."

(B) is mentioned in regards to Murray's view, not the author's.

(C) is tempting because it mentions access to jobs. However, it's a little too specific in pointing out "former jobs" when, in fact, a woman didn't even have to have previous work experience. The perception was that the woman, whether she'd ever worked or not, could find a job if necessary.

(E) is wrong because health isn't mentioned in the passage. This is a tempting answer because it makes sense in the real world, i.e., good health is helpful to a woman hoping to conceive.

Question 29

Difficulty: **Medium** · Percent Correct: **58%**

Answer: **C**

"However" indicates that the author disagrees with Murray. The author then presents what he or she believes is a more reasonable view. In this sense, it doesn't seem that the author would be talking about the accepted view. Rather, he or she would be mentioning a view that's more likely or more believable. This points to **(C)**, which means "believable."

You know that it is a view the author finds more likely. To say it's worthy, as in choice (D), is going a little too far.

Question 30

Difficulty: **Medium** · Percent Correct: **54%**

Answer: **B**

The passage implies that Murray overlooks the role middle- and lower-middle-class women might have on his conclusion. This points best to **(B)**.

(A) is tempting. Ultimately, Murray does ignore the role of women in dual-income households. But more specifically he ignores middle- and lower-middle-class women— those who continued working in factories.

(C) is wrong because Murray focuses on state of mind, i.e. optimism, not wealth.

(D) is wrong because Murray overlooks, rather than overemphasizes, women who continued working in factories.

(E) is wrong. Notice that the passage, in regards to Murray's view, says both "women and men's perspectives changed."

Write your own GRE adventure! Use some of your favorite GRE vocabulary words to fill in the blanks and complete the story below.

I didn't just study for the GRE—I was married to the GRE. For three months, I would _____ vocabulary words until three in the morning. I would _____ mental math games while I shopped at the supermarket and would get so distracted I'd forget to remove my credit card from the chip reader at the register. When friends called me to hang out, I'd tell them I already had a date—with the Powerprep practice test. When I did actually meet my friends for coffee, I couldn't help but use words like _____, _____, and _____. I didn't have to worry that my friends would try to interrupt me during the second Powerprep practice test—they'd stopped calling me altogether. While I should have felt _____, I thought that it was all worth it. I was getting close to perfect scores on test prep materials in both sections.

The test itself seemed like a mere formality. I just had to show up and _____ would be mine. But things didn't quite go that way. The night of the test, a neighbor of mine decided to _____ at 3:30 in the morning. Though I tried to go back to sleep, I discovered that a mosquito had crept into my room and decided to _____ me until the sun came up. At least I didn't need an alarm clock to wake up for my eight a.m. GRE test appointment.

The trip to the testing center is when things started getting complicated. Though I had _____ planned my route, I somehow managed to get off the bus one stop too late. I blamed it on that mosquito, which seemed to be _____ in my ear. I figured instead of simply getting back on the train in the opposite direction, I'd _____—how complicated could it be? Little did I know that the local baseball team had won the World Series and today was the _____, which happened to be taking place at the stop where I got off. I had to _____ my way through screaming fans with painted faces and little patience for somebody with the GRE Official Guide tucked under their _____ trying to elbow through.

1. A GRE verb
2. A regular verb
3. A long GRE word
4. An even longer GRE
5. A funny-sounding GRE word
6. A negative GRE adjective

7. Regular positive noun
8. Negative GRE verb
9. Negative regular verb

10. GRE adverb
11. –ing regular verb
12. Action verb
13. Type of event
14. GRE verb
15. GRE noun

By the time I reached the testing center, I was already twenty minutes late. The person behind the desk gave me a _____ look. (16) Luckily, I was still able to take the test. The only problem was that the fingerprint reader _____ (17), and I had to wait fifteen minutes for the testing center staff to fix it. Then, it turned out that I brought too many personal belongings—how could I possibly part with my shoebox filled with flashcards of the _____ (18) most important GRE vocabulary words? Luckily, I was able to recycle my shoe box and cram my GRE study paraphernalia into the lockers provided at the testing center. By the time, I actually started to take the test, it was almost ten in the morning.

I was so stressed by my travel experience to take the test that I assumed I'd perform terribly on the GRE. After all, halfway through the Issue essay, I felt my eyelids _____ (19). By the time I got to the second math section, I didn't know my _____ (20) from my _____ (21). And all of those words that I thought I knew inside out suddenly seemed like a foreign language. _____ (22) and _____ (23) started to blend into one definition, and I didn't even know what that definition was. And it was during the long reading passage that I started to hear the mosquito again. Suddenly it dawned on me that I had forgotten to have my usual _____ (24) cups of morning coffee and was likely experiencing caffeine withdrawal symptoms. By the time I got to the screen asking me if I wanted to accept my score, I was so confused as to why this _____ (25) only had two possible answers. Luckily, I clicked "yes," because somehow I had earned a 160 in both sections. Nonetheless, I promptly dozed off at the keyboard. A _____ (26) proctor had to wake me up and tell me to go home.

I was so exhausted I missed my stop again on the way back. But it didn't matter. All my _____ (27) brain could think about was the little light of _____ (28) it felt now that the test was over. Three months later, I found out that all that studying and test prep paid off when I was accepted into my dream school; though I never did find that pesky mosquito.

16. Strong negative GRE word
17. Regular verb
18. A really large number

19. –ing verb
20. Difficult math concept
21. Even more difficult math concept
22. A really difficult GRE word
23. An even more difficult GRE word
24. A single-digit number
25. GRE question type
26. Strong negative adjective

27. GRE synonym for confused
28. Super positive GRE word

Chapter 5

GRE Analytical Writing Assessment

Brought to you by Chris from Magoosh

Meet the GRE AWA

Many people studying for the GRE give short shrift to the Analytical Writing Assessment (AWA). After all, it's not included in the 130–170 score range. However, a very low writing score could hurt your chances of getting accepted to many graduate programs. So it's important to carve out some time for writing practice in your busy GRE-prep schedule.

Just enough?

The AWA is scored on a scale from 0.0 to 6.0, in 0.5 increments. While very few people are able to get a perfect 6, most graduate programs aren't too concerned about your score, as long as you're able to get a 4.0 and above. Of course, you know best whether your target graduate program falls into that group. Are you looking to get a degree in journalism? Well, then anything less than a 5.0 is problematic. Looking to study computer science or engineering? For most programs, a 4.0 should be sufficient.

A 4.0 translates to roughly the 50th percentile. Basically, you're able to write the two essays better than half of the other GRE test takers. Getting to a 4.0 should be your goal. If you find out later that your program looks for at least a 4.5, which some do, you'll then be only 0.5 off and can double down on writing to make that extra improvement.

Two essays

The AWA isn't just one long, taxing essay, but two relatively long, taxing essays. For the first, you'll have to take a side on a complex issue and craft a four- to five-paragraph essay, offering logical supporting examples to explain your reasoning. This is the "Analyze an Issue" task, which, for most, is the more difficult of the two essays.

Next is the "Analyze an Argument" task. Instead of having to argue your own position, the way you must do on the Issue task, you must criticize someone else's argument. This someone else happens to be the GRE test-writers. But don't worry: they aren't going to ask you to challenge an essay written on Marxist theory. The arguments are always based on straightforward real-world examples. Better yet, the arguments are typically filled with gaping logical holes that make them relatively easy for you to take apart.

How to Do Well on the AWA

So what are the graders looking for? Well, for both the Issue and Argument tasks, you will want to write essays that are

Well-structured: Each essay should have an introduction, body paragraphs, and a conclusion. Your introduction should end with a clearly defined thesis so the person reading it knows what you're trying to prove. Your body paragraphs should be driving toward your main point. It's a good idea to make sure the final sentences of the body tie back to your thesis. Finally, the conclusion should recap what you said in the essay and shouldn't start introducing entirely new points.

Well-reasoned: The body paragraphs in the Issue task should contain examples, either actual or hypothetical, that cogently defend your position. Your position should be nuanced and your examples should be developed so that they support this nuanced position. You don't want to just summarize some historical event. For the Argument task, you need to use analysis to show why the argument is weak. You will need to identify the underlying assumptions and ways in which the argument can be made valid.

Well-expressed: The GRE scorers want to get a sense of how well you write. And by "write," we mean, do you use relatively sophisticated diction? Do you vary your sentences? Do grammar issues interfere with your expression? Writers typically refer to this as *style*.

So don't be afraid to flaunt your style!

At the same time, don't think whipping out highfalutin words like "indefatigable," "prognosticate," or "approbatory" is going to win you points. Even if used correctly, your writing will come across as contrived. Use these complex words incorrectly and your attempt at sophistication will smack of desperation.

The GRE scorer will use the three categories (structure, reason, and expression) to formulate an overall impression (what they call a holistic approach) of your writing ability. However, the scoring is a little more complex than this, as we'll explain below.

How are the essays scored?

Deep in a dark room, far, far away, resides a poor soul who must sort through an interminable stack of GRE essays. In a mere thirty seconds, they must award a score of 0.0–6.0. The grader is typically a university literature/writing professor who, according to ETS, has undergone rigorous training.

But that's only half of the story.

This next part sounds a little nefarious, so hold onto your seats. Over the course of the last decade or so, ETS has developed *e-rater*, an automated essay grader. While it may seem that HAL, the diabolical talking computer from Stanley Kubrick's *2001: A Space Odyssey*, has been unleashed to wreak grading havoc on your essays, *e-rater* is only used as a second "grader" to ensure that the human grader isn't napping on the job. If the *e-rater*'s score differs by more than one point (on the 0.5-point scale) from the human grader's score, your essay is sent to another human grader, the master grader—who, presumably, resides in an even darker room. Your final score is the average of the two essays, rounded up to the nearest 0.5.

What exactly does it mean to get a 0.0, or for that matter a 6.0? Well, a 0.0 means you fell asleep, your forehead planted firmly on the keyboard, an endless series of gobbledygook forming on screen. A 6.0, by contrast, is a consistently insightful and well-crafted essay that runs a good eighty-plus lines.

You may think we're joking about the 0.0, but not really: those essays are deemed "Ungradeable," possibly because they're blank, not in English, or entirely off topic. Hence, very few students end up getting a 0.0, or, for that matter, a score below a 2.0. The vast majority of grades fall between a 3.0 and a 5.0.

A scoring rubric can be found at ets.org/gre. But for now, here's an overview of the different scores.

2.0: This is a "seriously flawed" essay in which the writer has been unable to support his or her position with relevant examples or points. The writing is very simplistic and the essay is marred by poor, unclear, or grammatically incorrect writing.

4.0: This is an "adequate" essay. The essay has a clear position, some relevant examples, and a proper essay structure. What the essay doesn't have is deeper analysis of the issue. The position is usually one-sided and, as a result, the examples are short and superficial (we'll delve into this much more in the issue section). An argument essay of this same 4.0 range also doesn't explore ways in which the argument could be strengthened.

6.0: This is an "outstanding" essay. Only 2–5 percent of students achieve this score. Such an essay develops a nuanced and insightful position with compelling supporting examples. Ideas flow together logically, and each paragraph is well-organized and coherent. Finally, the writer uses sophisticated sentence structure and displays a strong grasp of vocabulary and sentence mechanics.

As we analyze examples of the Issue and Argument tasks, we'll give you a sense of how well the excerpts would likely score. We hope these examples will give you a better sense of the kind of writing the scores above correspond to.

Given the inordinate stack of essays the human grader is faced with, it's rumored that they spend as little as thirty seconds per essay.

The Issue Task

Both the issue prompt and argument prompt you'll see test day are actually on the ets.org site. That said, there are almost 200 of each prompt so your chances of actually getting a prompt you've written an essay on aren't that high. But still . . .

We're going to give you some advice here that many writing teachers would frown upon: don't stress about structure of introduction, body paragraphs, and conclusion. You know what they are. You know they need to be included.

Instead, we at Magoosh believe there's an even *more* important component to the Issue task, one that's most often overlooked: analysis.

This shouldn't be a surprise; after all, AWA stands for "Analytical Writing Assessment." Nevertheless, many students think they need only provide concrete examples supporting a thesis. What usually happens is they end up writing very one-sided essays, with three concrete examples supporting a strong "yes" or "no" position.

The GRE, though, wants to see how you *analyze* a complex issue. It chooses prompts that it wants you to explore before arriving at a nuanced position. What the GRE is *not* looking for is a simple "yes" or "no" response, followed by three examples that, while heavy on details, are devoid of analysis. But as the following example shows, many students fail to elaborate or offer analysis.

Because organization is critical for a high score, we wanted to let you know exactly what GRE essay graders are looking for. And *look* they will, since organization—or lack thereof—will be one of the things they notice as soon as they see your essay. So you need a clear introduction, followed by two to three body paragraphs. Each should be preceded by a paragraph break—avoid writing one massively long paragraph! Finally, you should have a conclusion that does just that: concisely sums up your essay. But again, this is only a small part of the story.

Below is an official prompt, taken from the official GRE site, along with the directions. (Note: these directions will change slightly based on the prompt, so it's always important to read them carefully.)

> As people rely more and more on technology to solve problems, the ability of humans to think for themselves will surely deteriorate.
>
> *Write a response in which you discuss the extent to which you agree or disagree with the statement and explain your reasoning for the position you take. In developing and supporting your position, you should consider ways in which the statement might or might not hold true and explain how these considerations shape your position.*

Example Introduction

Technology is becoming a bigger part of our lives each day. People are always on their cellphones or in front of a computer. This is not good for our ability to think clearly. **Therefore, humans will not be able to think for themselves as time goes on.**

We've bolded the thesis. What do you notice about it? Some people might think this an excellent thesis statement. It's clear and directly answers the question. After all, that's what many of us learned about essay writing: a quick introduction, and a clear and direct thesis. For such organizational diehards, this essay is off to a favorable start.

However—and this is a big *however*—the thesis makes what is quite possibly the single biggest mistake on the GRE. It addresses the instruction, "discuss the extent to which you agree or disagree," by completely agreeing. Now, if you're thinking, *Oh, all I have to do is completely disagree*, you're equally wrong. The GRE intentionally makes statements that are one-sided so that you can basically say, *Actually, it's not that simple; the issue is much more complex and nuanced. Here is why and here is my position.*

At this point, there may be alarm bells going off. You may think that you always have to take a position to avoid being wishy-washy. This is 100 percent correct. Nevertheless, there's a major difference between saying technology is both helpful and harmful, and the following:

> *Technology clearly has given us great benefits, from increasing the quality of life to destroying the barrier of distance by allowing us to connect face-to-face over smartphones or computers. But technology also has offloaded many skills that we once used our brains to rely on: crunching numbers, memorizing the location of a friend's home amongst byzantine streets, or remembering an important date. And while it is easy to think that human beings are headed for a life in which we are mere biological automata, our thinking highly diminished, technology has—and most likely will— continue to supplant thought processes that are generally tedious, allowing us to focus on what really matters and thus sharpening our thinking in these critical areas.*

Notice that this introduction started off by introducing not only the topic but also both sides of the issue—the 100 percent agree and the 100 percent disagree. In a mere two sentences, it paints both positions as gross simplifications of a complex debate. Yet it doesn't take the easy road out by saying that both are equally right; instead, it describes a nuanced position that's far closer to the "disagree" side than to the "agree" side. That position is in a somewhat wordy thesis, though. You should err on the side of brevity when it comes to your main position. In this case, the thesis can be simplified to the following:

> *Technology doesn't deteriorate our thinking in issues that are important—that is, those that can't simply be offloaded to the nearest smartphone or computer.*

It's important to take a nuanced position like this not only so the essay can start on an analytical note, but also so analysis can inform your body paragraphs. Had you taken an extreme view, your body paragraphs might have looked like this (introduction paragraph reproduced immediately below):

In ancient Greece, it was not uncommon for well-educated people to memorize long works, such as the *Iliad* and the *Odyssey*. Even before the advent of electronic technology, the human capacity for memory has been generally underappreciated and underused in the modern age.

313

Introduction

Technology is becoming a bigger part of our lives each day. People are always on their cellphones or in front of a computer. This is not good for our ability to think clearly. **Therefore, humans will not be able to think for themselves as time goes on.**

1st body

The iPhone, when it first came on the market, seemed like a great thing to have. It could do everything for you and was very popular. For instance, it had a calculator on it, a calendar in which you could set important meetings, and an alert so you remembered to do things. There were also GPS and an Internet connection so you could figure out where things were. But now that we have that capability, people are bumping into each other on the streets because they are so engrossed in their phones. They read constant news reports or update their social media posts. This all shows how our thinking is deteriorating because the smartphone is doing it for us.

Did you find that paragraph persuasive? The paragraph is basically constructed to show how the iPhone does things that we used to do and therefore it deteriorates our thinking. That's highly simplistic thinking. Even colorful writing cannot make up for the lack of analysis, as the next example shows.

What was once the province of our highest brain regions has been co-opted by a mere black box. Pandora thought she had it bad? There's no hope for us with an iPhone constantly in our hand doing our thinking for us. We are already a platoon of zombies in lockstep through crowded city streets, our thumbs frenetically at our phones: update, update, update.

Yes, that was cute—though the test writers won't necessarily think so. Sadly, we've seen many able writers go down this very path.

By coming up with a nuanced position in your introduction, on the other hand, you allow yourself to analyze your example throughout the body paragraph. When showing instances in which your example doesn't hold true, it will be over a subtle point, not something major that might compromise your thesis.

Let's return to the directions for a moment. Look at how the boldfaced part encourages you to analyze, not merely explain:

> Write a response in which you discuss the extent to which you agree or disagree with the statement and explain your reasoning for the position you take. **In developing and supporting your position, you should consider ways in which the statement might or might not hold true and explain how these considerations shape your position.**

So you aren't just saying the iPhone or technology is bad. You're saying that the iPhone is bad in some cases because it, say, cuts people off from real social interaction. You could give a quick example. But then you could qualify that further by saying, "only if those social media interactions don't lead to actual social interactions." For instance, if I use Facebook to facilitate meet-ups I have with people who share common interests, then the program is actually *enhancing* social interaction.

That's analysis. It shows that the issue is complex, that it *depends*, e.g., social media isn't inherently bad; it depends on how you use it. Describing what those ways are and using concrete examples will lend your paragraph further support. You can sum each body paragraph up by pointing out in your final sentence how your example links back to your thesis. Then you can move on to the next body paragraph.

Here are some specific ways to thread analysis into your paragraph:

1. **Anticipate the objection.** One way to show that you're not extreme in either agreeing or disagreeing is by showing the other side of the argument. One way to do this is to anticipate what the objection might be. For instance, let's say you're arguing that social media keep us from real-life interactions, thereby eroding our ability to think:

   While many may argue that not all forms of social media are bad and that social media does have advantages, from being able to keep in touch with far-away friends and family to venting your thoughts at three o'clock in the morning, they overlook something important. There is a cost to such convenient connections: we are less likely to reach out to those who matter most.

   The first sentence addresses an objection to your position. The second sentence shows a weakness in this objection.

2. **Concession point.** Another way to show the other side of the argument is with a concession point. This specifically gets at the part of the instructions that say, "In developing and supporting your position, you should consider ways in which the statement might or might not hold true."

   Essentially, you're getting back to the idea of "it depends." That is, you're describing what your position depends on. For instance, consider the example with social media:

   True, not all forms of social media harm our ability to function in social contexts. Indeed, one could argue that many conflicts that might become more contentious in a face-to-face scenario would be better hashed out with a smiley-face and a "like." But for the most part, social media can eat away at the fabric of our most intimate bonds.

   Notice that we've pointed out an instance in which our position doesn't hold true (conflict). We didn't go on to show how that objection was incorrect as we did with "anticipate an objection." The reason this shows critical thinking/analysis and isn't an example of being wishy-washy or uncertain is that you admit that the issue isn't black and white, that there are little shades of grey in there, but that your position still holds in general.

Interestingly, concession points can be reserved for an entire paragraph. One strategy is to write two body paragraphs with a fair amount of analysis, followed by one in which you offer a concession point and perhaps anticipate some objections. In other words, include a paragraph that's mostly analysis.

In terms of structure for the Issue task, there's no one right way. Still, you must include a hefty amount of analysis and show the grader that you're aware of the complexity of the issue, and that you have carefully thought out and defended a nuanced position. Threading that analysis throughout will prevent your essay from appearing too one-sided, something that might clash with a sudden concession paragraph at the end.

3. **If/then statements.** One way to show that you're thinking critically about an issue is to bring up *if/then*, or hypothetical scenarios. Note that these shouldn't make up most of your essay, since hypotheticals aren't as convincing. But peppering them here and there can add an extra dimension of analysis.

If people spend their time constantly "plugged in" to their cell phones, then it will diminish the quality of connections they have. For instance, if a person cannot stop thinking of the latest sports scores or whether they got a "like" on a photo they just posted, then the level of engagement they have with a real-life human being suffers.

Now let's take a look at an essay. You should note what the essay does well and what it could improve on.

Below are the first two paragraphs of an essay: the introduction and the first body paragraph:

From the mundane—virtual calendars that have each minute of each day planned out for the next three months—to the profound—diagnostic tools that allow physicians to capture cancer in its earliest stages—technology is greatly shaping the way we live and think. With this increased reliance, some argue, surely our ability to think for ourselves becomes diminished. After all, many of us are unable to recall our home phone number, or those of any of our close friends, since everything is stored on an electronic device. While it is tempting to think that such dependence portends an apocalypse in thinking skills, much of the technology we use today actually allows us to function more efficiently and focus our attention on thinking about those things that matter most.

Nowhere are information and the ability to use that information more critical to our lives than in medicine. Doctors inundated with patients and the recordkeeping this entails are more prone to making errors. Some of these errors might seem venial— thinking an allergy is a cold. Other oversights, however, can be downright lethal. Fortunately, in the last decade, technology has played a far greater role in both informing and guiding the decisions of physicians. Patient histories that were previously lost if the patients moved to another provider can now be easily accessed via electronic devices. Timely and redundant procedures can now be dispensed with a quick flick of the wrist. Physicians can use an iPad to access a patient's history—one that has sedulously been stored in a database. They can now focus on those fields in which technology has yet to catch up with the human intellect—the diagnosis, the ability to read an X-ray. Indeed, they will have more time to hone such skills, to augment their thinking, as much of the minutiae of medicine can be "outsourced" to technology. That is not to say that technology has become a panacea, as it were, for the medical profession; human error can pop up in anything from transfer of records to a doctor becoming overly reliant on the Internet to the detriment of her clinical skills. Yet those very oversights technology itself will be able to redress, as doctors become better at documenting any oversights and making such discoveries available, via technology, to a wider audience. In sum, as technology becomes a greater part of the medical profession, physicians will better be able to focus and refine their uniquely human thinking abilities.

That's a pretty solid body paragraph, though it's a bit on the long side. The author probably should have summarized a little less at the beginning. Again, it's not so much the specifics of the example as the analysis. As a result, the writer might only have had time to furnish a much shorter second body paragraph before moving on to the conclusion.

It's important to note that you do *not* need three body paragraphs. In fact, we'd argue that two well-executed body paragraphs is the best way to go given the thirty minutes you have.

Back to the essay. Here is what this body paragraph does well in terms of analysis: it anticipates an objection and clearly addresses it:

That is not to say that technology has become a panacea, as it were, for the medical profession; human error can pop up in anything from transfer of records, to a doctor becoming overly reliant on the Internet to the detriment of her clinical skills. Yet those very oversights technology itself will be able to redress, as doctors become better at documenting any oversights and making such discoveries available, via technology, to a wider audience.

It also clearly links back to the thesis in the middle of the paragraph, before it goes into the analysis:

They can now focus on those fields in which technology has yet to catch up with the human intellect.

But the paragraph isn't perfect. Had it explained in even more detail how technology isn't a panacea, or fleshed out the idea of "detriment to clinical skills," while showing that these things didn't detract from the overall force of the thesis, it would have been an excellent paragraph. For now, it's a strong beginning, but the writer should be careful not to spend too much time summarizing in the next paragraph.

We've included two different versions of the next paragraph to this essay. One would likely lead to a 5 essay score, style notwithstanding, the other a 6 score. Which body paragraph do you think should earn the 6 score, and why?

Body paragraph #2—version 1

Likewise, our daily lives are inundated with menial tasks. Do I really need to be able to have the hippocampal development of a taxi driver and know where every street in my city is so I never get lost? Do I need to be able to do rapid mental math so I don't end up undertipping the waiter? The list of items that once cost people valuable time and bandwidth is long. But technology has evolved to the point that such concerns need no longer worry us. Instead, we can give full attention and passion to whatever our specialty or passion in life is. As a concert pianist, I'd rather have a ream of a Brahms concerto running through my head than wonder if I have to take a left up the next hill. With GPS leading the way, the music can keep playing in my head.

Body paragraph #2—version 2

At the same time, technology does threaten important aspects of our critical thinking. While many are too pessimistic on this account, there are still innovations of which we need to be wary. There is an inherent element of addiction built into the Internet, whether it be the alerts from a social media or the video game that lures you in by comparing your performance to that of other avid players. This "gamification" is the result of programmers and designers finding what works best at ensuring that we do not leave a certain site or stop playing a certain game. Immured in such a world, we will surely see our thinking skills deteriorate, beyond, of course, whatever improvement in hand-eye coordination we get from a game. Yet even with these downsides, if one is aware of them and learns to steel oneself against the temptations of being compulsively online, he or she can reap the aspect of technology that frees us up to think about matters that are truly important.

Grades

Version 1

The first paragraph lapses into one-sidedness. It suggests technology can free us from all the menial stuff. It then goes on to—entertainingly, we might add—list quite a few of these. But where is the analysis of the issue? It definitely gives specific examples, which can help bring a 4 essay up to the 5 range. But without digging deeper into the debate and showing how their position is shaped, this paragraph really only becomes convincing to those who already agree with what the writer has to say.

Assuming this essay has a standard conclusion, we'd give it a 5. There was too much summary and not enough analysis in the first body paragraph, and no real analysis in the last body paragraph. That said, the essay does well in terms of style. Both the vocabulary used ("sedulously," "inundated")—and used correctly—and the complex sentence structure will positively influence the graders. Had the essay been less well-written, the lack of analysis—especially in the second paragraph—would have stood out more. Not to be overlooked, the wealth of detail allows the writer to write more. And though it might sound ridiculous, the length of the essay contributes to the grade. To be fair, the first thing graders will likely notice when they look at your essay is the length. Provided the essay doesn't ramble nonsensically, the longer the essay the better.

Version 2

This paragraph starts with a concession point: there's some validity to the other side. But it's not saying, "Yes, the other side is equally valid." That would be fence-sitting, or being wishy-washy. It's saying there's an aspect of the other side that has some merit and shows that my argument doesn't always hold true. This is the type of critical thinking that the test graders like. You'll of course have to be specific. Here, the essay describes those technologies that can threaten our ability to think.

Now you don't actually have to agree with this essay. In fact, you might be an avid gamer and bristle at the writer's contention that your critical thinking has been impaired. But the graders aren't grading essays on how closely the writer's views conform to their own. They're looking at the analysis the writer brings to the issue. In this case, the writer does very well and this essay merits a 6.

What about the conclusion?

We'd say the conclusion is the least important part of the essay. It's almost like the period that comes at the end of this sentence. Omitting it would have been an egregious lapse in punctuation. By including it, you hardly notice.

So as long as the conclusion recaps the essay's main point and perhaps ends with an apt parting thought, it doesn't need to be longer than three sentences. Even two sentences would suffice.

And don't forget the period at the end!

First sentence recaps: *Though many feel that technology, in taking over many of the roles that were once under our cognitive domain, will harm our ability to think, they miss the point that much of what is being "outsourced" was not what made us critical thinkers in the first place.*

Second sentence quickly mentions examples: *Instead, technology can augment those critical thinking skills that will always be a part of our uniquely human roles— whether they be that of a doctor or a concert pianist.*

Third sentence offers a parting thought: *To think otherwise is to forget what truly makes us human.*

A perfect score doesn't mean a perfect essay

If you're a picky reader with an editorial bent, you might be thinking, *That's not a 6. I can poke more holes in that than I could a paper boat. I give it a 4.5.* (Admittedly, the examples we've walked through are fairly sophisticated, at least stylistically, so that may not be the case.)

By looking only at the rubric of scores, you could certainly come to that conclusion. Nonetheless, we have to remember that students have only thirty minutes to write on a topic they've likely never written on before. With such time constraints, it's difficult to write anything immaculate. Also, these are grad school candidates, not journalists trying to land a story on the front page of the *New York Times*.

To really get a sense of what a 2 essay, a 6 essay, and anything in between looks like, visit ets.org for actual sample essays. That will also give you an idea of where your writing is and what you'll need to do to get there. We hope the strategies you learn here will help!

So how do I get better at writing an Issue essay?

Once you have a sense of what the essay expects—a nuanced position and thoughtful analysis on a complex issue—you should get in the habit of coming up with an introduction that reflects this.

Once you're adept at coming up with a thesis statement that isn't one-sided or directly in the middle, start coming up with examples to support your position. As soon as you come up with an example, though, think of a counterargument. Then, think of ways that the counterargument is valid and ways that it is not valid. If you keep thinking to yourself, "There are so many objections to my position!" that's not a bad thing. Simply choose a few likely objections and address them using critical analysis. Again, there are supposed to be plenty of objections to any position, since an issue featured on the GRE tends to be complex and affords many perspectives. By acknowledging that you're aware of them and by handling them in a way that leaves your main thesis intact, you're well on your way to a strong score in the Issue task.

The Argument Task

Each paragraph argument will be riddled with logical fallacies. Luckily, these fallacies tend to fall into predictable categories. Once you know what to look for, you'll have a far easier time spotting—and elaborating on—the logical flaws in the paragraph.

Here are the six categories that fallacies on the GRE tend to fall into.

#1: Mistaken cause and effect

> After instituting a comprehensive bilingual program, Miramonte Prep School has graduated a higher percentage of students this year than the previous year. Therefore, if Miramonte wants to continue to increase the percentage of students graduating from next year's class, it should continue the bilingual program.

Fallacy: There can be many causes for the increase in the percent of graduates. Therefore, it's wrong to assume that the bilingual program was the sole reason—or even a reason—for this observed effect.

A further—and subtler—fallacy is one that's specific to the example, not necessarily cause and effect. Nonetheless, we thought we'd point it out to show that once you've identified a fallacy as falling into one of these categories, you can dig a little deeper. In this case, assuming that the bilingual program actually played a major role in the number of students graduating—that is, assuming that many were not passing their foreign language requirement—the conclusion incorrectly assumes that the graduation rate will "continue to increase" the following year, when it's possible the gains of the program have already been made.

#2: Confusing number and percent

> In 2014, MakeTech had the lowest percentage of defective products in its five-year history. Therefore, there were fewer defective MakeTech products released to the market in 2014 than there were in previous years.

Fallacy: It's wrong to conclude, based on the percentage of defective products, that the total number of defective products is lower than in previous years. For example, let's say 5% of MakeTech's products were defective in 2014, and they released 100,000 products. The total number of defective 2014 products released is 5,000. On the other hand, if 2012 was a sloppy year, and the defect rate was 10%, but MakeTech only released 40,000 products, the number of defective products is only 4,000. So in this case, the percent of products released in 2012 that were defective may be higher than that of 2014, but the number of physical products is lower.

#3: Things change

In the 1990s, ManCorp significantly boosted profits by starting a new line of haircare products, Fresh Scent, to appeal to the burgeoning single male market. Since 2010, ManCorp has been experiencing a significant decline in annual profits. In order to boost profits again, ManCorp should appeal to the single male market by releasing a new line of grooming products.

Fallacy: What was successful in one time period is not necessarily going to be successful in another time period. The idea is that many factors shift over time. In this case, the market in the 1990s is not the same as the market today. For instance, is the single male market "burgeoning" the way it was in the 1990s? Even if it is growing, there could be many competitors targeting the same market. After all, ManCorp isn't doing well. There can be many reasons for this, but those reasons aren't necessarily going to disappear simply because ManCorp releases a new line of products.

#4: Vague language

Studies have shown that those who eat three Maxomeal fruit bars a day are in better shape than those who eat a normal diet.

Fallacy: When language is vague, it's open to interpretation, making it difficult to draw any valid conclusions. In this case, what does "better shape" mean exactly? Lower fat percentage? Higher cardiovascular functioning? Bulging biceps? Then there's also "normal diet": this could mean almost anything. Indeed, for a fan of Maxomeal bars, eating three a day might be part of a "normal diet." Again, when language is so vague that it's open to wildly divergent interpretations, it essentially becomes meaningless.

#5: Apples aren't oranges

Five years ago, to offset a recession, Clarksburg built a new outdoor shopping area, filled with luxury outlets and fine dining establishments. The city has since been reinvigorated economically. Therefore, Gaptown, which is currently in a recession, should build a similar shopping establishment if it wants to escape its economic slump.

Fallacy: Based on the example, we know very little about Clarksburg and Gaptown. They could be different in any number of ways. Therefore, it's wrong to conclude that what works for one will work for the other. For instance, Clarksburg might have many high-income families (those who can afford a high-end shopping area), or at least be close to a city that has such residents. If Gaptown is a middle-class town and is nowhere near any town with big spenders, then having a shopping area filled with luxury outlets, if anything, portends economic disaster.

You might have noticed several other fallacies we've already talked about. Indeed, this example—albeit shorter—is very much like what you'll see in an actual GRE AWA Argument Task: multiple fallacies in one sentence. Here are some other fallacies you may have seen:

#1: Mistaken cause and effect: How do we know for sure that the reason Clarksburg escaped its recession was because of the shopping area? Perhaps there was a bounce back in the economy at large.

#4: Vague language: What does it mean exactly to be "reinvigorated economically"? And what exactly constitutes "escape its economic slump"? Is this the same thing as being "reinvigorated economically"? With such vague language the answers to these questions are "yes," "no," and "maybe so." Essentially, the phrases are meaningless.

Here's one last type of fallacy that you might see in the GRE AWA:

#6: Surveys

According to a survey by AminoCorp, its workers are happy with the current office layout: 75% of those polled say they prefer the current office layout to the old one. Therefore, the current office layout should not be changed.

Fallacy: Surveys don't necessarily give us accurate pictures, especially if the sample (who was surveyed) and the sample size (how many were surveyed) are unknown. In the GRE AWA, this information is seldom, if ever, given. Therefore, the mention of a survey is an opportunity for you to point out a fallacy. In this case, it says "of those polled." How do we know if this is representative of the entire company and therefore how people really feel about the office layout? In this example, the survey is misleading in another way: the paragraph concludes that the office layout should not be changed, even though the survey is comparing the old layout to the current one. Even if all of AminoCorp was surveyed, if the old office layout was terrible, many are going to say they prefer the current layout, even if the current layout is mediocre. Had they been surveyed on the question of whether they would be open to a new office layout, that would provide us with more helpful information to draw the conclusion above.

Sample Argument Task

The "best place to live" in the USA is an idea promoted by many websites and surveys, but because there are a panoply of possible rating systems one could use, it seems that different rankings seldom wind up picking exactly the same lists. Various recent contenders for #1 include Apex, NC; Denver, CO; Fargo, ND; Rochester, MN; and of course, San Francisco, CA, where, according to the song, people leave their hearts!

> SuperCorp recently moved its headquarters to Corporateville. The recent surge in the number of homeowners in Corporateville proves that Corporateville is a superior place to live compared to Middlesburg, the home of SuperCorp's previous headquarters. Moreover, Middlesburg is a predominately urban area and according to an employee survey, SuperCorp has determined that its workers prefer to live in an area that is not urban. Finally, Corporateville has lower taxes than Middlesburg, making it not only a safer place to work but also a cheaper one. Therefore, SuperCorp clearly made the best decision.
>
> *Task: Write a response in which you examine the stated and/or unstated assumptions of the argument. Be sure to explain how the argument depends on the assumptions and what the implications are if the assumptions prove unwarranted.*

Step one: Attack the assumptions

Don't agree with any part of the argument—assume it's full of logical gaps. Your job on this task is to expose those gaps. Of course, you don't only want to cite what is wrong with the argument: you want to elaborate on how the argument can be improved.

The first step is to brainstorm the logical gaps or unwarranted assumptions the argument makes. Thinking of the assumptions before writing is key—don't just rush into the essay. Planning before you write will, in the end, save you time.

Assumption #1: The argument assumes that the increase in homeowners is directly correlated with improved living, or, as the argument states, "a superior place to live." Housing could simply be cheaper, causing an influx of people. That is, the increase of population doesn't mean that everybody wants to live in Corporateville because it's such a great place.

Assumption #2: Even if everybody wants to move to Corporateville because it's a superior place to live, that doesn't mean what is "superior" for residents is "superior" for a corporation. Remember, working and living are two very different things.

Assumption #3: We don't know anything about the survey. Is it really indicative of how employees feel? Perhaps the survey only asked upper management. Maybe only the engineering department was questioned. Basically, there's no way for us to know whether the sample was representative. Anyhow, the survey—even if it is representative—found that SuperCorp's workers preferred to live, not to work, in areas that aren't urban.

Assumption #4: There's nothing in the argument that says that Corporateville isn't urban. Perhaps Corporateville is also somewhat urban. We don't know. And be careful not to assume that people typically leave urban areas for the suburbs. Never bring your own preconceived notions into the argument.

Assumption #5: Toward the end, the argument mentions that Corporateville is safer. In this same sentence, you also find mention of lower taxes. If the argument is setting out to prove that Corporateville is a superior place to work than Middlesburg, it has to be more specific about how lower taxes will improve quality of workplace.

Assumption #6: The argument ends by saying that SuperCorp clearly made the right decision. Even if Corporateville is a better place for SuperCorp, to say that the company made "the best decision" is stretching it. Perhaps SuperCorp could have moved to a different city, one even better suited to its needs.

A Look at an Example Argument Task

Let's start with the introduction. The introduction should be short and sweet. In fact, the introduction in the Argument task should really not contain any novel ideas. You simply want to say that the argument you're evaluating is unwarranted for a number of reasons. If you find yourself hung up on the introduction, write it later, after finishing the body paragraphs. The key to the essay is the body, in which you identify the unwarranted assumptions. You don't want to waste precious minutes fiddling with the introduction.

Introduction

The argument makes a number of unwarranted assumptions regarding the corporation's proposed move from Middlesburg to Corporateville. Taken as a whole, these unstated assumptions render the argument highly suspect. Indeed, if these unstated assumptions do not hold true, then the argument totally falls apart.

Next we have the body paragraphs, in which you'll point out the unstated assumptions that make the argument invalid. You can lump all into one massive paragraph or you can—as done here—spread them into three paragraphs, one for each unstated assumption.

Body paragraph #1

The argument assumes that the increase in homeowners is directly correlated with improved living, or, as the argument states, "a superior place to live." Housing could simply be cheaper, causing an influx of people. That is, the increase of population does not mean that everybody wants to live in Corporateville because it is such a great place. In fact, low-priced housing and overcrowding clearly would make Corporateville an inferior place to live.

325

Notice how we ended the argument by carrying out what the instructions asked us to do: *"Be sure to explain how the argument depends on the assumptions and **what the implications are if the assumptions prove unwarranted**."*

Body paragraph #2

Another unstated assumption the argument makes is that what is superior for residents is the same as what is superior for corporations. Thus, even if everybody wants to move to Corporateville because it is a superior place to live, that doesn't mean it is a superior place for a company to move its headquarters. For instance, perhaps Corporateville has an excellent public school system and/or natural parks. Neither of these would make Corporateville a superior place to work. Unless the argument can show that there is clear reason that Corporateville is superior to Middlesburg for a corporation, then the corporation could be making the wrong decision in moving to Corporateville.

Body paragraph #3

We won't actually write this one out. But if we did, it would focus on the survey. This is probably the strongest unstated assumption remaining (the survey as a valid measure). Nonetheless, you can choose to focus on taxes or urban vs. non-urban. Don't, however, try to jam all the assumptions into your essay. Your focus is to show that the essay makes many unproven assumptions and is thus invalid. Pointing out several assumptions is enough. Unless you have time, don't be exhaustive.

Conclusion

Like the introduction, the conclusion should be short and sweet. Don't add new information; simply give a brief summary of what you've already said. Write something along the lines of the following:

The argument makes a number of unstated assumptions that seriously undermine its validity. Unless these assumptions are addressed, the argument falls apart and the corporation could very well make a major mistake shifting operations from Middlesburg to Corporateville.

Parting thought

The goal of the brainstorming session isn't to see how many assumptions you can find. Instead, you want to choose the few that you think best invalidate the argument.

So how do I improve?

Essay writing is tough. Practicing for the GRE AWA—given that it's difficult to get feedback—makes things even tougher. In other words, you write and write without knowing if you're really improving. But don't despair: there are sample essays, as well as friends and family.

1. **Write.** By simply writing often, you'll be able to write with greater command and facility. With frequent practice, words won't feel like they're so hard to come by. Give it enough time and they'll spring to life on the page.

2. **Don't forget to outline/brainstorm.** You have to think about what you're going to write before you begin. When practicing for the GRE, avoid trying to go full steam ahead, hoping the words that come from your fingers are the right ones. Instead, spend a few minutes coming up with a roadmap either in your head or on the computer screen. At first this step will slow you down, and you'll want to go back to the old method. Be patient. Once you become adept at outlining, the essay will write itself.

3. **Spend lots of time editing your practice essays.** Though you won't get much of an opportunity to edit your essay on test day, carefully editing your practice essays will make you more aware of your mistakes, both grammatical and logical. Correcting these mistakes will help you anticipate them in the future, which will make the writing and logic in those future essays clearer.

4. **Constantly read sample essays**. By reading other students' essays, you'll develop a sense of what the GRE AWA is looking for. You'll also be able to better judge your own essays. During practice sessions, you should keep tweaking your essays so they get closer and closer to the next score up. If you started by writing an essay that looked similar to a sample of a 3, then focus on writing an essay that looks more like a 4.

5. **Improve grammar.** ETS explicitly states that it's looking for quality and clarity of thought, and not grammar per se. Yet the two are closely related. So if you struggle to articulate something—and in doing so break a grammatical rule (or three!)—you'll sacrifice clarity. Even minor grammatical errors (faulty pronouns, subject/verb agreement) can hurt the overall quality of your writing.

How do I improve my grammar and style?

Between grammar and style, grammar is much easier to improve. Great style is much more elusive. Indeed, many writers cultivate their prose style over years of practice. Rest assured, though, to score well on the GRE, your writing doesn't have to be fit for the *New Yorker*. You do want to avoid choppy sentences by varying your sentence structure, but you shouldn't be worried about trading a simple word for a more complex one, as long that word is appropriate for the context.

A great book that offers writing advice, from dangling modifiers to how to construct compelling, dynamic sentences, is William Zinsser's *On Writing Well*.

For a sterner approach to writing, Strunk and White's *The Elements of Style* has helped students for over half a century.

The only reason we mention both of these books is that they focus not only on grammar but also on style. Many grammar books suffice as far as grammar goes—but they're short on teaching writing style, which is a great skill to have for the GRE AWA (and beyond!).

Practice Writing Tasks

These examples should help you get an idea of what to expect from writing tasks on the GRE. There are even more practice questions in the GRE practice test in chapter 6.

Question 1

The best leaders are those who encourage feedback from the people they lead.

Write a response in which you discuss the extent to which you agree or disagree with the statement and explain your reasoning for the position you take. In developing and supporting your position, you should consider ways in which the statement might or might not hold true and explain how these considerations shape your position.

Question 2

Universities should require students to take courses only within those fields they are interested in studying.

Write a response in which you discuss your views on the policy and explain your reasoning for the position you take. In developing and supporting your position, you should consider the possible consequences of implementing the policy and explain how these consequences shape your position.

Question 3

The following was presented as part of a business plan by Apex Corporation.

"To answer the increased demand for artisanal coffee, Apex Corporation is releasing a new line of coffee, 'Gourmet Select.' Apex Corporation will first introduce the coffee into major supermarkets, where it hopes word-of-mouth advertising will sustain sales. After a few months Apex Corporation will run an advertising campaign aimed at television and radio while simultaneously releasing the brand to several major chain restaurants. Based on this strategy, Apex Corporation hopes to make 'Gourmet Select' one of the top sellers in the coffee market."

Write a response in which you examine the stated and/or unstated assumptions of the argument. Be sure to explain how the argument depends on these assumptions and what the implications are for the argument if the assumptions prove unwarranted.

Question 2

The business district of downtown Laughton is thriving during the weekdays but is virtually uninhabited during the weekends. As a result, many of the shops and restaurants close during this time, though the proprietors must still pay rent. Since many such businesses have struggled over the last year, the mayor of Laughton has proposed that a nearby, abandoned twenty-acre plot of land that houses a few dilapidated warehouses be converted into a park. Once completed, the park will serve as a weekend attraction for many families living in Laughton. As a result, many will frequent the restaurants and shops, thereby reinvigorating these struggling businesses.

Write a response in which you examine the stated and/or unstated assumptions of the argument. Be sure to explain how the argument depends on these assumptions and what the implications are for the argument if the assumptions prove unwarranted.

Need a study break? Color in the shapes below to make whatever pattern you'd like. Have fun!

Chapter 6

GRE Practice Test

On the following pages, you'll find a mock GRE test that we've created using a variety of questions from the Magoosh vault. While this practice test is built to help you experience the types of questions you'll see on the GRE, remember that the *real* test is online. For a more accurate experience of the GRE, including online, timed practice tests, check out Magoosh online. The online Magoosh offerings that people know and love are very similar to what you'll experience on test day.

For now, though, you're working your way through this paper test, and we commend you for that. Take any opportunity to practice you can get—online, on paper, on an app—wherever!

Here's what to expect on the following pages:

1. **A mock GRE AWA.** You'll find an "Analyze an Issue" task and an "Analyze an Argument" task. Set your time for thirty minutes for each task and have at it. We've provided some space to use for brainstorming, but we recommend using a computer to type the essays.

2. **GRE Quantitative section 1.** You'll complete twenty questions in thirty-five minutes. Remember that on test day you'll have an onscreen calculator. For this practice test, use whatever calculator you have handy, other than the one on your phone—no distractions!

3. **GRE Verbal section 1.** You'll complete twenty questions in thirty minutes. Get ready to flex those vocab skills.

4. **GRE Quantitative section 2.** Here you'll find another twenty questions to be completed in thirty-five minutes.

5. **GRE Verbal section 2.** And another twenty questions to be completed in thirty minutes.

Tips

- Set aside four uninterrupted hours to complete the practice test.
- Find a place to work where you won't be disturbed.
- Turn off your cellphone and leave it in another room.
- Have a timer handy and don't forget to restart it for each section.
- Try to attack the whole practice test at one time, rather than sitting down for different sections at different times.
- Try not to skip the AWA section in any mock test. Although an accurate assessment of the AWA section might not be possible, writing the essays first does build up your test-taking endurance.
- Take a ten-minute break in between the first GRE Verbal section and the second GRE Quantitative section.
- Eat healthy snacks before sitting down to practice—not during the test.
- Check out the Magoosh online practice tests to experience the GRE as it will be on the actual test day.

Good luck!

GRE Practice Test Questions

GRE Analytical Writing

Remember, you get thirty minutes on the test for EACH response.
Set your timer!

Analyze an Issue Task #1

Those who see their ideas through, regardless of doubts or criticism others may express, are the ones who tend to leave a lasting legacy.

Write a response in which you discuss the extent to which you agree or disagree with the statement and explain your reasoning for the position you take. In developing and supporting your position, you should consider ways in which the statement might or might not hold true and explain how these considerations shape your position.

Analyze an Argument Task #1

The following is a memorandum from the office of Mayor Harrison Peter Jones.

"In order to relieve Briggsville's notorious traffic congestion, Mayor Harrison Peter Jones plans to build a multi-million-dollar subway system. The subway will run through the major downtown areas, a part of the town where buses serve as the only form of public transportation. For years, residents have been complaining both about inconsistent buses and the general lack of safety while riding the buses. Additionally, the subway will be running twenty-four hours a day. Since motorists will spend less time in traffic, Mayor Harrison Peter Jones expects to see an immediate increase in worker productivity, which will improve the economy of Briggsville."

Write a response in which you examine the stated and/or unstated assumptions of the argument. Be sure to explain how the argument depends on these assumptions and what the implications are for the argument if the assumptions prove unwarranted.

STOP

Take a 1-minute break before moving on to the next section.

GRE Quantitative Section 1

Remember, you get thirty-five minutes on the actual GRE for this section. Set your timer before you get started.

Test Question 1

The numbers p and q are both positive integers.

Column A	Column B
$\dfrac{p}{q}$	$\left(\dfrac{p}{q}\right)^2$

- (A) The quantity in Column A is greater
- (B) The quantity in Column B is greater
- (C) The two quantities are equal
- (D) The relationship cannot be determined from the information given

Test Question 2

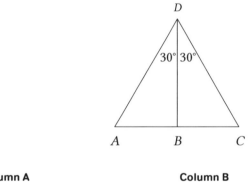

Column A	Column B
AB	BC

- (A) The quantity in Column A is greater
- (B) The quantity in Column B is greater
- (C) The two quantities are equal
- (D) The relationship cannot be determined from the information given

Test Question 3

Ashley's score was 20% higher than Bert's score. Bert's score was 20% lower than Charles's score.

Column A	Column B
Ashley's score	Charles's score

- (A) The quantity in Column A is greater
- (B) The quantity in Column B is greater
- (C) The two quantities are equal
- (D) The relationship cannot be determined from the information given

Test Question 4

For positive numbers p and q, $\dfrac{p \cdot q}{p + q} = \dfrac{2}{3}$

Column A	Column B
$p + q$	5

- (A) The quantity in Column A is greater
- (B) The quantity in Column B is greater
- (C) The two quantities are equal
- (D) The relationship cannot be determined from the information given

Test Question 5

K = sum of the integers from 1 to 500 inclusive that are divisible by 5.

Column A	Column B
K	25,000

- (A) The quantity in Column A is greater
- (B) The quantity in Column B is greater
- (C) The two quantities are equal
- (D) The relationship cannot be determined from the information given

Test Question 6

Main course: Chicken, Beef, Tofu
Side dish: Rice, Salad, Soup, Pasta
Dessert: Pie, Cake

A meal at a certain restaurant consists of 1 main course, 2 different side dishes, and 1 dessert.

Column A	Column B
Number of different meals possible	36

- (A) The quantity in Column A is greater
- (B) The quantity in Column B is greater
- (C) The two quantities are equal
- (D) The relationship cannot be determined from the information given

Test Question 7

Column A	Column B
22 percent of x	$\frac{2}{9}$ of x

Ⓐ The quantity in Column A is greater

Ⓑ The quantity in Column B is greater

Ⓒ The two quantities are equal

Ⓓ The relationship cannot be determined from the information given

Test Question 8

If the circle with center O has area 9π, what is the area of equilateral triangle ABC?

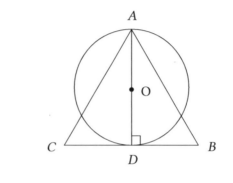

Ⓐ $9\sqrt{3}$

Ⓑ 18

Ⓒ $12\sqrt{3}$

Ⓓ 24

Ⓔ $16\sqrt{3}$

Test Question 9

What are the x-intercepts of the parabola defined by the equation $y = 2x^2 - 8x - 90$?

Indicate <u>all</u> x-intercepts.

A −10

B −9

C −5

D −4

E 4

F 5

G 9

H 10

Test Question 10

If $8^{n+1} + 8^n = 36$, then $n =$

(A) $\frac{1}{3}$

(B) $\frac{1}{2}$

(C) $\frac{3}{5}$

(D) $\frac{2}{3}$

(E) $\frac{4}{5}$

Test Question 11

In a large bucket of screws, the ratio of slot screws to Phillips screws is 11 to 4. There are no other varieties of screws in the bucket. If there are 320 Phillips screws in the bucket, what is the total number of screws in the bucket?

Test Question 12

If $2^k = 3$, then $2^{3k+2} =$

(A) 29

(B) 54

(C) 81

(D) 83

(E) 108

Test Question 13

Televisions in Town X, and Population per Television

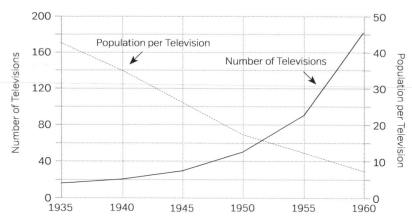

In 1955, the ratio of the number of televisions to the number of people was approximately

(A) 1 to 13
(B) 1 to 23
(C) 1 to 26
(D) 1 to 50
(E) 1 to 90

Test Question 14

Televisions in Town X, and Population per Television

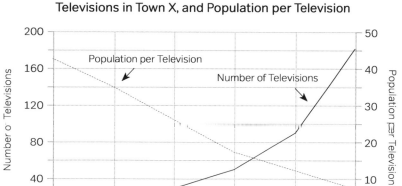

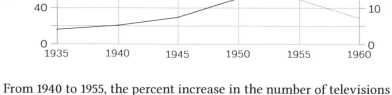

From 1940 to 1955, the percent increase in the number of televisions was closest to

(A) 30
(B) 130
(C) 350
(D) 450
(E) 650

Test Question 15

Televisions in Town X, and Population per Television

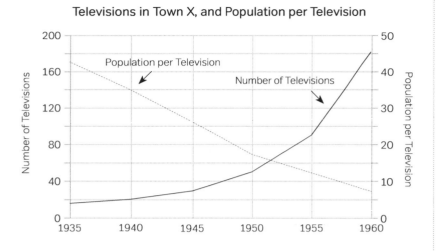

What was the approximate population of Town X in 1945?

Ⓐ 150

Ⓑ 750

Ⓒ 1500

Ⓓ 3000

Ⓔ 6000

Test Question 16

The average (arithmetic mean) of two numbers is $4x$. If one of the numbers is y, then the value of the other number is

Ⓐ $x - 4y$

Ⓑ $4x + 4y$

Ⓒ $8x - 4y$

Ⓓ $4y - 8x$

Ⓔ $8x - y$

Test Question 17

The figure shows the graph of the equation $y = k - x^2$, where k is a constant. If the area of triangle ABC is $\frac{1}{8}$, what is the value of k?

Give your answer to the <u>nearest 0.01</u>

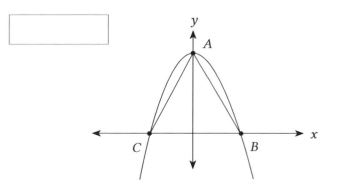

Test Question 18

If a and b are integers and $(\sqrt[3]{a} \times \sqrt{b})^6 = 500$, then $a + b$ could equal

(A) 2

(B) 3

(C) 4

(D) 5

(E) 6

Test Question 19

From a group of 8 people, it is possible to create exactly 56 different k-person committees. Which of the following could be the value of k?

Indicate <u>all</u> such values.

A 1

B 2

C 3

D 4

E 5

F 6

G 7

Test Question 20

In the xy-coordinate system, a circle with radius $\sqrt{30}$ and center $(2, 1)$ intersects the x-axis at $(k, 0)$. One possible value of k is

(A) $2 + \sqrt{26}$

(B) $2 + \sqrt{29}$

(C) $2 + \sqrt{31}$

(D) $2 + \sqrt{34}$

(E) $2 + \sqrt{35}$

STOP

Take a 1-minute break
before moving on to the
next section.

GRE Verbal Section 1

Allow yourself thirty minutes to complete this section!

For questions 1 to 7, select one word that best completes the sentence. For questions with multiple blanks, select <u>one</u> word from each corresponding column that best completes the sentence.

Test Question 1

Much of the consumer protection movement is predicated on the notion that routine exposure to seemingly _____ products can actually have longterm deleterious consequences.

- (A) outdated
- (B) banal
- (C) litigious
- (D) virulent
- (E) benign

Test Question 2

That the nightmarish depictions common to most early twentieth-century dystopian novels are exaggerated should by no means diminish the _____ power of these works, for many of the visions they conjure up are reflected, albeit in less vivid form, in many totalitarian governments today.

- (A) synoptic
- (B) ephemeral
- (C) comprehensive
- (D) apolitical
- (E) prophetic

Test Question 3

In conservative scientific circles, embracing an unorthodox theory, especially one that is backed up by little empirical evidence, is tantamount to (i) _____; indeed, any scientist who does so may be (ii) _____.

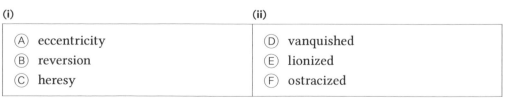

(i)	(ii)
(A) eccentricity	(D) vanquished
(B) reversion	(E) lionized
(C) heresy	(F) ostracized

Test Question 4

No less incendiary amongst the populace than many other "hot button" issues of the day, "fracking"—or hydraulic fracturing of the earth's surface to acquire gas, a practice that mostly takes place in remote parts of the country—has been (i) _____ the national dialogue come election time, perhaps because voters are typically (ii) _____ environmental problems that do not occur in their own backyards, so to speak.

(i)	(ii)
(A) unfairly tarnished in	(D) misinformed about
(B) a prominent theme in	(E) worked up over
(C) curiously absent from	(F) unmoved by

Test Question 5

To the (i) _____ eye, the jungle canopy can seem little more than a dense latticework of branches and leaves. For the indigenous peoples of the Amazon, even a small area can serve as a veritable (ii) _____ of pharmaceutical cures. The field of ethnobotany, which relates to both the natural pharmacy offered up by the jungle and the peoples who serve as a store of such knowledge, has become increasingly popular in the last decades as many anthropologists, hoping to take advantage of this vast bounty, learn the language and customs of the tribes in order to (iii) _____ them thousands of years worth of knowledge.

(i)	(ii)	(iii)
(A) untutored	(D) cornucopia	(G) glean from
(B) sophisticated	(E) invasion	(H) allot to
(C) veteran	(F) dissemination	(I) purge from

Test Question 6

The contention that Hopkin's extensive anthropological fieldwork led to a unified theory is (i) _____; close scrutiny reveals a (ii) _____ of observations that, at times, even prove (iii) _____ one another.

(i)	(ii)	(iii)
(A) redoubtable	(D) mere hodgepodge	(G) inimical to
(B) specious	(E) coherent system	(H) convergent with
(C) unbiased	(F) meticulous scaffolding	(I) susceptible to

Questions 7 to 9 are based on the following reading passage. For each of these questions, select <u>one</u> answer choice unless instructed otherwise.

PASSAGE

Researchers, investigating the link between daily coffee consumption and learning, claim that subjects who consumed one cup of coffee a day for one week (the equivalent of 50 mg per day) exhibited improvements in declarative memory. Furthermore, the study revealed that such improvements were longer-lasting than those witnessed in a control group served decaffeinated coffee (decaffeinated coffee contains negligible amounts of caffeine). After a week of learning a list of facts, the subjects who consumed one cup of coffee were able to recall these facts with significantly more accuracy.

While daily coffee consumption may aid in the process of forming a greater number of short-term memories and increase the likelihood that these memories will be stored in long-term memory, the study glosses over an important fact. Many exhibit sensitivities to caffeine, including headaches (both migraine and non-migraine), sleeplessness, heightened anxiety, and any number of factors that, when working either alone or in tandem, may actually lead to a decrease in the observed link between caffeine and learning. Nevertheless, despite the fact that the study represents a random sampling—and thus any number of subjects can exhibit any number of reactions to caffeine—if enough subjects continue to display signs of improvements in learning, then this result would not be inconsistent with the study's findings. Still, until the researchers either release more details of this study, or subsequent studies are conducted, the extent to which those with caffeine sensitivity influenced the observed link between coffee consumption and memory will not be fully known.

Test Question 7

The primary purpose of the passage is to

(A) discredit the findings of a study due to flaws in the design of the study
(B) point out a factor that may modify the extent of certain findings
(C) show how results in a finding were unintentionally fabricated
(D) bolster an argument concerning the interaction of learning and caffeine intake
(E) expand on several oversights of a noteworthy study

Test Question 8

Regarding coffee's effectiveness on memory amongst those who do not display "sensitivities to caffeine," the author assumes that

(A) more rigorous analysis in the form of follow-up studies must be conducted
(B) the researchers must be more forthcoming in their findings
(C) this group displayed a uniform tendency
(D) any positive effects will be negated by the effects exhibited by those with sensitivities to caffeine
(E) this effectiveness was fleeting and tended to all but disappear within a week of the study

Test Question 9

Select the sentence in which the author expresses an opinion toward the results of the study. In the computer-based test, you'll click on the sentence in the passage. For this paper-based test, circle the sentence in the passage above.

Questions 10 to 11 are based on the following reading passage. For each of these questions, select <u>one</u> answer choice unless instructed otherwise.

PASSAGE

What little scholarship has existed on Ernest Hemingway—considering his stature— has focused on trying to unmask the man behind the bravura. Ultimately, most of these works have done little more than to show that Hemingway the myth and Hemingway the man were not too dissimilar (Hemingway lived to hunt big game, so should you be surprised at his virility, not to mention that of many of the author's— chiefly male—protagonists?). In the last few years, several biographies have reversed this trend, focusing on Hemingway near the end of his life: isolated and paranoid, the author imagined the government was chasing him (he was not completely wrong on this account). Ironically, the hunter had become the hunted, and in that sense, these latest biographers have provided—perhaps unwittingly—the most human portrait of the writer yet.

Test Question 10

It can be inferred from the passage that the author considers the latest Hemingway biographies a departure from traditional biographies since the newer ones

(A) focus on a much overlooked aspect of the writer's body of work
(B) depict Hemingway in a manner that is at odds with the myth of Hemingway
(C) claim that Hemingway was similar to several of his chief protagonists in his books
(D) suggest that Hemingway lacked the virility many associated with him
(E) do not attempt to explore the link between Hemingway the man and Hemingway the myth

Test Question 11

With which of the following would the author of the passage agree? Select <u>all</u> that apply.

[A] The prevalence of scholarship on Hemingway is commensurate with his renown as a writer.
[B] The latest Hemingway biographies consciously intended to show Hemingway's vulnerabilities.
[C] Until recently, Hemingway biographies had shown a similar trend.

Test Question 12

Recently, a team of scientists digging through a tar pit unearthed a jawbone fossil. Initially, the team hypothesized that the jawbone came from a young gomphothere, a now extinct distant relative of the elephant, since the teeth were those of a juvenile. The gomphothere, however, is known for its large molars, and the teeth on the jawbone would not allow enough room for the molars of an adult gomphothere to fit. Based on this evidence, the scientists conclude that the jawbone fossil provides evidence of a distinct species closely related to the gomphothere.

Which of the following, if true, would best provide evidence showing that the conclusion above is possibly flawed?

(A) The manner in which teeth grow provides sufficient evidence for the accurate classification of a bygone species.

(B) In order for the molars of an adult gomphothere to emerge, several juvenile teeth are first forced out of the gums to accommodate the molars.

(C) The molars of an adult mastodon, a close relative of the gomphothere, are similar in size to those of an adult gomphothere.

(D) Many fossils exist that have yet to be conclusively attributed to any one species.

(E) The juvenile jawbone of a species related to a gomphothere is longer than the juvenile jawbone of a gomphothere.

For questions 13 to 16, select exactly <u>two</u> words that best complete the sentence and produce sentences that are alike in meaning.

Test Question 13

The heckler, hiding amongst the amorphous crowd, is the epitome of _____—as soon as he has been identified, he goes scuttling off, head down, grumbling to himself.

A stealthiness

B outspokenness

C shyness

D aloofness

E cravenness

F spinelessness

Test Question 14

In the last few decades, technological progress has proceeded at such a dizzying rate that, beyond the obvious advantages a given technology confers on the user, the non-specialist becomes _____ when pressed to explain how anything really works.

A elegiac
B belligerent
C confident
D baffled
E complacent
F perplexed

Test Question 15

After years of assiduously cultivating an image of integrity, the mayor was acutely aware that just one scandal could forever _____ his reputation in the public's eyes.

A bolster
B besmirch
C tarnish
D promulgate
E mollify
F solidify

Test Question 16

If good taste has _____ the vampire genre to be tired and trite, the entertainment industry surely is not listening: for every bloodsucker baring fangs, there is a hack bearing some script.

A found
B deemed
C expected
D discovered
E demeaned
F anticipated

For questions 17 to 20, select <u>one</u> answer choice unless instructed otherwise.

Test Question 17

Scientists have created double-blind studies so that neither the subjects of the experiment nor scientists know whether a patient is receiving an actual drug or a placebo, which is nothing more than a sugar pill. Essentially, if one knows that one is receiving an actual pill, such knowledge can affect the outcome of a study. A recent study on the effectiveness of the selective serotonin reuptake inhibitor (SSRI) fluvoxamine on depression found that those subjects administered the drug were 15 percent more likely to have a decrease in symptoms than the control group, which was comprised of those who received a placebo. Since neither group knew which they were receiving, the placebo or the SSRI, the observed drop in depression can only be attributed to fluvoxamine.

Which of the following, if true, best calls into question the conclusion of the argument?

(A) Neither the patients nor the doctors in either group (the control group or the fluvoxamine group) knew which drug they were receiving.

(B) Since patients in both groups were briefed on the potential side effects of an SSRI, which can often be pronounced, many in the fluvoxamine group, upon exhibiting side effects, concluded that they were being administered the SSRI.

(C) Fluvoxamine does not exhibit a uniform effect in all patients, with many reporting little improvement in symptoms of depression, even after several months of taking the drug.

(D) At dosages two-fold of those employed in the trial, fluvoxamine has been shown to cause brief episodes of psychosis.

(E) One subject from the fluvoxamine group experienced debilitating side effects and was forced to drop out of the trial before its completion.

That some dinosaurs could fly has long been established. That these very same species may have been able to walk—using their wings no less—has been far more controversial. However, the latest computer simulations suggest that the pteranodon, a pterosaur with a wingspan of up to twenty-five feet, while no rapid runner, was able to walk by retracting its wrists so as to walk on its palms. Why the pteranodon did so remains unanswered.

One theory is that walking allowed it to forage for food on the ground. While this idea is enticing, proponents of this theory have yet to propose a reasonable answer as to what led to such a dramatic change in both physiology and locomotion. Another explanation is that flying was the evolutionary advantage conferred upon these creatures: in times of scarcity, a flying creature has access to a far greater abundance of fauna than does one limited to terrestrial movement.

Test Question 18

In the sentence that begins, "Another explanation is that flying was the evolutionary advantage," the author implies that

- (A) most flying dinosaurs underwent similar transformations
- (B) only a theory that accounts for the scarcity of resources can account for the physiological adaptations of the pteranodon
- (C) dinosaurs only underwent evolutionary change if doing so provided an obvious advantage
- (D) the pteranodon had originally only been able to walk before evolving the ability to fly
- (E) the pteranodon would be able to access sufficient food while in flight

Test Question 19

Which of the following can be substantiated based on information found in the passage? Select all that apply.

- [A] Scientists consider evidence based on computer simulations sufficient for backing up a theory.
- [B] The pteranodon had other adaptations, besides the ability to retract its wrists, that allowed it to walk.
- [C] Even if a theory is compelling, that theory should not be immune to analysis.

Test Question 20

The waters off the coast of Iceland are filled with pods of killer whales, which migrate there during the summer. Wildlife parks that rely on the killer whales for entertainment hunt them almost exclusively in the water of Iceland, because strict sanctions forbid them from doing so off the coast of North America, an area also abundant in killer whales. Since Iceland recently gave into pressure from international groups opposed to the hunting of killer whales, it too will forbid the hunting of killer whales off its coast. Therefore, all wildlife parks will be forced to end their shows featuring killer whales once their current killer whales are unable to perform.

All of the following cast doubt on the conclusion of the argument EXCEPT

(A) The recent ban only extends to within one hundred miles of Iceland, though killer whales are plentiful along the shores of Greenland, which fall outside this range.

(B) The incoming prime minister of Canada, who is more conservative, is planning on lifting the ban on hunting killer whales off the coast of Canada.

(C) In-park killer whale births have become increasingly common, especially in those wildlife parks that harbor a large number of killer whales.

(D) Some wildlife parks are involved in the illegal trade of killer whales.

(E) It is nearly impossible to catch killer whales in deep waters, so hunters typically rely on luring killer whales into coves.

STOP

Take a 10-minute break before moving on to the next section.

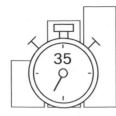

GRE Quantitative Section 2

Remember, you get thirty-five minutes on the actual GRE for this section. Set your timer before you get started.

Test Question 1

For positive numbers a, b, and c, $\frac{a \times b}{c} = 1$ and $\frac{c}{a} = 4$

Column A	Column B
b	4

Ⓐ The quantity in Column A is greater

Ⓑ The quantity in Column B is greater

Ⓒ The two quantities are equal

Ⓓ The relationship cannot be determined from the information given

Test Question 2

1. n is a positive integer.

2. n is not divisible by 4.

3. n is not divisible by 5.

Column A	Column B
The remainder when n is divided by 4	The remainder when n is divided by 5

Ⓐ The quantity in Column A is greater

Ⓑ The quantity in Column B is greater

Ⓒ The two quantities are equal

Ⓓ The relationship cannot be determined from the information given

Test Question 3

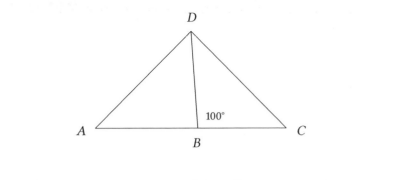

Column A	Column B
$AB + AD$	$DC + BC$

(A) The quantity in Column A is greater
(B) The quantity in Column B is greater
(C) The two quantities are equal
(D) The relationship cannot be determined from the information given

Test Question 4

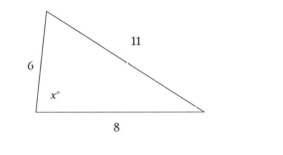

Column A	Column B
x	90

(A) The quantity in Column A is greater
(B) The quantity in Column B is greater
(C) The two quantities are equal
(D) The relationship cannot be determined from the information given

Test Question 5

When a coin is flipped, the probability of getting heads is 0.5, and the probability of getting tails is 0.5

A coin is flipped 5 times.

Column A	Column B
Probability of getting exactly 2 heads	Probability of getting exactly 3 heads

- (A) The quantity in Column A is greater
- (B) The quantity in Column B is greater
- (C) The two quantities are equal
- (D) The relationship cannot be determined from the information given

Test Question 6

1. x and y are integers greater than 5.
2. x is y percent of x^2

Column A	Column B
x	10

- (A) The quantity in Column A is greater
- (B) The quantity in Column B is greater
- (C) The two quantities are equal
- (D) The relationship cannot be determined from the information given

Test Question 7

In a group of 200 workers, 10% of the males smoke, and 49% of the females smoke.

Column A	Column B
Total number of workers who smoke	59

- (A) The quantity in Column A is greater
- (B) The quantity in Column B is greater
- (C) The two quantities are equal
- (D) The relationship cannot be determined from the information given

Test Question 8

A sum of money was distributed among Lyle, Bob, and Chloe. First, Lyle received \$4 plus one-half of what remained. Next, Bob received \$4 plus one-third of what remained. Finally, Chloe received the remaining \$32. How many dollars did Bob receive?

Ⓐ 10

Ⓑ 20

Ⓒ 26

Ⓓ 40

Ⓔ 52

Test Question 9

If the sales tax on a \$12.00 purchase is \$0.66, what is the sales tax on a \$20.00 purchase?

Ⓐ \$1.08

Ⓑ \$1.10

Ⓒ \$1.16

Ⓓ \$1.18

Ⓔ \$1.20

Test Question 10

If $\dfrac{2 + \frac{3}{n}}{3 + \frac{2}{n}} = \dfrac{5}{4}$, what is the value of n?

Enter your answer as a fraction. Fractions do not need to be in their simplest forms.

Test Question 11

The probability is 0.6 that an "unfair" coin will turn up tails on any given toss. If the coin is tossed 3 times, what is the probability that at least 1 of the tosses will turn up tails?

Ⓐ 0.064

Ⓑ 0.36

Ⓒ 0.64

Ⓓ 0.784

Ⓔ 0.936

Test Question 12

The sides of a triangle are 1, x, and x^2. What are the possible values of x?

Indicate <u>all</u> possible values.

- [A] 0.5
- [B] 1
- [C] 1.5
- [D] 2
- [E] 2.5
- [F] 3
- [G] 3.5

Test Question 13

The following tables show the revenues and costs, in thousands of dollars, for a small company in the year 2007.

Revenues

Sales	753
Investments	53
Subsidiaries	246
Total	1052

Costs

Materials & Resource	83
Production	16
Payroll & Benefits	452
Insurance & Plant	123
Research & Development (R&D)	75
Total	749

Profit = Revenue − Costs. If costs remain constant from 2007 to 2008, and if revenues increase by 10% in that same period, by what percent will profits increase from 2007 to 2008?

- (A) 11.6%
- (B) 25.8%
- (C) 34.7%
- (D) 71.2%
- (E) 116.3%

Test Question 14

The following tables show the revenues and costs, in thousands of dollars, for a small company in the year 2007.

Revenues

Sales	753
Investments	53
Subsidiaries	246
Total	1052

Costs

Materials & Resource	83
Production	16
Payroll & Benefits	452
Insurance & Plant	123
Research & Development (R&D)	75
Total	749

Investments and Subsidiary revenues combined constitute what percent of total revenue?

Ⓐ 5.0%

Ⓑ 14.2%

Ⓒ 22.6%

Ⓓ 28.4%

Ⓔ 39.9%

Test Question 15

The following tables show the revenues and costs, in thousands of dollars, for a small company in the year 2007.

Revenues

Sales	753
Investments	53
Subsidiaries	246
Total	1052

Costs

Materials & Resource	83
Production	16
Payroll & Benefits	452
Insurance & Plant	123
Research & Development (R&D)	75
Total	749

Suppose in the following year, 2008, the sales are the same value, and half of those sales are directly due to the 2007 investment in R&D. The revenue received from these sales would be what percent greater than the money invested in R&D?

Ⓐ 85%

Ⓑ 110%

Ⓒ 200%

Ⓓ 402%

Ⓔ 503%

Test Question 16

Which of the following is equal to 8^{24}?

Indicate <u>all</u> possible values.

A. 2^{96}

B. 4^{36}

C. 12^{12}

D. 16^{18}

E. 24^{8}

F. 32^{15}

Test Question 17

For all numbers a and b, the operation $\oplus$ is defined by $a \oplus b = a^2 - ab$.
If $xy \neq 0$, then which of the following can be equal to zero?

I. $x \oplus y$

II. $xy \oplus y$

III. $x \oplus (x + y)$

(A) II only

(B) I and II only

(C) I and III only

(D) II and III only

(E) All of the above

Test Question 18

In the figure below, ABC is a circular sector with center A. If arc BC has length 4π, what is the length of AC?

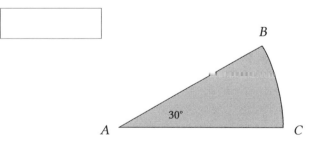

Test Question 19

The sum of k consecutive integers is 41. If the least integer is -40, then $k =$

(A) 40

(B) 41

(C) 80

(D) 81

(E) 82

Test Question 20

In the equation $n^2 - kn + 16 = 0$, n is an integer. Which of the following could be the value of k?

Indicate <u>all</u> such values

A. 8

B. 15

C. −17

STOP

Take a 1-minute break before moving on to the next section.

GRE Verbal Section 2

Remember to allow yourself thirty minutes to complete this section!

For questions 1 to 6, select <u>one</u> word that best completes the sentence. For questions with multiple blanks, select <u>one</u> word from each corresponding column that best completes the sentence.

Test Question 1

Critics who charged that the technology start-up had blatantly appropriated the laptop design of the leading manufacturer failed to take into account a recent report citing that the start-up had been anything but _____, as not only was it the first to market, but pictures of its original design had initially surfaced publicly.

Ⓐ hesitant

Ⓑ dominant

Ⓒ innovative

Ⓓ unscrupulous

Ⓔ posthumous

Test Question 2

There are few _____ thrills to be gleaned from Kafka's writing, for his characters, which typically embody ideas, are not fleshed out enough for the reader to become fully immersed in their plights.

Ⓐ novel

Ⓑ vicarious

Ⓒ tangential

Ⓓ precarious

Ⓔ substantive

Test Question 3

Mulcahy, in averring that most literary criticism has become so filled with abstruse jargon as to be practically indecipherable to anyone save its practitioners, is himself (i) _____: his main point will be discernible only to the very community he seeks to (ii) _____.

(i)	(ii)
Ⓐ uncertain	Ⓓ defend
Ⓑ complicit	Ⓔ impugn
Ⓒ enlightened	Ⓕ inform

Test Question 4

The latest biography on J. R. Oppenheimer, in attempting to dispel the pervasive notion that he was a(n) (i) _____, only (ii) _____ such a view: seemingly every one of Oppenheimer's quirks is related with gleeful fondness.

(i)	(ii)
Ⓐ egomaniac	Ⓓ overturns
Ⓑ eccentric	Ⓔ perpetuates
Ⓒ reactionary	Ⓕ invalidates

Test Question 5

According to Lackmuller's latest screed, published under the title *Why We Can't Win at Their Game*, special interest groups not nominally tied to ecological concerns have become so (i) _____ the process of environmental policymaking that those groups who actually aim to ensure that corporate profit does not trump environmental health have been effectively (ii) _____. Lackmuller's contention, however, is (iii) _____ in that it fails to account for the signal achievements environmental groups have effected over the last twenty years—often to the chagrin of big business.

(i)	(ii)	(iii)
Ⓐ marginalized in	Ⓓ vindicated	Ⓖ somewhat tentative
Ⓑ indebted to	Ⓔ squelched	Ⓗ rarely myopic
Ⓒ influential in	Ⓕ lionized	Ⓘ highly misleading

Test Question 6

The question as to what constitutes art is hardly a (i) _____ one. Today, artists exist whose main goal seems only to subvert work that no longer warrants the trite tag "cutting-edge." Once the proverbial envelope is pushed even further, the public inevitably scratches its collective head—or furrows the collective brow—thinking that this time the "artists" have (ii) _____. That very same admixture of contempt and confusion, however, was not unknown in Michelangelo's day; only what was considered blasphemous, art-wise, in the sixteenth century, would today be considered (iii) _____.

(i)	(ii)	(iii)
Ⓐ perennial	Ⓓ served their purpose	Ⓖ hackneyed
Ⓑ contemporary	Ⓔ gone too far	Ⓗ reverent
Ⓒ controversial	Ⓕ failed to provoke	Ⓘ tame

Questions 7 to 10 are based on the following reading passage. For each of these questions, select <u>one</u> answer choice unless instructed otherwise.

PASSAGE

The question of when the first people populated the American subcontinents is hotly debated. Until recently, the Clovis people, based on evidence found in New Mexico, were thought to have been the first to have arrived, some thirteen thousand years ago. Yet evidence gathered from other sites suggests the Americas had been settled at least one thousand years prior to the Clovis people's arrival. The "Clovis-first" idea, nevertheless, was treated as gospel, backed by supporters who, at least initially, outright discounted any claims that suggested precedence by non-Clovis people. While such a stance smacked of fanaticism, proponents did have a solid claim: if the Clovis crossed the Bering Strait thirteen thousand years ago, only after it had become ice-free, how would others have been able to make a similar trip but over ice?

A recent school of thought, backed by Weber, provides the following answer: pre-Clovis people reached the Americas by relying on a sophisticated maritime culture, which allowed them to take advantage of refugia, or small areas in which aquatic life flourished. Thus, they were able to make the long journey by hugging the coast as far south as what is today British Columbia. Additionally, they were believed to have fashioned a primitive form of crampon so that they would be able to dock in these refugia and avail themselves of the microfauna. Still, such a theory raises the question as to how such a culture developed.

The Solutrean theory has been influential in answering this question, a fact that may seem paradoxical—and startling—to those familiar with its line of reasoning: the Clovis people were actually Solutreans, an ancient seafaring culture along the Iberian peninsula, who had—astoundingly, given the time period—crossed into the Americas via the Atlantic Ocean. Could a similar Siberian culture, if not the pre-Clovis people themselves, not have displayed equal nautical sophistication?

Even if one subscribes to this line of reasoning, the "Clovis-first" school still has an objection: proponents of a pre-Clovis people rely solely on the Monte Verde site in Chile, a site so far south that its location raises the question: what of the six thousand miles of coastline between the ice corridor and Monte Verde? Besides remains found in a network of caves in Oregon, there has been scant evidence of a pre-Clovis people. Nevertheless, Meade and Pizinsky claim that a propitious geologic accident could account for this discrepancy: Monte Verde was located near a peat bog that essentially fossilized the village. Archaeologists uncovered two of the wooden stakes, which, at one time, were used in twelve huts. Furthermore, plant species associated with areas one hundred and fifty miles away were found, suggesting a trade network. These findings indicate that the Clovis may not have been the first to populate the Americas, yet more excavation, both in Monte Verde and along the coast, must be conducted in order to determine the extent of pre-Clovis settlements in the Americas.

Test Question 7

In the context in which it appears, the phrase "avail themselves of" most nearly means

(A) locate
(B) exploit
(C) regard
(D) fathom
(E) distribute

Test Question 8

It can be inferred from the passage that the reason the author finds the Solutrean hypothesis both startling and paradoxical is that

(A) ancient cultures were most likely unable to develop such a sophisticated form of maritime transport that they were able to cross the Atlantic
(B) it supports the Clovis school of thought and posits the existence of a capacity not commonly associated with ancient people
(C) the Clovis people had crossed from Siberia navigating across a difficult ice corridor, whereas the pre-Clovis people had sailed, with far less difficulty, across the Atlantic Ocean
(D) it suggests that the pre-Clovis people had a way to circumvent the ice corridor, yet were unlikely to have traveled as far south as modern day Chile
(E) it runs counter to one of the chief tenets of the "Clovis-first" school of thought

Test Question 9

It can be most reasonably inferred from the passage that, in regard to the manner in which the Monte Verde village was preserved,

(A) unless evidence of other pre-Clovis people was fossilized the same way it was in Monte Verde, archaeologists will be unable to determine the extent of the settlement of pre-Clovis people
(B) major discoveries can sometimes result from random processes in the environment
(C) plant species can offer valuable clues into the origin of other pre-Clovis settlements
(D) sites dated from slightly after the period of the Clovis people did not offer archaeologists such a trove of information
(E) archaeologists are unlikely to find any other significant evidence of pre-Clovis people unless they venture as much as one hundred and fifty miles from the site

Test Question 10

If it is true that a trade network between pre-Clovis people had been established, then which of the following could be expected to be found at settlements near Monte Verde? Select <u>all</u> that apply.

[A] other villages that have been preserved in a peat bog
[B] plants species similar to those uncovered at Monte Verde
[C] the same number of wooden stakes for supporting dwellings

Questions 11 and 12 are based on the following reading passage. For each of these questions, select <u>one</u> answer choice unless instructed otherwise.

PASSAGE

The two realms of Vladimir Nabokov's genius, that of a scientist and that as an author, have been treated as discrete manifestations of a prodigious and probing mind, until now. In her recent biography on Nabokov, Temoshotka makes the bold assertion that these two apparently disparate realms of Nabokov's polymorphous genius were not so unrelated after all. While Temoshotka cannot be faulted for the boldness of her thesis—that Nabokov's hobby as a lepidopterist (a butterfly collector) and his experience as a novelist informed each other—she fails to make a convincing case. Surely, with enough ingenuity, one can find parallels, as Temoshotka does, between the creative products of Nabokov the naturalist and Nabokov the writer: the intricate butterfly wings that he pored over in his laboratory and the intricate prose that he crafted with sedulous care. But to say the prose of *Lolita* and *Speak, Memory* would not have coalesced into their current incarnations had Nabokov's hobby been, say, lawn tennis is simply reaching too far.

Test Question 11

The primary purpose of the passage is to

(A) analyze several conflicting interpretations of an author's work
(B) champion a specific interpretation of a writer's work
(C) challenge a common understanding of a well-known writer
(D) applaud an undertaking but question the validity of its claims
(E) support a claim regarding an author's creative process but doubt the extent of that claim

Test Question 12

According to the author of the passage, Temoshotka, in her estimation of Nabokov, does which of the following? Select <u>all</u> that apply.

[A] Reconcile two antagonistic tendencies that coexisted in the author
[B] Make a claim without providing any evidence to this claim
[C] Present a thesis that while at points is valid is also overly ambitious

For questions 13 to 16, select exactly <u>two</u> words that best complete the sentence and produce sentences that are <u>alike in meaning</u>.

Test Question 13

As the job fair neared an end, the recent college graduate became ever more
_____, desperately trying to befriend prospective employers he had earlier not even deigned to give so much as a cursory glance.

- [A] ingratiating
- [B] fawning
- [C] withdrawn
- [D] volatile
- [E] vociferous
- [F] direct

Test Question 14

Montreaux, initially _____ as the forerunner to the evolving twentieth-century cinematic idiom, experienced a decline that was as precipitous as his rise was meteoric.

- [A] identified
- [B] snubbed
- [C] hailed
- [D] unseated
- [E] lauded
- [F] rejected

Test Question 15

Yet another creation in line with the _____ melodramas the director is so well known for, the latest effort is likely to have a similar effect: a tiny subset of the population will extol the deliberate pacing, while the majority will dismiss the film as soporific drivel.

- [A] plodding
- [B] convoluted
- [C] exacting
- [D] sadistic
- [E] tedious
- [F] shocking

Test Question 16

Through mere _____, Hirasaki, in her delightful vignettes of a childhood spent living in two divergent cultures, is able to communicate far more cogently about alienation and belonging than those of her contemporaries who believe verbosity is tantamount to profundity.

A suggestion

B artfulness

C intimation

D illumination

E contrivance

F abbreviation

For questions 17 to 20, select one answer choice unless instructed otherwise. Questions 17 to 19 are based on the following reading passage.

PASSAGE

The proliferation of social media tools allowing for communication within corporations has recently been the subject of two studies. Meyers and Tassleman find that such tools tend to exert a positive effect but that such effect tends to diminish the larger the organization is. The two speculate that one of the reasons is that the kind of communication in social media presumes a level of comfort that is not consistent with that typically found in larger companies. Consequently, many employees are reluctant to use social media tools because they feel constrained by a workplace culture that is not consistent with the social values these tools promote. Such a result undermines the very relaxed spirit that upper-level management hopes to foster by using such tools.

Gershin focuses on the extent to which social media tools have displaced other forms of office communication, notably email and in-person interactions. Additionally, he uses data collected from surveys, from both middle management and upper management, to assess the effect, if any, that such displacement has had. His findings are twofold: social media is in many cases deemed extraneous since it adds a layer of redundancy to communication. In other words, employees have adequately communicated something via traditional channels but simply echo such communication on social network channels. However, Gershin found that social media tools fostered company culture because they provided employees a means of planning social events, something they might not have done using traditional forms of communication.

Test Question 17

Which of the following, if true, best calls into question the validity of Gershin's findings regarding the effect of social media tools in the workplace?

(A) Some of those who plan social events use only traditional forms of communication to do so.

(B) Of those surveyed, more mentioned the negative effects of social media in the workplace than the positive effects.

(C) Redundancy can serve as a way of reinforcing and emphasizing communication pertaining to social events.

(D) The thoughts of middle and upper-level managers do not accurately reflect the thoughts of those most likely to use social media in the workplace.

(E) Redundant communication is found both in traditional forms of office communication and on social media.

Test Question 18

According to Meyers and Tassleman, social media tools tend to be less effective the larger the company because

(A) communication is often lost between different levels of an organization

(B) the values of larger companies tend not to be closely aligned with those of social media

(C) the cultural values of upper management and middle management are not consistent with those of other employees

(D) there is a greater amount of redundancy as the number of employees using office-based social media increases

(E) small companies are better able to communicate the limitations that using social media in the workplace presents

Test Question 19

The primary purpose of the passage is to

(A) discuss how the implications of two schools of thought are likely to lead to divergent conclusions

(B) discuss two findings regarding an issue

(C) promote the benefits of a practice common in the workplace

(D) assess the validity of two findings

(E) criticize the methodology used in two different studies

Test Question 20

The rates of health complications of patients on intravenous (IV) therapy at a particular hospital were higher than usual. Government inspectors found that the typical IV solutions used in this hospital had somewhat high concentrations of sodium and potassium, which were raising patients' blood pressure and taxing their kidneys. The government inspectors mandated lowering the sodium and potassium in these IV preparations, and threatened the hospital with a possible government fine. In compliance, the hospital lowered the sodium and potassium levels in the IV solutions to the correct levels. Nevertheless, patients on IV therapy at that hospital continued to have a high rate of health complications.

Which of the following, if true, most helps to explain why acting on the government inspectors' recommendations failed to achieve the hospital's goal?

(A) The change in IV solution procedure meant a number of related legal documents had to be renegotiated and rewritten, at great cost.

(B) When sodium and potassium levels in the blood fall below their baseline level, it can damage cells throughout the body by reverse osmosis.

(C) It is typical for a patient's appetite to increase to healthy levels once they have completed a course of IV therapy.

(D) A high proportion of patients at this hospital are older, and older patients are more vulnerable to infections that can accompany IVs.

(E) Because the findings were published in the news, some patients have chosen to use another hospital in the region.

You have completed the test!

Answer Key

GRE Quantitative Section 1	GRE Verbal Section 1	GRE Quantitative Section 2	GRE Verbal Section 2
1. D	1. E	1. C	1. D
2. D	2. E	2. D	2. B
3. B	3. C F	3. D	3. B E
4. D	4. C F	4. A	4. B E
5. A	5. A D G	5. C	5. C E I
6. C	6. B D G	6. C	6. B E I
7. D	7. B	7. C	7. B
8. C	8. C	8. B	8. B
9. C G	9. The first sentence of the second paragraph	9. B	9. B
10. D	10. B	10. $\frac{2}{7}$	10. B only
11. 1,200	11. C only	11. E	11. D
12. E	12. B	12. B C	12. C only
13. A	13. E F	13. C	13. A B
14. C	14. D F	14. D	14. C E
15. B	15. B C	15. D	15. A E
16. E	16. A B	16. B D	16. A C
17. 0.25	17. B	17. B	17. D
18. B	18. D	18. 24	18. B
19. C E	19. A C	19. E	19. B
20. B	20. E	20. A C	20. D

GRE Practice Test Explanations

GRE Analytical Writing Assessment

At the beginning of this mock test, we had you write the two GRE AWA essays to get the feel of the full GRE experience. With all the subsequent sections, we provide objective answers and explanations. Obviously, there's no way to do this with essays.

This leaves the question: now that you have these two essays, what are you going to do with them? Here are a few suggestions.

If you have a friend, family member, or a study buddy who is a good writer, have them go to the GRE AWA score level descriptions at www.ets.org/gre/revised_general /scores and then grade your essay against the standards of the official rubric as best they can. You can also find the rubric in *The Official Guide to the GRE*. If you're on good terms with an English teacher or professor, you might be able to persuade that person to critique your essay. If you're really ambitious, you could hire a writing tutor, make the official rubric available to your tutor, and have your tutor grade your essay. That tutor probably would be in a good position to give you recommendations about how to strengthen your writing.

Failing all this, simply set the essays aside for a while, maybe a week, and then grade them yourself against the official rubric. It's very hard to be objective about your own writing right after you have written something, but if you put it aside long enough to forget about it, then mistakes and ambiguities become clearer. It's not important to get a precise score for the GRE AWA. Just getting a rough idea of how you did is enough. It's more important to understand where you fell short, so you can produce a tighter and more persuasive essay on test day!

GRE Quantitative Section 1 Answers and Explanations

Question 1

Difficulty: **Easy** · Percent Correct: **70%** · Concept(s): **Number Sense** · Type: **Quantitative Comparison**

Answer: **D**

When you square a fraction smaller than one, it gets smaller. When you square any number bigger than one, it gets bigger. Lastly, if p and q are equivalent (for example, $p = 5$, $q = 5$), that means column A will be equal to 1 $\left(\frac{5}{5} = 1\right)$, as will column B $\left(\left(\frac{5}{5}\right)^2 = 1^2 = 1\right)$. Depending on choices, the square could be greater than, less than, or equal to the original, so the answer cannot be determined.

Question 2

Difficulty: **Medium** · Percent Correct: **52%** · Concept(s): **Geometry** · Type: **Quantitative Comparison**

Answer: **D**

This question is a great test of what you *can* assume and what you *can't* assume on a GRE geometry diagram, especially on the quantitative comparison questions.

You *can* assume the following: that the two angles marked as 30° actually are 30°; and that points A and B and C are collinear, i.e., that there's no hidden "bend" at point B.

You *can't* assume that something that appears perpendicular is exactly perpendicular or that lines that appear as horizontal or vertical actually are horizontal or vertical.

On a side note, many students get confused about the word *straight*. The word *straight* means "collinear," and you can assume lines that look straight actually are straight. Unfortunately, many people make the mistake of using the word *straight* as a synonym for "horizontal." On the GRE, you can assume a line is straight; you can't assume a line is horizontal.

Where does all this leave us with this diagram? Well, it may be that BD is perfectly vertical and that AC is perfectly horizontal, and therefore, the triangle ADC is a perfect isosceles triangle with perfect symmetry. That *could* be true, and of course you know by now that the primary sin on any GRE geometry question is blindly believing the diagram; if you do this, you're guaranteed to get the question incorrect.

It could also be true that AC is not the least bit horizontal, and therefore it could be slanted in either direction—this way:

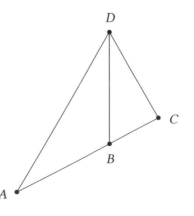

... or this way:

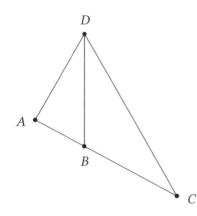

Clearly, all of these are consistent with the little you're able to assume from a GRE diagram. In some cases, $AB > BC$, and in others $AB < BC$, and in still others, $AB = BC$. There isn't a mathematical way to decide.

**Aren't sides opposite of equal angles equal? Both those sides are opposite 30°
angles.** That property refers to two angles in the *same* triangle. That would be an isosceles triangle, and this statement is 100 percent true for two angles and two sides in an isosceles. But that does *not* mean that equal angles in two different triangles will be opposite equal sides. The two 30° angles here are in different triangles: one on the left, one on the right.

Together, they're contained in one bigger triangle, but that gives us just one angle of 60° (from the two smaller angles added together) and no other angle measurements.

Question 3

Difficulty: **Medium** · Percent Correct: **62%** · Concept(s): **Percents / Fractions / Ratios** · Type: **Quantitative Comp.**

Answer: **B**

This question, like many on the GRE, is designed to exploit a typical student misunderstanding. This can lead to one of the most predictable mistakes on the entire GRE. So many students mistakenly think if you increase by 20%, then decrease by 20%, you'll be back at the original value.

In general, an increase of P%, followed by a decrease of that same P%, does *not* lead back to the original value.

It's easiest to start with Charles (though you can start with Bert or Ashley, if that seems to make more sense to you). Suppose Charles's score is 1,000, just to pick a round number. Bert is 20% less than this. Well, 20% of 1,000 is 200, and 200 less than 1000 is 800. That's Bert's score. Now, Ashley's score was 20% higher than 800. Well 10% of 800 is 80, so 20% is twice that, 160. Of course, 160 higher than 800 is 960. That's Ashley's score. Charles scored 1,000, and Ashley scored 960, so Charles's score is higher. Column B is higher.

Why start with Charles? Why not Ashley? Or Bert? Charles is the logical starting place simply because the math is easier. You *could* solve it starting with Ashley or Bert, but you would have to do much more complicated math.

Think of it this way. Take these two terms: K and M. Now, let's say K is $P\%$ of M. The term after the word "of" is the 100% term, the whole, the standard to which the other, the part, is being compared. [PART] is $P\%$ of [WHOLE]: the "whole" is what comes after the word "of." In this example, M is the standard, the whole, and K is the part being compared to M. Therefore, it makes much more sense to start with M, and make that equal to 100. In this problem, you compare Ashley (A) to the whole of Bert (B), and then Bert to the whole of Charles (C). So C is the ultimate whole, the anchor, to which all else is compared. That's why it makes the most sense by far to start with C and let it equal 100 or 1,000.

Question 4

Difficulty: **Hard** · Percent Correct: **45%** · Concept(s): **Algebra** · Type: **Quantitative Comparison**

Answer: **D**

There are a couple tricky things about this problem. The first is one of the GRE's favorite traps: the word "number." Of course, a positive number could be a whole number, such as 7 or 6,000, or a fraction, such as $\frac{1}{13}$, or a decimal such as π, or a square root—all of which are positive. Don't fall for the trap that "number" must be a whole number, a positive integer—that kind of thinking is severely penalized on the GRE.

Next, you cannot equate the numerators and denominators separately. You should never consider "across the numerators" and "across the denominators" as two separate equations. That's another gigantic trap. You have to consider the fraction as a whole. You have no guarantee that the fraction on the left is written in simplest form. When a fraction equals $\frac{2}{3}$, the numerator and denominator could be both very big or both very small. For example:

$$\frac{2}{3} = \frac{2000}{3000} = \frac{0.0002}{0.0003}$$

The algebraic fraction given in the prompt has a numerator of $(p - q)$ and a denominator of $(p + q)$. Notice that column A is the denominator. Well, as you see above, the denominator $(p + q)$ could equal 3,000, or it could equal 0.0003, so for different choices, it could be much greater than 5 or much less than 5.

Question 5

Difficulty: **Medium** · Percent Correct: **59%** · Concept(s): **Number Sense** · Type: **Quantitative Comparison**

Answer: **A**

$$K = 5 + 10 + 15 + 20 + 25 + \ldots + 490 + 495 + 500$$

The greatest common factor of every term in the series is 5, so factor this out.

$$K = 5(1 + 2 + 3 + 4 + 5 + \ldots + 98 + 99 + 100)$$

Now, what's in parentheses is a series of consecutive integers from 1 to n, so you can use:

$$\text{sum} = \frac{n(n + 1)}{2}$$

$$K = 5\left(\frac{100(101)}{2}\right) = 5(50 \times 101) = 5(5050)$$

You don't have to even calculate this last product. You know 25,000 = 5 × 5,000, so five times anything bigger than 5,000 has to be bigger than 25,000.

Alternate method of solution: Think about this sum. If you pair the members from the two ends, you get

5 + 500 = 505
10 + 495 = 505
15 + 490 = 505
20 + 485 = 505
25 + 480 = 505
etc.

Each pair has the same sum. That will *always* be true for an evenly spaced list! There are 100 numbers on the list, so that's fifty pairs, each with a sum of 505.

$$K = 50 \times 505 > 50 \times 500 = 25,000$$

Is it possible to start with $n = 500$ and then divide by 5? Why was the 5 factored out first? In this problem, you aren't calculating the sum of ALL numbers from 1 to 500. If you did that—500(500+1)/2 = 125,250, then divide by 5—that's the sum of *every* positive integer from 1 to 500, divided by five. This would be equivalent to the sum of the set of all the integers from 1 to 500, each divided by five, which would be this set: {0.2, 0.4, 0.6, 0.8, 1.0, 1.2, 1.4, ... , 99.0, 99.2, 99.4, 99.6, 99.8, 100.0}. Notice that there are 500 numbers in that set!

Instead, you want the sum of the multiples of 5 between 1 and 500. Since it's a little difficult to use the formula $\frac{n(n+1)}{2}$ with multiples of five {5, 10, 15, 20, ...}, you factor out a 5 so that you can use the set {1, 2, 3, 4, ...}, which fits much more nicely with the formula. Then, after you calculate this sum, you can multiply by 5 to get our total sum.

Question 6

Difficulty: **Medium** · Percent Correct: **59%** · Concept(s): **Probability / Combinatorics** · Type: **Quant. Comparison**

Main course: Chicken, Beef, Tofu

Side dish: Rice, Salad, Soup, Pasta

Dessert: Pie, Cake

A meal at a certain restaurant consists of 1 main course, 2 different side dishes, and 1 dessert.

Column A	Column B
Number of different meals possible	36
$nCr = \dfrac{n!}{r!(n-r)!}$ $\underset{\text{Main}}{3} \times \underset{\text{Side}}{6} \times \underset{\text{Dessert}}{2} = \mathbf{36}$ ⇧ $_4C_2$	**36**

Why did the counting principle (4 × 3) not work for the side dishes? It would have if the question had asked the side dishes to be in a particular order, e.g. if you were designating a clear "first side dish" and a "second side dish." In this case, though, since each meal has two side dishes, and we don't care which order those two sides are chosen in, you have to use a combination. You have to choose two out of four possibilities, which isn't the same as (4 × 3).

Why are the different stages multiplied and not added (3 + 6 + 2 = 11)? They're multiplied because you're using the fundamental counting principle.

Why not use a permutation here? Doesn't order matter in selecting the main course and dessert? Although order matters in a sense—you can't choose a side dish in the "main course" slot, for instance—we typically think of permutations when we are pulling items from a single pool and are concerned with the order they end up in. These are three separate pools (main, side, and dessert), so we use the fundamental counting principle instead. It may look deceivingly like a permutation problem because you happen to be multiplying integers together, but you're simply using the fundamental counting principle.

If you think about it, you're using combinations for each dish—the main dish, the two sides, and the dessert. The only difference between the sides and the rest of the dishes is that you're choosing two sides instead of one.

Look at it this way:

C = Choice

MAIN DISH: 3C1: You get one option out of three main dish choices. This simplifies out to 3.

SIDE DISHES: 4C2: You get two options out of four side dish choices. This simplifies out to 6.

DESSERT: 2C1: You get one option out of two choices. This simplifies out to 2.

Then, using the fundamental counting principle, you would multiply them all together to get all possible combinations of meals.

Remember, with combinations, order doesn't matter.

Question 7

Difficulty: **Hard** · Percent Correct: **21%** · Concept(s): **Percents / Ratios / Fractions** · Type: **Quantitative Comparison**

Answer: **D**

Column A	Column B
22 percent of x	$\frac{2}{9}$ of x
22% of x	22.$\overline{2}$% of x
If $x = 0$, then 22% of $x = 0$, which is equal to column B.	If $x = 0$, then 22.$\overline{2}$% of $x = 0$, which is equal to column A.
If $x = 1000$, then 22% of $x = 220$, which is less than column B.	If $x = 1000$, then 22.$\overline{2}$% of $x = 222.\overline{2}$, which is greater than column A.

$\frac{1}{9} = 11.\overline{1}\% \Rightarrow \frac{2}{9} = 22.\overline{2}\%$

Question 8

Difficulty: **Medium** · Percent Correct: **60%** · Concept(s): **Geometry** · Type: **Multiple Choice**

Answer: **C**

You're told the circle has an area of $9 \times \pi$. From Archimedes' famous formula ($A = \pi r^2$), you know that the radius of the circle must equal $r = 3$. This means $AO = OD = 3$, which means $AD = 6$. Now, you have the length of the side of triangle ABD.

ABD is the kind of triangle you get when you bisect an equilateral. The angle B is still 60°, the angle at D is a right angle, and the angle at A has been bisected, so that angle $DAB = 30°$. This is a 30-60-90 triangle, which has special properties.

Suppose you don't remember all those properties. Look at side DB. It's exactly half the side of the equilateral triangle. If you call $DB = x$, then a full side, like BC or AB, must equal $2x$. Given that $AD = 6$, $BD = x$, and $AB = 2x$, you can use the Pythagorean theorem in right triangle ABD.

$$AD^2 + BD^2 = AB^2$$
$$6^2 + x^2 = (2x)^2$$
$$36 + x^2 = 4x^2$$
$$36 = 3x^2$$
$$12 = x^2$$

$$BD = x = \sqrt{12} = \sqrt{4 \times 3} = \sqrt{4} \times \sqrt{3} = 2\sqrt{3}$$

This means that a full side of the equilateral is twice this:

$$AB = BC = 4\sqrt{3}$$

Incidentally, if you remembered your 30-60-90 triangle properties, you could have found:

$$\frac{AB}{BD} = \frac{2}{\sqrt{3}} \quad \Rightarrow \quad \frac{AB}{6} = \frac{2}{\sqrt{3}}$$

$$AB = \frac{12}{\sqrt{3}} = \frac{12}{\sqrt{3}} \times \frac{\sqrt{3}}{\sqrt{3}} = \frac{12\sqrt{3}}{3} = 4\sqrt{3}$$

Now you have a height, $BD = 6$, and a base,

$$AB = BC = 4\sqrt{3}.$$

So now you can find the area.

$$Area = \tfrac{1}{2}bh = \left(\tfrac{1}{2}\right)(6)(4\sqrt{3}) = 12\sqrt{3}$$

That's the area of the equilateral triangle ABC.

Can the problem be solved to $\frac{36}{\sqrt{3}}$? Is this wrong? That answer is correct—just not in its final form. Ultimately, never leave a root in a denominator.

Why isn't $\frac{18}{\sqrt{3}}$ an answer? You're so close to the right answer. You found the area for half of the triangle. Multiply $\frac{18}{\sqrt{3}}$ by 2 to find the total area of the triangle.

$$\left(\frac{18}{\sqrt{3}}\right) \times 2 =$$

$$\frac{36}{\sqrt{3}} =$$

$$\frac{36}{\sqrt{3}} \times \left(\frac{\sqrt{3}}{\sqrt{3}}\right) =$$

$$\frac{(36 \times \sqrt{3})}{(\sqrt{3} \times \sqrt{3})} =$$

$$\frac{(36 \times \sqrt{3})}{3} = 12\sqrt{3}$$

Question 9

Difficulty: **Easy** · Percent Correct: **61%** · Concept(s): **Algebra** · Type: **Multiple Answer**

What are the x-intercepts of the parabola defined by the equation $y = 2x^2 - 8x - 90$?

Answers: **C** **G**

Indicate <u>all</u> x-intercepts.

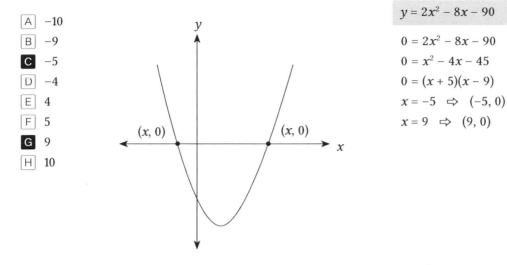

A −10
B −9
C −5
D −4
E 4
F 5
G 9
H 10

$y = 2x^2 - 8x - 90$

$0 = 2x^2 - 8x - 90$
$0 = x^2 - 4x - 45$
$0 = (x + 5)(x - 9)$
$x = -5 \Rightarrow (-5, 0)$
$x = 9 \Rightarrow (9, 0)$

Question 10

Difficulty: **Medium** · Percent Correct: **59%** · Concept(s): **Exponents** · Type: **Multiple Choice**

If $8^{n+1} + 8^n = 36$, then $n =$

Answer: **D**

(A) $\frac{1}{3}$

(B) $\frac{1}{2}$

(C) $\frac{3}{5}$

(D) $\frac{2}{3}$

(E) $\frac{4}{5}$

$8^{n+1} + 8^n = 36$
$8^n (8^1 + 1) = 36$
$8^n (9) = 36$
$8^n = 4$
$(2^3)^n = 2^2$
$2^{3n} = 2^2$
$3n = 2$
$n = \frac{2}{3}$

Question 11

Difficulty: **Easy** · Percent Correct: **63%** · Concept(s): **Percents / Ratios / Fractions** · Type: **Numeric Entry**

The ratio of slot screws to Phillips screws is 11:4, which means that, for some k, there are $11k$ slot screws and $4k$ Phillips screws.

Answer: **1,200**

$4k = 320$
$k = \frac{320}{4} = 80$

The total number of screws in the bucket is $11k + 4k = 15k$, and you know the value of k.
When you multiply, use the doubling and halving trick.

total number $= 15 \times 80 = 30 \times 40 = \textbf{1,200}$

Question 12

Difficulty: **Medium** · Percent Correct: **59%** · Concept(s): **Algebra, Exponents** · Type: **Multiple Choice**

Answer: **E**

If $2^k = 3$, then $2^{3k+2} =$

(A) 29

(B) 54

(C) 81

(D) 83

E 108

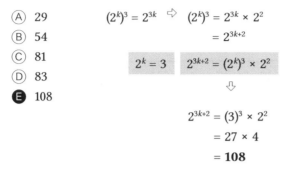

$(2^k)^3 = 2^{3k}$ ⇨ $(2^k)^3 = 2^{3k} \times 2^2$

$\qquad\qquad\qquad = 2^{3k+2}$

$2^k = 3$ $\qquad$ $2^{3k+2} = (2^k)^3 \times 2^2$

⇩

$2^{3k+2} = (3)^3 \times 2^2$

$\qquad\quad = 27 \times 4$

$\qquad\quad = \mathbf{108}$

Question 13

Difficulty: **Medium** · Percent Correct: **63%** · Concept(s): **Data Interpretation** · Type: **Multiple Choice**

Answer: **A**

In 1955, the ratio of the number of televisions to the number of people was approximately

A 1 to 13

(B) 1 to 23

(C) 1 to 26

(D) 1 to 50

(E) 1 to 90

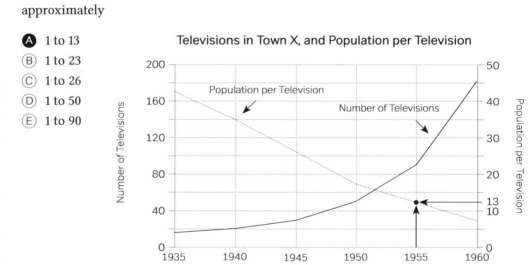

Televisions in Town X, and Population per Television

people to televisions ≈ 13 to 1

⇨ televisions to people ≈ **1 to 13**

Question 14

Difficulty: Easy · Percent Correct: 65% · Concept(s): Data Interpretation · Type: Multiple Choice

From 1940 to 1955, the percent increase in the number of televisions was closest to

Answer: **C**

(A) 30

(B) 130

(C) 350

(D) 450

(E) 650

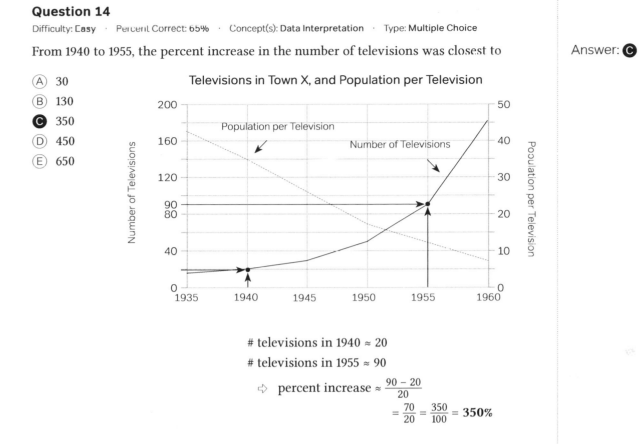

Televisions in Town X, and Population per Television

televisions in 1940 ≈ 20

televisions in 1955 ≈ 90

⇨ percent increase ≈ $\dfrac{90 - 20}{20}$

$= \dfrac{70}{20} = \dfrac{350}{100} = \mathbf{350\%}$

Question 15

Difficulty: Hard · Percent Correct: 48% · Concept(s): Data Interpretation · Type: Multiple Choice

What was the approximate population of Town X in 1945?

Answer: **B**

(A) 150

(B) 750

(C) 1500

(D) 3000

(E) 6000

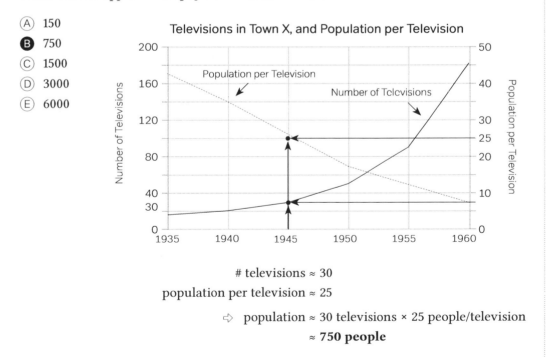

Televisions in Town X, and Population per Television

televisions ≈ 30

population per television ≈ 25

⇨ population ≈ 30 televisions × 25 people/television

≈ **750 people**

Question 16

Difficulty: **Easy** · Percent Correct: **92%** · Concept(s): **Algebra** · Type: **Multiple Choice**

Answer: **E**

The average (arithmetic mean) of two numbers is $4x$. If one of the numbers is y, then the value of the other number is

(A) $x - 4y$

(B) $4x + 4y$

(C) $8x - 4y$

(D) $4y - 8x$

E $8x - y$

> If m is the mean of n numbers, then the sum of the numbers is nm

⇨ sum of two numbers $= 2(4x)$

$$= 8x$$

$$(1\text{st }\#) + (2\text{nd }\#) = 8x$$

$$(y) + (2\text{nd }\#) = 8x$$

$$2\text{nd }\# = 8x - y$$

Question 17

Difficulty: **Hard** · Percent Correct: **35%** · Concept(s): **Algebra** · Type: **Numeric Entry**

Answer: **0.25**

The figure shows the graph of the equation $y = k - x^2$, where k is a constant. If the area of triangle ABC is $\frac{1}{8}$, what is the value of k?

Give your answer to the <u>nearest 0.01</u>

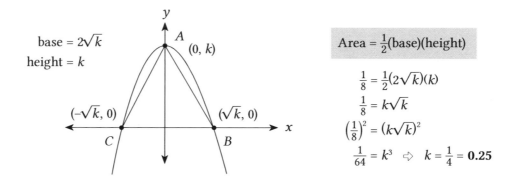

base $= 2\sqrt{k}$

height $= k$

> Area $= \frac{1}{2}(\text{base})(\text{height})$

$$\frac{1}{8} = \frac{1}{2}(2\sqrt{k})(k)$$

$$\frac{1}{8} = k\sqrt{k}$$

$$\left(\frac{1}{8}\right)^2 = (k\sqrt{k})^2$$

$$\frac{1}{64} = k^3 \quad ⇨ \quad k = \frac{1}{4} = \mathbf{0.25}$$

For the purposes of the GRE, if you're rounding to the nearest digit or decimal, you round 0 to 4 down and 5 to 9 up, as simply as that.

Question 18

Difficulty: **Hard** · Percent Correct: **50%** · Concept(s): **Algebra, Exponents** · Type: **Multiple Choice**

Answer: **B**

If a and b are integers and $\left(\sqrt[3]{a} \times \sqrt{b}\right)^6 = 500$, then $a + b$ could equal

(A) 2

B 3

(C) 4

(D) 5

(E) 6

$$\left(\sqrt[3]{a} \times \sqrt{b}\right)^6 = 500$$

$$\left(a^{\frac{1}{3}} \times b^{\frac{1}{2}}\right)^6 = 500 \qquad \boxed{\sqrt[n]{x} = x^{\frac{1}{n}}}$$

$$a^2 \times b^3 = 500 \qquad \boxed{(x^a y^b)^c = x^{ac} y^{bc}}$$

$$a^2 \times b^3 = 2 \times 2 \times 5 \times 5 \times 5$$

$$a^2 \times b^3 = 2^2 \times 5^3$$

$$⇨ \quad b = 5 \quad ⇨ \quad a + b = 5 + 2 = 7$$

$$a = \pm 2 \qquad a + b = 5 + (-2) = \mathbf{3}$$

Question 19

Difficulty: Hard · Percent Correct: 40% · Concept(s): Probability / Combinatorics · Type: Multiple Answer

From a group of 8 people, it is possible to create exactly 56 different k-person committees. Which of the following could be the value of k?

Answers: C E

Indicate all such values.

[A] 1
[B] 2
[C] 3
[D] 4
[E] 5
[F] 6
[G] 7

$_nC_r = {_n}C_{n-r}$

$_8C_3 = {_8}C_5$

$_8C_k = 56$

$_nC_r = \dfrac{\text{first } r \text{ values of } n!}{r!}$

$_8C_1 = \dfrac{8}{1} = 8 \quad \Rightarrow \quad {_8}C_7 = 8$

$_8C_2 = \dfrac{8 \times 7}{2 \times 1} = 28 \quad \Rightarrow \quad {_8}C_6 = 28$

$_8C_3 = \dfrac{8 \times 7 \times 6}{3 \times 2 \times 1} = 56 \quad \Rightarrow \quad {_8}C_5 = 56$

$_8C_4 = \dfrac{8 \times 7 \times 6 \times 5}{4 \times 3 \times 2 \times 1} = 70$

Question 20

Difficulty: Medium · Percent Correct: 57% · Concept(s): Geometry, Coordinate Geometry · Type: Multiple Choice

In the xy-coordinate system, a circle with radius $\sqrt{30}$ and center $(2, 1)$ intersects the x-axis at $(k, 0)$. One possible value of k is

Answer: B

(A) $2 + \sqrt{26}$
(B) $2 + \sqrt{26}$
(C) $2 + \sqrt{31}$
(D) $2 + \sqrt{34}$
(E) $2 + \sqrt{35}$

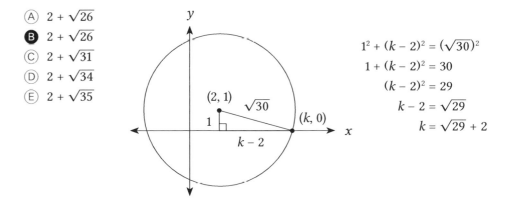

$1^2 + (k - 2)^2 = (\sqrt{30})^2$

$1 + (k - 2)^2 = 30$

$(k - 2)^2 = 29$

$k - 2 = \sqrt{29}$

$k = \sqrt{29} + 2$

Can the problem be solved by directly computing the value of k and plugging the coordinates into the distance formula? That's actually a great way to solve this problem, though it may not be as evident to those who haven't memorized the distance formula. Here is the whole thing worked out just in case you ran into trouble:

$$\sqrt{(30)} = \sqrt{\left[(0 - 1)^2 + (k - 2)^2\right]}$$
$$30 = (0 - 1)^2 + (k - 2)^2$$
$$30 = 1 + (k - 2)^2$$
$$29 = (k - 2)^2$$
$$\sqrt{(29)} = k - 2$$
$$2 + \sqrt{(29)} = k$$

GRE Verbal Section 1 Answers and Explanations

Question 1

Difficulty: **Medium** · Percent Correct: **55%** · Type: Single-Blank Text Completion

Answer: **E**

The sentence is structured as follows: "Routine exposure" to something that is "seemingly" (or apparently) BLANK can actually be bad ("deleterious"). This indicates that the word in the blank should be the opposite of deleterious or bad. **(E)** *benign* works best.

(A) is wrong because nowhere does the sentence mention that the products are old.

(B) is wrong because *banal* means "commonplace." Make sure not to associate this with the word "routine," which modifies "exposure," not the products themselves.

(C) is wrong because *litigious* relates to lawsuits.

(D) is wrong because *virulent* means "harmful," which is the opposite of the answer you seek.

Question 2

Difficulty: **Medium** · Percent Correct: **54%** · Type: Single-Blank Text Completion

Answer: **E**

Notice the time period at the beginning of the sentence: early twentieth century. That was when the dystopian novels were written. Yet these works foretold, for the most part, how totalitarian governments today would act. **(E)** means "having predictive powers," which these novels definitely had.

(A) means "providing an overview."

(B) means "short-lived."

(C) means "thorough." The word is too general to modify power, since you're seeking a word that specifically shows how these books' predictions turned out to be correct in some cases.

(D) is the opposite of "political."

Question 3

Difficulty: **Medium** · Percent Correct: **56%** · Type: Double-Blank Text Completion

Answers: **C** **F**

A clash between the conservative and the unorthodox provides the best support for **(C)** *heresy*. Used figuratively, heresy means to go against the prevailing beliefs. As a result, any scientist who does so may be **(F)** *ostracized*, or excluded from conservative scientific circles.

Question 4

Difficulty: **Medium** · Percent Correct: **59%** · Type: Double -Blank Text Completion

Answers: **C** **F**

This is a subtle question, since the "shift" actually happens in the answer choice. The "no less incendiary" at the beginning of the sentence leads us to believe that "fracking" is going to be a major issue come election time. The second blank, however, is a much easier solution: people will be affected by problems that occur in their immediate environments; that is, they'll be **(F)** *umoved by* the "environmental problems." Thus fracking, which "takes place in remote parts," doesn't fall into this category. Therefore, fracking is **(C)** *curiously absent* from the national dialogue. The second part of the sentence gives us the reason.

Question 5

Difficulty: **Medium** · Percent Correct: 54% · Type: Triple-Blank Text Completion

Answers: **A D G**

The contrast is between the indigenous peoples—who know a lot about the jungle—and those who are not indigenous and therefore don't notice anything more than a "dense lattice." The non-indigenous are **(A)** *untutored*. The indigenous people can discern an abundance, or a **(D)** *cornucopia* of cures.

Ethnobotanists hope to learn, or **(G)** *glean*, the knowledge from the indigenous peoples.

Question 6

Difficulty: **Hard** · Percent Correct: 36% · Type: Triple-Blank Text Completion

Answers: **B D G**

First we want to look for clues in the paragraph. "Close scrutiny" implies that that the "contention" was misleading, or **(B)** *specious*. Instead of presenting a unified theory, Hopkin's fieldwork does the opposite: it's a **(D)** *mere hodgepodge* of observations. The "even" suggests an apposition, and thus the word in the third blank is more extreme. **(G)** *inimical to* works because it implies that the observations are at odds with one another.

Question 7

Difficulty: **Medium** · Percent Correct: 53% · Type: Reading Comprehension

Answer: **B**

The point of the passage is to mention that the study failed to take into account those who have adverse reactions to caffeine. As a result, the findings in the study are likely to change. This matches up best with **(B)**.

(A) is tempting, but the passage isn't completely discrediting the findings.

(C) is wrong, as nowhere does it say that researchers fabricated or made up data.

(D) is wrong since it contradicts the overall tone and direction of the passage. The second paragraph raises doubts about the connection between learning and coffee consumption. (D) doesn't include these doubts, and therefore needs to be eliminated.

(E) is incorrect because of the words "several oversights." The passage mentions only one oversight.

Question 8

Difficulty: **Hard** · Percent Correct: 31% · Type: Reading Comprehension

Answer: **C**

(C) is the best answer because the author assumes that those who didn't display sensitivities to caffeine all had improvements in memory. That is, the passage implies that only those who had adverse reactions to caffeine intake didn't exhibit the improvements noted in the study.

(A) is supported by the passage but doesn't answer the question.

(B) is also supported but doesn't answer the question.

(D) is incorrect because the author implies the opposite: that the positive effects will be more pronounced.

(E) isn't supported by the passage.

Difficulty: **Very Hard** · Percent Correct: **25%** · Type: **Reading Comprehension**

Answer:

The first sentence of the second paragraph

The first sentence of the second paragraph, "While daily coffee … glosses over an important fact," cites the author's opinion of the study. The word "important" is worth noting. Whether or not the study is missing "important" facts is subjective. You can say objectively that the study doesn't include some information, but whether that information is important is subjective.

The final sentence of the passage, in contrast, serves as a conclusion (which may or may not be correct) that includes no subjective detail, and therefore isn't exactly an "opinion." It's a tempting choice, because it's the author's main argument, but it's not stated subjectively; it's meant to be a fact. An opinion, unlike a conclusion, would include an assessment of something, as in the above, where the study is said to be missing "important" facts.

Here is another way to think about this: a conclusion is likely to come, as the word implies, at the end of an argument. Conclusions are based on reason and facts. After describing key facts, a conclusion might be stated, as is the case in this passage. An opinion, in contrast, is a personally and subjectively held "conclusion" that doesn't necessarily rely on facts and reason. In this passage, the final sentence is a summation—a conclusion—of the information given in the preceding sentences. The "While daily coffee …" sentence, on the other hand, is at the beginning of the paragraph, with the relevant facts about the "glossed over" pieces coming *after it*, which is a good indication that it's an *opinion* and not a *conclusion*.

Why isn't the second to last sentence ("Nevertheless, despite the …") correct? Isn't it a statement of an opinion? Let's look at the penultimate sentence:

> *Nevertheless, despite the fact that the study represents a random sampling—and thus any number of subjects can exhibit any number of reactions to caffeine—if enough subjects continue to display signs of improvements in learning, then this result would not be inconsistent with the study's findings.*

In this sentence the author is certainly giving her or his own thoughts. However, this sentence doesn't express an opinion toward "the results of the study," which is what the question is asking. Rather, the sentence focuses on a hypothetical: "if enough subjects continue to display." The sentence is talking about further research and results, and how those might affect the results of the original study. Thus, this sentence is discussing a topic beyond the original study more than expressing an opinion directly about the study.

Question 10

Difficulty: Medium · Percent Correct: 57% · Type: Reading Comprehension

The myth of Hemingway relates to how earlier biographies tried to "unmask the man …." The new biographies show Hemingway as "the hunter … the hunted." Therefore **(B)** is correct.

Answer: **B**

(A) is incorrect because while they explore a different side of Hemingway the man, they don't explore a different side of his work.

(C) is the opposite of what the passage implies about the latest biographies.

(D) is going a little too far in saying that Hemingway lacked virility or manliness.

(E) is an appealing answer choice. (E) can be generally inferred from the passage. But the question relates to why the author thinks the latest biographies are different, and (B) is therefore the best answer choice.

Question 11

Difficulty: Very Hard · Percent Correct: 23% · Type: Reading Comprehension

[A] is wrong because the first sentence clearly states the opposite: for someone of Hemingway's stature, few biographies have been published.

Answer: **C** only

[B] is wrong because the passage uses the language "perhaps unwittingly," meaning the biographies didn't consciously set out to depict Hemingway's vulnerabilities.

[C] is clearly supported in the passage: "What little scholarship … bravura."

Question 12

Difficulty: Easy · Percent Correct: 68% · Type: Reading Comprehension

Premise #1: The fossil of a jawbone is that of a juvenile animal (one theory is that it's the remains of a gomphothere).

Answer: **B**

Premise #2: The jawbone doesn't have enough space to accommodate big molars (the gomphotheres are known for this).

Conclusion: Jawbone is not that of a gomphothere.

(A) is tempting since it's an assumption upon which the argument rests. However, we're looking for a statement showing the *conclusion* is possibly flawed.

(B) is correct because it provides evidence that the lack of space on the jawbone of a juvenile gomphothere isn't a reason to discount the theory that the jawbone is that of a gomphothere. Before gomphotheres become adults, teeth are forced out of the jawbone, and that allows room for the massive molars to grow.

(C) provides information that, on the basis of the logic in the conclusion, discounts the mastodon as a viable candidate for the fossil. In other words, an adult mastodon also has large molars that wouldn't be able to fit on the jawbone fossil. This doesn't weaken the conclusion, since yet another species may still have existed.

(D) doesn't specifically address the connection between the jawbone and the molars.

(E) is irrelevant. The conclusion is focused on the lack of space on the jawbone fossil for big molars. That another species has an even longer jawbone than the gomphothere doesn't point to the fossil at all. The fossil is discounted as coming from a gomphothere because there isn't enough space for the molars, not because the jawbone isn't long enough.

Question 13

Difficulty: **Hard** · Percent Correct: **48%** · Type: **Sentence Equivalence**

Answers: **E** **F**

"Amongst the amorphous" shows that when the heckler cannot be identified, he hurls aggressive, inflammatory comments. As soon as he's identified, he sneaks away, "head down."

[A] *stealthiness* is an attractive answer choice, especially with the first half of the sentence. It doesn't, however, capture the overall meaning of the sentence, and there's no similar word in the other answer choices.

[B] *outspokenness*, another attractive answer choice, ignores the contrast between the time before and after the heckler is identified.

[C] *shyness* doesn't fit the context.

[D] *aloofness* means "standing apart." A heckler embroils himself in possible conflict and is not aloof.

[E] *cravenness* is "cowardliness." The heckler, when anonymous, is very bold. As soon as he's identified, he cowardly goes "scuttling off."

[F] *spinelessness* connotes the same lack of courage as cravenness.

Question 14

Difficulty: **Easy** · Percent Correct: **80%** · Type: **Sentence Equivalence**

Answers: **D** **F**

Technology has progressed so quickly that somebody who isn't an expert has difficulty explaining how technology really works. You're seeking a word in the blank that suggests the non-specialist is out of his/her element.

[A] *elegiac* means "mournful."

[B] *belligerent* means "inclined to fight."

[C] *confident* is the opposite of what should go in the blank.

[D] *baffled* shows confusion, which fits the context: the non-specialist becomes totally confused when ask to explain how technology really works.

[E] *complacent* means "satisfied."

[F] *perplexed* means "confused," which also fits the context.

Question 15

Difficulty: **Easy** · Percent Correct: **76%** · Type: **Sentence Equivalence**

Answers: **B** **C**

The mayor has worked very hard ("assiduously") to make sure he's seen as honest. He is thus aware that one scandal could forever hurt his reputation.

[A] *bolster* means "to support."

[B] *besmirch* means "to damage someone's standing or reputation," and so this fits the context.

[C] *tarnish* means "to damage someone's reputation," and so also fits the context.

[D] *promulgate* means "to make widely known."

[E] *mollify* means "to soothe."

[F] *solidify* doesn't work in the context.

Question 16

Difficulty: **Hard** · Percent Correct: **45%** · Type: **Sentence Equivalence**

This is a tough question because the word [A] *found* is being used in a different sense than is typical. To make matters worse, the usual sense of *found* has the synonym *discover*, answer choice [D]. The fact that [D] sounds right if you plug it into the blank makes this a fiendishly difficult question.

What, though, does it mean to discover something to be "trite"? Would you say, after watching a generic film, that you discovered it to be trite? Perhaps not. You would, however, say that you found it trite. In this sense, found means that you offered a judgment. The only synonym is [B].

Need this sentence explained in more detail? Breaking the sentence apart makes it easier to analyze.

If good taste has _____ the vampire genre to be tired and trite,

"Good taste" refers to people who have good taste in art/movies. They have _____ vampire movies to be a bad type of movie. What would people with good taste do to a movie when they judge it to be bad? They would be describing or labeling it. The closest fit for these are: **[A]** *found* and **[B]** *deemed*. Potentially, [D] *discovered* and [F] *anticipated* could work, but as discussed above, "discovered" doesn't really match the sense of judgment we need (it's more about finding out an objective fact), and "anticipated" refers to a something that hasn't happened yet, whereas this sentence is talking about a current discussion.

the entertainment industry surely is not listening

At the beginning of the sentence ("If good taste has _____ the vampire genre to be tired and trite ..."), it's determined that people with good taste probably don't like vampire films. However, the sentence follows this up by saying, "the entertainment industry surely is not listening": this means that even though people with good taste dislike vampire films, the entertainment industry is "not listening" to their opinion, since they continue to create more and more vampire films (described by the third part of the sentence, below).

for every bloodsucker baring fangs there is a hack bearing some script.

This is a figure of speech: when you say, "for every X, there is a Y," that means that there are a lot of both Xs and Ys.

In this sentence, it's saying that there are a lot of vampires ("bloodsucker baring fangs") and a lot of bad scriptwriters ("a hack bearing some script").

Here's an example of the "for every X, there is a Y" structure: *For every pair of shoes she buys, there is a purse that she needs to buy to match.* This sentence is describing a woman who buys a lot of shoes, and every time she buys shoes, she also buys a purse that matches it. It's a pretty trivial sentence, but it implies that the

Answers: **A** **B**

woman buys a lot of shoes and also a lot of purses.

Knowing this, you can make the following summary: "people don't like vampire movies, but the entertainment industry keeps on making them; there are a lot of scripts for vampire movies."

Question 17

Difficulty: **Medium** · Percent Correct: **51%** · Type: **Reading Comprehension**

Answer: **B**

The conclusion of the argument is that the effects observed in the fluvoxamine group can only be attributed to the use of the drug. The correct answer must show that something else could explain the effect. **(B)** provides information that shows that those in the fluvoxamine group, due to the obvious side effects, were aware that they were receiving fluvoxamine. As the argument states, "essentially, if one knows that one is receiving an actual pill, such knowledge can affect the outcome of a study."

(A) is wrong because it simply restates the protocol for double-blind studies noted at the beginning of the argument.

(C) doesn't provide an alternative explanation to the observed drop in depression.

(D) doesn't relate to the conclusion.

(E) indicates that not all of the members in the fluvoxamine group had a successful outcome. It doesn't, however, provide another factor that could account for the successful outcome.

Question 18

Difficulty: **Hard** · Percent Correct: **39%** · Type: **Reading Comprehension**

Answer: **D**

"Flying … evolutionary advantage" implies that the pteranodon walked before it evolved the ability to fly. **(D)** restates this conclusion.

(A) is out because the passage doesn't mention other dinosaurs.

(B) is tempting because the theory does mention "scarcity of resources." However, "only" (in the sequence "only a theory that accounts") is a very strong word. The quoted lines don't imply that the only theory that can explain the pteranodon's adaptations is one that includes "scarcity of resources."

(C) is tempting as well, but ultimately this is too general to be well linked to the target text. It may be background information that the topic of evolution relies on, but the author isn't trying to communicate this; the passage isn't making an argument about how and why evolution happened among dinosaurs in general. This sentence instead implies some information specifically about the pteranodon.

(E) is limited to the bird being able to find food while flying. The sentence mentions flying in contrast to "terrestrial movement." Thus, you can only infer that the creature was able to access more food because it was in flight—not that it was able to live using food gathered only in flight.

Need help with those confusing questions asking what the author implies?
These questions can be very tricky! The test doesn't really want you to make any large logical leaps. These are very, very small inferences you have to make; they have to be supported directly by the text.

Look again at the sentence that's under consideration here: "One explanation is that flying was the evolutionary advantage conferred upon these creatures ..." It's clear there's some "evolutionary advantage" which was developed in the pteranodon. And there seems to be some question as to what that advantage was—the sentence suggests that flying was the development, as opposed to ... Well, as opposed to *what*? What's the other option? Walking!

So this sentence tells us that between two options, walking and flying, one of them (flying) was an evolutionary change, which helped the creature. So what did the animal do before it started flying? You already know that the creature could both fly and walk; it must have gained the ability to fly after already having the ability to walk.

Question 19

Difficulty: **Hard** · Percent Correct: **31%** · Type: **Reading Comprehension**

[A] is supported by the passage, because the author—along with other scientists—is basing theories on the computer models.

Answers: A C

While [B] may have been true, it's not supported by the passage.

[C] is supported by the sentence starting with "while this idea is enticing ..." This shows that the author would agree—and thus [C] can be substantiated—that regardless of how compelling a theory is, it should be analyzed further.

Why is [A] correct? The passage says that the simulation *suggested* the pteranodon could walk. That's not sufficient support, right? This is actually very subtle, so it's a great question. The passage doesn't explicitly state this, but it's implied in the way the passage is written. Take another look at the end of that first paragraph:

> "*was able to walk by retracting its wrists so as to walk on its palms. Why the pteranodon did so remains unanswered.*"

Notice that it doesn't say "why the pteranodon *might have done* so." Instead, the sentence expresses a certainty: "*did* so." Following that, you have a paragraph that continues with the assumption that the pteranodon did walk. The only thing up for debate is *why* the pteranodon walked. Nobody seems to be refuting the idea that it walked; it seems widely accepted, and the only evidence you're provided is the computer model.

Why isn't [B] correct? Since the passage says that the pteranodon had a wingspan of up to twenty-five feet, this means that it could fly. Doesn't flying count as an adaptation? Flying *does* count as an adaptation, but look again at what answer choice [B] says: "The pteranodon had other adaptations, besides the ability to retract its wrists, *that allowed it to walk.*"

Did flying allow it to walk? That's a bit strange and never supported in the passage. The only adaptation that we know allowed it to walk is the wrist adaptation. Since no other adaptations are listed in the passage besides the pteranodon's wrists, there isn't adequate support for [B], and thus it's incorrect.

Question 20

Difficulty: **Hard**   ·   Percent Correct: **37%**   ·   Type: **Reading Comprehension**

The argument states that the only place wildlife parks can find killer whales is off the coast of Iceland but that with an imminent ban there, wildlife parks will be unable to replenish their respective in-park killer whale populations. Eliminate all the answer choices that call this conclusion into question.

(A) provides a source of killer whales (Greenland), thereby weakening the conclusion.

The argument states that North America is also abundant in killer whales. If Canada lifts its ban, then wildlife parks can find killer whales there. (B) is out.

(C) provides a great place to replenish the killer whale population: the park itself. Therefore, (C) directly attacks the argument that wildlife parks will run out of killer whales.

(D) provides a clear means by which parks will acquire killer whales despite all the bans.

(E) doesn't provide a new means by which parks will acquire new killer whales. It only describes how killer whales are generally caught. Therefore **(E)** is the answer.

GRE Quantitative Section 2 Answers and Explanations

Question 1

Difficulty: **Easy** · Percent Correct: **71%** · Concept(s): **Algebra** · Type: **Quantitative Comparison**

Let's start with the second ratio. That one has c in the numerator and a in the denominator, but the first ratio has the opposite arrangement of these variables, so you'll begin by taking the reciprocal of the second ratio:

$$\frac{c}{a} = 4 \quad \Rightarrow \quad \frac{a}{c} = \frac{1}{4}$$

Because you're free to multiply and divide factors in any order, you're going to rearrange the first ratio a bit:

$$\frac{(a \times b)}{c} = \left(\frac{a}{c}\right) \times b = 1$$

Now, substitute the value from the second ratio into this equation:

$$\left(\frac{a}{c}\right) \times b = 1 \quad \Rightarrow \quad \left(\frac{1}{4}\right) \times b = 1 \quad \Rightarrow \quad b = 4$$

Thus, **(C)** the two columns are equal.

Answer: **C**

Question 2

Difficulty: **Medium** · Percent Correct: **62%** · Concept(s): **Number Sense** · Type: **Quantitative Comparison**

1. n is a positive integer.
2. n is not divisible by 4.
3. n is not divisible by 5.

Answer: **D**

Column A	Column B
The remainder when n is divided by 4	The remainder when n is divided by 5
n = 1 $\Rightarrow$ remainder = 1 n = 6 $\Rightarrow$ remainder = 2	remainder = 1 remainder = 1

The best way to approach this question is by plugging in possible values and seeing which of the four answers you end up with. A good start is to choose an easy number—hence 1 (though you could have chosen any number that obeys the criteria regarding n). Plugging in 1 gives us an answer of (C).

The next step is to plug in another value. In doing so, three things can happen: column A is greater; column B is greater; or, once again, the two columns are equal, pointing to (C).

If either of the first two things happens, the answer is (D), since the relationship between the two columns cannot be determined. That is, the answer cannot be both (C)—as was initially determined—and (A). When multiple answers result based on the values plugged in, the answer is always (D). If you plug in several more values and the columns are still equal, try to plug in numbers that might disprove this (where applicable: negative numbers, small fractions, or negative fractions). But if you notice a pattern, such that the columns are always the same, then the answer is very likely (C).

With this question, we don't have to plug in many numbers. Sure, we can plug in 3 and still get (C) since the remainder is going to equal 3 when you divide it into both 4 and 5. But as soon as we choose a number that's greater than the highest possible remainder when dividing by 4 or 5, which is 3, a different relationship emerges. For instance, plugging in 6 gives us 2 in column A and 1 in column B, resulting in (A). Again both (A) and (C) can't be the answer, so the answer must be **(D)**.

Question 3

Difficulty: **Medium** · Percent Correct: **63%** · Concept(s): **Geometry** · Type: **Quantitative Comparison**

Answer: **D**

All you know is that angle $DBC = 100°$, which tells us that angle $ABD = 80°$. You know nothing about the lengths of the various sides. For example, you could start to slide point C to the right ...

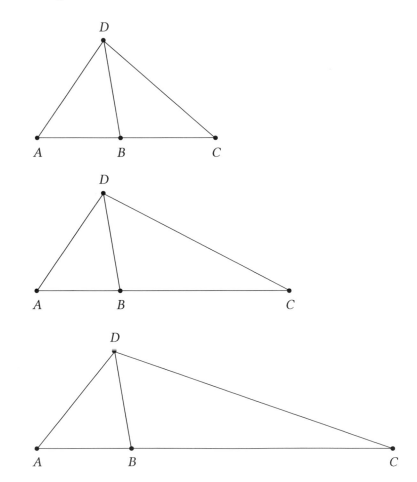

which makes $DC + BC$ much bigger than $AB + AD$. Or you could slide point A to the left ...

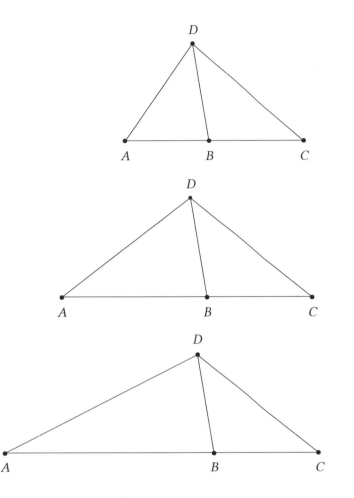

which makes $AB + AD$ much larger than $DC + BC$.

Any of the above diagrams could be correct because lengths aren't specified. Because you can construct diagrams that make the inequality go either way between the two columns, you know that **(D)** is the correct answer since you don't have sufficient information to determine the relationship.

Question 4

Difficulty: **Medium** · Percent Correct: **59%** · Concept(s): **Geometry** · Type: **Quantitative Comparison**

The three side lengths of the triangle are all specified. There's a theorem from geometry called SSS congruence, which says that if the three sides of a triangle are specified, then there can only be one triangle shape that has those three sides. In other words, specifying all three sides uniquely determines the shape of the triangle.

Answer: **Ⓐ**

Remember, GRE math diagrams are automatically accompanied by the caveat "not drawn to scale." Therefore, even though this triangle has a fixed shape, it might not look anything like the diagram appearing in the problem.

What you have here, essentially, is another misleading GRE diagram. Your job is to ignore the diagram and discover what you can about the shape of the triangle.

The numbers in this problem were actually chosen to evoke a pattern in your mind. The pattern involves what are called "Pythagorean triples," or sets of three positive integers that satisfy the Pythagorean theorem. For example, (3, 4, 5) is the simplest Pythagorean triple. If you multiply all those numbers by 2, you get (6, 8, 10). Ideally, when you looked at the (6, 8, 11) triangle of this problem, it was supposed to remind you of the (6, 8, 10) triangle, and you solve the problem by comparison. This is an example of why it's essential to have the basic Pythagorean triples memorized.

Remember this about the theorem:

1. If you know the triangle is a right triangle, then you can conclude that the sides obey the equation $a^2 + b^2 = c^2$

AND

2. If you know the sides of a triangle obey the equation $a^2 + b^2 = c^2$, then you can conclude that it is a right triangle.

This means that, if you know the sides are any Pythagorean triple, (6, 8, 10), that's an absolute guarantee the angle is a right angle. If the sides in this problem were (6, 8, 10), then you would know with certainty that the angle was 90°.

Instead of a (6, 8, 10) triangle, you have a (6, 8, 11) triangle. Think about what you would have to physically do to the triangle to make that change. Suppose you have a 6' × 8' × 10' triangle made out of wood. Of course, this triangle has to have a right angle opposite the side of 10', because the sides satisfy the Pythagorean equation. If you then attempt to remove that 10' board that currently makes the hypotenuse and cram an 11' board in its place, you'll have to wrench the two legs apart to a wider angle.

Here is a "to scale" diagram of the (6, 8, 11) triangle.

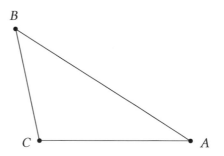

You are **not** responsible for knowing how to come up with that exact angle. You just need to see that, by comparison with the (6, 8, 10) triangle, the angle would have to be greater than 90°. So **(A)** is the answer: the quantity in column A is greater.

Generalizing, you can say the following: suppose the three sides of any triangle are $a < b < c$. Then you can say:

(i) if $a^2 + b^2 = c^2$, then the angle opposite c is a right angle
(ii) if $a^2 + b^2 < c^2$, then the angle opposite c is an obtuse angle
(iii) if $a^2 + b^2 > c^2$, then the angle opposite c is an acute angle

Case (i) is none other than the Pythagorean theorem itself. In case (ii), the longest side c is longer than it would be in right triangle, so the angle has to open wider to accommodate it. In case (iii), the longest side c is shorter than it would be in right triangle, so the angle has to close up, get narrower, in order to fit this side. You can think of this as a "generalized Pythagorean theorem."

Question 5

Difficulty: Medium · Percent Correct: 59% · Concept(s): Probability/Combinatorics · Type: Quantitative Comparison

This is a deeply conceptual question and, like many on the GRE, it really doesn't involve a single calculation. It requires imagination and the ability to shift perspectives.

Answer: **C**

> Scenario A is a result of 2 Hs (heads) and 3 Ts (tails).
> Scenario B is a result of 3 Hs and 2 Ts.

If you were to do a calculation, you would use combinations.

> $_nC_r$ = the number of ways to choose r items from a pool of n items

Here's another way to think about this:

> $_nC_r$ = the number of ways r identical items can be placed in n possible positions

Let's arbitrarily say that getting a single H when you flip the coin is a "success." Then the probability of one success is $\frac{1}{2}$. To figure out the number of ways exactly 2 successes could be distributed among the 5 trials, you would use combinations.

> $5C2$ = the number of ways 2 successes could be distributed among 5 trials

For the purposes of this question, though, you don't even need that numerical value. You just need to know (a) there are 5 trials; (b) the probability of success in each trial is exactly $\frac{1}{2}$; and (c) you want exactly 2 successes in 5 trials, so there are $5C2$ ways these successes could be distributed among the 5 trials. That's enough to allow you to calculate P, the probability of getting exactly 2 H's in 5 tosses. P is the value in column A.

But wait! Notice that, at the very beginning, we said to pretend that H is a "success." That was completely arbitrary. We could have said that T was a "success." If you treat T as a success, then conditions (a), (b), and (c) in the previous paragraph would remain true, and the probability that results from those conditions, P, now would be the probability of getting exactly 2 Ts in 5 tosses. If you toss the coin 5 times, and get exactly 2 Ts, then you would have to get exactly 3 Hs. Thus, P is also the value in column B, and therefore the answer is **(C)** since the columns are equal.

Here are some more details on that calculation:

As it happens, $5C2 = 10$. Let's say S is a "success" and F is a "failure":

SSFFF	SFFSF	FSSFF	FSFFS	FFSFS
SFSFF	SFFFS	FSFSF	FFSSF	FFFSS

Those are the 10 ways that 2 successes can be distributed among 5 trials. For column A, you would replace the Ss with Hs and the Fs with Ts, and for column B, you would replace the Ss with Ts and the Fs with Hs.

Question 6

Difficulty: **Hard** · Percent Correct: **37.8%** · Concept(s): **Percents/Fractions/Ratios** · Type: **Quantitative Comparison**

Answer: **C**

1. x and y are integers greater than 5.
2. x is y percent of x^2

Column A	Column B
x	10
10	10

x is y percent of x^2

$$x = \frac{y}{100}x^2 \ \Rightarrow \ 1 = \frac{y}{100}x \ \Rightarrow \ 100 = xy$$

$x = 1, y = 100$	$x = 5, y = 20$	$x = 25, y = 4$
$x = 2, y = 50$	$\mathbf{x = 10, y = 10}$	$x = 50, y = 2$
$x = 4, y = 25$	$x = 20, y = 5$	$x = 100, y = 1$

Question 7

Difficulty: **Hard** · Percent Correct: **27%** · Concept(s): **Percents/Fractions/Ratios** · Type: **Quantitative Comparison**

Answer: **C**

You have 200 workers, some of whom are women and some of whom are men. If you write that as an equation, it looks like this:

200 total workers = total males + total females

Next:

"10% of males smoke" is $\frac{10}{100}$.
"49% of females smoke" is $\frac{49}{100}$.

This is our equation for the total number of smokers:

total # of smokers = $\left(\frac{10}{100}\right)M + \left(\frac{49}{100}\right)F$

You have two equations and three variables at this point, so substitution won't work to solve this problem. Instead, there's another way to arrive at the answer. Let's step back to find it.

You can figure out F and M with a little reasoning and logic. The key to solving quickly is noticing that you're dealing with people. You can't have a fraction or decimal result when you multiply our percent and the number of total females $(\frac{49}{100})F$ or the number of total males $(\frac{10}{100})M$.

For example, if there were 150 female employees and 50 male employees, then you would end up with the following fraction of women smoking:

$$\left(\frac{49}{100}\right) \times 150 = 73.5$$

This doesn't make sense, since you can't have 0.5 of a person smoking.

So if you accept that you need a whole number, an integer, then you next need to consider the 49% of women who smoke. This is a highly restrictive number since you only have two options for our total number of women. All others would yield a decimal when multiplied to $\frac{49}{100}$ (like the example above).

The total number of female employees is either 100 or 200.

But wait! There can't be 200 women working at this company. You know that 10% of the men smoke, which means you need at least 10 men at the company. You can't have 10% of 0.

So you can eliminate the possibility of 200 female workers. There must be 100 females. And if there are 100 females, that means that there are 100 male workers (100 + 100 = 200 total workers).

Now you can plug in our numbers to find the total number of smokers

$$\left(\frac{10}{100}\right) \times 100 + \left(\frac{49}{100}\right) \times 100 = 49$$
$$10 + 49 = 59$$

A total of 59 women and men smoke at the company, and so the answer is **(C)** since quantity is equal to the amount listed in column B.

How do we know that 10% is actually 10%? When a percent is given in a GRE word problem, ETS means that exact value; 10% on the screen is exactly 10.00000%. In news sources and pop media, when people say 10%, they might mean 9.7% or 11.3%, but on the GRE Quantitative, you have to assume that every single number given in a word problem is precise. If it's not the exact stated value, ETS will indicate this by saying "approximately."

Why can't the number of male workers be equal to 0? Couldn't it be assumed that 0 male workers smoke and 98 female workers smoke, making 98 smokers overall? It's correct that the question doesn't specifically say that the number of men (or women) is a non-0 number. But it still isn't possible to treat the number of men as "0." If the question tells us that 10% of the male workers smoke, then you should answer the question as though there's a non-0 number of men. Because if you don't, then things get crazy!

If 10% of 0 men = 0, then so does 75% or 90% or 100% of the men! They all equal 0, because any number multiplied by 0 is 0. It would make the use of percentages meaningless. There would be too many cases to think of. If you used the same reasoning you could also conclude that 59% of zero women is 0.

When the question gives a percentage for both men and women, then you can assume that there are both men and women in the group. In a situation like this, you must assume that the "percent of" number is non-0, because a percent of 0 doesn't make sense in a real-world scenario.

Question 8

Difficulty: **Hard** · Percent Correct: **37%** · Concept(s): **Algebra, Word Problems** · Type: **Multiple Choice**

A sum of money was distributed among Lyle, Bob, and Chloe. First, Lyle received $4 plus one-half of what remained. Next, Bob received $4 plus one-third of what remained. Finally, Chloe received the remaining $32. How many dollars did Bob receive?

(A) 10

(B) 20

(C) 26

(D) 40

(E) 52

Let A = $ remaining AFTER Lyle received his amount

Let B = $ Bob received

$$B = 4 + \frac{1}{3}(A - 4) \ \Rightarrow \ 3B = 12 + A - 4$$

$$3B = A + 8$$

$$A - 3B = -8$$

$$- \ [A - B = 32]$$

$$\overline{}$$

$$-2B = -40$$

$$B = \mathbf{20}$$

Why can Lyle's share of the money be ignored? Imagine that there's a nice stack of money on the table to be split between the friends. Lyle grabs his cash and leaves the room. Now you're left with Bob and Chloe in the room. You've got a (smaller) stack of money on the table. You know that Chloe ends up with the remaining $32, so all you really need to know is how much money was there *after Lyle left.*

To make this clearer, you might try working backward using the 32. Directly before the $32 were left on the table, Bob took $\frac{1}{3}$ of the money that was there. That means there must have been an amount of money divisible into 3 parts on the table. Bob took 1 of those 3 parts and then there were $32 left. So there were $48 on the table before Bob took the $\frac{1}{3}$, since $48 - \left(\frac{1}{3}\right) \times 48 = 32$. And before that, he had taken $4. Add that onto the 48, and you know that there were $52 before Bob took his share. $52 - 32 = 20$

Why is $B = 4 + \left(\frac{1}{3}\right)(A - 4)$ instead of $4 + \left(\frac{1}{3}\right)A$? Let's think about it this way: Lyle takes his money and leaves the room. There's now A dollars. Bob takes $4 from that and puts it in his pocket. There's now $A - 4$ dollars. Bob's a little selfish, so he decides to take $\frac{1}{3}$ of the remaining money. So he takes $\frac{1}{3} \times (A - 4)$, and since he already had 4 dollars in his pocket, he's got $4 + \frac{1}{3} \times (A - 4)$ dollars now.

Need help working backwards? Let's start out with just Bob's and Chloe's amounts. After Lyle took his amount of money and left, there were A dollars. Bob takes $4, so now there are $(A - 4)$ dollars left. Then Bob takes $\frac{1}{3}$ of the remaining $(A - 4)$ dollars.

This means that the $20 Bob has are equal to $4 + \frac{A-4}{3}$. You solve for A and get that the following:

$$20 = 4 + \frac{A-4}{3}$$
$$60 = 12 + (A - 4)$$
$$52 = A$$

This confirms what you know, that Bob and Chloe together took $52: Bob took $20 and Chloe took $32.

If you'd like to work backwards further and get Lyle's amount (*you absolutely don't need to*, but for those of you out there who like to leave no unknown unsolved), you can work backwards again.

Lyle first received $4. If you call the total "T," then there's "$T - 4$" left afterward. Then Lyle takes $\frac{1}{2}$ of what remains, which is $\frac{T-4}{2}$. This is the remaining amount. You already know that when Lyle leaves, there are $52 left.

$$\frac{T-4}{2} = 52$$
$$(T-4) = 104$$
$$T = 108$$

So the original total was $108. Lyle got $56, Bob got $20, and Chloe got $32.

When you check, you should use the order of events. You have to be careful about when the taking away of $4 occurs and when division of remaining money occurs:

A sum of money was distributed among Lyle, Bob and Chloe: $108

1. Lyle received $4 plus $\frac{1}{2}$ of what remained:
   1a. $108 − 4 = 104$
   1b. Then, $\frac{104}{2} = \$52$ remaining

2. Next, Bob received $4 plus $\frac{1}{3}$ of what remained.
   2a. $52 − 4 = 48$
   2b. $48 - \left(\frac{1}{3}\right)$ of $48 = 48 - 16 = \$32$

3. Finally, Chloe received the remaining $32. There's no more taking away. Chloe just received what's left.

Question 9

Difficulty: **Easy** · Percent Correct: **91%** · Concept(s): **Percents/Ratios/Fractions** · Type: **Multiple Choice**

If the sales tax on a $12.00 purchase is $0.66, what is the sales tax on a $20.00 purchase?

Answer: **B**

(A) $1.08

(B) $1.10

(C) $1.16

(D) $1.18

(E) $1.20

$$\frac{\text{purchase price}}{\text{sales tax}} : \frac{12}{0.66} = \frac{20}{x}$$

$$\frac{2}{0.11} = \frac{20}{x}$$

$$2x = (0.11)(20)$$

$$2x = 2.20$$

$$x = \mathbf{1.10}$$

Question 10

Difficulty: **Medium** · Percent Correct: **53%** · Concept(s): **Algebra** · Type: **Numeric Entry**

Answer: $\dfrac{2}{7}$

If $\dfrac{2 + \frac{3}{n}}{3 + \frac{2}{n}} = \dfrac{5}{4}$, what is the value of n?

If $\dfrac{a}{b} = \dfrac{c}{d}$ then $ad = bc$

$$\frac{2 + \frac{3}{n}}{3 + \frac{2}{n}} = \frac{5}{4}$$

$$5\left(3 + \frac{2}{n}\right) = 4\left(2 + \frac{3}{n}\right)$$

$$n\left(15 + \frac{10}{n}\right) = n\left(8 + \frac{12}{n}\right)$$

$$15n + 10 = 8n + 12$$

$$7n + 10 = 12$$

$$7n = 2$$

$$n = \frac{2}{7}$$

Question 11

Difficulty: **Medium** · Percent Correct: **55%** · Concept(s): **Probability/Combinatorics** · Type: **Multiple Choice**

Answer: **E**

The probability is 0.6 that an "unfair" coin will turn up tails on any given toss. If the coin is tossed 3 times, what is the probability that at least 1 of the tosses will turn up tails?

- (A) 0.064
- (B) 0.36
- (C) 0.64
- (D) 0.784
- **(E) 0.936**

$\text{P(tails)} = 0.6 \Rightarrow \text{P(heads)} = 1 - 0.6$
$= 0.4$

$\text{P(at least 1 tails)} = 1 - \text{P(no tails)}$
$= 1 - \text{P(all heads)}$
$= 1 - \text{P}(H_1 \text{ AND } H_2 \text{ AND } H_3)$
$= 1 - [\text{P}(H_1) \times \text{P}(H_2) \times \text{P}(H_3)]$
$= 1 - [0.4 \times 0.4 \times 0.4]$
$= 1 - [0.064]$
$= \mathbf{0.936}$

Isn't the probability of at least one tails (0.6)(0.4)(0.4) + (0.6)(0.6)(0.4) + (0.6)(0.6)(0.6)? The basic thinking is correct, but there are actually more than 3 cases here that would satisfy our requirement for at least one tails. They are …

One tails: THH, HTH, HHT
Two tails: TTH, THT, HTT
Three tails: TTT

Now you need to analyze the probability for each of these cases and add them:

THH = (0.6 × 0.4 × 0.4) = 0.096
HTH = (0.4 × 0.6 × 0.4) = 0.096
HHT = (0.4 × 0.4 × 0.6) = 0.096
TTH = (0.6 × 0.6 × 0.4) = 0.144
THT = (0.6 × 0.4 × 0.6) = 0.144
HTT = (0.4 × 0.6 × 0.6) = 0.144
TTT = (0.6 × 0.6 × 0.6) = 0.216

When you add all of those up, you get 0.936 as your answer. Of course, this is much more complicated than noting that there's only one possible scenario in which no tails are flipped (HHH), finding that probability and then subtracting it from 1.

Question 12

Difficulty: **Hard** · Percent Correct: **36.8%** · Concept(s): Geometry · Type: **Multiple Answer**

The sides of a triangle are 1, x, and x^2. What are the possible values of x?

Answers: **B C**

Indicate <u>all</u> possible values.

- A 0.5
- **B** 1
- **C** 1.5
- D 2
- E 2.5
- F 3
- G 3.5

The triangle inequality states that the sum of any two sides of a triangle must be bigger than the third side. If we can identify which side is the largest, then the other two sides must have a sum larger than that largest side in order for the triangle to be possible.

Consider the first option:

$$x = 0.5 = \frac{1}{2} \quad \Rightarrow \quad x^2 = \frac{1}{4}$$

The longest side is 1, and the sum of these two fractions is $\frac{3}{4}$, less than 1. This doesn't satisfy the triangle equality, so this is not a possible triangle.

The next option, $x = 1$, produces a triangle with three sides equal to 1—in other words, an equilateral triangle. This, of course, is possible.

Consider the next option:

$$x = 1.5 = \frac{3}{2} \quad \Rightarrow \quad x^2 = \frac{9}{4}$$

The longest side is $\frac{9}{4} = 2.25$. The sum of the other two sides is $1 + 1.5 = 2.5$, and this is bigger than the longest side. This is a possible triangle, so this works.

Consider the next option, $x = 2$, a triangle with sides {1, 2, 4}. Of course, $1 + 2 = 3 < 4$, so this doesn't satisfy the triangle inequality, and therefore this is not a possible triangle.

The problem with $x = 2$ is that, by this point, the squared term has increased enough that it's larger than the sum of the other two terms. If you think about how larger numbers, when squared, produce even larger results, you realize that the square will continue to increase more and more, totally outracing the sum of the other two terms.

$$x = 2.5 = \frac{5}{2} \quad \Rightarrow \quad x^2 = \frac{25}{4} = 6.25 \quad \Rightarrow \quad 1 + 2.5 = 3.5 < 6.25$$

$$x = 3 \quad \Rightarrow \quad x^2 = 9 \quad \Rightarrow \quad 1 + 3 = 4 < 9$$

$$x = 3.5 = \frac{7}{2} \quad \Rightarrow \quad x^2 = \frac{49}{4} = 12.25 \quad \Rightarrow \quad 1 + 3.5 = 4.5 < 12.25$$

Notice that the squared term is not only bigger than the sum of the other two terms, but gets further and further away from this in each case as x increases. The only two cases that work as triangles are $x = 1$ and $x = 1.5$.

Question 13

Difficulty: **Easy** · Percent Correct: **76%** · Concept(s): **Data Interpretation** · Type: **Multiple Choice**

Answer: **C**

Current profit is about $300K, which we can call the "whole" of the percent change. If revenues increase by 10%, that's approximately $100K extra, all of which is added to the profits because costs remain fixed. That's the "part." Percent $= \frac{100}{300} = \frac{1}{3} = 33.3\%$, which is very close to **(C)**—and close enough to be the correct answer.

In a more precise calculation, current profit is $1,052,000 − $749,000 = $303,000. If revenues increase by 10%, that's an additional $105,200.

$$\text{percent increase} = \frac{\$105,200}{\$303,000} \times 100\% = 34.7\%$$

Question 14

Difficulty: **Easy** · Percent Correct: **90%** · Concept(s): **Data Interpretation** · Type: **Multiple Choice**

Answer: **D**

The sum of subsidiaries + investments is approximately $300K: that's the "part." The total revenues are approximately $1,000K: that's the "whole." Percent $= \frac{300}{1,000} = 0.3 = 30\%$. But revenues are a little more than $1,000K, which makes the denominator bigger, which makes the whole fraction smaller, so you expect answer just under 30%.

In a more precise calculation, the sum of subsidiaries + investments = $246,000 + $53,000 = $299,000 is the "part," and the total revenues, $1,052,000, is the "whole." The calculation gives us answer **(D)**:

$$\text{percent} = \frac{\$299,000}{\$1,052,000} \times 100\% = 28.4\%$$

Question 15

Difficulty: **Hard** · Percent Correct: **48%** · Concept(s): **Data Interpretation** · Type: **Multiple Choice**

Answer: **D**

Notice that the value of the sale is approximately 10 times bigger than the value of the R&D budget. If R&D is responsible for half the sales, that's a value 5 times bigger. An increase from 100% to 5 times bigger, 500%, is an increase of 400%. A very quick approximation leads to answer **(D)**!

In a more precise calculation, the 2008 sales are the same, so half of those sales, the part due to R&D, would be

$$\text{sales due to R\&D} = \frac{\$753,000}{2} = \$376,500$$

The "whole" is the 2007 R&D budget, $75,000, and the "part" would be the difference between $75,000 and $376,500, which becomes the "return on the investment."

$$\text{percent increase} = \frac{\$376,500 - \$75,000}{\$75,000} \times 100\% = 402\%$$

Question 16

Difficulty: **Hard** · Percent Correct: **44%** · Concept(s): **Exponents** · Type: **Multiple Answer**

Which of the following is equal to 8^{24}?

Answers: **B** **D**

Indicate <u>all</u> possible values.

First, express 8 as a power of 2.

$$8^{24} = (2^3)^{24} = 2^{3 \times 24} = 2^{72}$$

In that process, you used the power rule from the laws of exponents.

$$(a^m)^n = a^{n \times m}$$

| A | 2^{96} | ⇨ | This has the wrong power of 2. |

B 4^{36} ⇨ Express 4 as a power of 2. ⇨ $4^{36} = (2^2)^{36} = 2^{2\times36} = 2^{72}$

| C | 12^{12} | ⇨ | 12 isn't a power of 2; this expression contains factors of 3, which 2^{72} does not. |

D 16^{18} ⇨ Express 16 as a power of 2. ⇨ $16^{18} = (2^4)^{18} = 2^{4\times18} = 2^{72}$

| E | 24^8 | ⇨ | 24 isn't a power of 2; this expression contains factors of 3, which 2^{72} does not. |

| F | 32^{15} | ⇨ | Express 32 as a power of 2. ⇨ $32^{15} = (2^5)^{15} = 2^{5\times15} = 2^{75}$ ⇨ Wrong power of 2. |

Question 17

Difficulty: **Medium** · Percent Correct: **54%** · Concept(s): **Number Sense** · Type: **Multiple Choice**

For all numbers a and b, the operation ⊕ is defined by $a \oplus b = a^2 - ab$. If $xy \neq 0$, then which of the following can be equal to zero?

Answer: **B**

I. $x \oplus y$ ⇨ $x \oplus y = x^2 - xy$ | $a \oplus b = a^2 - ab$
$= x(x - y)$, which can equal 0 if $x = y$

II. $xy \oplus y$ ⇨ $xy \oplus y = (xy)^2 - (xy)y$
$= x^2y^2 - xy^2$
$= xy^2(x - 1)$, which can equal 0 if $x = 1$

~~**III.**~~ $x \oplus (x + y)$ ⇨ $x \oplus (x + y) = x^2 - x(x + y)$
$= x^2 - x^2 - xy$
$= -xy$, which can never equal 0 because $xy \neq 0$

(A) II only

B I and II only

(C) I and III only

(D) II and III only

(E) All of the above

Question 18

Difficulty: **Medium** · Percent Correct: **53%** · Concept(s): **Geometry** · Type: **Numeric Entry**

Answer: **24**

In the figure below, ABC is a sector with center A. If arc BC has length 4π, what is the length of AC?

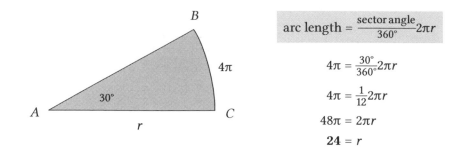

Question 19

Difficulty: **Medium** · Percent Correct: **56%** · Concept(s): **Number Sense** · Type: **Multiple Choice**

Answer: **E**

The sum of k consecutive integers is 41. If the least integer is -40, then $k =$

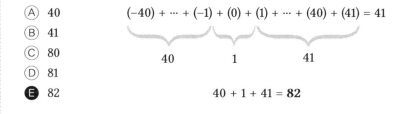

(A) 40

(B) 41

(C) 80

(D) 81

E 82

Question 20

Difficulty: **Hard** · Percent Correct: **38%** · Concept(s): **Algebra** · Type: **Multiple Answer**

Answers: **A C**

Since n is an integer, you won't get some ugly irrational numbers. First, we want to see that we have an equation in the form $ax^2 + bx + c$, and we're looking for the "middle" value b which corresponds to k.

$$n^2 - kn + 16$$

From this equation, we know that c has to equal 16.

Since we don't know the value of k, we have to figure out what two numbers give us a product of 16. Using FOIL, we can test out these cases and see what the resulting values of k are. The following numbers give us a product of 16: 1 and 16, 2 and 8, and 4 and 4. We also need to remember that two negatives, when multiplied together, give us a positive number. Therefore, -1 and -16, -2 and -8, and -4 and -4 are possibilities.

Luckily, we don't need to try out all those combinations, because we're only looking for which of the three answers—[A], [B], and [C]—are valid.

[A] 8 is correct. $(n - 4)(n - 4) = n^2 - 8n + 16$, so k can equal 8. Notice that the original form contains a negative sign in front of the k. So the positive 8 in [A], when written in the original equation, has a negative sign in front of it.

[B] 15 is incorrect. Though k looks like it might equal 15, $(n - 16)(n - 1)$ gives us a value of 17, and $(n + 16)(n + 1)$ gives us a value of -17. Remember that if we make one sign negative and one sign positive, $(n - 16)(n + 1)$, we end up with -16 as a product.

Therefore, [B] is not an answer.

[C] –17 is also correct. We can get this number by multiplying the following: $(n + 16)(n + 1) = n^2 + 17n + 16$. Though k looks like it equals positive 17, remember the original equation has a negative sign in front of k. Therefore, in the equation $n^2 + 17n + 16$, $k = -17$.

GRE Verbal Section 2 Answers and Explanations

Question 1

Difficulty: **Hard** · Percent Correct: **45%** · Type: Single-Blank Text Completion

Answer: **D**

The key to this sentence is to notice "blatantly appropriated," which means "obviously stolen," and the latter parts of the sentence "not only was … market" and "initially surfaced publicly." Therefore, the company didn't steal the design. They were "anything but" (which means "not at all") thieves or unscrupulous people.

(A) is a great trap because the start-up was "the first to market." This would imply that they weren't *hesitant*. The focus of the sentence, however, is whether they illegally copied the design of the other company.

To say that they were not at all (B) *dominant* is a little misleading. First off, the company was the first to market, suggesting that they were somewhat dominant. Granted, this is a weak connection and, in general, the sentence isn't about whether the start-up was dominant, but whether it stole the design from the leading manufacturer.

As for (C), the sentence suggests that the start-up had been *innovative*. Therefore (C) is out.

(D) *unscrupulous*, which means "unethical," best creates a meaning that's consistent with the information in the passage: the start-up didn't steal the design because they were the first ones to come up with it. Therefore, the start-up was anything but unethical.

(E) *posthumous* means "occurring after death." Had the company's product been released after the company had been dissolved, then this word might make sense. But as is, there's no mention of the end of the company's existence. The trap here is the root *post-* which means "after." Since the company was first, posthumous might sound tempting. But remember, you can't separate a root from the entire word, since the more specific meaning is often contained in other roots in the word.

Question 2

Difficulty: **Hard** · Percent Correct: **41%** · Type: Single-Blank Text Completion

Answer: **B**

On the surface this seems like a pretty straightforward question. But there are some sneaky traps. First off, (A) *novel*, which means "new," is a trap because its definition as a noun is related to the content of the sentence: Kafka is an author. We can rule it out because it's too general. The sentence is focusing more on the thrills we get from reading a book and putting ourselves in the shoes of the hero or heroine.

There's a specific word that means that—and it's not (E) *substantive*, which suffers from the same fate as (A): it's too general. In other words, Kafka's writing may or may not offer substantive thrills; these thrills just won't relate to losing yourself in a character. **(B)** is correct because *vicarious* is that specific word. It means "to experience something second-hand, or through another character or person." For instance, if you watch the Travel Channel at home, you travel vicariously through the host, though you don't actually leave your place.

(C) *tangential* means "not directly relevant to the topic at hand." Had Kafka frequently wandered from the main plot, there might be tangential thrills. However, there are no clues in the sentence supporting this interpretation.

(D) *precarious* means "situated in a dangerous spot or likely to collapse." There's no text to support this word.

Question 3

Difficulty: **Hard** · Percent Correct: **43%** · Type: Double-Blank Text Completion

The word **(B)** *complicit* means "guilty." Mulcahy is guilty of using too many big words in trying to tell us that literary criticism uses too many big words. Of course, the only ones who will be able to understand all these big words are the literary critics themselves—the very group Mulcahy seeks to criticize or **(E)** *impugn*. More specifically, (E) means "call into question."

Answers: **B** **E**

Question 4

Difficulty: **Medium** · Percent Correct: **49%** · Type: Double-Blank Text Completion

"In attempting to ... only ..." shows that the two blanks are in contrast. The fact that the biography relates Oppenheimer's quirks shows that it **(E)** *perpetuates* or reinforces the view that Oppenheimer was **(B)** *eccentric*.

Answers: **B** **E**

Question 5

Difficulty: **Hard** · Percent Correct: **31%** · Type: Triple-Blank Text Completion

The best way to approach this sentence is by seeing the clue at the very end: "environmental groups ... effected." Therefore, you know that environmental groups are doing good and that Lackmuller is ignoring them (the "however" tips the reader off that the third blank represents a shift from the rest of the sentence). Lackmuller, then, believes that groups not tied to the environment have become more **(C)** *influential* than groups that are actually protecting the environment from the government (these groups, he believes, have been suppressed). **(E)** *squelched*, which means "silenced," works best.

Answers: **C** **E** **I**

For the third blank, it's clear Muller is wrong in believing the first part of the sentence because he ignores all the great things environmental groups have done. Therefore, **(I)** is the best.

How is "nominally" used in the prompt? Also, how can the right answer choice for the second blank be figured out? Nominally usually means "in name only; not in reality." But here, when the sentence says "not nominally tied ..." it means that groups who aren't tied to ecological concerns by name (that is, their group doesn't specifically promote dealing with these concerns) have become really influential in environmental policymaking.

Let's go to the question now. Here it is for reference:

According to Lackmuller's latest screed, published under the title, Why We Can't Win at Their Game, *special interest groups not nominally tied to ecological concerns have become so (i)* _____ *the process of environmental policymaking that those groups who actually aim to ensure that corporate profit does not trump environmental health have been effectively (ii)* _____.

Now, you may simplify this:

> *According to Lackmuller's latest screed, special interest groups not tied to ecological concerns have become so (i) _____ policymaking that those groups that are tied to ecological concerns have been effectively (ii) _____.*

So you can see a contrast between two groups—those tied to ecological concerns and those not tied to ecological concerns. Basically, the influence of those that aren't ecologically concerned in policymaking has had some kind of impact on those that are ecologically concerned. So you would expect opposites for the two blanks. (C) *influential in* and (E) *squelched* would make the most logical sense here, though you'll need some clues from the second sentence to confirm this. (D) *vindicated* doesn't seem to fit well as a contrast to *influential in*. These aren't good opposites. But let's dig deeper to find out:

> *Lackmuller's contention, however, is (iii) _____ in that it fails to account for the signal achievements environmental groups have effected over the last twenty years—often to the chagrin of big business.*

Let's rephrase this:

> *However, his argument fails to account for the achievements environmental groups have effected over the last twenty years—often to the chagrin of big business—therefore his argument is _____.*

So there's something wrong with Lackmuller's argument because it doesn't account for the success of the environmental groups against those other groups seeking corporate profit (non-ecological groups). Therefore, the logic is that Lackmuller considers the non-ecological groups to be powerful while the ecological groups have been ignored. Squelched has a very similar meaning, so it's a good fit here, and it's much better than (D) *vindicated*, which means "to clear from blame." The author argues that this isn't exactly true, and, in fact, Lackmuller's argument is (I) *highly misleading*.

Question 6

Difficulty: **Very Hard** · Percent Correct: 20% · Type: **Three-Eyed Text Completion**

Answers:

There's a time shift that contrasts the beginning of the sentence, "today …" with "Michelangelo's day." Therefore, the first blank is **(B)** *contemporary*. "The proverbial envelope … further" indicates that artists are very much challenging convention. (E) *gone too far* captures this pushing of what is considered normal. "Contempt" and "confusion" further back up this answer. The final blank is a contrast. Notice the second time shift at the very end, between the sixteenth century and today. The two time periods in this case are contrasted: what is shocking in the sixteenth century would today not be considered shocking at all. **(I)** *tame* is the best answer.

Isn't "blasphemy" an antonym of "reverence" and not tame, in which case the answer to blank three would be (H) *reverent*? For the third blank, you want to select a contrast with the word "blasphemous." However, you don't necessarily want the exact opposite, as that would change the meaning of the sentence. In the context of the sentence, blasphemous means "shocking": artists these days are producing art that's so shocking ("gone too far …") that they would make what was deemed shocking art in the sixteenth century seem *not* shocking, *not* offensive. "Tame" matches this meaning well. Reverent would mean sixteenth-century art that was at that time viewed as shocking would now be viewed as "showing deep and solemn respect." This isn't what the sentence implies; it's just saying that you wouldn't view this art as offensive or shocking anymore.

Why isn't (G) *hackneyed* correct for the last blank? Isn't it a synonym for "trite"? The structure implies that you want a contrasting word to blasphemous. Hackneyed has nothing to do with something being blasphemous (or the opposite of it).

It's true that hackneyed does mean the same as trite, but trite is referring to the "tag" of cutting-edge in the first sentence. For the third blank, you're dealing with the perception of art. The best choice will be a word that means the opposite of "blasphemous" or "shocking" in the context here, so *tame* is the correct answer.

Question 7

Difficulty: **Medium** · Percent Correct: **59%** · Type: **Reading Comprehension**

Answer: **B**

The context is that the pre-Clovis people are able to "take advantage of" local microfauna, which basically means "little sea creatures." The phrase "take advantage of" matches nicely with **(B)** *exploit*. Note that "exploit" doesn't always have a negative connotation.

(A) is tempting because if you plug the word *locate* into the text, the answer seems to make sense—they have to locate the microfauna so they can eat it. However, in a GRE "Vocabulary-in-Context" question, the answer must always be a dictionary definition of the word in quotations marks (though often the answer isn't the first definition—which tends to be the trap). In other words, the definition of the phrase "to avail oneself of" would be "to locate physically," which it isn't.

(C) *regard* doesn't capture the positive relationship between the microfauna and the pre-Clovis people.

(D) *fathom* means "to determine the depth of something or to understand at a deep level." It doesn't make sense to say they wanted to determine the depth of the microfauna or to understand it on a profound level. They are simply relying on the microfauna for subsistence as they make these really long sea journeys.

There's no context implying that they (E) *distribute* the microfauna. Even if one argues that they're distributing the microfauna amongst themselves to eat, the answer to a "Vocabulary-in-Context" question must always be a dictionary definition of the word in quotations (see answer choice (A) for further explanation).

Question 8

Difficulty: **Very Hard** · Percent Correct: **23%** · Type: **Reading Comprehension**

The Solutrean hypothesis, which is used by the Clovis-first school, is now being used by the pre-Clovis school to give their ice corridor story more credibility. This is paradoxical because the Clovis-first school's own theories are being used to undermine their claims. The author finds the Solutrean hypothesis startling because the Solutreans had, "astoundingly, given the time period … crossed into the Americas." So the answer is **(B)**.

(A) isn't correct because the author doesn't disagree with the Solutrean hypothesis.

(C) is wrong because the author never mentions that the Clovis had an easier time crossing the Atlantic.

(D) may be startling but doesn't address the "paradoxical" aspect of the question.

(E) is partially correct in that it provides the "paradoxical" aspect, since the Solutrean hypothesis has been used by the pre-Clovis. However, (E) doesn't address the "startling" aspect.

How can the passage be summarized to make it more understandable? People debate over who populated the American subcontinent first. One group believes that the Clovis people were there first; however, other evidence suggests that a group of people arrived one thousand years before the Clovis people did. The supporters of the Clovis people had a point: if the Clovis people crossed the Bering Strait thirteen thousand years ago, only after it had become an ice-free land bridge, how would others have been able to make a similar trip but over ice?

Weber's school of thought has an answer to this question that proves the Clovis were not first: pre-Clovis people got to the American subcontinent on boats and thus didn't need to cross the Bering Strait. But how did such a sophisticated maritime culture develop in pre-Clovis people?

The Solutrean theory explains this: the Clovis people were actually Solutreans, an ancient seafaring culture along the Iberian Peninsula, who had—astoundingly, given the time period—crossed into the Americas via the Atlantic Ocean. Couldn't there be a similar Siberian culture (i.e., NOT Clovis, but the people who came before) who could also sail boats?

The Clovis-first (i.e., those who think the Clovis arrived first) have an objection to this: the pre-Clovis supporters don't take into account all of the land leading up to the ice corridor, and they don't base their assumptions on what could have happened here. On the other hand, archaeologists argue that there are findings that support the idea that pre-Clovis people existed in these areas.

Question 9

Difficulty: **Very Hard** · Percent Correct: 22% · Type: Reading Comprehension

The Monte Verde discovery resulted from a random process: had a peat bog not engulfed a village, there would be no remains at the Monte Verde site. This matches **(B)**.

Answer: **B**

(A) is incorrect because the passage doesn't say that the only way pre-Clovis remains will be found is if a settlement was also fossilized by a peat bog.

(C) is incorrect because, while the passage mentions plant species, it doesn't relate to the way in which the Monte Verde village was preserved.

There's no information in the passage to support (D).

The passage only mentions plant species in the context of a trade network. That doesn't mean that there were no other pre-Clovis sites less than 150 miles from Monte Verde. Thus, (E) is incorrect.

Question 10

Difficulty: **Hard** · Percent Correct: 33% · Type: Reading Comprehension

[A] isn't supported because there's nothing in the passage suggesting that other villages were also submerged in a peat bog.

Answer: **B** only

[B] can reasonably be inferred because the passage mentions that similar plant species were found as far as 150 miles away. Therefore, it's reasonable to conclude that, if there was a trade network, such a plant species would be found in other settlements.

[C] isn't supported by the passage.

Question 11

Difficulty: **Hard** · Percent Correct: 35% · Type: Reading Comprehension

(D) is the best answer because the passage does commend Temoshotka on the boldness of her thesis but ultimately questions the validity of the claim.

Answer: **D**

(A) is wrong. There are no "conflicting interpretations" involved.

(B) is wrong because the author calls attention to the dubious nature of Temoshotka's claims.

The passage challenges a specific interpretation of an author's work. That isn't the same as (C).

(E) is wrong because the text applauds/supports the cleverness and the boldness of the claim but not the claim itself.

Question 12

Difficulty: **Very Hard** · Percent Correct: 22% · Type: Reading Comprehension

[A] is wrong because nowhere in the passage does it say the two tendencies (Nabokov the writer and Nabokov the butterfly scientist) were antagonistic.

Answer: **C** only

[B] is wrong because Temoshotka does use evidence (*Lolita* and *Speak, Memory*).

[C] is correct, because the author mentions that she "cannot be faulted" for coming up with an interesting theory on Nabokov's creativity, but she "fails to make a convincing case." Notice too the last sentence, which implies that Temeshotka was overly ambitious in her theory.

Question 13

Difficulty: **Medium** · Percent Correct: **55%** · Type: **Sentence Equivalence**

Answer: **A** **B**

"Trying to befriend" and "not even deigned" show a shift from an aloof condescension to a desperate need to make friends or come across as likeable.

[A] *ingratiating* means "trying desperately to win the affection of others."

[B] *fawning*, while slightly different from "ingratiating," captures the college graduate's attempts to win the affection of others through excessive flattery.

[C] *withdrawn* is the opposite of the blank.

[D] *volatile* means "prone to changing one's mood suddenly and unpredictably."

[E] *vociferous* means "outspoken."

[F] *direct* doesn't capture the college graduate's sense of desperation to seem likeable.

Question 14

Difficulty: **Easy** · Percent Correct: **67%** · Type: **Sentence Equivalence**

Answers: **C** **E**

"Initially" signals a time shift. At first, Montreaux was declared or trumpeted as an important person in cinema. But then he experienced a precipitous or steep decline after his meteoric (or sudden) rise to fame. Therefore, the answers have to be synonyms for declared or trumpeted. [A] *identified* is close but is a little too neutral and isn't part of a synonym pair. Only [C] *hailed* and [E] *lauded* work.

[B], [D], and [F] all describe what likely happened *after* the decline, but the blank describes Montreaux's "initial" reception.

Question 15

Difficulty: **Medium** · Percent Correct: **46%** · Type: **Sentence Equivalence**

Answers: **A** **E**

The film is very slow ("deliberate pacing"), to the point that many find it sleep-inducing ("soporific"). [A] *plodding* and [E] *tedious* both match this context best. The phrase "in line" implies that this latest creation is similar to the director's melodramas. Therefore, [A] and [E] fit in the blank.

You could argue, in a *convoluted* fashion, as it were, that [B] makes sense. That is, a convoluted melodrama is one that's likely to drag on and cause people to fall asleep because it takes forever to get to the point, if it even has one. However, none of the other words are close in meaning to "convoluted." Without a synonym, this cannot be the answer.

[C] *exacting* means "requiring a lot of attention." Since the "deliberate pacing" causes many to fall asleep, the film could be seen as exacting, with only a few being able to handle the pacing. Nonetheless, like [B], there's no word amongst the six answer choices that has a similar meaning.

[D] *sadistic* means "to enjoy inflicting suffering on others." It's a stretch to say that a boring film is inflicting suffering.

[F] *shocking* implies something surprising, the opposite of soporific.

Question 16

Difficulty: **Very Hard**   ·   Percent Correct: 29%   ·   Type: **Sentence Equivalence**

Hirasaki is being compared to her contemporaries who are verbose. Therefore, you want to select a word that's the opposite of *verbose*.

[A] *suggestion* implies that Hirasaki is using few words but conveying a great amount.

[B] *artfulness* implies a craftiness that doesn't fit with the context.

[C] *intimation* is the act of implying or hinting at something. This is a good contrast to being verbose.

[D] *illumination* doesn't contrast with verbosity.

[E] *contrivance* means "to pull off something in an artificial or unnatural manner." This doesn't match the context.

[F] *abbreviation*, while apparently opposite to verbosity, doesn't match stylistically. Also, there's no similar word among the answer choices.

Answers: **A** **C**

Question 17

Difficulty: **Medium**   ·   Percent Correct: **50%**   ·   Type: **Reading Comprehension**

Relevant text: "Additionally, he uses data collected from surveys, from both middle management and upper management, to assess the effect, if any, that such displacement has had."

Answer: **D**

The fact that only middle and upper management were surveyed and not the company as a whole limits the scope of the findings. Therefore, if **(D)** is true, then the validity of Gershin's findings is challenged: we don't actually know what those who use social media feel.

(A) is wrong. Gershin finds that social media tools can help in the planning of social events. That some people don't use social media to plan social events doesn't fundamentally challenge the validity of Gershin's findings: many people do use social media to plan social events and, according to the study, they find it helpful in doing so.

(B) is also wrong. Gershin's findings describe both the positive and negative effects of social media. Even if more managers did mention the negative effects, that's still consistent with what Gershin describes regarding redundancy. That is, a few could mention the positive effects of social events, while the majority focus on redundancy.

(C) is a close answer. However, Gershin's focus on redundancy pertains to traditional communication. In (C), redundancy pertains to the planning of social events.

(E) is wrong. The fact that social media tends to be redundant with traditional forms of communication, one of Gershin's findings, isn't incompatible with (E). Gershin describes how social media serves as a redundant layer of communication. That redundancy also happens in other forms of communication doesn't weaken Gershin's claim that redundant communication happens when people use social media.

Question 18

Difficulty: **Easy** · Percent Correct: **77%** · Type: **Reading Comprehension**

Answer: **B**

Relevant text: "The two speculate that one of the reasons is that the kind of communication in social media presumes a level of comfort that isn't consistent with that typically found in larger companies." This points to **(B)**.

(A) is tempting because it describes something that's true in reality. However, information becoming lost is never mentioned in the passage.

(C) is tricky because it's an ever-so-slight variance from what the passage actually says. Remember the relevant text above: social media's level of comfort (its value) doesn't match those of larger corporations. The differentiation isn't between the values of management and those of the rest of the company.

(D) seems to be common sense: the more people communicating, the more likely there will be redundancy. But the passage never explicitly mentions this.

(E) is wrong since the ability of companies to communicate the limitations of social media is never mentioned in the passage.

Question 19

Difficulty: **Easy** · Percent Correct: **79%** · Type: **Reading Comprehension**

Answer: **B**

The passage is concerned with describing two theories regarding social media tools in the workplace. At no point does the passage actually compare the two studies. This points to **(B)**.

(A) is wrong. Meyers and Tassleman focus on whether these tools exert a positive effect (their answer is "yes" and "no," depending on the size of the company), whereas Gershin focuses on whether social media tools are displacing other forms of office communication (in some areas "yes," but not overall). (A) says that these two conclusions (the ones in parentheses above) lead to divergent, or opposite, conclusions. Since the two studies are focused on different aspects, they aren't really that relevant to each another. There's nothing contradictory about them since we don't know the size of the company on which Gershin was focused. This researcher found that there was some use—and positive use (social events)—so this is consistent with what Meyers and Tassleman could have learned about a smaller company, one that sees some positive benefit to social media tools in the office place.

(C) is also wrong. The author never takes a position on his/her views regarding the use of social media tools in the workplace. Therefore, it's a stretch to say that the passage "promotes the benefits …"

(D) is wrong. Again, the author simply describes the findings of the two studies. He/she doesn't take a position on the findings.

(E) is wrong. There's no criticism of either of the two studies. He/she is simply relating the findings.

Question 20

Difficulty: **Medium** · Percent Correct: **55%** · Type: **Reading Comprehension**

The ostensible cause of health complications is the IV therapy, the specific culprit being excess concentrations of sodium and potassium. Once the concentration of sodium and potassium is lowered, however, nothing changes. Thus, we're looking for an alternative cause to the high rate of health complications. **(D)** nicely provides this; the cause is nothing more than old age, i.e., those who are older are likely to have more health complications.

(A), (C), and (E) are out of scope.

(B) is tempting, but remember the paragraph says that sodium and potassium levels were returned to correct levels. (B) only refers to extremely low levels.

Answer: **D**

Off to the Test!

Wow! You made it. You've prepared for weeks, and the GRE test sits there on the horizon, ready to be conquered!

You've spent hours and hours prepping with us. You have attacked practice problems, tested out new strategies, read long passages, worked through tough equations, and taken mock practice tests. And now the time has come for us to step aside and let you apply all that you've learned.

Is there something in our eyes over here at Magoosh? Maybe. We're just really proud of all you've accomplished.

Getting ready for the big day requires you to keep the study intensity high and continue to work toward your achievement goals. Don't change anything at this point!

If you're unsure what to do in the final week leading up to the test, here are some suggestions:

- Take a practice test five to seven days before the actual exam so that you can practice your pacing and build up your stamina for the long test ahead. Make sure to do all the essays and do an extra math or verbal section from a practice book (preferably ETS or this one).
- Review your notes, especially problems and concepts that you have struggled with. It's important to have everything you've learned fresh in your mind on test day.
- Any practice you do at this point should be timed.
- Work on your weaknesses as much as you can.

Then, the day before the test, don't forget to follow our very important advice: do nothing! That's right. It might seem counterintuitive and it might seem like the last thing you should do, but you need to rest up for the big day. Cramming will hurt you more than it will help you. So what should you do?

The parasympathetic nervous system (PNS) generates the "relaxation response" of the body; it's the natural opposite of stress. The "on-switch" for the PNS is a sustained rhythm of slow, deep breathing. This is precisely why meditation and yoga focus so much on breathing. During the test, stress won't help you. If you remember to practice deep breathing in a sustained way, this may well eliminate stress so you can perform at your highest potential.

- No test preparation all day! Seriously!
- Eat a large, healthy, leisurely dinner—no alcohol!
- Lay out everything that you'll need for test day.
- Go to bed earlier than usual.

And then we come to the day of the test. We're serious about not cramming last minute. Don't even think about it! Instead,

- Eat a large breakfast, full of protein.
- Do relaxing, fun activities to pass time until the test.
- Burn off anxiety and prime your mind for the test with some light exercise.
- Give yourself more than enough time to arrive at the test center, find parking, and take your seat.

And when you head out for the testing site, don't forget to bring

- A valid ID that includes your full name, photo, and signature
- A bottle of water
- Healthy, energy-packed snacks like nuts or a protein bar

Oh, and during the test,

- Make sure to get up and move during breaks. Moving and stretching the large muscles of the body (legs, torso, and back) will get oxygen flowing, which will help keep you awake and keep you thinking clearly.

Okay, okay, we're done with the reminders. We're ready to watch you walk into that testing center with some swagger. We're behind you as you stand tall and choose to be positive when facing the tough stuff on the test. We support your decision to totally dominate the GRE.

Be confident in your abilities and trust that you're ready for the test. We have no doubt that you are—after all, you're part of the Magoosh family.

P.S. Let us know how the GRE went for you by emailing **book@magoosh.com**. We love throwing a celebratory bash in the office to honor work well done.

Off to the Test!

How to Score Your Practice Test

To score the test, figure out the number of questions you answered correctly in each category of the test. Then, add together the numbers for the two GRE Quantitative sections, and add together the numbers for the two GRE Verbal sections. This will be your raw score for GRE Quantitative and GRE Verbal, respectively.

Raw Score	Scaled Verbal Score	Scaled Quantitative Score	Raw Score	Scaled Verbal Score	Scaled Quantitative Score
40	170	170	19	150	148
39	170	170	18	150	147
38	169	168	17	149	146
37	168	167	16	148	145
36	167	165	15	147	144
35	165	164	14	146	143
34	164	163	13	145	142
33	163	161	12	144	141
32	162	160	11	143	140
31	161	159	10	142	139
30	160	158	9	140	138
29	159	157	8	139	136
28	158	156	7	138	134
27	157	155	6	136	132
26	156	155	5	134	130
25	155	154	4	132	130
24	154	153	3	130	130
23	154	152	2	130	130
22	153	151	1	130	130
21	152	150	0	130	130
20	151	149			

Make sure you take a GRE Powerprep test from ETS so you can get the most accurate assessment of your current abilities. The good news is this software is free to download here: www.ets.org/gre/revised_general/prepare/powerprep2.

If for some reason, the program doesn't load on your computer, you can always take the "paper-based" version found here: www.ets.org/s/gre/pdf/practice_book_GRE_pb _revised_general_test.pdf.

Magoosh Vocabulary Word Lists

While it might be tempting to dive in and just start studying the words below as you read through them, let us suggest a different method. Why? Well, reading might be fun, and it might *seem* that you're learning the words, but the truth is you're likely not retaining what you read.

Instead, scan this list for words whose meanings you don't have any clue about. Read the entries and example sentences for those words and then (and here's the important part) turn each word into a flashcard, writing the definition on the back. That way you can study the words that are totally new to you, taking advantage of the retentive powers that flashcards give you.

We also have a Magoosh GRE Vocabulary Flashcard app, so if you want to learn vocabulary on your smartphone, this is a great way to go. You can download them for free here: gre.magoosh.com/flashcards/vocabulary.

High-Frequency GRE Words

Alacrity (n.)

The GRE has a predilection for words that don't really sound like what they mean. *Alacrity* is no exception. Many think the word has a negative connotation. *Alacrity*, however, means "an eager willingness to do something."

So imagine it's the first day at a job that you've worked really hard to get. How are you going to complete the tasks assigned to you? With alacrity, of course.

An interesting correlation: the more *alacritous* (adjective form) you are when you're learning GRE vocabulary, the better you'll do.

The first three weeks at her new job, Mary worked with such alacrity that upper management knew they would be giving her a promotion.

Contrite (adj.)

Word roots are often misleading. This word doesn't mean "with triteness" (*con-* meaning "with"). To be *contrite* is to be "remorseful and affected by guilt."

Though he stole his little sister's licorice stick with malevolent glee, Chucky soon became contrite when his sister wouldn't stop crying.

Disparate (adj.)

If two things are fundamentally different, they're *disparate*. For instance, verbal skills and math skills are disparate and, as such, are usually tested separately—the GRE being no exception.

With the advent of machines capable of looking inside the brain, fields as disparate as religion and biology have been brought together as scientists try to understand what happens in the brain when people pray.

Egregious (adj.)

Greg is the Latin root for "flock." At one point, *egregious* meant "standing out of the flock in a positive way." This definition went out of vogue sometime in the sixteenth century, after which time *egregious* was used ironically. Thus for the last five hundred years, *egregious* meant "standing out in a bad way." In sports, an egregious foul or penalty would be called on a player who slugged another player.

The dictator's abuse of human rights was so egregious that many world leaders asked that he be tried in an international court for genocide.

Laconic (adj.)

A person is described as *laconic* when he/she says very few words. Think of either John Wayne, the quintessential cowboy, who, with a gravelly intonation, muttered few words at a time, or Christian Bale in *Batman*—the laconic caped crusader.

While Martha always swooned over the hunky, laconic types in romantic comedies, her boyfriends inevitably were very talkative—and not very hunky.

Maintain (v.)

The second definition of this word—and one the GRE favors—is "to assert." People can *maintain* their innocence. A scientist can maintain that a recent finding supports her theory. The latter context is the one you'll encounter on the GRE.

The scientist maintained that the extinction of dinosaurs was most likely brought about by a drastic change in climate.

Paucity (n.)

Paucity is "a lack of something." In honor of paucity, this entry will have a paucity of words.

There is a paucity of jobs for which companies are hiring today that require menial skills, since most jobs have either been automated or outsourced.

Prosaic (adj.)

Prosaic conjures up a beautiful mosaic for some. But, once again the GRE confounds expectations. *Prosaic* means "dull and lacking imagination." It can be used to describe plans, life, language, or just about anything inanimate that has become dull; however, it's not used to describe people.

A good mnemonic: prose is the opposite of poetry. And where poetry, ideally, bursts forth with imagination, prose (think of text-book writing), lacks imagination. Hence, prose-aic.

Unlike the talented artists in his workshop, Paul had no such bent for the visual medium, so when it was time for him to make a stained glass painting, he ended up with a prosaic mosaic.

Veracity (n.)

Veracity sounds a lot like *voracity*. Whereas many know *voracity* means "full of hunger, whether for food or knowledge" (the adjective form *voracious* is more common), few know the meaning of *veracity*. Unfortunately, it's easy to confuse the two on the test. *Veracity* means "truthful." Also, *veracious*, the adjective form of *veracity*, sounds a lot like *voracious*. So be careful.

After years of political scandals, the congressman was hardly known for his veracity; yet despite this distrust, he was voted for yet another term.

Top Five Basic GRE Words

Bleak (adj.)

If a person has a very depressing take on life, we say that he or she has a *bleak* outlook. Landscapes (Siberia in April, the Texas of *No Country for Old Men*) and writers (Dostoevsky, Orwell) can be bleak.

Unremitting overcast skies tend to lead people to create bleak literature and lugubrious music—compare England's band Radiohead to any band from Southern California.

Candid (adj.)

A straightforward and honest look at something is a *candid* look. Many great photographers have created enduring work because they turned their respective lenses on what is real. Whether these photos are from the Dust Bowl, the Vietnam War, or the Arab Winter, they move us because they reveal how people felt at a certain moment.

A person can also be *candid* if they're being honest and straightforward with you.

Even with a perfect stranger, Charles was always candid and would rarely hold anything back.

Erratic (adj.)

Unpredictable, often wildly so, *erratic* is reserved for pretty extreme cases. An athlete who scores the winning point one game and then botches numerous opportunities is known for his or her erratic play. The stock market is notoriously erratic, as is sleep, especially if your stocks aren't doing well.

Erratic can also mean "strange and unconventional." Someone may be known for his or her erratic behavior. Regardless of which meaning you're employing, you shouldn't be erratic in your GRE prep.

It came as no surprise to pundits that the president's attempt at re-election floundered; even during his term, support for his policies was erratic, with an approval rating jumping anywhere from 30 to 60 percent.

Innocuous (adj.)

Something *innocuous* is harmless and doesn't produce any ill effects. Many germs are innocuous, as are most bug bites. Even television, in small doses, is typically innocuous. *Innocuous* can also mean "inoffensive." An innocuous question is unlikely to upset anyone.

Everyone found Nancy's banter innocuous—except for Mike, who felt like she was intentionally picking on him.

Profuse (adj.)

If something pours out in abundance, we say it's *profuse*. A person who apologizes ceaselessly does so *profusely*. Or, to be more vivid, certain men who fail to button up their shirts completely let the world know of their profuse chest hairs.

During mile twenty of the Hawaii Marathon, Dwayne was sweating so profusely that he stopped to take off his shirt and ran the remaining six miles clad in nothing more than skimpy shorts.

Common GRE Words That Don't Sound Like What They Mean

Ambivalent (adj.)

Students often believe that to be *ambivalent* toward something is to be indifferent. The truth is almost the opposite. See, when you're *ambivalent*, you have mixed or conflicting emotions about something. This word might also pop up in the reading comprehension section in questions asking about the author's tone.

Sam was ambivalent about studying for the GRE because it ate up a lot of her time, yet she learned many words and improved at reading comprehension.

Auspicious (adj.)

This word sounds very sinister but actually means the opposite of "sinister." If an occasion is *auspicious*, it's favorable.

The opposite, *inauspicious*, is also common on the GRE. It means "unfavorable."

Despite an auspicious beginning, Mike's road trip became a series of mishaps, and he was soon stranded and penniless, leaning against his wrecked automobile.

Contentious (adj.)

This GRE word doesn't mean "content," as in feeling happy. It comes from the word *contend*, which means "to argue." If you're *contentious*, you like to argue. *Contentious* is a very common GRE word, so unless you want me to become contentious, memorize it now!

> *Since old grandpa Harry became very contentious during the summer when only reruns were on TV, the grandkids learned to hide from him at every opportunity.*

Enervate (v.)

Most people think *enervate* means "to energize." It actually means "to sap the energy from."

> *John preferred to avoid equatorial countries; the intense sun would always leave him enervated after sightseeing.*

Equivocate (v.)

People tend to think that *equivocate* has to do with "equal." It actually means "to speak vaguely, usually with the intention to mislead or deceive." More generally, *equivocal* can mean "ambiguous." The related word *unequivocal* can also be confusing. To state something *unequivocally* is to state it in such a way that there is no room for doubt.

> *The findings of the study were equivocal, because the two researchers had divergent opinions on what the results signified.*

Extant (adj.)

Many think this word means "extinct." *Extant* is actually the opposite of extinct.
A great mnemonic is to put the word "is" between the "x" and the "t" in extant. This gives you *existant* (don't mind the misspelling).

> *Despite many bookstores closing, experts predict that some form of book dealing will still be extant generations from now.*

Sedulous (adj.)

To be *sedulous* is to be anything but idle. If you're *sedulously* studying for the GRE, you're studying diligently and carefully—making flashcards, writing down important words and formulas, and, of course, checking out the Magoosh blog every day.

> *An avid numismatist, Harold sedulously amassed a collection of coins from over one hundred countries—an endeavor that took over fifteen years.*

Tricky "Easy" GRE Words with Multiple Meanings

Base (adj.)

When the definition of this word came into existence, there were some obvious biases against the lower classes (assuming that lexicographers were not lower class). It was assumed that those from the *base*, or the lowest, class were without any moral principles. They were contemptible and ignoble. Hence, we have this second definition of *base* (the word has since dropped any connotations of lower class).

> *She was not so base as to begrudge the beggar the unwanted crumbs from her dinner plate.*

Check (v.)

To *check* is "to limit," and it's usually used to modify the growth of something.

> *When government abuses are not kept in check, that government is likely to become autocratic.*

Expansive (adj.)

The common definition of *expansive* is "extensive, wide-ranging." The lesser-known definition is "communicative, and prone to talking in a sociable manner."

> *After a few sips of cognac, the octogenarian shed his irascible demeanor and became expansive, speaking fondly of the "good old days."*

Hedge (v.)

If you're really into horticulture—which is a fancy word for gardening—you'll know *hedges* are shrubs, or small bushes that have been neatly trimmed. If you know your finance, then you've probably heard of *hedge funds* (where brokers make their money betting against the market). *Hedge* can also be used in a verb sense. If you *hedge* your bets, you play safely. If you *hedge* a statement, you limit or qualify that statement. Finally, *hedge* can also mean "to avoid making a direct statement, as in equivocating."

> *When asked why he had decided to buy millions of shares at the very moment the tech company's stock soared, the CEO hedged, mentioning something vague about gut instinct.*

Imbibe (v.)

Literally, to *imbibe* is "to drink," usually copiously. Figuratively, *imbibe* can refer to an intake of knowledge or information.

> *Plato imbibed Socrates's teachings to such an extent that he was able to write volumes of work that he directly attributed, sometimes word for word, to Socrates.*

Intimate (v.)

Just as *tender* doesn't relate to two people in love, neither does *intimate*, at least in the GRE sense. The secondary meaning for *intimate* is to "suggest something subtly."

> *At first Manfred's teachers intimated to his parents that he was not suited to skip a grade; when his parents protested, teachers explicitly told them that, notwithstanding the boy's precocity, he was simply too immature to jump to the sixth grade.*

Inundate (v.)

Inundate is a synonym for "deluge," which means "flood." Figuratively, to be *inundated* means "to be overwhelmed by too many people or things."

> *The newsroom was inundated with false reports that only made it more difficult for the newscasters to provide an objective account of the bank robbery.*

Involved (adj.)

We are *involved* in many things, from studying to socializing. For something to be *involved*, as far as the GRE is concerned, means it's complicated and difficult to comprehend.

> *The physics lecture became so involved that the undergraduate's eyes glazed over.*

Moment (n.)

A *moment* is a point in time. We all know that definition. If something is *of moment*, it's significant and important (think of the word *momentous*).

> *Despite the initial hullabaloo, the play was of no great moment in Hampton's writing career, and, within a few years, the public quickly forgot his foray into theater arts.*

Qualify (v.)

This is possibly the most commonly confused secondary meaning, and one that's very important to know for the GRE. To *qualify* is to limit, and this word is usually used in the context of a statement or an opinion.

> *I love San Francisco.*

> *I love San Francisco, but it's always windy.*

The first statement shows an *unqualified* love for San Francisco. In the second statement, that love is *qualified*.

In the context of the GRE, the concept of qualification is usually found in the reading comprehension passage. For example, an author usually expresses qualified approval or some qualified opinion in the passage. As you may have noticed, the authors of reading comprehension passages never feel 100 percent about something. They always think in a nuanced fashion. Therefore, they're unlikely to be gung-ho or downright contemptuous. That is, they qualify, or limit, their praise/approval/disapproval.

Retiring (adj.)

Sure, many dream of the day when they can *retire* (preferably to some palatial estate with a beachfront view). The second definition doesn't necessarily apply to most. To be *retiring* is to be shy, and to be inclined to retract from company.

Nelson was always the first to leave soirees—rather than mill about with "fashionable" folk, he was retiring and preferred the solitude of his attic.

Stem (v.)

To *stem* means "to hold back or limit the flow or growth of something." You can stem bleeding, and you can stem the tide—or at least attempt to do so. However, don't stem the flow of vocabulary coursing through your brains. Make sure to use GRE words whenever you can.

To stem the tide of applications, the prestigious Ivy requires that each applicant score at least 330 on the GRE.

Unchecked (adj.)

This word describes something undesirable that has grown out of control.

Deserted for six months, the property began to look more like a jungle and less like a residence—weeds grew unchecked in the front yard.

Wanting (adj.)

Wanting means "lacking." So if your knowledge of secondary meanings is wanting, this book is a perfect place to start learning.

She didn't find her vocabulary wanting, yet there were so many GRE vocabulary words that inevitably she didn't know a few of them.

Commonly Confused Sets

Artless (adj.) vs. Artful (adj.) vs. Artifice (n.)

Van Gogh, Picasso, Monet … surely they relate to the second word, and definitely not the first, which would be reserved for people who reached their artistic apotheosis with the drawing of stick figures.

Well, as far as the GRE is concerned, neither word relates to art (in both the lower-case and upper-case sense). To be *artful* means "to be cunning and wily." To have *artifice* is to be artful. Maybe you've read Dickens, and remember the character Jack Dawkins, whose nickname was the "Artful Dodger." The Artful Dodger didn't have a penchant for watercolors, but was instead a devious, wily lad. This trait, presumably, allowed him to dodge tricky situations.

If somebody is *artless*, on the other hand, that person is innocent, guileless. It should come as little surprise, then, that the literary canon doesn't include an "Artless Dodger," as he would be too innocent and naive to dodge much of anything.

Finally, *artful* and *artless* can refer back to the original usage of "art." However, the GRE rarely, if ever, tests these definitions.

Beatific (adj.) vs. Beautiful (adj.)

A *beatific* person is someone who radiates bliss. This person is so happy, they almost seem blessed and holy (think of a saint, or the Buddha). As for *beautiful*, well you may be beatific if you're beautiful, or you may be totally unhappy. The two words are totally unrelated.

Marred by the ravages of time, the idols were hardly beautiful, yet each seemed to emanate a beatific aura that not even five hundred years could diminish.

Censure (v.) vs. Censor (v.)

Speaking of beeping out the F-word, we have a synonym for *expurgate*: *censor*. *Censure*, the much more common GRE word, has nothing to do with removing objectionable words and/or material. However, if you decide to start dropping the F-bomb in public—and we don't mean "facetious"—then you can easily expect someone to censure you.

To *censure* someone is to express strong disapproval of that person.

Demur (v.) vs. Demure (adj.)

To *demur* means "to object or show reluctance."

Wallace dislikes the cold, so he demurred when his friends suggested they go skiing in the Alps.

To be *demure* is to be modest and shy. This word is traditionally used to describe a woman, so don't call a man demure, as they'll surely demur.

Errant (adj.) vs. Arrant (adj.) vs. Errand (n.) vs. Err (v.)

To be *errant* is to be wandering, not sticking to a circumscribed path. It can also connote deviating from accepted behavior or standards.

Unlike his peers, who spent their hours studying in the library, Matthew preferred errant walks through the university campus to help his brain function.

Arrant means "complete and utter." It usually modifies a noun with a negative connotation, e.g., liar, fool, etc.

An arrant fool, Lawrence surprised nobody when he lost all his money in a pyramid scheme that was every bit as transparent as it was corrupt.

An *errand* is a small chore.

Maria carried out her errands with dispatch, completing most before noon.

To *err* is (surprise!) to make an error.

He erred in thinking that errant and arrant were synonyms.

Expurgate (v.) vs. Expunge (v.)

They both mean to remove but in different ways. To *expurgate* means "to remove objectionable material." If you've ever watched a R-rated film that has been adapted for prime time TV, you'll probably note that all those F-words—factitious, facetious, and fatuous—have been removed.

That's expurgation (think of the "beep").

To *expunge* simply means "to wipe out or remove any trace of." Many people who commit petty crimes have those crimes expunged from their records, granted they don't decide to start running every other red light. So if you've been a good driver over the last ten years, then that one incident when 85 became the new 65 ... well, that's probably been expunged from your record.

Histrionic (adj.) vs. History (n.)

Histrionic is totally unrelated to history. It comes from the Latin for "actor." To be *histrionic* isn't to have a penchant for bad Pacino or Brando imitations but to be overly theatrical.

Though he received a B– on the test, he had such a histrionic outburst that one would have thought that he'd been handed a death sentence.

Indigent (adj.) vs. Indigenous (adj.) vs. Indignant (adj.)

Indigent means "poor, having very little means."

In the so-called developing world, many are indigent and only a privileged few have the wherewithal to enjoy material luxuries.

Indigenous means "relating to a certain area." Plants and animals are often indigenous, as are people.

The flora and fauna indigenous to Australia are notably different from those indigenous to the US—one look at a duck-billed platypus and you know you're not dealing with an opossum.

Imagine you're waiting in line to order your morning coffee. Right as you're about to ask for a nice steaming cup, someone cuts in front of you and places an order for six people. How would you feel? *Indignant.*

Indignant means "to feel anger over a perceived injustice."

You don't want to be indignant the day of the test, when ETS just happens to pick that one word you always end up confusing with another word.

Miserly (adj.) vs. Frugal (adj.)

This is one of the most commonly confused pairs. These words, despite popular opinion, aren't the same. *Frugal* has a positive connotation, i.e., you spend money wisely, and *miserly* has a negative connotation, i.e., you pinch every penny.

> *Monte was no miser but was simply frugal, wisely spending the little that he earned.*

Perfunctory (adj.) vs. Preemptive (adj.) vs. Peremptory (adj.)

Ever done dishes before? As far as daily experiences go, this one represents the nadir for most. As a result, when we do dishes, we do them in a routine way. We're hardly inspired.

To do something in such a manner is to be *perfunctory*. The word also carries with it the connotation of carelessness. That is, if you do something in which you're merely going through the motions, you're probably not doing your best.

To act before someone else does is to act *preemptively*.

> *Just as Martha was about to take the only cookie left on the table, Noah preemptively swiped it.*

Preemptive is often times heard in a political context. A country that strikes before another country can do so is launching a preemptive strike.

If you're *peremptory*, you're bossy and domineering.

> *Alan's older brother used to peremptorily tell him to do the dishes, a chore he would either do perfunctorily or avoid doing altogether.*

Ponderous (adj.) vs. Imponderable (adj./n.)

Ponder means "to think over." So *ponderous* must mean "thinking," right? Not the case. The word is derived from *pondus*, which means "weight" (think of a pound). So to be *ponderous* means "to be weighed-down, and to move slowly and in a labored fashion."

Imponderable isn't the opposite of *ponderous*. It actually relates to thinking.

An *imponderable* is something that's impossible to estimate, fathom, or figure out. Say a child was to ask, "How long would it take driving in a car to go from one end of the universe to the other?" Unless you have a really big calculator—and a very fast car—the answer to this question would be imponderable.

Eponyms

English is highly promiscuous, absorbing languages as unrelated as Sanskrit and Finnish into its bulging lexicon. So you might not always want to rely on Latin/Greek roots to figure out what unfamiliar words mean. Thwarting a root-based approach even more is the fact that English not only takes from any language it stumbles across, but also blithely appropriates a person's name, trimming a few letters here and there (adding the Latin *-ian*, or *-esque* for true mongrel effect) and begetting a Franken-word that would confound a seasoned etymologist.

This kind of word, which is derived from a person's name, is known as an *eponym*. What makes eponyms fascinating—and even more indecipherable—is that just about anyone can bequeath the world his or her name: a fictional anti-hero who thought windmills were dragons; a jingoistic veteran of Napoleon's army; a figure from the Bible.

But the GRE doesn't include just any old eponyms. For instance, you don't need to know that a *jeroboam* is a massive wine bottle named for an ancient Israeli king (who apparently was quite the wino). So we have collected a list of eponyms that may actually show up test day.

Byzantine (adj.)

"Byzant" wasn't a medieval philosopher (nor an industrious ant). The word *byzantine* isn't derived from a person's name, but from Byzantium, an ancient city that was part of the Byzantine Empire (the word can also refer to the empire itself). Specifically, Byzantium was known for the intricate patterns adorning its architecture. Bulbous domed turrets were emblazoned with ornate latticing (think of the towers on a Russian church). The modern usage of *byzantine* refers not to architecture per se but to anything that's extremely intricate and complex. It actually carries a negative connotation.

Getting a driver's license is not simply a matter of taking a test; the regulations and procedures are so byzantine that many have found themselves at the mercy of the DMV.

Chauvinist (n.)

Many have heard this word, and some may even have a visceral reaction to it. However, this word is often misused. Nicolas Chauvin, a one-time recruit in Napoleon's army, used to go about town, thumping his chest about how great France was. In its modern day incantation, *chauvinism* can also mean anyone who thinks that their group is better than anybody else's group. You can have male chauvinists, political party chauvinists, and even female chauvinists.

The chauvinist lives on both sides of the political spectrum, outright shunning anybody whose ideas are not consistent with his own.

Galvanize (v.)

Like many late eighteenth-century scientists, Luigi Galvani was fascinated with electricity (you may recall a certain Ben Franklin who had a similar penchant). Galvani's breakthrough came a little more serendipitously than playing with metal in lightning storms: he noticed that an electric current passing through a dead frog's legs made those legs twitch. This observation sparked—pardon the pun—a series of connections: could it be that electric shock could cause muscles to twitch? Today, *galvanize* can mean "to shock" but in a different sense than through raw electricity. To *galvanize* is "to shock or urge somebody/something into action."

The colonel's speech galvanized the troops, who had all but given up.

Maudlin (adj.)

Mary Magdalene was the most important female disciple of Jesus. After Jesus had been crucified, she wept at his tomb. From this outward outpouring of emotion, today we have the word *maudlin*. Whereas Mary's weeping was noble, *maudlin* has taken on a negative connotation. A person who is *maudlin* cries in public for no good reason, or feels the need to share with the stranger sitting next to them all of his deepest feelings.

Just as those who were alive during the 70s are mortified that they once cavorted about in bellbottoms, many who lived during the 80s are now aghast at the maudlin pop songs they used to enjoy— really, just what exactly is a "total eclipse of the heart"?

Mesmerize (v.)

Franz Mesmer, an Austrian physician prominent at the turn of the nineteenth century, was renowned for hypnotizing people. His method included kneeling near a patient, touching his/her knees, and looking into the person's eyes (we're curious if he ever proposed to one of his clients). Today, we have the word *mesmerize*, which doesn't necessarily mean to hypnotize (though it could), but is used figuratively and means "to hold spellbound."

The plot and the characters were so well developed that many viewers were mesmerized, unable to move their eyes from the screen for even a single second.

Quixotic (adj.)

Don Quixote is possibly one of the most well known characters in all of literature, probably because there's something heartbreaking yet comical at a man past his prime who believes he's on some great mission to save the world. In fact, Don Quixote was so far off his rocker that he thought windmills were dragons. As a word that means "somebody who mistakes windmills for dragons" would have a severely limited application, *quixotic* has taken the broader meaning of "someone who is wildly idealistic." It's one thing to want to help end world hunger; it's another to think you can do so on your own. The latter approach would be deemed quixotic.

For every thousand startups with quixotic plans to be the next big thing in e-commerce, only a handful ever become profitable.

Words with Strange Origins

Mercurial (adj.)

From the element mercury, which has no fixed form and constantly changes, we have the word *mercurial*. *Mercurial* refers to personality; anyone who unpredictably changes his or her mood is *mercurial*. This is a very common GRE word, so make sure you learn it.

The fact that Alex's moods were as mercurial as the weather was problematic for his relationships—it didn't help that he lived in Chicago.

Protean (adj.)

Protean is an eponym derived from the Greek god Proteus, who could change into shape or forms at will. To be *protean*, however, doesn't mean you wow party guests by shifting into various kinds of lawn furniture. The consummate adaptability implied by the word is used to describe a person's ability. So an actor, musician, or writer who is very versatile is *protean*.

Peter Sellers was truly a protean actor—in Doctor Strangelove *he played three very different roles: a high-strung group captain, a sedate president, and a deranged scientist.*

Saturnine (adj.)

The etymology of this curious word can be traced to two sources: alchemy and astrology. For alchemists, Saturn was related to the chemical element lead. When a person has severe lead poisoning, he or she takes on a very gloomy and morose disposition. Astrologers, on the other hand, believed that the person

associated with Saturn was gloomy and morose. Usually, we would be loathe to attribute human characteristics to large floating rocks, but remember—these were astrologists. Either way you look at it, to be *saturnine* is to be morose.

Deprived of sunlight, humans become saturnine; that's why in very northerly territories people are encouraged to sit under an extremely powerful lamp, lest they become morose.

Supercilious (adj.)

Cilia are small, thick hairs, or, in Latin, eyelashes. Above those eyelashes are eyebrows, of course—and in Latin, that becomes "supercilia." *Supercilious* is derived from the raising of these brows. Of course, a word that means "raising your eyebrows" would probably have limited use. It's what the raising of eyebrows connotes. Apparently, to be *supercilious* is to be haughty and disdainful. That is, when we look down at someone in a demeaning way, we might be tempted to lift our brows.

Nelly felt the Quiz Bowl director acted superciliously toward the underclassmen; really, she fumed, must he act so preternaturally omniscient each time he intones some obscure fact—as though everybody knows that Mt. Aconcagua is the highest peak in South America?

People You Wouldn't Want to Meet

Martinet (n.)

Not to be confused with a doll dangled on strings (that's a marionette), a *martinet* is a person who is a strict disciplinarian. Think of a drill sergeant who barks an order and a platoon of cadets jump to attention—the slightest misstep and it's toilet duty. If anything, the martinet is the one holding the strings.

This military example is no coincidence; *martinet* is an eponym, meaning "a word derived from a person's name." The guilty party in this case is the seventeenth-century French drillmaster Jean Martinet.

The job seemed perfect to Rebecca, until she found out her boss was a martinet; after each project he would come by to scrutinize—and inevitably criticize—every detail of her work.

Misanthrope (n.)

You thought a curmudgeon was bad? A *misanthrope*—or hater of humankind—walks down the street spewing vitriol at all those who walk by. College campuses are famous for misanthropes, those disheveled types who haunt coffee shops, muttering balefully as students pass by. Some say they're homeless; others think that they didn't get tenure. Regardless, steer clear of the misanthrope.

Hamilton had been deceived so many times in his life that he hid behind the gruff exterior of a misanthrope, lambasting perfect strangers for no apparent reason.

Reprobate (n.)

This word comes from "reprove," a popular GRE word, which means (nope, not "to prove again") "to express disapproval of." A *reprobate* is a noun and is the recipient of the disapproval. *Reprobate* is a mildly humorous word, meaning that you would use it to describe someone who isn't a highly principled individual but is someone for whom you nonetheless have a fondness.

Those old reprobates drinking all day down by the river—they're not going to amount to much.

Religious Words

Cardinal (adj.)

When it comes time to elect the pope, who gets together? The cardinals, of course. And when you're watching baseball in St. Louis, and the players all have red birds on their uniforms, which team are you seeing? The Cardinals, of course. And when you're on the GRE and you see the word *cardinal*? Well, it has nothing to do with birds, baseball, or popes. *Cardinal* means "of primary importance,

fundamental." That makes sense when you think of the cardinals in the church—after all they do elect the pope. The bird happens to be the same color as the cardinals' robes. As for what St. Louis has to do with cardinals, we have no clue. As if you needed any more associations—the expression "cardinal sin" retains the GRE definition of the word and means "primary." It doesn't refer to naughty churchmen.

Most cultures consider gambling a cardinal sin and thus have outlawed its practice.

Desecrate (v.)

If a person willfully violates or destroys any sacred place, he (or she) is said to *desecrate* it. Tombs, graves, churches, shrines, and the like can all be victims of desecrations. A person can't be desecrated, regardless of how holy he or she may be.

The felon had desecrated the holy site, damaging relics that were of great value to the church.

Iconoclast (n.)

This is an interesting word. The definition that relates to the church is clearly negative, i.e., an *iconoclast* is someone who destroys religious images. Basically, this definition applies to the deranged drunk who goes around desecrating icons of the Virgin Mary. The applicability of this definition to the GRE is clearly suspect. The second definition, however, happens to be one of the GRE's top one hundred words. An *iconoclast*—more broadly speaking—is somebody who attacks cherished beliefs or institutions. This use of the word isn't necessarily negative:

According to some scholars, art during the nineteenth century had stagnated into works aimed to please fusty art academies; it took the iconoclasm of Vincent van Gogh to inject fresh life into the effete world of painting.

Parochial (adj.)

This word comes from *parish*, a small ecclesiastical district, usually located in the country. *Parochial* still has this meaning, i.e., "relating to a church parish," but we're far more concerned with the negative connotation that has emerged from the rather sedate original version. To be *parochial* is to be narrow-minded in point of view. The idea is if you're hanging out in the country, you tend to be a little cut off from things. The pejorative form—at least to our knowledge—is not a knock at religion.

> *Jasmine was sad to admit it, but her fledgling relationship with Jacob didn't work out because his culinary tastes were simply too parochial. "After all," she quipped on her blog, "he considered Chef Boyardee ethnic food."*

Sanctimonious (adj.)

This is a tricky word, and thus you can bet it's one of GRE's favorites. *Sanctimonious* doesn't mean "filled with sanctity or holiness." Instead, it refers to that quality that can overcome someone who feels that they're holier than (read: morally superior to) everybody else. Colloquially, we hear the term "holier-than-thou." That's a very apt way to describe the attitude of a sanctimonious person.

> *Even during the quiet sanctity of evening prayer, she held her chin high, a sanctimonious sneer forming on her face as she eyed those who were attending church for the first time.*

Words from Political Scandals

Embroiled (adj.)

To become caught up in a scandal is to become *embroiled* in it. In the last couple of months, a few well-known politicians (not naming any names) have become embroiled in scandals. From the verb *embroiled*, we get the noun *imbroglio*, which is an embarrassing, confusing situation.

> *These days we are never short of a D.C. imbroglio—a welcome phenomenon for those who, having barely finished feasting on the sordid details of one scandal, can sink their teeth into a fresh one.*

Malfeasance (n.)

Malfeasance is wrongdoing, usually by a public official. Oftentimes, you hear the term "corporate malfeasance"—this type of wrongdoing occurs when somebody in the business world is up to no good. Typically, though, *malfeasance* is used in the context of politics.

> *Not even the mayor's trademark pearly-toothed grin could save him from charges of malfeasance: while in power, he'd been running an illegal gambling ring in the room behind his office.*

Prevaricate (v.)

If you've ever seen a politician caught in a lie (never!), and that person is trying to wiggle their way out of a pointed question, he or she is *prevaricating*. Not that a US president would ever prevaricate by talking about the household pet when confronted with charges of venality (we're alluding to Richard Nixon and his dog Checkers).

> *Bobby learned not to prevaricate when his teacher asked him where his homework was; by giving a straightforward answer, he would avoid invoking the teacher's wrath.*

Turpitude (n.)

Sometimes lechery and its synonymous friends are just too soft when describing certain acts of malfeasance. At the far ends of the political spectrum, where outrage is felt most keenly, people feel the need to invoke far harsher vocabulary when condemning naughty behavior. One such word is *turpitude*, which gained prominence in the late 90s (Google will fill in the blanks). A synonym for *depravity*, *turpitude* is only reserved for those acts deemed to be downright wicked and immoral.

> *During his reign, Caligula indulged in unspeakable sexual practices, so it not surprising that he will forever be remembered for his turpitude.*

Venality (n.)

If you've ever heard of a government taking bribes, well, that's an example of *venality*. To be *venal* is to be corrupt. Of late, charges of venality tend to be few, though such charges simply don't make the same headlines as scandals of the lecherous kind.

If our legal system becomes plagued with venality, then the very notion of justice is imperiled.

Money Words

Avarice (n.)

One of the seven deadly sins, *avarice* means "greed." Of note, this word doesn't necessarily mean "greed for food" but usually pertains to possessions or wealth. *Gluttony* describes "greed for food."

The conquistadors were known for their avarice, plundering Incan land and stealing gold.

Cupidity (n.)

This word is similar to *avarice* in that it means "greedy." But the word is even more relevant to this list in that it means "greed for money." Surprising, right? We think of Cupid the flying cherub, firing his arrow away and making Romeos and Juliets out of us. To avoid any confusion, imagine Cupid flying around shooting arrows into people's wallets/purses and then swooping in and taking the loot.

Grover already owned two fifty-foot yachts and beachfront property in the Hamptons—yet he continued to relish in swindling people out of millions, so great was his cupidity.

Impecunious (adj.)

The word *pecuniary* means "relating to money." *Impecunious*, on the other hand, means "not having any money." *Pecunious*, now mainly obsolete, means—as you can probably guess—"wealthy."

In extremely trying times, even the moderately wealthy, after a few turns of ill fortune, can become impecunious.

Parsimonious (adj.)

A synonym for *miserly* and *stingy*, *parsimonious* is GRE-speak for "extremely frugal." Multimillionaires dining from the discount rack at the donut shop and Silicon Valley tech moguls sporting Birkenstocks and Bermuda shorts are likely parsimonious. Like *miserly*, this word has a negative connotation.

Even with millions in his bank account, Fred was so parsimonious that he followed a diet consisting of nothing more than bread and canned soup.

Penurious (adj.)

This is a synonym for *impecunious*. *Penurious* also can be a synonym for *miserly*, so this word can be a little tricky. Whenever you have a word with two meanings, even if those meanings are closely related, make sure to come up with example sentences for both.

Truly penurious, Mary had nothing more than a jar full of pennies.

Sarah chose to be penurious and drive a beat-up VW, though with her wealth she could have easily afforded an Italian sports car.

Prodigal (adj.)

The provenance of this word—like many GRE words—is the Bible. One of Jesus's most famous parables, the story is of a young man who squanders his father's wealth and returns home destitute. His father forgives him, but to posterity he will forever be remembered as the *prodigal* son. To be *prodigal* is to squander or waste wealth (it doesn't necessarily have to be familial wealth). Don't confuse this word with *prodigious*, which means "vast or immense."

Successful professional athletes who do not fall prey to prodigality seem to be the exception—most live decadent lives.

Profligate (adj./n.)

This word means "spending recklessly almost to the point of immorality." *Profligate* pops up in politics, when the media really wants to heat up the rhetoric. So if the government is spending wastefully, the debt skyrocketing, look for newspapers to whip this word out. A *profligate* (n.) is a person known for his or her *profligacy*.

Most lottery winners go from being conservative, frugal types to outright profligates, blowing millions on fast cars, lavish homes, and giant yachts.

Spendthrift (n.)

Though the word *thrifty* is a synonym for *frugal* (wise with spending), *spendthrift* is someone who does just that: spend. So if you embrace consumerism as though it were going out of style, you are likely a spendthrift.

Taking weekly trips to Vegas and eating at five-star restaurants on Tuesday evenings, Megan was a spendthrift whose prodigality would inevitably catch up with her.

Sybarite (n.)

There is pampering yourself with a ninety-minute massage, followed by a three-course dinner; and then there is being a *sybarite* by indulging in a three-hour massage and facial, followed by a five-course meal at Michelin starred restaurant, and then a side trip to the Ferrari dealership. *Sybarite* describes anybody who overly indulges in luxury. You don't necessarily have to be rich to be a sybarite, though it surely helps.

Despite the fact that he'd maxed out fifteen credit cards, Max was still a sybarite at heart: when the feds found him, he was at a $1,000-an-hour spa in Manhattan, getting a facial.

In a way, "sybarite" is an eponym, only the origin here is not a person but a city. The ancient Greek city of Sybaris, in southern Italy, was noted for the exceptionally luxurious lifestyle with which it was associated.

Preposterous Prepositions

Upbraid (v.)

Upon seeing this word, you may imagine a hair stylist busily braiding patrons' hair. *Upbraid*, however, relates neither to "up" nor "braiding." It means "to scold or berate," a meaning it shares with many other words: *reprimand, reproach, chide,* and *castigate*.

Bob took a risk walking into the "Students' Barbershop"—in the end he had to upbraid the apparently hungover barber for giving him an uneven bowl cut.

Underwrite (v.)

If you're writing below the margins of a paper, you're not *underwriting*—you're simply writing below the margins of a piece of paper. *Underwrite* means to "support financially."

The latest symphony broadcast was made possible with the underwriting from various arts and humanities associations.

Overweening (adj.)

What exactly does it mean to *ween*? "To go out on Halloween," making an *overweening* person one who takes a little bit too zealously to candy-collecting and wakes up the next morning with a sugar hangover? The answer, of course, is "no." To be *overweening* is to be presumptuously arrogant. What exactly does that mean? Say the aforementioned trick-or-treater grabs three times as much candy as everyone else because he assumes he's entitled to as much candy as he wants. He would be overweening while Halloweening (okay, we'll stop before our humor becomes overweening!*).

Overweening can also refer to ideas/opinions/appetites that are excessive or immoderate.

Mark's overweening pride in his basketball skills made it impossible for him to fathom how his name was not on the varsity list. "Coach," he blurted, "you forgot to put my name on the list."

Them's Fighting Words

Bellicose (adj.)

From the Latin root "bell-," which means "war," we get *bellicose*. Someone who is *bellicose* is warlike, and inclined to quarrel. The word is similar to *belligerent*, which also employs the "bell-" root.

Known for their bellicose ways, the Spartans were once the most feared people from Peloponnese to Persia.

Jingoist (adj.)

Jingoism is what happens when bellicosity meets patriotism, and both drink too much whiskey. A person who thinks their country should always be at war is a *jingoist*. The word is similar to *hawkish*, a word that means "favoring conflict over compromise."

In the days leading up to war, a nation typically breaks up into the two opposing camps: doves, who do their best to avoid war, and jingoists, who are only too eager to wave national flags from their vehicles and vehemently denounce those who do not do the same.

Pugnacious (adj.)

Pugnacious means "having an inclination to fight and be combative." A useful mnemonic is a pug dog—you know, those really small dogs that always try to attack you while releasing a fusillade of yaps. Okay, fine; they're freaking adorable, because for all their *pugnacity*, they're about as lethal as ladybugs.

The comedian told one flat joke after another, and when the audience started booing, he pugnaciously spat back at them, "Hey, you think this is easy—why don't you buffoons give it a shot?"

Truculent (adj.)

A person who is *truculent* has a fierce, savage nature. Drivers of small cars find trucks—from the eighteen-wheeler to the four-by-four—to be quite truck-ulent when they drive. A silly mnemonic, but next time you're cut off by a truck, instead of giving the proverbial middle finger, you can just mutter, "What a truculent fellow."

Standing in line for six hours, she became progressively truculent, yelling at DMV employees and elbowing other people waiting in line.

Vocab from the Lab

Amalgam (n.)

An *amalgam*, in the chemistry sense, is an alloy made of mercury and some other metal (formerly used, before the health scare, as part of dental fillings). Generally speaking, an *amalgam* is a mixture of two or more things.

The band's music was an amalgam of hip-hop and jazz.

Precipitate (adj./n./v.)

There aren't too many words in the English language that, without any change in spelling, can be a noun, verb, or an adjective. *Precipitate*, one such word, conjures up the image of technicians in lab coats, mixing test tubes. The *precipitate* is part of the solution left inside a test tube (or any other container used in labs these days). This definition, though, isn't important for the GRE. The verb and adjective definitions, however, are. To be *precipitate* is to be hasty or rash. To *precipitate* something, such as a government precipitating a crisis, means "to make something happen suddenly."

Instead of conducting a thorough investigation after the city hall break-in, the governor acted precipitately, accusing his staff of aiding and abetting the criminals.

A-Words

Aberration (n.)

A deviation from what is normal or expected: this word is tinged with a negative connotation. For instance, in psychology there's a subset of behavior known as *aberrant* behavior. So, basically, if you're narcissistic, psychotic, or just plain old cuckoo, you're demonstrating *aberrant* behavior.

Aberrations in climate have become the norm: rarely a week goes by without some meteorological phenomenon making headlines.

Acrimony (n.)

Acrimony means "bitterness and ill will." Don't forget the adjective form, *acrimonious*, which describes relationships filled with bitterness and ill will.

The acrimonious dispute between the president and vice-president sent an unequivocal signal to voters: the health of the current administration was imperiled.

Affable (adj.)

Likeable, easy to talk to: *affable* is similar to *amiable*. The differences are subtle, and as far as the GRE is concerned, you can treat them as the same word. Like *amiable*, this word is great to use to describe people we know. After all, everyone knows an affable person.

For all his surface affability, Marco was remarkably glum when he wasn't around other people.

Ambiguous (adj.)

Ambiguous means "open to more than one interpretation." Let's say you have two friends, Bob and Paul. If you tell us, "he's coming to my house today," then that's ambiguous. Who do you mean? Paul or Bob?

The coach told his team, "Move toward that side of the field"; because he didn't point, his directions were ambiguous, and the team had no idea to which side he was referring.

Amenable (adj.)

Amenable means "easily persuaded." If someone is cooperative and goes along with the program, so to speak, that person is *amenable*. *Amenable* can also be used in the medical sense: if a disease is amenable to treatment, that disease can be treated.

Even though she didn't like bad weather, Shirley was generally amenable and decided to accompany her brother to the picnic.

Amiable (adj.)

Amiable means "friendly." It's very similar to *amicable*, another common GRE word. *Amicable*, however, doesn't refer to a person the way that *amiable* does, but rather refers to relationships between people. You'll notice that *amicable* is, therefore, the opposite of *acrimonious* (see above).

Amy's name was very apt: she was so amiable that she was twice voted class president.

Amorphous (adj.)

Amorphous means "shapeless." *Morph-* comes from the Latin for "shape." The root *a-*, as in *atypical*, means "not or without." Therefore, if something is *amorphous*, it lacks shape.

His study plan for the GRE was at best amorphous; he would do questions from random pages in any one of seven test prep books.

Animosity (n.)

Meaning "intense hostility," *animosity* should be reserved for extreme cases. That is, if you really loathe someone, and that person feels the same way, then you can say animosity exists between the two of you. A related word, and a synonym, is *animus* (though *animus* can also mean "motivation," as in *impetus*).

The governor's animosity toward his rival was only inflamed when the latter spread false lies regarding the governor's first term.

Anomalous (adj.)

Anomalous means "not normal, out of the ordinary," and is simply the adjectival—and scarier-looking—form of *anomaly*, which is a noun. *Anomalous* can be used in cases to describe something that isn't typical, like an unusually cold California spring.

According to those who don't believe in climate change, the extreme weather over the last five years is simply anomalous—average temperatures should return to normal, they believe.

Attenuate (v.)

Attenuate means "to weaken (in terms of intensity), to taper off/become thinner." *Attenuate* can refer to both abstract and tangible things.

Her animosity toward Bob attenuated over the years, and she even went so far as to invite him to her party.

The stick is attenuated at one end to allow the villagers to forage for ants.

C-Words

Calumny (n.)

Calumny is the making of a false statement meant to injure a person's reputation.

With the presidential primaries well under way, the air is thick with calumny and the mud already waist-high.

Castigate (v.)

To *castigate* someone is to reprimand harshly. This word is very similar to *chastise*. They even have the same etymology (word history).

Drill sergeants are known to castigate new recruits so mercilessly that the latter often break down during their first week in training.

Chary (adj.)

Chary rhymes with *wary*, and it also means "to be cautious." They're synonyms.

Jack was wary of GRE words that looked similar, because they usually had different definitions; not so with "chary," a word that he began to use interchangeably with "wary."

Chastise (v.)

Very similar to *castigate*, it also means "to reprimand harshly."

Though chastised for his wanton abuse of the pantry, Lawrence shrugged off his mother's harsh words and continued to plow through jars of cookies and boxes of donuts.

Churlish (adj.)

Someone who is *churlish* lacks manners or refinement. A *churlish* person lacks tact, civility, and is often outright rude.

The manager was unnecessarily churlish to his subordinates, rarely deigning to say hello, but always quick with a sartorial jab if someone happened to be wearing anything even slightly unbecoming.

Cogent (adj.)

Something that's *cogent* is clear and persuasive.

His essay writing, while full of clever turns of phrases, lacks cogency: the examples he uses to support his points are at times irrelevant and, in one instance, downright ludicrous.

Commensurate (adj.)

To be *commensurate* to is to be in proportion or corresponding in degree or amount. The definition of this word tends to be a little unwieldy, regardless of the source. Therefore, it's a word that screams to be understood in context (for this very reason, the GRE loves *commensurate*, because they know that those who just devour flashcards won't understand how the word works in a sentences). Speaking of a sentence ...

The convicted felon's life sentence was commensurate to the heinousness of his crime.

Conciliate (v.)

To *conciliate* is to make peace with.

His opponents believed his gesture to be conciliatory; yet as soon as they put down their weapons, he unsheathed a hidden sword.

Contentious (adj.)

Contentious has two meanings: "controversial (in terms of an issue)" and "inclined to arguing (in terms of a person)." This word doesn't mean "content." It comes from *contend*, which means "to argue." Be chary (see above) of this word.

As soon as the discussion turns to politics, Uncle Hank becomes highly contentious, vehemently disagreeing with those who endorse the same positions.

Corroborate (v.)

To *corroborate* something is to confirm or lend support to (usually an idea or claim).

Locals, who reported that many species of frogs had seemingly vanished overnight, corroborated her claim that frog populations were falling precipitously in Central America.

Re- Doesn't Always Mean "Again"

Remiss (adj.)

Remiss doesn't mean to "miss again." It means "to be negligent in one's duty."

Remiss in his duty to keep the school functioning efficiently, the principle was relieved of his position after only three months.

Remonstrate (v.)

You've probably guessed already that this doesn't mean "to demonstrate again." To *remonstrate* means "to make objections while pleading."

The mothers of the kidnapped victims remonstrated to the rogue government to release their children, claiming that the detention violated human rights.

Repine (v.)

The verb *pine* means "to yearn for." Like *remiss*, however, the addition of the prefix *re-* doesn't signify "again." To *repine* means to "complain or fret over something." Note: the verb *pine* can also mean "to waste away."

The tragedy's hero, stoic till the bitter end, neither whimpered nor repined as he entered the throes of death.

Restive (adj.)

Restive sounds like *rest*. It's actually the opposite, and means "restless." Though most of the *re-* words are common, *restive* is definitely the *re-* word you're most likely to see test day. It can be used to describe both people and groups of people.

The crowd grew restive as the comedian's opening jokes fell flat.

Vicious Pairs of "V"s

Venal (adj.) vs. Venial (adj.)

You definitely don't want to confuse these two. To call someone *venal* is to say they're corrupt and likely to accept bribes.

To be *venial* actually doesn't refer to a person but rather a sin or an offense. A venial offense is one that's minor and pardonable.

His traffic violations ran the gamut from the venial to the egregious—on one occasion he simply didn't come to a complete stop; another time, he tried to escape across state lines at speeds in excess of 140 mph.

Venerate (v.) vs. Enervate (v.)

Okay, fine—this one is deviating from the agenda a little. Still, despite not starting with a "v," *enervate* actually contains all the letters found in *venerate*, only scrambled. As for their meanings, these two words are anything but similar. To *venerate* someone is to respect that person deeply. To *enervate*, on the other hand, is to sap that person of energy.

The medieval Western Church traditionally distinguished venial sins from mortal sins. In this perspective, a venial sin might be a one-time bad thing to do, such as losing your temper at a good friend on one occasion. By contrast, a mortal sin would involve a whole-life-consuming attitude, such as the person who walks around angry at everyone and everything.

Appendix

444

Dave found the professor's lecture so enervating that not even a potent cup of joe could keep his eyes from drooping. The professor, despite his soporific lectures, was venerated amongst his colleagues, publishing more papers yearly than all of his peers combined.

Vicarious (adj.) vs. Vicissitude (n.)

Isn't travel great? You get to experience other cultures and see the world. Well, actually, sometimes traveling can be more stressful than a rush-hour commute—lost luggage, stolen items, and inclement weather are just a few of the many woes that can beset the traveler.

So why not stay at home and watch the Travel Channel? With just one flick of the wrist, you can journey to the distant lands of Machu Picchu or Angkor Wat. To travel so, enjoying something through another person's experiences—in this case the host of the travel show—is to live *vicariously*. The contexts, of course, can vary widely. Maybe your best friend has told you all about his or her graduate school experiences via weekly blog posts. Now you, too, feel that you've gone through grad school. That's living vicariously.

A *vicissitude* is any change in circumstances, usually for the worse. That is, life is full of ups and down that are beyond our control. Those are vicissitudes. Speaking of, traveling—especially any of those quit-your-job, six-week jaunts through Europe—is full of vicissitudes, so again, sometimes it's better to stay at home and tune into the Travel Channel (as long as the remote control doesn't go traveling off somewhere).

Vindictive (adj.) vs. Vindicate (v.)

These words look very similar, so their definitions must be somewhat related, right? Actually, the two words are very different. To be *vindictive* means "to have a very strong desire for revenge."

As for *vindicate*, it means "to prove oneself right." What, exactly, does this mean? Say you claim to your friends that you'll score at the 95th percentile on the verbal. They doubt your claim and lightly tease you on your lofty and seemingly unattainable goal. Now, it's up to you to prove that you can do it. If you score at the 95th percentile on test day, then you've vindicated yourself: you've proven that your original claim was correct. If you score way below that … well, then you may want to avoid your friends for some time.

X-Words

Excoriate (v.)

To yell at someone is one thing; to *excoriate* them is a whole other matter. A martinet of a boss whom you've once again upset; a drill sergeant berating a feckless, smirking recruit; now, we're closer. So to criticize really, really harshly is to *excoriate*. Interestingly, the second definition of the word is to tear a person's skin from his/her body.

Entrusted with the prototype to his company's latest smartphone, Larry, during a late night karaoke bout, let the prototype slip into the hands of a rival company. The next day Larry was excoriated and then fired.

Execrate (v.)

This word just sounds awful. The good news is the meaning of *execrate* is consistent with the way it sounds. To *execrate* somebody is to curse and hiss at them. For instance, a certain American basketball player left his team of many years so he could make more money with another team. Fans of the original team execrated the player for his perfidy and what they claim were his mercenary motives. Interestingly, the adjective form of *execrate* is the relatively common GRE word *execrable*. If something is *execrable*, it's so awful that it's worthy of our hissing.

Though the new sitcom did decently in the ratings, Nelson railed against the show, saying that it was nothing more than execrable pastiche of tired clichés and canned laughter.

Exegesis (n.)

This word refers to a critical interpretation of a scholarly work. If you think that definition is intimidating, the adjective form is *exegetical*.

The Bible is fertile ground for exegesis—over the past five centuries there have been as many interpretations as there are pages in a Gideon.

Exhort (v.)

To *exhort* means "to strongly urge on, encourage." The encouragement is for a positive action. So a mentor figure will exhort you to make the most of your life, whereas the miscreant will cajole you into doing something you'll regret.

Neil's parents exhorted him to study medicine, urging him to choose a respectable profession; intransigent, Neil left home to become a graffiti artist.

Extenuating (adj.)

Extenuating means "making less guilty or more forgivable." The phrase "extenuating circumstances" is common courtroom lingo. Say somebody broke into a drugstore to steal some expensive medication. Later we learn that medication was for that person's wife, who was dying of some disease that only the medication could cure. Most of us, presumably, would be more likely to forgive the man. Why? Because of the extenuating factor of his wife's disease.

The jury was hardly moved by the man's plea that his loneliness was an extenuating factor in his crime of dognapping a prized pooch.

Negation Words with Misleading Roots

Immaterial (adj.)

While *immaterial* can describe a ghost, phantom, or run-of-the-mill ectoplasm, *immaterial* primarily means "not relevant."

The judge found the defendant's comments immaterial to the trial, and summarily dismissed him from the witness stand.

Impertinent (adj.)

Impertinent can actually be the opposite of *pertinent*, but this definition is seldom used. Most of the time, *impertinent* means "not showing the proper respect." You can think of it this way: if somebody's behavior isn't pertinent to the given social context, e.g., an occasion calling for formality, then you can think of that person as being impertinent. The definition usually only applies if a person is being rude where respect is expected and not staid where frivolity is apt.

Dexter, distraught over losing his pet dachshund, Madeline, found the police officer's questions impertinent—after all, he thought, did she have to pry into such details as to what Madeline's favorite snack was?

Insufferable (adj.)

Think of somebody, or something, that you simply can't tolerate. That person or thing is *insufferable*. A person bleating into their cell phones on a crowded bus is insufferable. So is a person who only talks about him or herself, and usually in the most flattering vein possible. Depending on the person, certain television shows or genres can be insufferable. This word is derived from the second definition of *suffer*, which means "to put up with, or tolerate."

Chester always tried to find some area in which he excelled above others; unsurprisingly, his co-workers found him insufferable and chose to exclude him from daily luncheons out.

Unconscionable (adj.)

If you're thinking of being knocked over the head and lying in a pool of blood on the sidewalk, you have the wrong word (not to mention a vivid imagination). In that case, the correct word is *unconscious*. If an act is so horrible and deplorable that it makes everyone around aghast, then that action is *unconscionable*. *Unconscionable* can also mean "something that's in excess of what is deemed tolerable." This second definition doesn't have the unethical smear of the first definition.

The lawyer's demands were unconscionable, and rather than pay an exorbitant sum or submit himself to any other inconveniences, the man decided to find a new lawyer.

Difficult Words the GRE Loves to Use

Belie (v.)

This is ETS's number one favorite word for harder questions. Period. If ETS needs to make a text completion or sentence equivalence question difficult, all it needs to do is throw in *belie*. The key to answering a text completion question that uses *belie* is to know how the word functions in context. Let's take a look below:

Her surface calm belied her roiling emotions.

Her upbeat attitude during the group project belied her inherent pessimism toward any collective endeavor.

In both cases, note how the outward appearance doesn't match up with the reality. That contradiction is the essence of *belie*.

Betray (v.)

To *betray* means "to go against one's country or friends." Right? Well, yes, but not always. Especially on the GRE. To *betray* means "to reveal or make known something, usually unintentionally."

As we age, our political leanings tend to become less pronounced; the once dyed-in-the-wool conservative can betray liberal leanings, and the staunch progressive may suddenly embrace conservative policies.

Disinterested (adj.)

Like *belie*, the addition of *disinterested* into a text completion question can make it more difficult. Why? Everybody assumes that *disinterested* means "not interested." While this is acceptable colloquially, the GRE, as you've probably come to learn by now, is anything but colloquial. The definition of *disinterested* is "unbiased, neutral."

The potential juror knew the defendant, and therefore could not serve on the jury, which must consist only of disinterested members.

Equivocal (adj.)

Equivocal doesn't mean "equal." It means "vague, undecided." *Equivocal*, especially in its more common form, *equivocate*, has a negative connotation. If a politician is *equivocating*, he/she isn't answering a question directly but is beating around the bush. In the academic GRE sense, if a phenomenon is open to multiple interpretations, it's *equivocal*.

Whether we can glean an artist's unconscious urges through his or her art remains equivocal—that we can ever even really tap into another person's hidden motives remains in doubt.

Feckless (adj.)

Feck, probably for its phonetic similarity to another word, has been dropped from the language. That or the lexicographers have become *feckless*, which means that they lacked the drive or initiative to include *feck* in the dictionary. *Feckless* means "lazy and irresponsible." So don't get feckless and drop the *-less*, lest somebody totally misinterpret you. In which case, you'll have to do a fair amount of propitiating.

By the way, I'm feckless—I won't include an example sentence (oops, I just walked into a contradiction).

Propitiate (v.)

Want to make an angry person less angry? Well, then you attempt to placate or appease. Or, if you like really big GRE words, you *propitiate* them.

> *The two sons, plying their angry father with cheesy neckties for Christmas, were hardly able to propitiate him—the father already had a drawer full of neckties he had never worn before or ever planned to.*

Sententious (adj.)

This word looks like it would relate to a sentence. If you know the GRE, you know this is probably not the case, as the GRE is likely to subvert people's gut reactions. *Sententious* means "to be moralizing, usually in a pompous sense."

> *The old man, casting his nose up in the air at the group of adolescents, intoned sententiously, "Youth is wasted on the young."*

Tendentious (adj.)

If you're promoting a controversial view, you're being *tendentious*. A good synonym for *tendentious* is *biased*, though if you're biased you aren't necessarily leaning toward a view that's controversial.

> *Because political mudslinging has become a staple of the twenty-four-hour media cycle, most of us, despite proclamations to the contrary, are tendentious on many of today's pressing issues.*

Undermine (v.)

Undermine is common in all sections of the GRE, not just difficult sections. It can pop up in reading comprehension answer choices just as commonly as text completion questions. *Undermine* means "to weaken" and is usually paired with an abstract term, such as *authority*. It can also have the connotation of slowly or insidiously eroding (*insidious* means "subtly harmful").

> *The student undermined the teacher's authority by questioning the teacher's judgment on numerous occasions.*

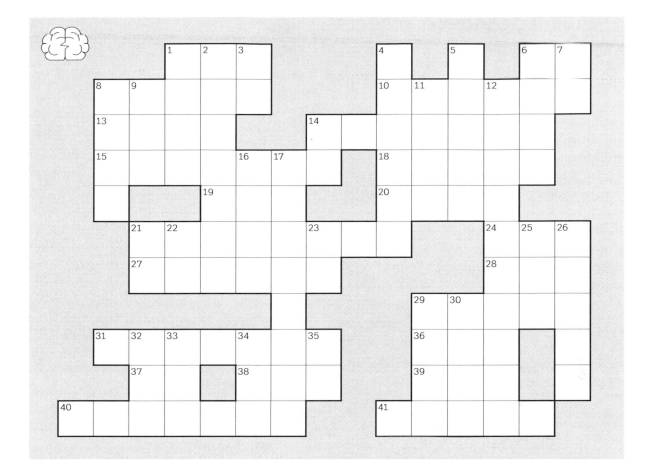

ACROSS

1. Busy first part of April
6. _____ the people
8. Cautious (GRE word)
10. Chaos over cured meat?
13. With "postale," teen apparel
14. Overly sentimental (GRE word)
15. Restless (GRE word)
18. Mother of nursery rhymes
19. Benz ender
20. 40 days long
21. Ready willingness (GRE word)
24. Gym unit
27. Headgear in Oz
28. Person A: "Tate beginner"
    Person B: "Tate beginner"
29. Openly disregard (GRE word)
31. Rhymes with "mosaic," but is not imaginative (GRE word)
36. Charged atom
37. Most of Trent's act
38. "Waterfalls" trio mix up
39. Happy inhibitor
40. To limit (GRE word)
41. To restrain (GRE word)

DOWN

1. "Revved-up" 2006 animated film
2. Versatile (GRE word)
3. Something Sparrow might say
4. Done too proudly (GRE word)
5. Power tower
6. To ebb (GRE word)
7. Wide dash
8. Fishy clue: find fault with puns
9. Haw's partner
11. A deer without antlers is _____
12. Overly dramatic (GRE word)
14. Before myself and I
16. Cause for one to take a mile
17. Truthfulness (GRE word)
21. Between a factorial and a pound
22. Famous Jet
23. King creepy
25. A big bird
26. Concise yet expressive (GRE word)
29. Typical nigiri ingredient
30. Poe: "Many a quaint and curious volume of forgotten _____"
32. Tiny messenger
33. Nigeria's big export
34. Long-snouted alien
35. Curt reply in Barcelona?

Answers can be found at the end of the book.

Student Acknowledgments

To make this the best possible GRE study tool it could be, we sent rough drafts of this book to actual Magoosh GRE students around the world and asked them for feedback. Below are the sixty-five amazing Magoosh superfans who dedicated their time and brainpower to help edit, refine, and perfect the pages of the book you hold in your hands.

Adrian Gilliam	GC Premsai	Nick Thornton
Aleksandr Belianov	Grace Van Ness	Nina Partha
Angela Green	Humayun Khan	Pratik Mishra
Anish Gupta	Ian Hutchinson	Reza Ali Lakhani
Anmol Vohra	Jasmine Jones	Ronald Drummer
Anshu Saha	Joel Thomas	Sabyasachi Mukherjee
Anshuman Nayak	Jonathan Fortman	Sanchari Ghosh
Avshalom Schwartz	Jonathan Pun	Sanchita Agarwal
Ayush Agarwal	Kaitlyn Nicholas	Seneca Erwin
Aziz Husain	Karan Desai	Sherry Budzisz
Bhadhri Prasad Raman	Kendra Holt Moore	Siddharth S
Bhogaraju Sreela Pavani	LaTresa Copes	Smriti Prasad
Charles Larson	Lin Rui Li	Soohyun Cho
Connor Phillips	Louis Alcorn	Stefanie Smith
Damaris Gomez	Luyan Yu	Syed Zubeen
Dashni Sathasivam	Maria O'Connor	Tanner Leach
David Moshons	Martha Yumiseva	Te'Quan Taylor
Debanjan Das	Mary (Lilli Anna) Henderson	Tuba Mansoor
Diego Guerrero	Mathias Longo	Vanessa Gil
Divya Sriram	Md Kishwar Shafin	Vinayak Shukla
Donna Hill	Meg Foulk	Vishakha Hanumante
Ephraim Schoenbrun	Ngozi Nwangwa	

Student Map

This map is just a glimpse at how diverse our Magoosh students are! Specifically, our student editors reviewed this book from the US, India, Mexico, Ecuador, Russia, Bangladesh, Singapore, and Israel. We can't thank them enough for the help they offered from every corner of the globe.

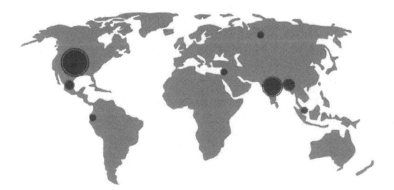

Answer key to the puzzle on page 449:

ACROSS

1. Busy first part of April: **CPA**
6. _____ the people: **We**
8. Cautious (GRE word): **Chary**
10. Chaos over cured meat?: **Mayham**
13. With "postale," teen apparel: **Aero**
14. Overly sentimental (GRE word): **Maudlin**
15. Restless (GRE word): **Restive**
18. Mother of nursery rhymes: **Goose**
19. Benz ender: **Ene**
20. 40 days long: **Lent**
21. Ready willingness (GRE word): **Alacrity**
24. Gym unit: **Rep**
27. Headgear in Oz: **Tin hat**
28. Person A: "Tate beginner"
    Person B: "Tate beginner": **Imi**
29. Openly disregard (GRE word): **Flout**
31. Rhymes with "mosaic," but is not
    imaginative (GRE word): **Prosaic**
36. Charged atom: **Ion**
37. Most of Trent's act: **NI**
38. "Waterfalls" trio mix up: **LTC**
39. Happy inhibitor: **SRI**
40. To limit (GRE word): **Qualify**
41. To restrain (GRE word): **Check**

DOWN

1. "Revved-up" 2006 animated film: **Cars**
2. Versatile (GRE word): **Protean**
3. Something Sparrow might say: **Ay**
4. Done too proudly (GRE word): **Smugly**
5. Power tower: **Pylon**
6. To ebb (GRE word): **Wane**
7. Wide dash: **Em**
8. Fishy clue: find fault with puns: **Carp**
9. Haw's partner: **Hee**
11. A deer without antlers is: **A doe**
12. Overly dramatic (GRE word): **Histrionic**
14. Before myself and I: **Me**
16. Cause for one to take a mile: **Inch**
17. Truthfulness (GRE word): **Veracity**
21. Between a factorial and a pound: **At**
22. Famous Jet: **Li**
23. King creepy: **It**
25. A big bird: **Emu**
26. Concise yet expressive (GRE word): **Pithy**
29. Typical nigiri ingredient: **Fish**
30. Poe: "Many a quaint and curious volume
    of forgotten _____": **Lore**
32. Tiny messenger: **RNA**
33. Nigeria's big export: **Oil**
34. Long-snouted alien: **Alf**
35. Curt reply in Barcelona?: **CC**

Redeem your 20% off coupon for Magoosh GRE Online

Get access to up to three full-length practice tests, over 200 lessons, customizable quizzes, 1000 practice problems, email assistance, and more!

Go to **gre.magoosh.com/plans** and enter your promo code at checkout:

Q1NyXSjEi94FpoBo

Made in the USA
San Bernardino, CA
15 May 2020

71806237R00262